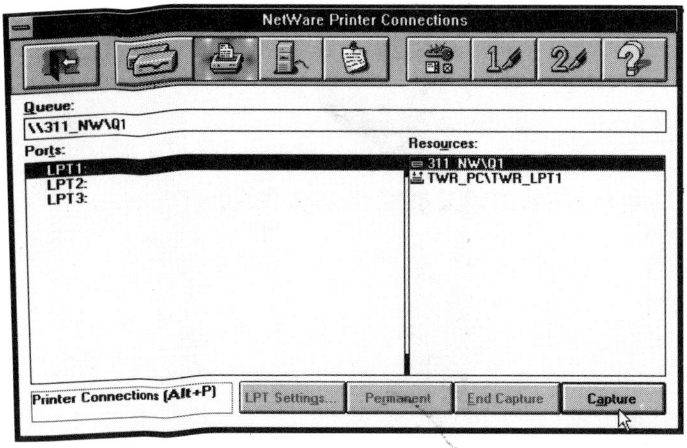

To Pri

(1) Pre

(2) Click on the printer button. (3) Click on the desired parallel port in the LPT: listing. (4) Click on the desired print queue in the Resources box. (5) Click on the Capture command button.

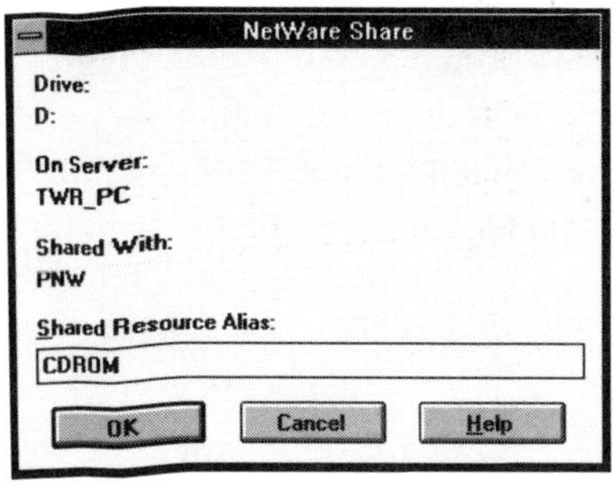

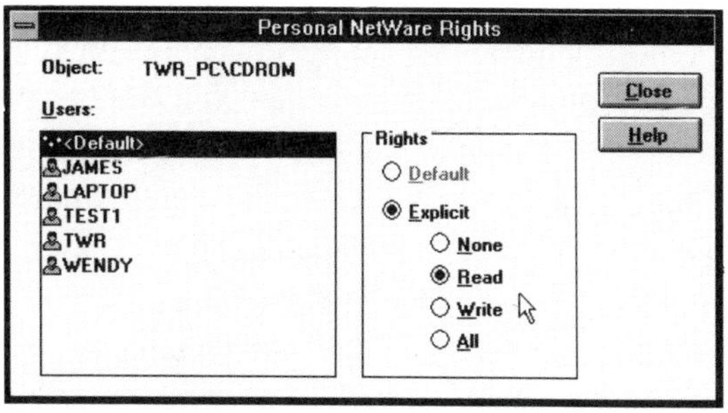

To Share a Directory (1) Double-click on the Personal NetWare icon in the Personal NetWare group. (2) In the NetWare view double-click on the server name. (3) Highlight the drive you want to share. (4) Choose Share from the File menu. (5) In the NetWare Share dialog box, enter a workgroup name for the shared directory into the Shared Resource Alias box, then click on OK. (6) In the Personal NetWare Rights dialog box, assign rights to the shared directory, then click on Close.

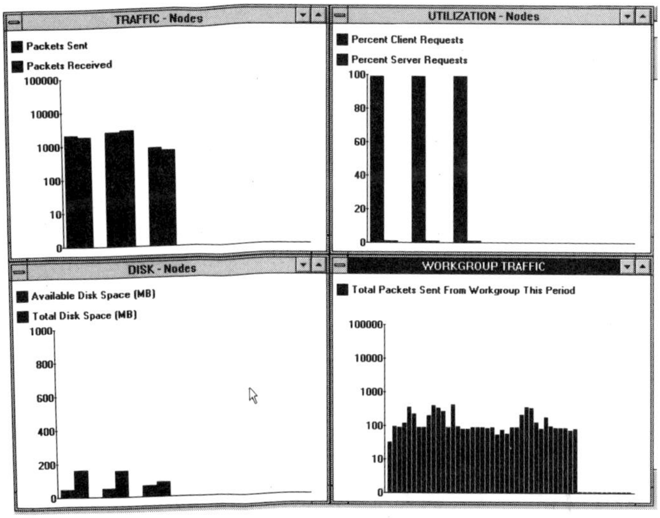

To See All the Network Diagnostics Graphs

(1) Double-click on the NetWare Diagnostics icon in the Personal NetWare group. (2) Click on an icon in the first group across the top of the screen to choose what type of network stations will be displayed (from left to right: all servers and clients, just servers, or just clients). (3) Choose All Graphs from the Graphs menu.

SYBEX is committed to using natural resources wisely to preserve and improve our environment. As a leader in the computer book publishing industry, we are aware that over 40% of America's solid waste is paper. This is why we have been printing the text of books like this one on recycled paper since 1982.

This year our use of recycled paper will result in the saving of more than 15,300 trees. We will lower air pollution effluents by 54,000 pounds, save 6,300,000 gallons of water, and reduce landfill by 2,700 cubic yards.

In choosing a SYBEX book you are not only making a choice for the best in skills and information, you are also choosing to enhance the quality of life for all of us.

NOVELL'S GUIDE TO Personal NETWARE

NOVELL'S® GUIDE TO Personal NETWARE®

JAMES E. GASKIN

with the assistance of
ROBERT WHITTLE,
Product Manager, Novell

NOVELL PRESS™

Novell Press, San Jose

PUBLISHER: *Rosalie Kearsley*
EDITOR-IN-CHIEF: *Dr. R.S. Langer*
EXECUTIVE EDITOR, NOVELL PRESS: *David Kolodney*
ACQUISITIONS EDITOR: *Dianne King*
DEVELOPMENTAL EDITOR: *David Kolodney*
EDITOR: *Marilyn Smith*
PROJECT EDITOR: *Michelle Khazai*
ASSISTANT EDITORS: *Valerie Potter, Kristen Vanberg-Wolff*
TECHNICAL EDITOR: *Merrill Smith*
NOVELL TECHNICAL ADVISOR: *Kelley Lindberg*
BOOK DESIGNER: *Helen Bruno*
PRODUCTION ARTIST: *Charlotte Carter*
TECHNICAL ART: *John Corrigan*
SCREEN GRAPHICS: *Aldo X. Bermudez*
TYPESETTER AND PAGE LAYOUT: *Helen Bruno*
PROOFREADER/PRODUCTION ASSISTANT: *Stephen D. Kullmann*
INDEXER: *Matthew Spence*
COVER DESIGNER: *Archer Design*
LOGO DESIGN: *Jennifer Gill*
COVER PHOTOGRAPHER: *Nicholas Pavloff*

Library of Congress Card Number: 93-87702
ISBN: 0-7821-1363-X

Manufactured in the United States of America

10 9 8 7 6 5 4 3 2 1

Acknowledgments

A book takes the patience and understanding of the entire family, and I have that. My lovely wife Wendy, along with my son Alex and daughter Laura, allowed me the time necessary to make this book real. I appreciate them for many things; this is just one more in a long list.

The people at Novell Press and SYBEX have done their usual outstanding job. Rose Kearsley, David Kolodney, and Michelle Khazai are my primary support group, and they deserve a nice round of applause. It's especially nice to see the Novell Press line grow as it has, and Rose deserves extra credit for this growth.

Working with a good editor makes the author's job easier, and I am happy to be working again with Marilyn Smith. She was warned and knew what to expect, but she signed on to this project anyway. The technical editor, Merrill Smith (no relation that I know of), gave me the backup needed when describing a new product.

My understanding of Personal NetWare was accelerated by Rob Whittle, the Product Manager at Novell.

My thanks to all those who helped directly and indirectly. Special thanks go to the production staff at SYBEX. Their hard work pushed this book out the door faster than normal, and I applaud them all.

CONTENTS AT A *Glance*

TABLE OF Contents

Introduction

Personal NetWare is Novell's vision for the future of computing. The technology of Personal NetWare includes three important components:

- **Single network login:** Clients access all the network resources with one login command.
- **Universal NetWare Client:** The software works with all Novell servers.
- **Single network view:** The software makes the resources of the entire network available.

A PC using the Personal NetWare software can do all these things and more. "How?" you ask. Novell engineers have blended the features of their most powerful new file server technology with the ease-of-use of software to support small business users. It's simple because it's so advanced.

Boy, is it getting thick in here! You're probably asking whether this helps you or just sounds good. Can it solve the problems you have at the office? Can it connect you to the new laser printer Diane has hidden in her office? Can it get you to the CD ROM drive that Rose has? Is there any way to use that big disk drive that David got last month?

All this and more is possible. You might even notice that sharing the resources of *your* PC may help the group. Do you have a CD ROM drive? Do you have a backup tape drive in your PC? Do you have a fancy printer others would like to use?

Let's take this one more step. Would you like to use the word processing files of a co-worker without putting files on a diskette and carrying them around in your shirt pocket? Wouldn't it be nice to let Marilyn use your spreadsheet files while they're still on your PC? That way, you know she's always using the latest version of your spreadsheet. With this technology, there's a good chance you won't have to redo any more budgets because Marilyn built her report around the spreadsheet you gave her last week instead of the correct one you finished this week.

Who Should Read This Book?

Personal NetWare will be used by two groups of computer users. The first set will use Personal NetWare to share computer resources such as printers and disk drives among a group. If you're familiar with NetWare Lite, Novell's first resource-sharing software for workgroups, you'll be comfortable with Personal NetWare. Personal NetWare builds upon NetWare Lite and adds new features.

The second group of Personal NetWare users are those who have Novell NetWare file servers up and running already. This group will use the software to provide a single, consistent view of the resources available across the entire network. Personal NetWare will be an upgrade of your current Novell NetWare client software.

There will be some overlap with these groups. Personal NetWare can turn any PC into a desktop file server, so that it can share disks and printers with any Personal NetWare user in the network. In fact, Personal NetWare works well when deployed as a departmental network group within a larger NetWare server network.

If you're the primary support person for either of these networks, this book will save you time and frustration. If you're a Personal NetWare user that shares the resources of your PC, this book will help you better share those resources. If your workstation is a Personal NetWare client but not a server, this book will help you gain access to the resources you need quickly.

How Do I Read This Book?

Different readers have different requirements and different levels of experience. Some of you prefer DOS; some prefer MS Windows. You'll find it easy to go directly to the information you need for either the MS Windows or DOS version of Personal NetWare. Peruse the table of contents a bit, and you'll see what I mean.

Some of you don't have the time to bother with details and just want the bare basics. Or you may need a quick refresher because you forgot the specific steps. This book offers a special new feature for those of you who are in a hurry for one reason or another. The arrows with the Fast Lane labels that pop into the margin here and there mark In-a-Hurry? sections. These sections provide a quick listing of the steps needed to perform the function described in that section of the book.

You can skim the margins for the Fast Lane arrow, then take a glance at the In-a-Hurry? task. Each set of instructions is numbered to reflect its position in the text. For example, the third set of In-a-Hurry instructions in Chapter 2 is numbered 2-3. Read the more detailed discussion that follows if you need to know more. The text explains the function in detail, including its options and alternatives. Where there is more than one way to perform a certain task, the In-a-Hurry? instructions also help by flagging the tool that works best for that task.

For even quicker reference, all the In-a-Hurry? instructions are gathered in the section that follows this Introduction. The instructions are listed in order of their appearance in text, with their corresponding number (2-3 for the third set in Chapter 2, for example) and the page number where the task is explained in the text.

What Does This Book Contain?

This book provides the information you need for networking with Personal NetWare. Chapter 1 starts you off with an answer to the question "What will Personal NetWare do for me?" and provides a foundation for working with your network. Chapters 2 and 3 explain how to log in and get connected under Microsoft Windows and under DOS, respectively.

Once you've mastered the basics, you'll get to file management in Chapter 4, printing in Chapter 5, and applications in Chapter 6. Chapter 7 describes Personal NetWare utilities that make networking easier.

Those of you who will be sharing your computer's resources with others will want to read Chapter 8, which details how to set up and manage shared disk drives and printers. Those of you who have Novell DOS 7 will be interested in Chapter 9, which provides an overview of the features in that version of DOS.

The first two appendices are about installing the software. Appendix A covers Personal NetWare installation, and Appendix B describes how to install and configure Novell DOS 7. The other appendices are handy references. Appendix C is a troubleshooting guide, which offers suggestions for solving common networking problems. Appendix D is a reference to Personal NetWare's NET commands, with a slight twist: ratings of how useful each command is (on a scale of one to four) and a straightforward answer to whether or not it's the best method for what you want to accomplish. Finally, those of you who aren't familiar with some of the networking terms can turn to the glossary in Appendix E for definitions.

You can relax and enjoy this book. This isn't Stephen King, so no monsters are going to jump from the sewer and eat you. True, one of Mr. King's books and the computer business are both full of clowns, but that's another story.

How to Contact the Author

You can contact me electronically using one of the following methods:

MCI Mail ID: jgaskin (455-3186)

CompuServe: 72470,1364

In-a-Hurry?

THE FAST LANE TO PERSONAL NETWARE

Do you want to get up to speed with Personal NetWare without bothering with details? Do you need a quick refresher on how to accomplish a particular task?

The In-a-Hurry? instructions throughout this book supply the basic steps without embellishments. These instructions are gathered here to provide a quick-and-easy reference. We've also included the number of the page where the steps appear in the chapter, so you can turn to the detailed discussion that follows the in-text set of instructions for details.

You'll notice that Chapters 1 and 9 are not included in the following listings. Chapter 1 provides an overview of Personal NetWare's capabilities. You'll need to read that chapter to understand the concepts, but you can still stay in the fast lane, since it's a short chapter. Chapter 9 is an introduction to the Novell DOS 7 operating system. It's like a fast-lane chapter in itself, because it gives you a quick guide to the handiest features of Novell DOS, without a detailed discussion of how the operating system operates.

Chapter 2: How Do I Log In and Get Connected under Microsoft Windows?

Send a message through Personal NetWare **2.1** **30**

1 • Double-click on the Novell icon.
2 • Double-click on the server.
3 • Double-click on the user name or group.

4 • Fill in the message text box.

5 • Click on Send.

Enable the NetWare Tools hotkey **2.2** **32**

1 • Open the Main group.

2 • Double-click on Control Panel.

3 • Double-click on the Network icon.

4 • Click on the Enable Hotkey box.

Send a message with NetWare Tools **2.3** **36**

1 • Press F6 to pop up NetWare Tools.

2 • Click on the icon showing paper with a push-pin button.

3 • Type your message in the text box just under the buttons.

4 • In the right box, double-click on the name of the recipient.

Turn off message reception **2.4** **38**

1 • Press F6 to pop up NetWare Tools.

2 • Click on the burning key (hotkey) button.

3 • Clear the Broadcasts check box in the Message Reception area.

Log in (attach) from NetWare Tools **2.5** **41**

1 • Press F6 to open NetWare Tools.

2 • Click on the server button.

3 • Double-click on the desired server in the Resources box.

4 • Type your name and password.

Log in to the workgroup

2.6 48

1 • Load all network drivers and files.
2 • Type NET LOGIN *YOUR-NAME* at the DOS prompt.
3 • When prompted, enter your password.
4 • Start MS Windows.

Start MS Windows before logging in

2.7 52

1 • Load all network drivers and files.
2 • Start MS Windows.
3 • Press F6 to pop up NetWare Tools.
4 • Click on either the drives or server button.
5 • Click on the Login button.
6 • Type your user name and password.
7 • Make drive and printer connections.

Connect to a workgroup printer

2.8 53

1 • Press F6 to start NetWare Tools.
2 • Click on the printer button.
3 • Click and hold down the mouse button on the desired printer.
4 • Drag the printer to the desired parallel port and drop it.

Disconnect a printer

2.9 55

1 • Press F6 to start NetWare Tools.
2 • Click on the printer button.
3 • Drag and drop the printer from the port back into the Resources box.

Connect to a workgroup drive **2.10** **56**

1 • Press F6 to pop up NetWare Tools.
2 • Click on the drives button.
3 • Click on the server and volume name you wish to map a drive to.
4 • Drag and drop the server name onto the drive letter that will now access that drive.
5 • Log in if prompted to do so.

Connect to a NetWare 4.*x* domain **2.11** **62**

1 • Press F6 to start NetWare Tools.
2 • Double-click on the NetWare 4.*x* tree icon.
3 • Fill in your name and password.

Connect to a NetWare 4.*x* printer **2.12** **63**

1 • Press F6 to start NetWare Tools.
2 • Click on the printer button.
3 • Drag and drop the desired printer to the desired parallel port.

Connect to a NetWare 4.*x* drive **2.13** **64**

1 • Press F6 to pop up NetWare Tools.
2 • Click on the drives button.
3 • Click on the server and volume name you wish to map a drive to.
4 • Drag and drop the server name onto the drive letter that will now access that drive.
5 • Log in if prompted to do so.

Make drive connections permanent **2.14** **67**

1. Press F6 to pop up NetWare Tools.
2. Click on the drives button.
3. Highlight a current drive mapping you want to keep.
4. Click on the Permanent button at the bottom of the window.
5. Check that the highlighted drive icon has a red stripe.

Make a printer connection permanent **2.15** **68**

1. Press F6 to pop up NetWare Tools.
2. Click on the printer button.
3. Highlight a current printer connection you want to keep.
4. Click on the Permanent button at the bottom of the window.
5. Check that the highlighted blank box becomes a printer icon.

Chapter 3: How Do I Log In and Get Connected under DOS?

Send a message **3.1** **77**

1. Pull down the File menu and choose Send Message (press Alt-F, then S).
2. Move the cursor through the Server/Workgroup list on the right until the user to receive the message appears in the Users list on the left.
3. Move the cursor to the Users list and highlight the user (press the spacebar or Enter key to mark multiple recipients).
4. Press Tab to move to the Message box, then type your message.
5. Press Tab to move the cursor to OK and press Enter.

1 • Type **NET** to start the NET program.
2 • Highlight your server, then press Enter.
3 • Provide your name and password, then press Enter.

1 • Type **NET** to start the NET program.
2 • Press Alt-O.
3 • Highlight LPT1, LPT2, or LPT3, then press Enter.
4 • Highlight the desired printer, then press Enter.

1 • Type **NET** to start the NET program.
2 • Press Alt-O.
3 • Highlight LPT1, LPT2, or LPT3.
4 • Press the Delete key.

1 • Type **NET** to start the NET program.
2 • Press Alt-D.
3 • Highlight the drive you want to connect to a NetWare server, then press Enter.
4 • Highlight the server that you want to map the drive to, then press Enter. The server must be one you're already connected to.
5 • Log in if you're prompted to do so.

Disconnect a drive mapping 3.6 84

1 • Type **NET** to start the NET program.
2 • Press Alt-D.
3 • Highlight the drive mapping to disconnect.
4 • Press the Delete key.

Connect to a NetWare 4.*x* server 3.7 90

1 • Type **NET** to start the NET program.
2 • Pick your 4.*x* server and press Enter.
3 • Provide your name and password, then press Enter.

Connect to a NetWare 4.*x* printer 3.8 91

1 • Type **NET** to start the NET program.
2 • Press Alt-O (remember, O for Output).
3 • Highlight LPT1 and press Enter.
4 • Highlight the desired printer and press Enter.

Map a drive to a NetWare 4.*x* directory tree 3.9 92

1 • Type **NET** to start the NET program.
2 • Press Alt-D.
3 • Highlight the drive you want to connect to a NetWare directory tree, then press Enter.
4 • Highlight the volume you want connected, then press Enter.

Save your setup 3.10 93

1 • Type **NET** to start the NET program.
2 • Press Alt-F to pull down the File menu.
3 • Press V to choose Save Script.

Save your setup with the NET SAVE command **3.11** **95**

1 • Configure your connections as you want them.
2 • Change to the \NWCLIENT directory.
3 • Type NET SAVE.

Chapter 4: Managing Files under MS Windows and DOS

Delete a directory with File Manager **4.1** **103**

1 • Open File Manager (through Program Manager, then Main group).
2 • Click on the drive letter where the directory resides.
3 • Highlight the directory in the directory tree display in the left box.
4 • Press the Delete key.
5 • Confirm your intentions to delete the directory.

Get a full directory listing with File Manager **4.2** **105**

1 • Open File Manager.
2 • Pull down the Tree menu.
3 • Click on Expand All.

Search for a file with File Manager **4.3** **109**

1 • Open File Manager.
2 • Choose Search from the File menu.
3 • Type the name of the file you want to find, then press Enter. You can include wildcards.
4 • Read the results in the Search Results window.

View your rights to a mapped drive 4.4 115

1 • Press F6 from an MS Windows program to pop up NetWare Tools.
2 • Click on the drives button.
3 • Highlight the mapped drive letter.
4 • Click on Drive Info.

View your rights to a Personal NetWare volume 4.5 118

1 • Press F6 to pop up NetWare Tools.
2 • Click on the drives button.
3 • Highlight the drive letter mapped to the Personal NetWare volume.
4 • Click on Drive Info.

Copy a single file with File Manager 4.6 121

1 • Open File Manager.
2 • Double-click on the network drive icon.
3 • Arrange the screen to see some of both drive windows.
4 • Click on the file you want to copy.
5 • Drag and drop the file to the desired directory.

Copy multiple files 4.7 123

1 • Open File Manager.
2 • Double-click on the network drive icon.
3 • Arrange the screen to see some of both drive windows.
4 • Shift-click or Ctrl-click on the files that you want to copy.
5 • Drag and drop the files to the desired directory.

1 • Open File Manager.
2 • Double-click on the network drive icon.
3 • Arrange the screen to see some of both drive windows.
4 • Click on the file that you want to copy.
5 • Press and hold down the Alt key.
6 • Drag and drop the file to the desired directory.

1 • Open File Manager.
2 • Double-click on the network drive icon.
3 • Arrange the screen to see some of both drive windows.
4 • Shift-click or Ctrl-click on the files that you want to move.
5 • Press and hold down the Alt key.
6 • Drag and drop the files to the desired directory.

1 • Open DOSSHELL (type **DOSSHELL** at the prompt).
2 • If you're not in a network drive, choose one from the top of the screen.
3 • Press Alt-T to pull down the Tree menu.
4 • Press A to choose Expand All.

1 • Open DOSSHELL.
2 • Choose Search from the File menu (press Alt-F, then H).

3 • Type the name of the file you want to find, then press Enter. The file name can include wildcards.
4 • Read the results in the Results box.

Find a directory with NET 4.12 131

1 • Open the NET program (type **NET** at the DOS prompt).
2 • Press Alt-D to open the Drives View screen.
3 • Place the highlight bar on the desired drive mapping.
4 • Press Alt-F, then P to see subdirectories.
5 • Press Enter on the directory name to search through.
6 • Press Alt-O to map that new directory.

Chapter 5: How Do I Print, and Where?

Connect to a NetWare system printer with MS Windows 5.1 143

1 • In MS Windows, press F6 to open NetWare Tools.
2 • Click on the printer button.
3 • Highlight an available print queue in the Resources box.
4 • Drag and drop the print queue to LPT1:.

Change printing settings with NetWare Tools 5.2 147

1 • Press F6 to open NetWare Tools.
2 • Click on the printer button.
3 • Highlight a connected printer.
4 • Click on LPT Settings.
5 • Make your changes, then click OK.

Connect to a workgroup printer under Windows **5.3** **152**

1 • From MS Windows, press F6 to open NetWare Tools.
2 • Click on the printer button.
3 • Highlight an available printer in the Resources box.
4 • Drag and drop the print queue to LPT1:.

Connect to a NetWare system printer under DOS **5.4** **155**

1 • Type **NET** at the DOS prompt to start the NET program.
2 • Press Alt-O to see your LPT settings.
3 • Highlight the parallel port of your choice and press Enter.
4 • Choose the printer you want to connect and press Enter.
5 • Exit NET and start your application.

Chapter 6: How Do I Use Applications across the Network?

Share the CD ROM drive with the workgroup **6.1** **163**

1 • Start the Personal NetWare program in the Personal NetWare group.
2 • Open the NetWare view, then double-click on the server name.
3 • Highlight drive D:, the CD ROM drive.
4 • Choose Share from the File menu, provide a workgroup name for the shared CD ROM, and then click on OK.
5 • In the next screen, configure rights to the CD ROM drive.

Share the CD ROM drive with the workgroup **6.2** **174**

1 • Type **NET ADMIN** from the DOS prompt.
2 • Press Alt-D, then press the Ins key to set up a new shared directory.

3 • Name the new directory for the workgroup.

4 • Highlight the server that's sharing this new resource, then press Alt-O.

5 • Set the directory path and rights to this new shared directory.

6 • Press Alt-O to accept the configuration and set up the new shared directory.

Chapter 7: What Other Utilities Are Included to Help Me?

Get context-sensitive help in NetWare Tools — 7.1 — 189

1 • Press F6 to pop up NetWare Tools.

2 • Open the screen that pertains to the topic about which you want to see help information.

3 • Press Alt-H.

Get help in NET — 7.2 — 192

1 • Type **NET** from the DOS command line.

2 • Move to the screen that pertains to the topic you want to see information about.

3 • Press function key F1.

Get help on NET commands — 7.3 — 193

1 • Type **NET HELP** from the DOS command line.

2 • Type **NET**, the name of the command you want to see information about, followed by **/ ?**.

Run the Personal NetWare Tutorial **7.4** **195**

1 • To install the Tutorial (if it isn't already), put Tutorial Disk 1 in a floppy drive, choose Run from the Program Manager File menu, and run WINTUTOR.EXE.
2 • Open the Personal NetWare Tutorial group.
3 • Double-click on the Personal NetWare Tutorial icon.

Run the Personal NetWare Tutorial under DOS **7.5** **197**

1 • To install the Tutorial (if it isn't already), put Tutorial Disk 1 in a floppy drive, change to that drive, and type **DOSTUTOR**.
2 • Type **PNWTRAIN** from the DOS command line.

Activate the Diagnostics Help display under Windows **7.6** **201**

1 • Open the Personal NetWare group.
2 • Double-click on the Network Diagnostics icon.
3 • Choose the Status Bar option from the Options menu.
4 • Check the Mouse Sensitive check box, then click on OK.
5 • Drag your mouse across the icons to see descriptions in the bottom-left corner of the screen.

Graph traffic for each node **7.7** **206**

1 • Open the Personal NetWare group.
2 • Double-click on the Network Diagnostics icon.
3 • Click on the Graph Traffic icon on the button bar.

Graph disk space for each node **7.8** **207**

1 • Open the Personal NetWare group.
2 • Double-click on the Network Diagnostics icon.
3 • Click on the Graph Disk Space icon on the button bar.

Graph local or remote utilization for each node **7.9** **208**

1 • Open the Personal NetWare group.
2 • Double-click on the Network Diagnostics icon.
3 • Click on the Server Utilization icon on the button bar.

Graph traffic for each workgroup **7.10** **208**

1 • Open the Personal NetWare group.
2 • Double-click on the Network Diagnostics icon.
3 • Click on the Workgroup Traffic icon on the button bar.

Select a different workgroup to monitor **7.11** **212**

1 • Type **NET DIAGS** from the DOS command line.
2 • Highlight the Select Data option on the Main menu, then press Enter.
3 • Highlight the Select a Workgroup option, then press Enter.
4 • Highlight the workgroup of your choice, then press Enter.

View available disk space **7.12** **213**

1 • Type **NET DIAGS** from the DOS command line.
2 • Highlight the Compare Data option on the Main menu, then press Enter.
3 • Highlight Servers, then press Enter.
4 • Highlight Resource Distribution, then press Enter.

View node traffic totals **7.13** **215**

1 • Type **NET DIAGS** from the DOS command line.
2 • Highlight the Compare Data option on the Main menu, then press Enter.
3 • Highlight All Nodes, then press Enter.
4 • Highlight Traffic, then press Enter.

View local and remote utilization **7.14** **216**

1 • Type **NET DIAGS** from the DOS command line.
2 • Highlight the Compare Data option on the Main menu, then press Enter.
3 • Highlight All Nodes, then press Enter.
4 • Highlight Local/Remote Utilization, then press Enter.

View server utilization **7.15** **218**

1 • Type **NET DIAGS** from the DOS command line.
2 • Highlight the Compare Data option, then press Enter.
3 • Highlight Servers, then press Enter.
4 • Highlight Server Utilization, then press Enter.

View node configurations **7.16** **219**

1 • Type **NET DIAGS** from the DOS command line.
2 • Highlight the View Configuration option, then press Enter.
3 • Highlight All Nodes, then press Enter.
4 • Press Enter on the node you wish to examine.

Test network connections **7.17** **221**

1 • Type **NET DIAGS** from the DOS command line.
2 • Highlight the Test Connections option, then press Enter.
3 • Highlight either Point to Point Test or All Points Test, then press Enter.

Back up the workgroup data **7.18** **225**

1 • Log in as a user with administrator privileges.
2 • Type **NET ADMIN** from the DOS command line.
3 • Highlight the server to backup.
4 • Press Alt-Enter.
5 • Press Alt-B.

Chapter 8: How Do I Share My PC with My Workgroup?

Grant workgroup administrator rights **8.1** **237**

1 • Open the Personal NetWare group, then double-click on the Personal NetWare icon.
2 • Double-click on the NetWare icon, then on the workgroup icon, then on the user name.
3 • Click on Configure.
4 • Check the Workgroup Administrator box, then click on OK.

Make a PC a workgroup server under MS Windows **8.2** **240**

1 • Open the Personal NetWare group, then double-click on the Personal NetWare Setup icon.
2 • Click on the check box labeled Share this computer's resources.

3 • Provide a unique name in the text box.

4 • Click on OK.

1 • Open the Personal NetWare group, then double-click on the Personal NetWare icon.

2 • Double-click on the NetWare icon, then on the workgroup icon.

3 • Press the Insert key.

4 • Highlight PNW User.

5 • Type the user name, then click on OK.

6 • Modify Personal NetWare User Account Configuration items as necessary, then click on OK.

1 • Open the Personal NetWare group, then double-click on the Personal NetWare icon.

2 • Double-click on the NetWare icon, then on the workgroup icon.

3 • Select the user whose account you want to modify.

4 • Change Personal NetWare User Account Configuration items as necessary, then click on OK.

1 • Open the Personal NetWare group, then double-click on the Personal NetWare icon.

2 • Double-click on the NetWare icon, then on the workgroup icon.

3 • Highlight the user's name, then press Alt-E.

4 • Confirm that you want to delete this user.

Share a directory on a workgroup server **8.6** **245**

1 • Open the Personal NetWare group, then double-click on the Personal NetWare icon.
2 • Double-click on the NetWare icon, then on the workgroup icon, then on the icon of the server with the directory to share.
3 • Double-click on the drive icon, then on each subsequent directory until the desired directory is displayed.
4 • Choose Share from the File menu.
5 • Provide a unique name (unique within this server) for the directory, then click on OK.
6 • Set the rights for the workgroup users.

Delete a shared directory **8.7** **249**

1 • Open the Personal NetWare group, then double-click on the Personal NetWare icon.
2 • Double-click on the NetWare icon, then on the workgroup icon.
3 • Highlight the directory you no longer want to share, then press Alt-E.
4 • Confirm the deletion.

Share a printer on a workgroup server **8.8** **249**

1 • Open the Personal NetWare group, then double-click on the Personal NetWare icon.
2 • Double-click on the NetWare icon, then on the workgroup icon, then on the icon of the server with the printer to share.
3 • Highlight the port where the printer is connected, then double-click on that port.
4 • Provide a name, unique to that server, for the printer, then click on OK.
5 • Change the rights profile for this printer as necessary, then click on Close.

Delete a shared printer **8.9** **253**

1 • Open the Personal NetWare group, then double-click on the Personal NetWare icon.
2 • Double-click on the NetWare icon, then on the workgroup icon.
3 • Highlight the printer you no longer want to share, then press Alt-E.
4 • Confirm the deletion.

Change workgroup server information **8.10** **260**

1 • Open the Personal NetWare group and double-click on the Personal NetWare icon.
2 • Double-click on the NetWare icon, then on the workgroup icon.
3 • Highlight the name of the server, then press Alt-Enter.
4 • Click on Configure.
5 • Make changes as necessary, then click on OK.

Display the audit or error log **8.11** **266**

1 • Open the Personal NetWare group, then double-click on the Personal NetWare icon.
2 • Highlight the workgroup name, then press Alt-Enter.
3 • Click on the Audit Log button or the Error Log button.

Grant workgroup administrator rights under DOS **8.12** **271**

1 • Log in to the workgroup as SUPERVISOR or as someone with administrator privileges.
2 • Type **NET ADMIN** from the DOS prompt.
3 • Press Alt-U to display the Users View screen.
4 • Highlight the user, then press Enter.

5 • Check the box for Workgroup Administrator.
6 • Press Alt-O to save and exit.

Make a PC a server under DOS — 8.13 274

1 • Type **SETUP** from within the \NWCLIENT directory.
2 • Check the box labeled Share this computer's resources.
3 • Select the Save Changes and Exit option.
4 • Reboot the PC.

Create a workgroup user account under DOS — 8.14 276

1 • Type **NET ADMIN** from the DOS prompt.
2 • Press Alt-U to open the Users View screen.
3 • Press Insert to create a new user.
4 • Provide a user name in the text box.
5 • Configure the new user's properties.
6 • Press Alt-O to save and exit.

Delete a workgroup user account under DOS — 8.15 277

1 • Type **NET ADMIN** from the DOS prompt.
2 • Press Alt-U to open the Users View screen.
3 • Highlight the name of the user, then press Delete.
4 • Confirm the deletion.

Add a shared directory under DOS — 8.16 278

1 • Type **NET ADMIN** from any DOS prompt.
2 • Press Alt-D to display the Shared Directories View screen.
3 • Press Insert to add a shared directory.
4 • Provide a name to be used by workgroup clients.

5 · Highlight the workgroup server where the directory is located, then press Alt-O to save this information.
6 · Configure the properties for the new shared directory.
7 · Press Alt-O to save and exit.

Remove a shared directory under DOS 8.17 279

1 · Type **NET ADMIN** from any DOS prompt.
2 · Press Alt-D to display the Shared Directories View screen.
3 · Highlight the directory you no longer want to share, then press Delete.
4 · Confirm the deletion.

Share a printer on a workgroup server under DOS 8.18 281

1 · Type **NET ADMIN** from any DOS prompt.
2 · Press Alt-P to display the Shared Printers View screen.
3 · Press Insert to add a new workgroup printer.
4 · Name the printer, choose its server, then press Alt-O.
5 · Modify the printer properties as necessary, then press Alt-O.

Delete a shared printer under DOS 8.19 282

1 · Type **NET ADMIN** from the DOS prompt.
2 · Press Alt-P to open the Shared Printers View screen.
3 · Highlight the printer that you no longer want to share, then press Delete.
4 · Confirm the deletion.

Back up the workgroup databases under DOS — 8.20 283

1 • Type **NET ADMIN** from the DOS prompt.
2 • Highlight the server to back up, then press Enter.
3 • Press Alt-B to choose Backup Databases.
4 • Provide a path to store the information.
5 • Press Alt-O to begin the backup operation.

Restore the workgroup databases under DOS — 8.21 285

1 • Type **NET ADMIN** from the DOS prompt.
2 • Highlight the server to restore, then press Enter.
3 • Press Alt-R to choose Restore Databases.
4 • Specify the path from your latest backup.
5 • Choose which part of the backup to restore.
6 • Press Alt-O to begin restoration.

Display server configuration information — 8.22 287

1 • Type **NET ADMIN** from the DOS prompt.
2 • Highlight the server, then press Enter.
3 • Press Alt-F to see the Configuration screen.
4 • Press Alt-A to display the Advanced Settings screen.

Display the audit or error log under NET ADMIN — 8.23 293

1 • Type **NET ADMIN** from the DOS prompt.
2 • Press Alt-W.
3 • Highlight Audit Log or Error Log, then press Enter.

CHAPTER 1

What Will Personal NetWare Do for Me?

Do you wish the computers in your department worked together better? Would you like to be able to get a file from Fred's PC, without having Fred copy it to the NetWare file server on a drive you can access? Without needing to ask for it again because Fred put it in the wrong place? Would you like to print to a close printer, not the system printer down the hall?

Personal NetWare for DOS and Microsoft Windows will, believe it or not, allow you to do all these things and many more. You will soon be able to share the resources of your PC with your co-workers, subject to the restrictions you set. You will be able to share the resources of your co-workers' PCs, subject to the restrictions they place on your access. These capabilities are added to, but separate from, your current ability to connect to the NetWare server you already have.

Changing Your View of Networking

Novell, the developer of NetWare, realized that people work in groups, but still need a central file server or two. More important, Novell noticed that these workgroups change from time to time, as people move from one project to another. So the flexibility to change your workgroup, dropping some resources (members, printers, groups of files, and so on) and adding others, is important.

This is actually quite radical thinking for a computer company. Most computer companies want you to either share exclusively with your workgroup, known as peer-to-peer networking, or always go to the server, known as client/server networking.

Although this is a convenient arrangement for the computer companies, it doesn't always help you get your work done. That's why Novell developed the Universal NetWare Client software in Personal NetWare. With this software installed on your computer, you have access to other PCs in your workgroup and to the central file server, all at the same time. Some resources, such as working files for a project, may be on a co-worker's PC.

Then you need the peer-to-peer features of the Universal NetWare Client software. Other resources, such as gateways to host computers and regular file backups, can be handled through the central file server.

The Universal NetWare Client software allows you the freedom to connect to a variety of resources. In fact, you may need to reorient your thinking just a bit. The view of the world, according to NetWare, has always been centered around the file server. Today, the view is of the network and available resources. Regardless of where a file or printer is, you'll be able to use it.

How the Universal NetWare Client Will Connect You Better Than Ever Before

Over the years, Novell has supported a wide variety of network types. In the past, each type had its own set of files for the client PCs. Today, the Universal NetWare Client gathers all the different support files and connection methods into a single, easy-to-use package. Think of it as "one-stop shopping" for all your network resources.

The Universal NetWare Client wasn't used before because NetWare was organized around the file server. This is what the term *server-centric* means. This focus on the server developed in the early days of NetWare, when a network had only one server.

Today, it's common to have many servers supporting scores and hundreds of users in one place. The focus on the server gets bothersome when each user wants to use some resources of a half-dozen or more servers. The administrator must carefully keep track of each user and his or her needs on each server. The access profiles and login scripts must be maintained separately, one set per server. Multiply this by a few hundred users, and you have a frazzled and overworked administrator.

NetWare 4.*x* has given us a "network" view of the world. NDS (NetWare Directory Services) provides network access based on the developing international directory specifications known as X.500. Now each user logs into the network one time, no matter how many (up to 50) servers the user accesses at any one time. The single database for user security and access privileges is replicated, or copied, to multiple servers. If one server is down, users can still log in and access the rest of the network resources.

So does this leave out all the users of NetWare 3.*x*, NetWare 2.*x*, and Personal NetWare? Not at all. With Personal NetWare and the Universal NetWare Client, the client software can gain access to multiple server resources automatically. Once a profile and resource list is set up in Personal NetWare, that same resource list will be available every time the user logs in from then on. The resource list is a nice bit of shorthand for the NetWare clients of the world. And the list can be modified at any time, either for that session alone or for all later sessions.

The New World of ODI Drivers and VLM Files

Before ODI (Open Data-Link Interface) drivers came along, there was no way to have one PC talk to both NetWare and another operating system, such as UNIX or LAN Manager, at the same time. This was a problem for many people, and Microsoft had a competing scheme, called NDIS (Network Device Interface Specification), for its network stations. ODI and NetWare have taken the lead away from Microsoft here, but most good network interface cards provide drivers for both ODI and NDIS.

Before ODI, the primary program NetWare used to communicate between the network interface card and the rest of the computer network software was a program named IPX.COM. This worked well, but since the details for every PC are different, the IPX.COM program needed to be recreated for every PC. Bummer.

With ODI, the IPX.COM file has been replaced with a file named IPXODI.COM. This file reads the configuration details for every PC in the

NET.CFG file when the network client software starts to load. The configuration file, a text file like your AUTOEXEC.BAT file, is much easier to modify than the old IPX.COM file. Cool.

Novell has been trying to move people over to the ODI drivers for several years. With Personal NetWare, NetWare 3.12, and NetWare 4.*x* all using this system, these ODI drivers are as close to mandatory as possible. Only the IPXODI.COM program supports the VLM (Virtual Loadable Module) files, and only the VLM files give you the real advantages of Personal NetWare and NetWare 4.*x*.

ROUTING OF NETWORK REQUESTS

If your PC has been configured using Personal NetWare or Novell DOS 7, all the files necessary to connect to a NetWare server have been installed for you. If your PC was set up as a NetWare client before Personal NetWare or Novell DOS 7, you will notice a few strange-looking files.

Before NetWare 4.0 and Personal NetWare, all Novell PC clients used "shell" programs. These programs ran ahead of DOS, intercepting NetWare requests. They ignored DOS and required extra memory to replace some of the functions that were in DOS (especially after DOS version 3.1). By working with DOS, the Personal NetWare files perform more network services in smaller amounts of memory.

NetWare 4.*x* and Personal NetWare now use what's termed a DOS Requester. In an unusually clear name for the computer business, the DOS Requester, sometimes called a Redirector, controls the routing of software requests from your local PC to the network. If your word processor issues a DOS command such as

```
GET FILE LETTERS.TXT
```

on a network drive letter, the DOS Requester redirects that command to the server the drive letter is pointing to.

For example, all the budget spreadsheets may be on the ACCTNG server in your workgroup. If your PC is configured with drive G: connected to the ACCTNG server, you might tell your spreadsheet program something like

```
GET G:\APPS\BUDGET\JANUARY.WK1
```

Then the program would send a request to DOS to find drive G: and that file. The request would be redirected to the server, without you or DOS worrying about the details.

BENEFITS OF THE NEW ORDER

What does all this Requester and VLM talk have to do with you in your daily grind? Here are some of the effects you will see:

- Less memory usage in your PC, since you can load the modules you need, rather than every piece of the client software as in the old days. VLMs make better use of high memory as well, leaving more RAM for your programs.
- Multiple protocol support, which means you can connect to your NetWare services and a UNIX system at the same time. This is one reason the ODI drivers are important.
- Easier updates when things change, since all the details are in configuration files rather than inside hard-to-modify programs.

The configuration files are all loaded by the STARTNET.BAT file, which the Personal NetWare installation program sets up for you. The STARTNET.BAT file is automatically called by your AUTOEXEC.BAT file. This means that you are connected to the network, ready to get to work, just by turning on your computer.

Connecting to the Workgroup under MS Windows

The support of multiple protocols comes in handy when you need to connect to the workgroup. Although NetWare servers and Personal NetWare use the same protocol, the VLMs required to support each system can be loaded separately. If you don't need to connect to a NetWare server, don't load those pieces of the Requester, and you'll save some memory. If you're using Personal NetWare or DOS 7 for better ways to connect to your NetWare server, you don't need to load the VLMs necessary for supporting the workgroup (Appendix A lists the VLMs required for each function).

After Personal NetWare is loaded, your Microsoft (MS) Windows system will have a new group. The Personal NetWare icon leads you into a completely mouse-driven MS Windows application to administer the workgroup. Everything that needs to be done, such as adding new users or making different resources available, can be done in the Personal NetWare program.

The Personal NetWare program will show you the workgroup available to you. If you double-click on the name, the login window pops up automatically. As shown in the example in Figure 1.1, the login window will usually have your name filled in for you, guessing that you are the one logging

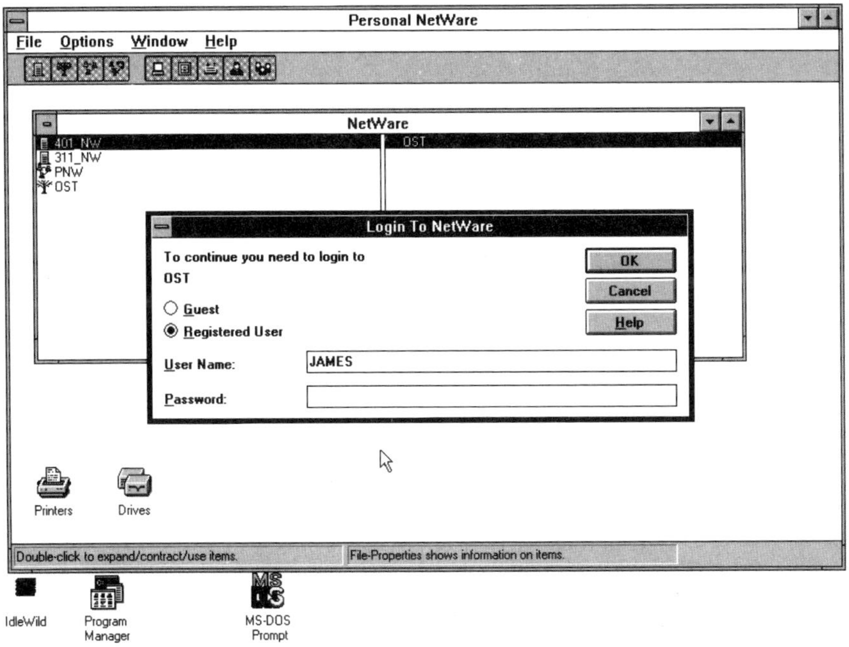

FIGURE 1.1
The Personal NetWare login window

in and not someone that has borrowed your computer. If you have borrowed another user's computer, just type your name in the space. Press the Tab key, type the password in the space provided, and then click on the OK button. Boom, there you are.

Connecting to the Workgroup under DOS

All the same tools available under Personal NetWare for MS Windows are available with the DOS version, they just don't have pictures. Typing NET LOGIN *YOUR-NAME* gets the same results as clicking with the mouse on the workgroup name under the Personal NetWare program. The same things happen, and the same database of security information about every user is used to determine whether or not you belong. Figure 1.2 shows the screen displayed by the NET program, with the view of NetWare servers available.

Use the NET program to get around, if you like menus. The Personal NetWare utility program NET looks just like the interface in DR-DOS (now Novell DOS) that won praise from many reviewers. It supports a mouse as well as plenty of shortcut keys, which get you the information you want quickly. From the main menu, you can perform the following tasks:

- Redirect your printing to a network printer.
- Change your context (more on that later in the book).
- Communicate with other users.
- Display information about your user account and privileges.
- Control which drive letters are pointing to which servers.
- Print to a network resource printer.
- Set or change your password.

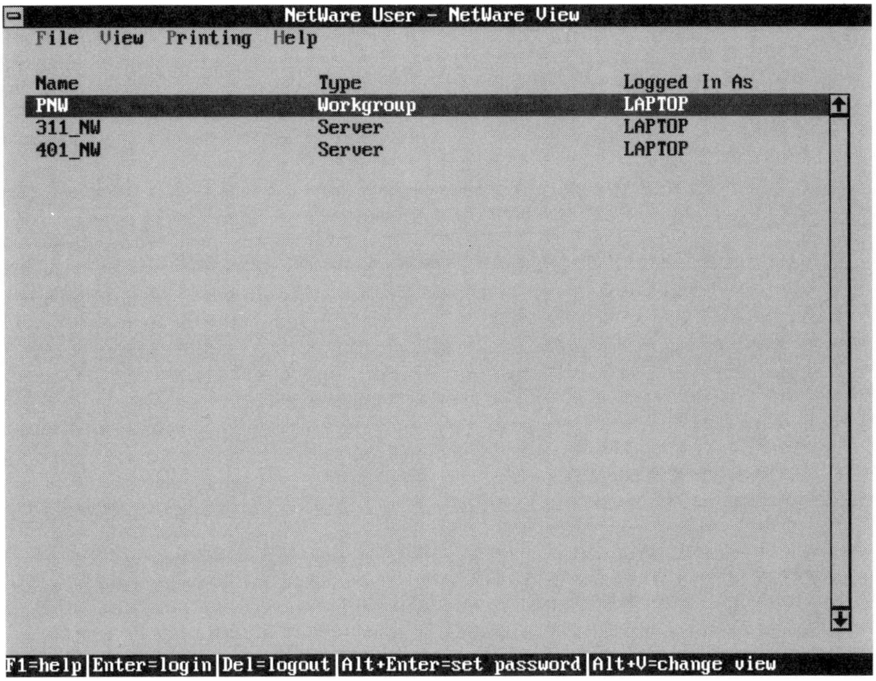

FIGURE 1.2

The Personal NetWare NET program opening screen

Typing NET /? from the DOS prompt displays a screen of the 30-plus workgroup commands, with instructions on how to get help on each specific command. The curious can type NET INFO and see what's running and what versions are in use. The busy can just get to work, since you're already logged in.

Connecting to NetWare Servers under MS Windows

Because MS Windows is the hot GUI (Graphical User Interface) today, Novell has included several helpful programs and put them all into their own group. In Personal NetWare, it's the Personal NetWare group. In DOS 7, these programs show up in the Novell DOS 7 group.

The Personal NetWare program lets you log in to a NetWare server just as easily as you log in to the workgroup, although it's more common to log in before you load MS Windows. You can also check and change your drive mappings, available printers, and available servers, and send a quick note to your colleagues. The Personal NetWare program is where you go to configure your PC as a server, if you choose to share your resources with the workgroup.

The Personal NetWare program works with NetWare servers as well, except you can't use it to configure new users and resources. That capability stays with the NetWare supervisor. You can send messages to users on those NetWare servers, however. You can also choose a NetWare server printer as one of your printers.

Connecting to NetWare Servers under DOS

To connect to a NetWare server under DOS, you don't need to use the NET LOGIN command, as you do to connect to the workgroup. Once you load the ODI drivers and VLM files, you will get a message that says

```
You are attached to server FS1
```

FS1 being replaced by the appropriate name. However, FS1 is the most popular server name in the world of small NetWare networks, so that name may work for you.

To log in, go to the drive letter listed in the NET.CFG program as FIRST NETWORK DRIVE, usually F:, and type LOGIN *YOUR-NAME*. The system will ask for your password, and then let you in (provided you remember your password and type it correctly). Don't put your login name and password on a sticky note on your monitor. Network administrators get all bent out of shape when they see that.

Fortunately, the Personal NetWare DOS utilities function well when you're connected to a NetWare server. Running the NET program gives almost as much control with the NetWare server as it does with the workgroup. Only the Display Account menu choice doesn't work when you're connected only to a NetWare server. This is because your user account information for the workgroup doesn't get copied to the NetWare server, and the NET utility doesn't read the NetWare server security files. For that, use SYSCON (SYStem CONsole), located in the \PUBLIC directory of all NetWare file servers.

Connecting to a NetWare 4.*x* Domain

NetWare 4.0 marks Novell's change from a server-centric operating system to a distributed, network-oriented operating system. With all the versions of NetWare before 4.0, each server was a kingdom unto itself. Like a monarchy, each server kept a list of subjects and resources for the kingdom. Like many times in history, if you weren't a subject of the kingdom, you were ignored at best or persecuted at worst. The only way to use the resources of kingdoms was to be granted access by royal decree, or by the system administrators, who sometimes confuse themselves with royalty.

With NetWare 4.0, the self-contained kingdom has been replaced by a federation of states. The entire network is a domain, stretching over multiple kingdoms. Subjects of one kingdom automatically have access to the resources of any other kingdom, without royal dispensation. Each kingdom goes farther now, and promises to be friendly to the subject of any kingdom. This means any user can pass freely through the network, once that user has been authorized by the NDS (NetWare Directory Service).

For a more modern analogy, think of the United States as the domain, with each state as a server. Being a resident of the entire United States gives you permission to travel to any state without being hindered. So you can visit Vermont to see maple trees, Wisconsin to see lakes, Florida to see Disneyworld, and

Texas to see cowboys astride their pickup trucks. Each region has something special to offer, and your United States travel citizenship gets you access to all of them.

What does this have to do with your network? With NetWare 4.*x*, you don't log in to a single server, just as you don't apply for United States citizenship on a state level; you apply to the federal government. You log in to the network, consisting of possibly many servers, rather than each server as you need it.

Network Diagnostics: See a Problem and Fix It

Under both DOS and MS Windows, Personal NetWare provides a full set of network diagnostics. The Network Diagnostics program gives plenty of detail about the workgroup servers, clients, and traffic levels. We'll cover this in more detail later, but if you're interested, you can try some of the choices in Diagnostics:

- Graph the amount of network traffic per network node (connected network drive).
- See how much disk space is available for you on every server's hard drive.
- See how busy the workgroup servers are.
- Graph traffic for the entire workgroup.
- Run a test to check connections to all nodes.

The MS Windows program PNWDIAG.EXE is part of the Personal NetWare group. The DOS counterpart, PNWDIAGS.EXE, gives the same information, and both are handy when things aren't going well. Or try it if you're just curious about how much traffic sending a message to Joe about lunch creates. Figure 1.3 shows the opening screen of Network Diagnostics.

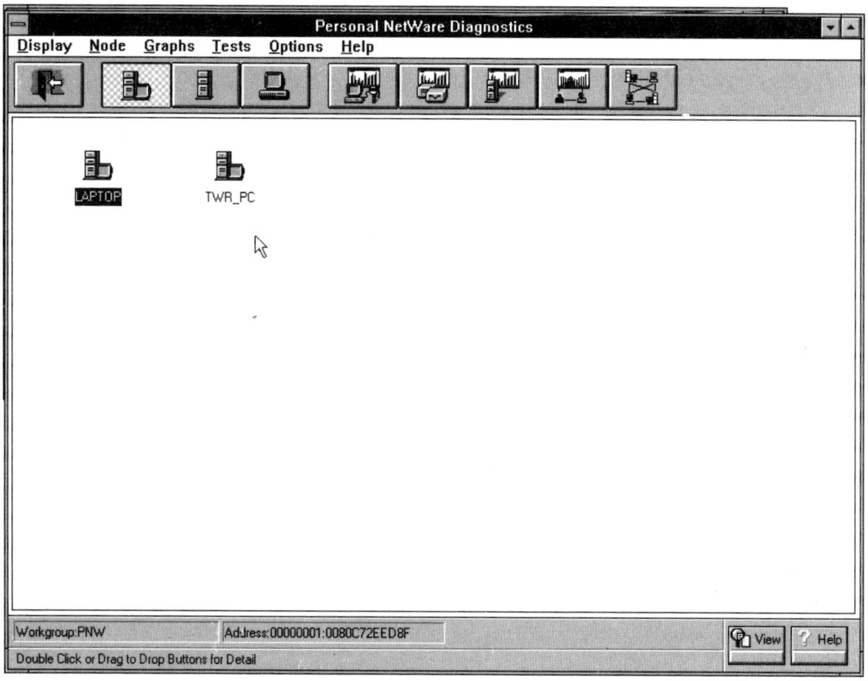

FIGURE 1.3
Network Diagnostics opening screen (MS Windows version)

Note that Network Diagnostics does not provide any information about the NetWare servers or network traffic between non-Personal NetWare clients and NetWare servers. Check the SETUP program for each user to make sure that they have the NMR.VLM loaded. It won't load automatically.

Client Monitoring: Who's Sharing My PC?

When you're sharing the resources of your PC, such as some hard disk space and your printer, you have a right to know who's using those resources. By using the NET CONSOLE command, you can get that information.

Once you see who's on first, and what's on second, you have the option to close files those computers are using and disconnect those people from your PC. This is not as cruel as it might seem. Some applications are touchy about being shut down without the files being closed. If Joe leaves his computer on and attached to your PC when he leaves for the day, NET CONSOLE allows you to gracefully close his application and disconnect him before you leave and turn off your system. Or just disconnect him before you leave, whether you turn off your system or not. Figure 1.4 shows the NET CONSOLE screen.

You might find that you don't turn off your system as much as you used to. If your machine is off, your workgroup won't have access to your files and printer and any other resource you have, such as a CD ROM player. Try leaving your system on, but turning your monitor off. If you leave the system on, perhaps no one will notice if you play hooky. If your system is off when everyone else gets to work, they will certainly know you're gone. They'll miss your hard disk, but then they'll notice you're gone as well. Be safe and leave it on, but get a battery backup system for your PC. Battery backups are fairly cheap now, and a backup system will help you avoid some scrambled files one of these days. Unscrambling files is about as much fun as unscrambling eggs, so get the battery backup.

FIGURE 1.4

The NET CONSOLE screen (after a bit, an interesting screen saver starts)

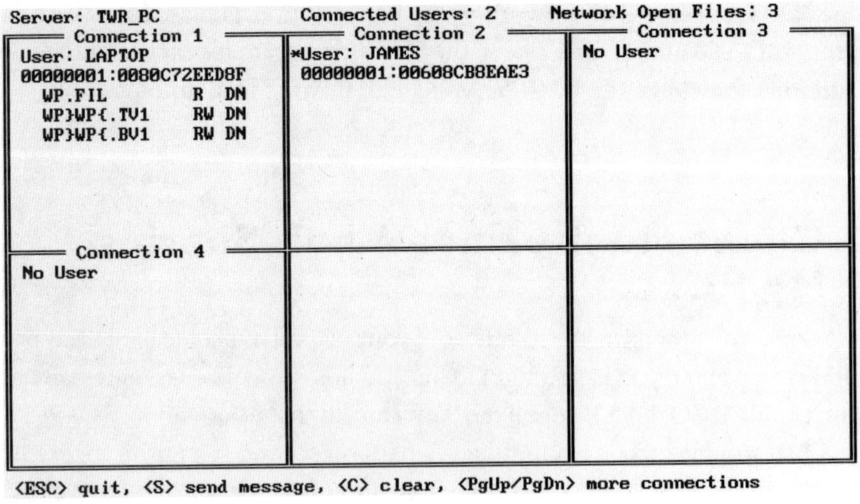

NETWARS: Stress Relief for One to Four Players (Sound Optional)

During a hard day at the keyboard, stress builds. One way to relieve that stress is to throw things through the window. A more socially acceptable way is to play NETWARS.

The single-player version pits you against some alien pirates that are intent on stealing your purple pods. The longer you save your pods and the more pirates you shoot, the more points you get. If stress is contagious in your office, invite up to three co-workers to play NETWARS with you. There are no pods to save in the multiple-player game, but you can shoot your friends. This relieves stress without the risk of being arrested.

The NETWARS program is in your \NWCLIENT directory. One of the options is to turn off the sound. If quiet and stealth are important when playing games in your office, remember not to yell, "Yahoo, I got him!" when you make a particularly good shot.

CHAPTER 2

How Do I Log In and Get Connected under Microsoft Windows?

The whole idea of a network is to share resources. These resources include, but are not limited to, programs, data files, hard disk space, printers, and messaging services. Other network resources include modems, CD ROM drives, computer fax servers, and host connections to larger computers such as UNIX systems or mainframes.

What's Available on the Network?

So, what's available on your network? There are several ways to find out, and several ways to connect once you know. Be prepared for the network to be somewhat "dynamic," which is a polite way to say "never the same way twice." Networks with NetWare file servers tend to be fairly stable and consistent, because there is usually at least one person dedicated to making sure the system is available for everyone. Some parts of the system, such as a fax server or a mainframe connection, may be separate from the file server itself. That explains why sometimes the file server is up but some of the resources aren't available. The goal, and the reality in the vast majority of cases, is for all the network resources to be available at all times.

Your workgroup is a different story. The workgroup servers that are sharing resources are other PCs like yours, run by other people just like you. If you feel this makes things a little less dependable than a NetWare file server, you're right. Ever see those bumper stickers that say, "Warning—I drive just like you"? You might want to print some that say, "Warning—I treat my PC as badly as you treat yours."

Just as people that work together depend on each other, people in a workgroup depend on each person using good computer manners. Remember, if you share some resources of your PC, the PC must be available at all times. When you leave, turn off the monitor, but not the PC. If you do this regularly, you can complain with a clean conscience when Marilyn forgets and turns her PC off.

Now that you know a bit about the overall capabilities of Personal NetWare for DOS and Microsoft (MS) Windows, let's get started. Your NetWare server awaits. Ready to log in? Well, hang on just a bit as we lay some foundation.

What Files Do I Need to Start the Universal NetWare Client?

If you look in the \NWCLIENT directory (or whatever directory you chose when installing either Personal NetWare or Novell DOS 7), you'll see some files with strange names. In the old days, NetWare started with one or two necessary files, and that was it. Today, you may need to load a baker's dozen or more small files to get things working. In spite of the larger number of files to load, however, the procedure is easier and more automatic than ever before.

Those old NetWare files, which you may still have on your system, still work when connecting to NetWare file servers versions 3.11 and below. For NetWare versions 3.12 and above, particularly NetWare 4.0 and above, you should use the new files. In the \NWCLIENT directory, the new files are all the ones with the .VLM (Virtual Loadable Module) extension.

THE STARTNET.BAT FILE

The default STARTNET.BAT file created by the installation procedures of both Personal NetWare and Novell DOS 7 is described in Table 2.1. The type is all in uppercase, which looks garish but doesn't matter to DOS. DOS is not case sensitive, meaning an *M* is the same to DOS as an *m*.

You don't need to create this file yourself, so stop sweating. The installation program automatically places this file in the directory you specify (the default is \NWCLIENT, and it's best to use this recommendation). Details of this installation, and changes that can be made, are described in Appendix A.

The STARTNET.BAT file can be modified in Novell DOS 7, PC DOS, or MS DOS by using the SETUP.EXE program. This program is found in the \NWCLIENT directory. Although the PATH statement will make the file available from anywhere, other programs (particularly MS Windows) also use a SETUP program. It's better to run SETUP from the \NWCLIENT directory so no unpleasant surprises pop up.

TABLE 2.1
STARTNET.BAT File

COMMAND OR FILE TO EXECUTE	EXPLANATION
SET NWLAN-GUAGE=ENGLISH	Tells NetWare to present messages in English
DPMS	DOS Protected Mode Services
NWCACHE 2909 1024 /LEND=ON /DELAY=ON	The NWCACHE program, which sets aside 2909K for a cache, but always keeping at least 1024K, lends memory to programs that can use it, and delays writing to disk for better performance
LH C:\DOS\SHARE.EXE /F:10240 /L:200	DOS program for controlling open files and file locking
LH C:\NWCLIENT\LSL	Link Support Layer, between the physical network board and the network protocol
LH C:\NWCLI-ENT\3C509.COM	The particular network interface card used in this PC
LH C:\NWCLI-ENT\IPXODI	Internetwork eXchange Open Data-Link Interface, the protocol for NetWare
LH C:\NWCLIENT\SERV-ER	The program that turns your PC into a workgroup server (optional)
C:\NWCLIENT\VLM	The VLM.EXE manager program that loads VLM modules based on NET.CFG details
C:\NWCLIENT\NET LOGIN	Starts the login process to the workgroup and any other connections in your PNWLOGIN,SCR file

Notice that each program name, except for VLM, has a ***LH*** at the beginning of the line. That tells the PC operating system to place the referenced program into high memory. This works only on any DOS 5 or above system. If you're still using DOS 4.*x*, now's a great time to upgrade.

The VLM.EXE program automatically looks above the 640 KB DOS barrier for space to load. There's nothing gained by putting the ***LH*** in for the VLM program in the STARTNET.BAT.

LOADING VLMS

The VLM manager mentioned on the last line of the STARTNET.BAT file starts another automatic sequence of program loading. Unlike much of DOS, the order in which the VLMs are loaded is important. You don't need to worry about this, unless you make lots of changes in the NET.CFG file. If you're starting up in the usual manner, like the vast majority of users, the VLM.EXE program will take care of the details. Your only concern is that all the files with the VLM extension are in the \NWCLIENT directory. The VLM manager program will pick each one out of the directory in the order needed.

Appendix A shows the names of the files in the order they load, although you rarely need to worry about this. If you are having problems, see Appendix C. That appendix contains troubleshooting information, including how to check your VLMs.

The AUTO.VLM file is the most interesting and useful to the majority of NetWare users. With this program loaded, your PC will reconnect to any workgroup servers that disappear and reappear. With earlier versions of NetWare client software, any connections lost because of network or server problems are gone until you log in again or reboot.

Do you need to understand everything about every VLM to make things work? No, not at all. However, understanding some of these files may come in handy one day. But aren't you glad the VLM.EXE file handles the vast majority of the work without being modified or configured?

THE NET.CFG FILE

The other file that is important to startup is NET.CFG. This is a configuration file, similar to the SYSTEM.INI file in MS Windows or CONFIG.SYS in DOS. It's an ASCII text file, like STARTNET.BAT, so your DOS editor will be fine for making any changes.

The basic NET.CFG file is created during installation of both Personal NetWare and Novell DOS 7. Some modification may be necessary, however, unless your installation is a brand new network.

NET.CFG is the configuration file used to specify things about your PC that are different from the default, normal settings. There's no problem with being "nondefault" or "not normal," because normal for a computer doesn't mean much to a human. Default settings tend to indicate settings that are the same for everyone, and that's rare in today's computer networks. In this context, nondefault may mean things like using the new Personal NetWare files to connect with just an existing NetWare server. Some of those settings will be different than if you were connecting only to a Personal NetWare workgroup or to a NetWare 4.*x* server.

Here is a sample NET.CFG file:

```
LINK DRIVER 3C509
 FRAME ETHERNET_802.3
NETWARE DOS REQUESTER
 FIRST NETWORK DRIVE = F
 VLM = AUTO.VLM
 VLM = NMR.VLM
SHOW DOTS = ON
```

So, what isn't "normal" about this NET.CFG file? Let's go down the listing, line by line.

The first line, LINK DRIVER 3C509, tells the system what type of network interface card is in your PC. This must be there, but the type of card used will vary among PCs. So there can never be a "default" NIC value, can there?

FRAME ETHERNET_802.3 describes the type of Ethernet data packet used on the network. This is the default frame type for all the NetWare systems up to NetWare 4.*x*, when the frame type changed to ETHERNET_802.2 for a default. This is a newer version of the packet, which provides some extra functions over the 802.3 version. However, if you are connecting to an existing NetWare server, chances are the type must be changed to 802.3, as in our example.

NETWARE DOS REQUESTER starts a section where many variables can be set for your particular PC. There are over 50 parameters that can be changed for particular situations. In our example, however, only two options out of the 50 have been used. Changing these variables are the exception, not the rule.

FIRST NETWORK DRIVE = F is our first parameter that affects the setup of our PC software. It keeps our drive mappings consistent. We're telling the NetWare software that the first drive letter that should point to a network resource is drive F:. The first five letters, A through E, are generally reserved for DOS. Drive F has traditionally been the drive NetWare starts with, but that's not a rule, only a custom. This parameter works with the line in your CONFIG.SYS file that says LASTDRIVE = Z. Before, the CONFIG.SYS file dictated where the NetWare drives started. Now the NET.CFG file does, and LASTDRIVE = Z in the CONFIG.SYS file makes the full range of drives available to NET.CFG.

VLM=AUTO.VLM tells the system to add the Auto-reconnect VLM to this station. If a NetWare server or a workgroup resource of any kind goes away for any reason (David mistakenly turns off his PC when he goes to lunch), the NetWare software will keep trying to find the resource. Once the server becomes available again (David comes back from lunch), the drive letters pointing to that resource will reconnect automatically.

VLM=NMR.VLM turns on the NetWare Management Responder inside the workstation software. Certain functions in Novell's IPX/SPX (Internetwork Packet eXchange/Sequenced Packet eXchange) protocol help monitor the network. Much of the software function provided by the Network Diagnostics program in Personal NetWare relies on this software.

SHOW DOTS = ON tells NetWare to show the current directory dot and parent directory dots. These are DOS directory attributes, but NetWare is not DOS and doesn't have these dots. When you tell the system that you want to see the DOS attributes for the current and parent directory, NetWare provides the information that your PC needs to recreate those dots for you. This is important for programs such as MS Windows File Manager, where you need the dots to move up to your parent directory.

More details on the NET.CFG file can be found in, you guessed it, Appendix A.

Logging In to the Server before Starting MS Windows

If Personal NetWare has just been installed on your PC, or you have made changes to any of the files mentioned in the previous sections, you must reboot before continuing. Some of the files are read by the system only at boot time. The network files are read each time you load the network drivers and workstation files. You can manually unload each and every file mentioned in STARTNET.BAT and NET.CFG, but it's easier to just reboot and start clean.

YOUR PC'S BOOT PROCESS

The boot process for your PC goes like this:

- Finish self-test, beep, and read the CONFIG.SYS file.
- Finish the CONFIG.SYS file and start reading the AUTOEXEC.BAT file.
- Finish the AUTOEXEC.BAT file and call the STARTNET.BAT file.
- Check for the NET.CFG configuration file.
- Load each program listed in STARTNET.BAT.
- Modify settings as described in NET.CFG.

YOUR LOGIN PROCESS

If there are no error messages on the screen after your PC reboots, the system will show the prompt

```
username:
```

Type the name your network administrator gave you as your user, or login, name. Please use this actual system name instead of YOUR-NAME. This isn't vaudeville, you know (George Burns is much funnier than your computer). Your user name may be three initials, or your first name and first letter of your last name, or first letter of your first name then all or part of your last name.

If your name is Rose B. Redd, your user name may look like one of these:

rbr
roser
rredd

There are other ways to do user names, of course, limited by imagination and the legal DOS character set.

After you enter your user name, the network will ask for your password, which you need to type now. After you enter the password correctly, you will be connected to the network.

The security system for the NetWare server will grant you access to those areas the administrator has previously defined for you. If you are a current NetWare user, the areas will probably be the same as before. If you have not been a NetWare user before this, from the DOS prompt, type the command

```
MAP
```

If you see a listing of drive letters, you have an account and can go on. If you get the DOS message "Bad command or file name," you haven't been set up properly by your administrator. Call and complain.

Logging in to the Server with MS Windows

Once you set up, log in, and get ready to work, how do you get around the network? How can you find out what's available to you? Where are the printers? Where are the resources you've been hearing about?

If MS Windows was on your system when you installed Personal NetWare (or Novell DOS 7), the installation program asked about including all the MS Windows-specific programs. The installation program even knew which directory MS Windows was in (usually C:\WINDOWS). If you installed MS Windows after Personal NetWare, check out Appendix A for instructions on adding the Personal NetWare files for MS Windows.

When you start MS Windows after installing Personal NetWare, there will be a new group: the Personal NetWare group. This has been placed there and configured for you by the installation program. The most used icon in the group is the one labeled Personal NetWare.

This is somewhat of a "quick start" section; all the gory details are described in later chapters. I would encourage you to play around here, however, and look behind each icon and menu choice. You can't hurt anything from here, except for rearranging some things that you might not understand too well yet. But when you start MS Windows again, everything goes back to normal. Feel free to experiment. The worst that can happen is you will need to restart MS Windows. You probably do that two or three times a day anyway, so what's once more?

Introduction to the Personal NetWare Program

Clicking on the Personal NetWare icon brings up a multipurpose window that controls drive mappings, printer availability, server connections, and more, as shown in Figure 2.1. Want to send a message to someone in the workgroup? Here's one place you can do it. Want to configure your server or your relationship to servers and resources across the network? This is the place.

To get out of Personal NetWare program, you can press Alt-F4, or click on the exit that hides inside the little box with the fat dash, in the upper-left corner of the window. The technical name for that thing is the Control menu box. Clicking once drops down the menu, and you can then move down and click on Exit. Clicking twice quickly, or double-clicking as they say, performs the same action.

FIGURE 2.1

The Personal NetWare program window, showing drive mappings

The information shown by the Personal NetWare program windows changes depending on the area you're in and what you want to do. First, let's look at the icons that will help you see what resources you have, where they are, and how you can use them.

See the line of little icons, just under the MS Windows menu bar? There's a picture of a tower PC server, a tree, a ring of people, and so on. Make sure all the buttons are depressed before starting. Depressed, in this context, means pushed in, not sad. If you're not sure which way is pushed in, click once on an icon. If there is a solid black line around the icon, it's depressed. If there is a white section line on the top and left of the icon, it isn't depressed. Push them all in for this exploration, so every type of resource will be visible to you.

Notice that when you move your mouse cursor on to each icon, an explanation appears in the bottom-left corner of the main Personal NetWare window. This is a handy introduction to the functions of the buttons. We'll go into detail on all of them later, but feel free to glide the cursor across them all and see the descriptions.

If the different views are closed, there will be a red Novell icon on the screen, a printer, and a pair of disk drives. Double-clicking on the icons will open a window covering much of the screen. All three can be open at one time without causing any problems. If you press Alt-W or click on the Window menu option, you'll see that you can arrange the windows or icons, just as you can in the Program Manager in MS Windows.

CHECKING YOUR DRIVES

The drives picture, or icon, is of two external hard disks. If you look closely, you can see the little green light in the bottom-left corner of the drive glowing, indicating drive activity. Double-clicking on this icon with the mouse shows all the drives you have available and lets you add or subtract drive definitions as you desire. The answer to "What disk resources do I have available?" is found right here.

The drives listed on the left side of the box show what you are connected to now, while the box on the right shows what's available to you. Double-clicking on the volume name on the right opens it up, showing all the directories on that server, or on the directory tree in NetWare 4.*x*.

CHECKING YOUR PRINTERS

The printer icon is for printer connections and resources. After you double-click on the icon of the printer, your three parallel printer ports, labeled LPT1:, LPT2:, and LPT3:, are listed on the left side of the window. On the right are all the available printer resources.

This is the format for most of the screens within Personal NetWare: your settings on the left, available resources on the right. If you can see it on the right, you can drag it with your mouse. Simply put the mouse on the line listing what resource you want, then press the left mouse button and hold it down while you move the arrow over to the left box. Place the resource on the line listing where you want the resource to be on your PC, and let go of the mouse button. If a password is necessary, a dialog box will open and await your password. Figure 2.2 shows this login dialog box.

CHECKING YOUR SERVERS

The red Novell icon depicts the available NetWare and Personal NetWare servers on your network. Opening that window shows the servers you are currently connected to, as well as which servers are available.

The right side of the box will be empty if you're already logged in to all the available servers on your network. If there are items listed in the right side, you can make connections by dragging and dropping once again. If you prefer, you can just highlight the resource by clicking one time on it,

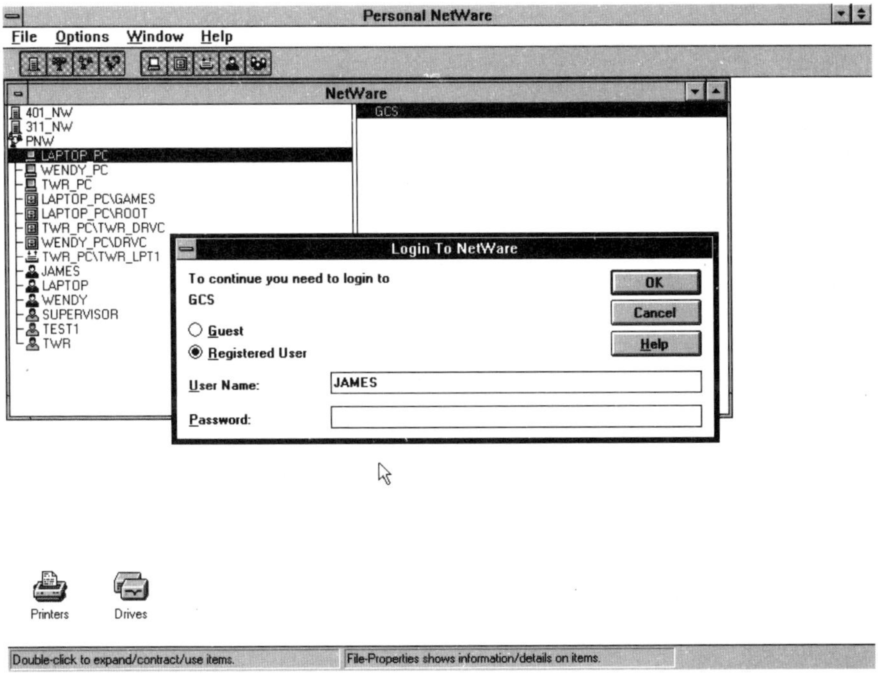

FIGURE 2.2

The Login to NetWare dialog box in the Personal NetWare program

then pull down the File menu and choose Connect. If you double-click on the resource, or click on the Connect button, the dialog box for logging in pops up again. Fill it out, and you're connected.

SENDING MESSAGES

2.1 THE FAST LANE

IN-A-HURRY? **Send a message through Personal NetWare**

1. Double-click on the Novell icon.
2. Double-click on the server.
3. Double-click on the user name or group.
4. Fill in the message text box.
5. Click on Send.

Want to send messages to your fellow networkers? When you double-click on the name of a server in the left window, the attached volumes, printers, users, and groups will appear underneath. By double-clicking on the name of the user you wish to annoy with a message, you bring up a dialog box, titled NetWare User Information, as shown in Figure 2.3. As you can see, this dialog box provides for more than just sending messages. We'll get to the details of the user information in Chapter 8. For now, though, let's just deal with message transmittal.

The bottom of the dialog box is for message text, and it is ready for your input. The vertical-bar cursor appears right at the beginning. Type your message inside that text box. If your addressee is running MS Windows, the message will word wrap, so type away. If the user runs DOS, only about half the message will show on his or her screen. It's best to make NetWare messages like this short and sweet. Something like, "Rose, let's eat," works the best. The message stays on the screen of the receiver until it is cleared off manually, interrupting the user's work, so use this facility judiciously.

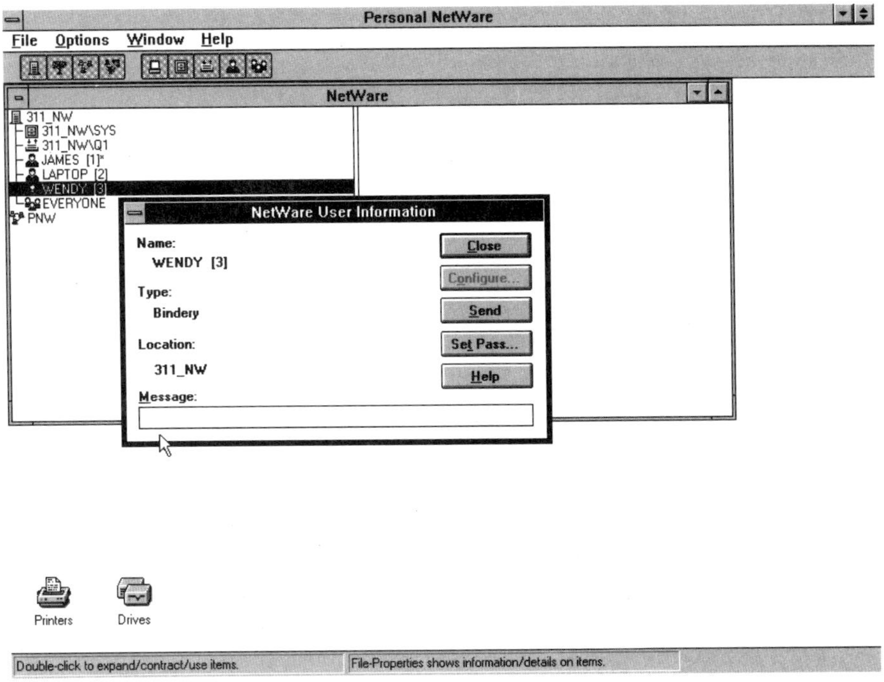

FIGURE 2.3

The NetWare User Information dialog box

RESIZING LIST BOXES

If you place your cursor exactly in the double lines separating the right and left sides of any of the windows in the Personal NetWare desktop, the cursor mutates. It turns into a line with arrows pointing right and left. This subtle clue indicates you can adjust the size of the two boxes.

To resize a list box, simply hold down the left mouse button and slide right or left. When you release the mouse button, the boxes will stay in the ratio you leave them. If you're more a Democrat, you can have more of the left box. If you lean more to the right, adjust the right box to be larger.

Introduction to the NetWare Tools Pop-Up Program

There's a lot of power behind some of the features in the Personal NetWare program: power to change, create, or delete users, servers, printers, file systems, and entire user groups. Since a misclick of the mouse in the wrong place can cause some level of mischief, Novell provided an easier, simpler, and more readily available set of tools for managing your connections to the network resources. Although the program isn't given a name in Personal NetWare, it's the same program that's called User Tools in NetWare 4.*x*. The program file is named NWTOOLS.EXE, as in NetWare Tools, so we'll refer to it as NetWare Tools.

SETTING THE HOTKEY FOR NETWARE TOOLS

2.2 THE FAST LANE

IN-A-HURRY? Enable the NetWare Tools hotkey

1 Open the Main group.
2 Double-click on Control Panel.
3 Double-click on the Network icon.
4 Click on the Enable Hotkey box.

NetWare Tools includes facilities for configuring drive mappings, assigning printers, connecting servers, and sending messages to your co-workers. There are two user-definable buttons as well. This set of tools is only a keypress away, once you tell MS Windows what F6 means.

In Program Manager, open the Main group if it's not already open, then double-click on Control Panel, the icon with the computer sitting under a clock. Double-click on the Network icon, the one illustrated, for some strange reason, with what looks like a printer cable writhing like a snake. Double-clicking on the snake brings up the NetWare Settings dialog box, shown in Figure 2.4.

Many of the settings don't have much value to us now, but the top box on the right, labeled NetWare Hotkey, is handy. This box contains a single

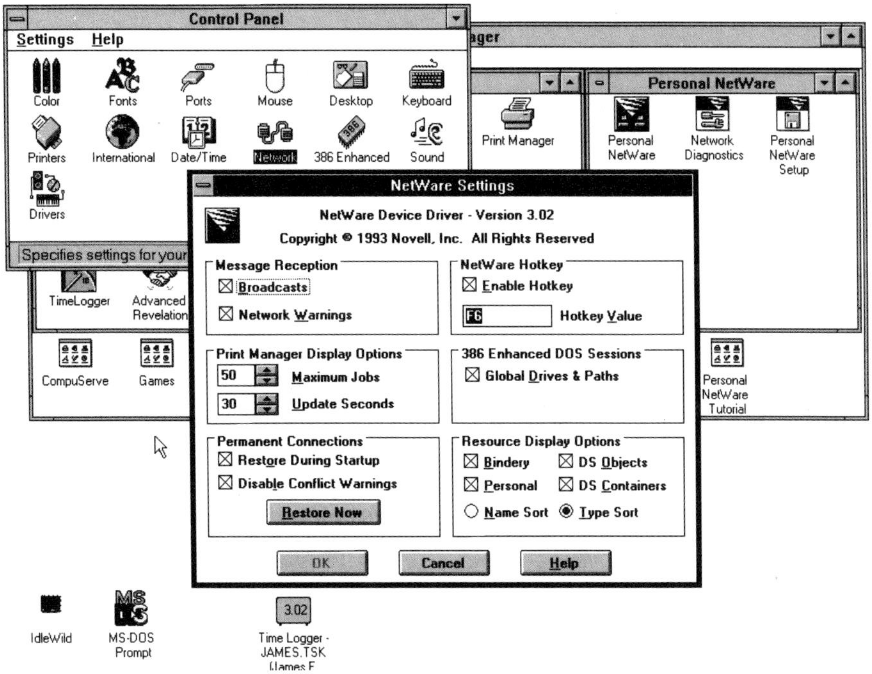

FIGURE 2.4

The NetWare Settings dialog box

check box to enable the NetWare Tools hotkey. The default key to use is F6 (function key 6 across the top of enhanced keyboards). If you don't like F6 for some reason, click on the text box containing F6 and press a few other keys. The ones that are available will appear in the text box—even stupid choices like Backspace. But since you can't put F6 back in there, be sure to click on the Cancel button at the bottom of the dialog box if you change your mind.

These fat rectangular boxes with commands inside are technically *buttons*. That's the truth. More technically, they are *command buttons*, because clicking on them (single-clicking, not double-clicking) executes the command listed on the button. If it says Cancel, for instance, clicking on the button will cancel your current activity. You'll see these all over the place.

Why should you bother with this hotkey? Because it gives you nearly instant access to network connections. With the hotkey enabled, anytime you want to check or change your NetWare connections while you're in MS Windows, you can just press F6. The NetWare Tools pop-up will appear on top of whatever you're working on. Be sure and press F6 only in MS Windows programs, however. Pressing F6 in a DOS window just puts a ^Z character, meaning end of file, on the screen wherever the cursor is sitting. If this happens, be sure to delete the ^Z, because it can cause problems if you leave it there. The NetWare Tools pop-up won't appear on top of a DOS session, but it's a nice trick everywhere else in MS Windows.

USING NETWARE TOOLS

The NetWare Tools pop-up provides a quick shortcut for doing the typical user things you will need to do in your daily networking. You may actually wind up using these tools more than the Personal NetWare program, since it's easier to pop up NetWare Tools than to load Personal NetWare from the Program Manager or expand its icon from the bottom of the screen if you minimized it.

The details of the NetWare Tools window change depending on your request. Look at Figure 2.5, which shows the window for server connections, for a second to get oriented.

The first large button, to the far left, shows a door and an arrow out. That's the exit. It works the same as the exit provided by MS Windows in the upper-left corner of the framing window. Using the red door exit is quicker, because it only requires a single click and is easier to hit for shaky mouse manipulators. You can also press the Escape key to close the NetWare Tools window.

The last big button, with the question mark, is for Help (or you can press F1 if you're a traditionalist).

Note that you can adjust the size of the right and left boxes in NetWare Tools in the same way as you resize list boxes in Personal NetWare. But don't be disappointed when they return in their default configuration the next time you pop up the window.

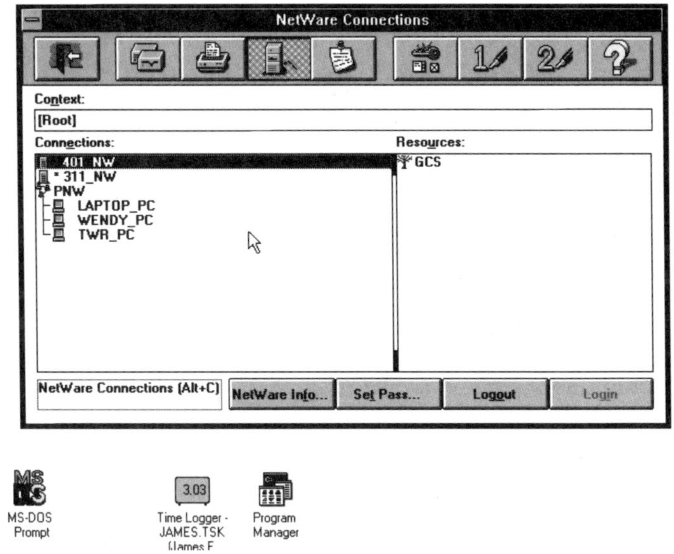

FIGURE 2.5

The NetWare Tools window, showing server connections

Checking Available Drives

The next large button to the right, slightly separated from the exit, is the drives button. The picture is of two external hard disks. If you look closely, you can again see the little green light glowing in the bottom-left corner of the drive. Clicking on this button shows all the drives you have available and lets you add or subtract drive definitions as you desire. The drives listed on the left side of the box show what you are connected to now, while the box on the right shows what's available to you.

Checking Available Printers

The next button is for printer connections and resources. When you click on the picture of the printer, you see the printers you can connect to. The left box lists your three parallel printer ports, labeled LPT1:, LPT2:, and LPT3:. On the right are all the available printer resources. This is the same format as used for most of the screens within Personal NetWare: your settings on the left, available resources on the right. As explained earlier, if you can see it on the right, you can drag and drop it with your mouse to set up your connections.

Checking Available Servers

To the right of the printer button is the server button, represented by a tower PC case. Servers don't need to be in those type cases, but they often are, so the picture is playing the percentages. When you click on this button, the window shows the servers you are connected to and those that are available.

In the left box, labeled Connections, your current connections are listed. You can tell which ones are active because they are in full color, rather than gray. If you have a monochrome monitor on your laptop, good luck. Unless, of course, you set your MS Windows color scheme to work on your mono screen by choosing one of the LCD color choices in Colors under Control Panel.

The right box will be empty if you are already logged in to all the available servers on your network. If items are listed in the Resources box, you can make connections by dragging and dropping once again. If you prefer, you can just highlight the resource by clicking once on it. The Login button at the bottom of the window will become active. You can tell it's active because it has a black outline and the letters become black rather than gray. If you double-click on the resource or click on the Login button, the dialog box for logging in pops up again.

Sending Messages

2.3 THE FAST LANE

IN-A-HURRY?? Send a message with NetWare Tools

1. Press F6 to pop up NetWare Tools.
2. Click on the icon showing paper with a push-pin button.
3. Type your message in the text box just under the buttons.
4. In the right box, double-click on the name of the recipient.

See the paper pinned to the wall in the button to the right of the server button? That indicates messaging services. NetWare Tools gives you a quick way to send a short message to anyone or everyone on the network. Click on this button, and you'll see the names of the attached servers on the left and a list of users on the right.

Type a short test message in the Message text box, just below the large buttons. Then highlight one of the names in the Resources box. Figure 2.6 shows a message ready to be sent.

Double-clicking on the name or clicking on the Send button at the bottom of the window does the same thing: writes your message on that person's screen. If the message recipient is using MS Windows, a little dialog box pops up smack in the middle of the screen. If the person you're sending the message to is using DOS, the message is placed on the top line of the monitor. Either way, remember that the person must clear the message before returning to work.

Don't make the mistake of choosing the person before typing your message: the message goes as soon as you pick the lucky recipient. If you

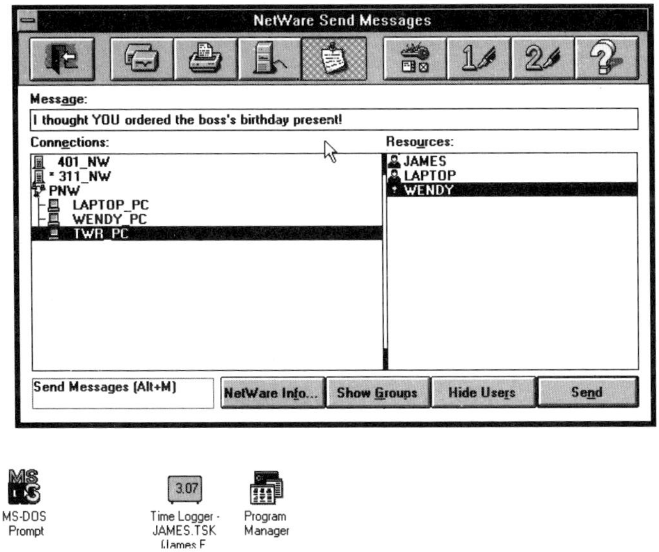

FIGURE 2.6

The NetWare Tools program messaging function

choose first, a blank message will be sent. Unfortunately, your name is attached to all messages, and if it's blank, you look either dumb or clumsy. Choose your defense now, because everybody sends a blank message or two by accident. Cursing your network administrator for lack of training will be allowed only once, then you'll need to step up and shoulder the blame or come up with a creative excuse.

Refusing Messages

2.4

IN-A-HURRY? **Turn off message reception**

1 Press F6 to pop up NetWare Tools.
2 Click on the burning key (hotkey) button.
3 Clear the Broadcasts check box in the Message Reception area.

You can set your PC so that messages are refused. This is particularly helpful if you have programs that churn a bit while you're at lunch.

To turn off messages from MS Windows, press F6 to pop up NetWare Tools. Then click on the fourth button from the right, the one showing a burning key (hotkey—get it?—must be a programmer's joke). This pops open the NetWare Settings dialog box, just as if you went through Program Manager and Control Panel again (see, Personal NetWare is saving you time already, by making this dialog box available more quickly than through normal MS Windows procedures).

In the NetWare Settings dialog box, the first box in the top-left area, just under the Novell icon, is labeled Message Reception. Clear the check box for the first item to turn off the receipt of NetWare broadcasts on your station. Leave the other option, NetWare Warnings, checked. If something bad is happening, you want to know as soon as possible. Click on OK to save the new settings and close the dialog box.

To turn off message receipt from the DOS prompt, type

```
NET RECEIVE OFF
```

and no messages will be received by your PC. If you don't want to be quite that hostile, type

```
NET RECEIVE 60
```

and the messages will stay on your screen for 1 minute (60 seconds), and then clear themselves.

Hiding Groups and Users

Notice that the buttons at the bottom of the NetWare Tools screen now offer you the choices to show or hide groups and users. When your network gets big, the Resources box fills up. Remember, this shows users and groups for the NetWare servers you're attached to, and servers often have hundreds of users connected. Excluding groups when you're looking for a particular user may save you some time and trouble.

Assigning Functions to the User-Definable Buttons

Across the top of the NetWare Tools window, the second and third buttons from the right (with the pictures of a pen drawing the numbers 1 and 2) are user-definable. This means that you can make them do anything you want, as long as the command can be put on a single command line. The best way to go is to add commands to run File Manager, Print Manager, Calculator, Terminal, or perhaps even a game. You want the buttons to be for programs you will run and then close, because if you click on your user-defined button while the program is still running, you'll have two copies of the program running.

When you first click on a user-definable button, you'll see a dialog box labeled User Defined Path, with a command line text box ready for your input. Enter the command carefully, because there's no easy way to edit this command line. Put the name, with full path listing, of the program you want to execute. If that program has an icon, it will take the place of the pen drawing a number. If it's a DOS file, a full-screen DOS window will open to run the program, but there won't be a new icon.

Did you mess it up the first time, like I did? And there's no way to edit that command string from within NetWare Tools, is there? And there's nothing in the manual about this either, is there? Aren't you glad you bought this book now?

Use a text editor to open the file \WINDOWS\NETWARE.INI. In the first section, labeled [Options], you'll see two lines, User1 and User2. That's where the command string is stored. Use your editor to either fix your mistake, or erase everything after User1= on that line. If you erase the line, you can try entering the command string again from NetWare Tools.

Connecting to a NetWare Server under MS Windows

There is a large installed base of NetWare file servers, and it's likely that the majority of Personal NetWare users will be connecting to at least one of them. The best way to connect to a NetWare file server is before starting MS Windows. With Personal NetWare, the NetWare Tools and Personal NetWare programs offer an easy way to attach to any file server, but not for a full login procedure. Attaching to a server verifies your right to use the server, but doesn't make any printer or drive connections. The login procedure sets up all your printer connections and drive mappings to a server. That's why it's easiest to make all the standard connections before you start MS Windows.

A NetWare server has a directory named \PUBLIC, with almost 150 files taking more than 8 MB of space. This directory holds all the NetWare utilities for all the NetWare clients. It's usually connected by means of a *search drive,* which is just a network drive in your PATH statement. The NetWare login procedure adds the search drive to your PATH statement when you log in. It puts this drive as the first search drive. That's one big reason logging in is important when you're going to a NetWare server under Personal NetWare.

Even if you don't want to log in to any servers immediately, you must still remember to have all your network files and drivers loaded before starting MS Windows. You can't forget, because MS Windows will give you an error message about missing the VLM files. This is why the STARTNET.BAT file is loaded by your AUTOEXEC.BAT file when your PC boots. Go back to the beginning of this chapter if you need to see which files should be loaded when. If you do get this error message, *do not* check the box that asks about disabling network warnings in the future. If those warnings don't show up when you start MS Windows, you might not know something is wrong until too late.

If you try to load the STARTNET.BAT file in a DOS window after you start MS Windows, you will be disappointed. It will work, but it will take up lots of memory, since MS Windows claims all the free memory it finds, leaving no upper memory for the network files. The connection will be good for that DOS window only, meaning none of the MS Windows or Personal NetWare utilities will know about the network. Even if you think you need a connection just for a moment, it's better to exit MS Windows, reboot or otherwise load the network files, and then restart MS Windows.

ATTACHING A NETWARE SERVER

IN-A-HURRY? **Log in (attach) from NetWare Tools**

2.5 THE FAST LANE

1 Press F6 to open NetWare Tools.
2 Click on the server button.
3 Double-click on the desired server in the Resources box.
4 Type your name and password.

It's perfectly fine to start MS Windows before you attach to a network file server. That's what the NetWare Tools program is all about: making and changing connections to your network resources. Press F6 to pop up the NetWare Tools window and click on the server button, or press Alt-C. Remember that the server button is the third one of the left group of four, with the tower PC case as an icon. You will see a list of connections in the left box and a list of available resources in the right box.

The servers running NetWare versions 2.*x* through 3.*x* will show up there as little gray lumps that are supposed to be server icons, but they're tough to see. NetWare 4.*x* servers are listed under the tree icon, which indicates NetWare Directory Services (NDS). The servers that you can connect to appear in the Resources box on the right.

There are three ways to start the attachment process:

- Double-click on the name of the server in the Resources box.
- Drag and drop the server from the Resources box to the Connections box.
- Click on the Login button at the bottom of the window.

No matter which method you use, a login dialog box will appear entitled, clearly enough, Login to NetWare, as shown in Figure 2.7. Be aware that *Login* should read *Attach;* don't be more confused than the software writers who mislabeled the boxes. When you connect through NetWare Tools, it won't run any login script that you might have on that server.

Here are the steps for completing the attachment procedure:

1. Click on either Guest or Registered User in the upper left of the dialog box to put a dot in the circle beside it. The default is Registered User, so you won't have to worry about this much, since you will probably log in to servers where your access is defined.
2. Fill in your user name in the first long text box across the bottom right of the dialog box.
3. Fill in your password. Click or press Tab to get from the User Name to the Password box.
4. Click on the OK button in the upper right, or press Enter.

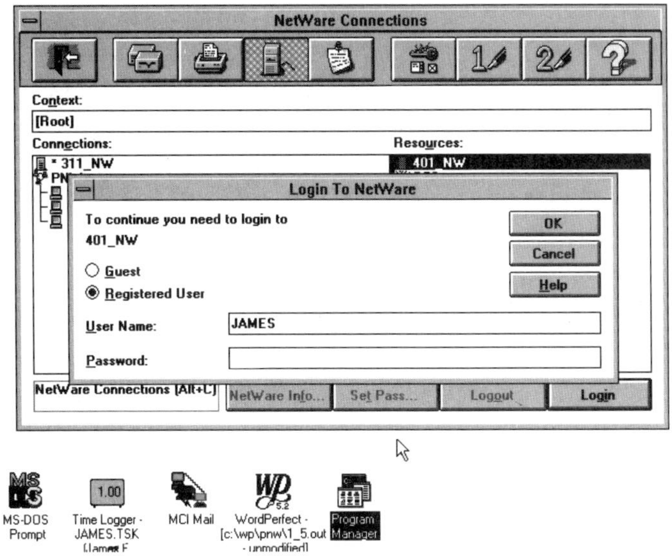

FIGURE 2.7 *The Login to NetWare dialog box, ready for a name and password*

Don't press Enter after typing your name and expect to go to the Password box. MS Windows will attempt to attach to the server before your password is entered, and you'll need to do it over.

After you complete the attachment sequence, you will notice that the name of the server no longer appears in the Resources box. In the Connections box, where it was once flat gray, the server icon is now filled with little disk drives and a red and a green light. Success!

If your login procedure happens as part of STARTNET.BAT before loading MS Windows, the appearance of the server icon will be in the "success" mode right away. The drive letters and printer connections will be filled in as well. See, it really is better to log in before loading MS Windows. Automating the process saves time and prevents mistakes. Computers do repetitive things like this well, so let yours take care of this login stuff for you.

CONNECTING TO NETWARE SERVER PRINTERS

In the NetWare Tools window, the second button in the left group of four is a printer, for NetWare printer connections. This icon is pretty clear, even if you have a laser printer instead of the dot-matrix printer shown. You click on this button, or press Alt-P (as shown in the bottom-left text box) to get to the Printer Connections view, shown in Figure 2.8.

The box on the left side of the window lists ports, and the box on the right, labeled Resources again, shows available printers. Under Queue at the top of the window the defined print queue on your connected server is shown. The print queues for other servers do not appear here. Workgroup shared printers appear as the printer itself, not as a print queue like the printers controlled by NetWare file servers. Print queues are referenced separately from the printers themselves. The queue may be changed from one printer to another, or the physical printer may be changed from one queue to another.

If printers seem to appear randomly, it's probably because you made different server connections at different times. The available printers shown will reflect that.

FIGURE 2.8

The NetWare Printer Connections window, with available printers listed on the right

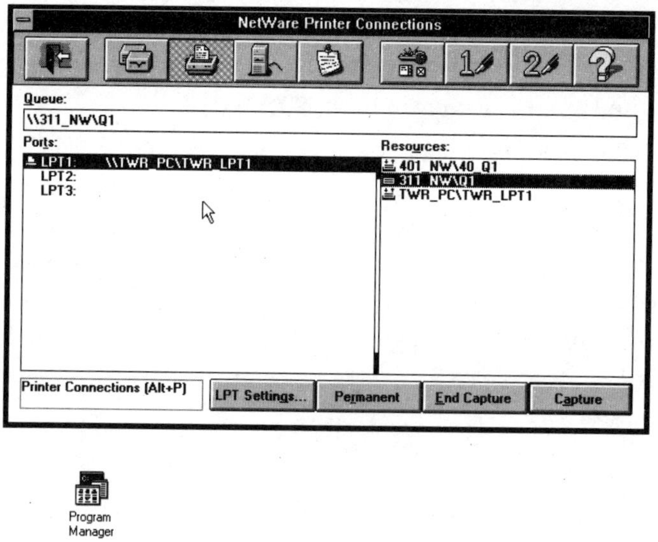

Notice that the rectangular button labeled Capture, in the very bottom right of the window, is active. Capture is NetWare's way of saying, "Capture all the print output from a particular parallel port and send it to a network printer." You can connect the print queue to a particular parallel port—LPT1:, LPT2:, or LPT3:—by dragging the print queue from the Resources box and dropping it on the desired printer port. Mouse-impaired users can simply click on Capture (or press Alt-A if you're truly mouse impaired), and the queue will be attached to whichever LPT: port is highlighted.

You will know the queue is connected, because the queue name, along with the server that controls it, will appear on the line with the LPT: port you specified. All print jobs that your application software sends to the specified LPT: port will now print through the network. This happens without requiring any changes in your application software.

Ready for a Famous Hypothetical Example? Diane captures LPT1: to a network queue, then later needs to print a quick note she typed in MS Windows Notepad. When she chooses File and Print from the Notepad menu, the file gets routed automatically to the network queue and printer she set up earlier. She doesn't need to lift a mouse button; it all happens automatically.

If Diane cares to, she can click on Print Setup under Files in Notepad. It will show that the default printer is currently set to the printer attached to the queue she defined. This is another example of how well Personal NetWare is integrated into MS Windows. If you want something more concrete than hypothetical, Figure 2.9 shows that exact setup.

What happens when you tire of your attached network print queue? There are two ways to "unhook" your PC from the queue. One way is just to click on the End Capture button (or press Alt-E), located just beside the Capture button at the bottom of the NetWare Printer Connections box. The other way is a reverse drag and drop. Drag the print queue name in the Ports box back into the Resources box and drop it there. The queue will once again be listed as available, and your LPT: port will be empty. The same procedure works similarly in both the NetWare Tools and Personal NetWare programs.

We'll go into excruciating detail in Chapter 5 about all the ways to control printing and printers, but this information will get you started and handle

FIGURE 2.9

The Printer Setup window within MS Windows Notepad showing a NetWare file server printer

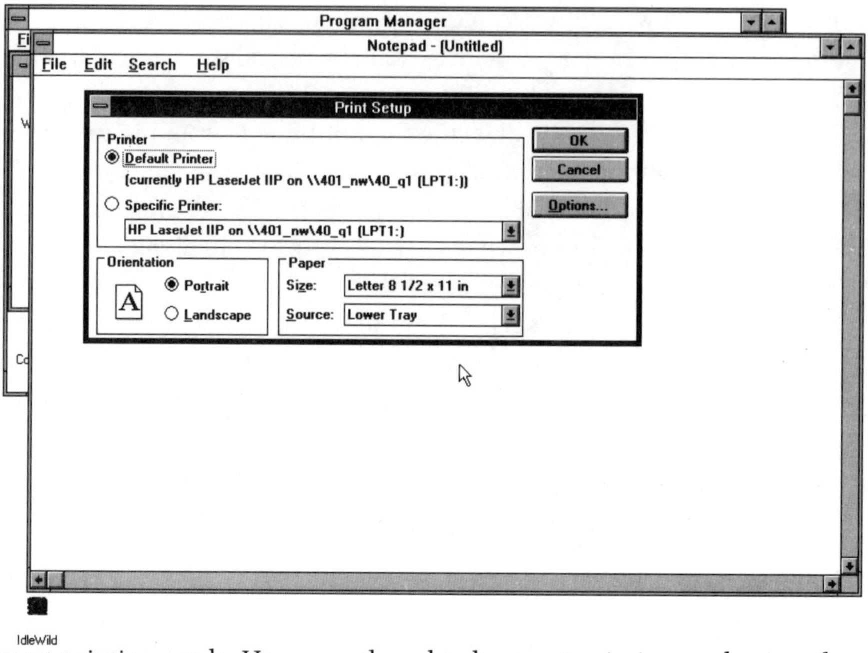

most printing needs. Have you thought about not printing, and using electronic mail and messaging instead? Save some trees? Save some money? We'll talk about that later, as well.

USING AND SAVING FILES ON THE NETWARE SERVER

Now that you have the printers under control, more or less, what are you going to print? Let's find some files.

First of all, your normal MS Windows File Manager works perfectly well. If you used File Manager before, and try it now with the Personal NetWare connections to a file server, it will offer you the same information it always did. But now it will offer information about drive letters pointing to a NetWare file server.

Once you start File Manager, all your mapped drives will show up as the little drive drawings (excuse me, icons) across the top of the File Manager window that opens at startup. The drive you were last on pops up, and you see that drive's contents. If you have most of your 26 drives mapped to one place or another, which is possible with NetWare, your drive icons may wrap to a second row. Figure 2.10 illustrates such a setup, showing more places to lose a file than you ever thought possible.

If you're curious, pull down the Disk menu and choose Network Connections. What do you see? The NetWare Tools screen again, right? And showing exactly the right view: the NetWare Drive Connections window. This window will show you exactly the same files and drive letters in a different format.

If you double-click on a program or batch file icon when you're back in File Manager, the program will execute, just as it should. The fact that the actual program is on another computer somewhere else in the building doesn't matter. If File Manager can see it, you can get it and do with it what you will (if you have the proper permissions to use that file, of course).

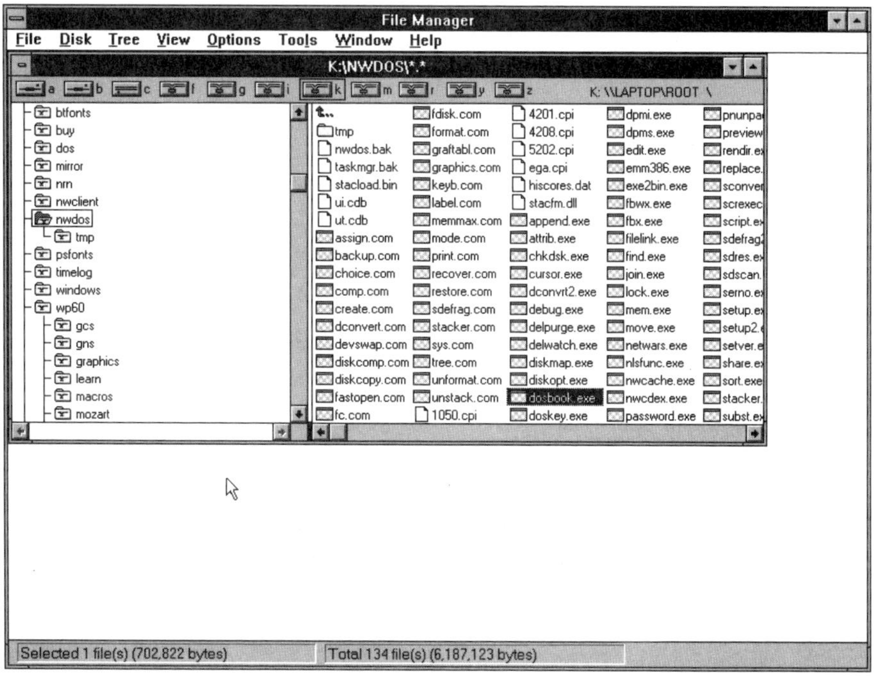

FIGURE 2.10

MS Windows File Manager managing server drives

File Manager works exactly the same way it works with your local hard or floppy drives. The whole idea is to make this easy, so you can concentrate on your work rather than your computer. This is another way to help make that happen.

Rather than File Manager, you can use the NetWare Drive Connections window to help you find directories. Once the NetWare Drive Connections window is open, you can double-click on any NetWare volume in the Resources box to see all the directories. Double-click on any directory to open that directory folder and see any subdirectories inside. Double-clicking again closes the directory folder.

Try going back to Program Manager, by closing File Manager. If you choose Run from the File menu, then click on the Browse button in the Run dialog box, the Browse window will appear. Click on the down arrow by the small text box on the bottom right. See what happens? Once again, all the different network drives spread out and are available. We're going vertically, rather than horizontally as in File Manager, but either way, there are lots of drives to choose from.

Logging In to the Workgroup

2.6

THE FAST LANE

IN-A-HURRY? Log in to the workgroup

1 Load all network drivers and files.
2 Type NET LOGIN ***YOUR-NAME*** at the DOS prompt.
3 When prompted, enter your password.
4 Start MS Windows.

The process for logging in to the workgroup is only a bit different from logging in to a NetWare server. You need to tell the computer software that you're using the NET.EXE program to connect to a Personal NetWare workgroup rather than a NetWare file server.

To log in to a workgroup, type

```
NET LOGIN SUPERVISOR
```

The answer from Personal NetWare is

```
You are logged in to workgroup YOUR-WORKGROUP as SUPERVISOR
```

The user you're logged in as is an important point, because if you logged in to a brand new Personal NetWare network, SUPERVISOR is the only user in the system. You must log in as SUPERVISOR to start defining all the other users. Setting up users is described in Chapter 8.

SETUP will configure STARTNET.BAT with your user name and start the login process. The computer's response will be

```
password:
```

which you then type. It's always a bad idea to put your password in an automatic login sequence, so don't even think about it. If your password is in the STARTNET file, anyone that starts your computer has access to everything you normally do. That's even worse than leaving your name and password on a sticky note on your monitor.

LOGGING IN AS A WORKGROUP CLIENT

If this is an existing network, you need to replace SUPERVISOR with your user name, as defined in the server security information. If you are new to the network, the administrator has probably given you a name and some level of access. If you were told, "Your name on the system is *new-guy* and your password is *rookie,*" you're in the system already. You would type

```
NET LOGIN NEW-GUY
```

and wait for Personal NetWare to ask for your password. When you type your password, it will seem like nothing is happening, since the cursor won't move. That's just a bit of security to thwart spies looking over your shoulder; the system will get your password. Your login procedure will be complete, and you'll be ready to get to work.

"Wait," you say, "how do I do that work? How can I use someone else's hard disk and printer?"

The easy answer is that you use another hard disk in exactly the same manner you use your own hard disk. The local disk, probably drive C:, is nothing special to your software. In the old days (before about 1987), applications regularly assumed C: was the only hard disk in town. Redirecting those applications to the network file server was hard work. There's no need for that kind of hard work today. If you do find a current application that won't accept any drive letter except C:, call and yell at the developer. Then get your money back, or demand a new version of the program that works properly.

One difference in Personal NetWare and regular NetWare 2.*x* and 3.*x* is what you actually connect to when you log in. In the earlier NetWare versions, you connect to a particular file server. You then have access to all the resources of that server only.

With Personal NetWare and NetWare 4.*x*, you connect to the entire network when you log in. All the resources of the network are available to you once you supply your password and get connected. That's why the system said you are logged in to WORKGROUP *YOUR-WORKGROUP* when you connected. That difference will be more exciting as you read what fun and advantages above and beyond any single server the workgroup holds for you.

Let's take that Famous Hypothetical Example and apply it here. Say Gus has his system set up as a workgroup server and is sharing his \WP60\CONTRACTS directory, and you have drive G: pointing there. If you want to edit a document that's on his system with your WordPerfect word processor, no problem. When WordPerfect asks for the file name and location, just tell it G:LINCOLN.NYC and get to work editing the file. WordPerfect will happily use the file across the network. You don't need to worry about what the directory structure is for Gus's machine, because the CONTRACTS directory looks like the root directory on your drive G:.

Remember that the file will be saved back on Gus's machine, unless you specifically tell WordPerfect to move that file to your machine. Of course, moving the file means there are now two copies, neither of which will ever be exactly the same. That's why you have a network: keep one copy of important files, but let everyone have access to that one copy. That gives you the security of a single copy of important data, while allowing full coordination between the team members.

STARTING UP YOUR PC AS A WORKGROUP SERVER

There is a line in the initial installation screen that asks

```
Will you be sharing the resources of this machine now?
```

If you said yes and gave a unique server name to your PC, your STARTNET.BAT file has an extra line. That line says:

```
LH SERVER
```

This line runs the SERVER.EXE program in the \NWCLIENT subdirectory. Your PC then loads the software program necessary to become a server to the workgroup. When you're a server, you can share your resources while still using the resources of the workgroup. And you can still access all the NetWare servers you used to connect to, as well.

The setup process is described in Chapter 8 (and also in Appendix A). Although running the SERVER.EXE command makes your system available to others, you need to describe which others have what kind of access. When you buy a house, you're happy to have your friends visit, but you still have a lock on the door. Chapter 8 will tell you how to set that lock.

You will need to log in to your own PC (seems strange, doesn't it?) to have access to some things. Entering NET LOGIN SUPERVISOR works just as well if your own PC is a workgroup server as it does if another PC is the server.

Remember, the server portion of your PC is separate from the client portion. This is one of the confusing parts about client/server computing you've heard about. The client part (you use resources available to you) and the server part (making your resources available to members of the workgroup) are distinctly separate. But to guarantee confusion, the client and server functions can run concurrently (at the same time) on one PC.

Having a server running on your PC will not affect your normal PC functions. You can still crunch numbers, type memos, and play solitaire when your boss isn't watching. But Fred can get a copy of the memo you typed last week without interrupting your game.

CONNECTING TO WORKGROUP SERVERS

2.7 THE FAST LANE

IN-A-HURRY? Start MS Windows before logging in

1. Load all network drivers and files.
2. Start MS Windows.
3. Press F6 to pop up NetWare Tools.
4. Click on either the drives or server button.
5. Click on the Login button.
6. Type your user name and password.
7. Make drive and printer connections.

Linking your PC to the workgroup server is much the same and a bit different than connecting to a NetWare file server. It's the same because making connections before loading MS Windows makes things neater and cleaner. It's different because not connecting to the workgroup before loading MS Windows is not much of a problem.

Unlike a NetWare server connection, for a workgroup connection, there is no search drive. All the utilities you need for Personal NetWare are included in your \NWCLIENT directory. Most of them are a combination of your NET.EXE program and a parameter, such as NET LOGIN SUPERVISOR. Since everyone already has a copy of these files, and since there are multiple servers supported in a workgroup, it wouldn't be an efficient use of space to copy a large set of files to every workgroup server. They're already installed during the normal Personal NetWare installation procedure.

With a NetWare file server system, all the clients on any physical network segment are connected to the file server. With the workgroup system, clients can only be logged in to one workgroup at a time. However, that workgroup can include as many servers as you want. This is why this is called *workgroup,* or *peer-to-peer,* computing: each PC can be both a client and server. And you thought the duality of existence was lessening in the nineties.

With Personal NetWare in the workgroup, it makes little difference if you connect to the workgroup before or after you start MS Windows. However, if you log in before you start MS Windows, you can read a batch file named PNWLOGIN.SCR, which establishes a series of connections all at once. What is the PNWLOGIN.SCR file and where does it come from? More later in the next chapter (in the section about saving your setup and connection information in PNWLOGIN.SCR). Since this is your book, you can skip to that part now if you must.

We've done this before, but here it is again. To log in to the workgroup, type

```
NET LOGIN YOUR-NAME
```

You must use the system name that has been given to you by your network administrator. That's the name that has been used on all the different workgroup servers to define your access privileges, similar to the user name used with the NetWare file servers. The same name can be used for both types of network connections, if you wish and your network administrator approves.

Within MS Windows, use the NetWare Tools program as described earlier to pick either drives or servers. Then click on the Login button. Enter your name and password, then press Enter or click on OK. To get connected and start working, you must point and click, or drag and drop, for each drive and printer connection. So perhaps you should just make it a habit to log in before starting MS Windows, no matter what system you're connecting to.

CONNECTING TO WORKGROUP PRINTERS

IN-A-HURRY? **Connect to a workgroup printer** 2.8

THE FAST LANE

1 Press F6 to start NetWare Tools.
2 Click on the printer button.

3 Click and hold down the mouse button on the desired printer.

4 Drag the printer to the desired parallel port and drop it.

Here we see one of the advantages of Personal NetWare: the way you connect to file server printers is exactly the same way you connect to workgroup printers. Handy, right? If you missed it earlier, here it is again.

Once in MS Windows, you must press F6. This brings back our now familiar NetWare Tools program, which will be showing the same view as the last time you closed it. If that view was not NetWare Printer Connections, click on the printer button to bring up that view. You're in the right place if the blue stripe across the top of the window says NetWare Printer Connections, as shown in Figure 2.11.

The box on the left is labeled Ports, and it shows your PC's LPT1:, LPT2:, and LPT3: ports, which are the three parallel ports supported by DOS. On the right is a box labeled Resources. The resources you have access to and authority to use, in this case printers, will be listed in the box. Each one will have a little printer icon, then the name of the server, backslash, then the

FIGURE 2.11

The NetWare Printer Connections window

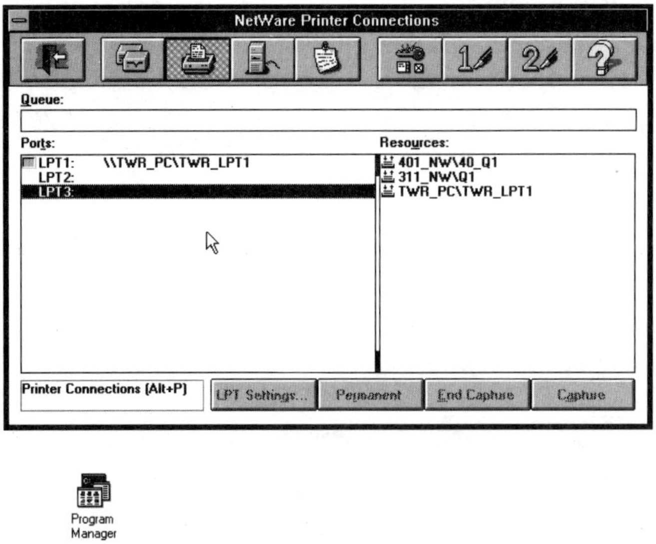

name of the printer, as in

```
TWR_PC\TWR_LPT1
```

The workgroup keeps track of which printers are available, and shows only the ones that are active. If a printer you like is missing, the PC owner of that printer has no doubt thoughtlessly turned off the computer. You're out of luck. You must choose from the resources (printers) listed in the Resources box.

When you decide which printer you want to use, there are two ways to make the connection between your parallel port and that printer. If you're a mouse maniac, simply drag and drop: click on the printer name with the left mouse button, hold down the mouse button, then drag the printer name over to the parallel port (usually LPT1:) you want to use to direct jobs to that printer. When you let the mouse button go, it will drop onto the printer port you selected. The highlight bar will move with your dragged printer, making it easy to see which LPT connection you're about to make. The printer will stay in the Resources box, since one printer can be connected to more than one printer port.

If you're more of the button-clicking type, click on the parallel port you want to connect to a printer. Then, click on the printer you want to connect. The Capture button, at the bottom right of the window, will become active. Click on the Capture button, and the printer's name will be placed on the same line as the parallel port you highlighted. Done.

Disconnecting Printers

IN-A-HURRY? Disconnect a printer 2.9 THE FAST LANE

1. Press F6 to start NetWare Tools.
2. Click on the printer button.
3. Drag and drop the printer from the port back into the Resources box.

To unhook the printer from the parallel port, the procedure is the reverse of the one for connecting the printer. You can either drag and drop the printer back into the Resources box, or highlight that printer and click on the End Capture button at the bottom of the window.

Either way, the printer connection will be cleared from your parallel port.

USING AND SAVING FILES ON THE WORKGROUP SERVER

After you log in to the workgroup and connect to a workgroup server, you must specify which drive letters point to which directories on which server. If you want your system configured for the same set of drive letters each time, look forward to the section about saving your setup and connection information in MS Windows, later in this chapter.

Since the workgroup servers are likely to be less permanent than NetWare file servers, it's common to make workgroup drive connections as you need them. Either the Personal NetWare or NetWare Tools program will do the job. Since NetWare Tools is a pop-up, it's generally quicker and easier to use that program. We'll look at this method first.

Connecting to Workgroup Drives with NetWare Tools

2.10 THE FAST LANE

IN-A-HURRY? **Connect to a workgroup drive**

1 Press F6 to pop up NetWare Tools.
2 Click on the drives button.
3 Click on the server and volume name you wish to map a drive to.
4 Drag and drop the server name onto the drive letter that will now access that drive.
5 Log in if prompted to do so.

When you press F6 to bring up NetWare Tools, once again, the view will be the same one that was on your screen the last time you used the program. The view you need now is the one showing your drive letter assignments, so click on the large button at the top showing the two hard drives.

There are two boxes in the NetWare Drive Connections view of the world, with Drives on the left and Resources on the right. Do you see all the servers you need there? If you're not connected to your workgroup or to a NetWare file server, it won't show up in the Resources box.

To get connected, go to the NetWare Connections window by clicking on the server button. If you see a server you wish to connect to, drag and drop the server from the right side of the box to the left. Drag the resource and drop it onto the connections side. A Login to NetWare dialog box will pop up then, asking for your name, password, and whether you're a regular user or a guest. When you make the connection, the resource will disappear from the right side and become a connection on the left side.

Once you're connected, click on the drives button. The servers you are connected to, both Personal NetWare and NetWare, will appear. On the left side is a listing of all your drive letters available under DOS. On the right are those resources, including Personal NetWare and all other NetWare servers, that are available to you.

Put your cursor on the server and volume name you wish to use for either storing or retrieving files. If you double-click, you will see all the directories available. That's interesting, but you don't need to drag the server name to the Connections box while the directories are showing. So double-click again to collapse the directory listing. Then drag the little drive icon over to the left side and release the mouse button on the drive letter of your choice. That drive letter will then point to the directory named when that particular shared directory was defined.

If you want a subdirectory of the file system that shows in the Resources list, however, the last trick about opening the file system is useful. Once you double-click on the NetWare volume listed as a resource, all the directories on that volume show up. If you double-click on one of the listed directories on a NetWare server, all the subdirectories will appear. You can highlight one of the subdirectories with the mouse, and drag that over to your drive letter. When you drop it, your drive letter will point to that subdirectory. When you highlight a subdirectory, the text box above the Connections listing will show the exact path. Figure 2.12 shows a subdirectory listing in the text box, already attached to a drive letter.

Back in MS Windows File Manager, check out the new drive letter you set up. If you pointed drive K: to JACK\MEMOS, for example, you could reach that directory by clicking on the K: icon in File Manager. All the contents of that directory will be available, depending on the access rights Jack set up when he offered that directory to the workgroup. If you have all rights, you can copy, move, rename, delete, or create files on that directory, exactly as you do your own local hard disk. You can create and delete subdirectories if you wish. As far as your PC and applications are concerned, drive K: on Jack's computer is just a regular hard disk, no questions asked.

FIGURE 2.12

Using NetWare Tools to map a volume's subdirectory

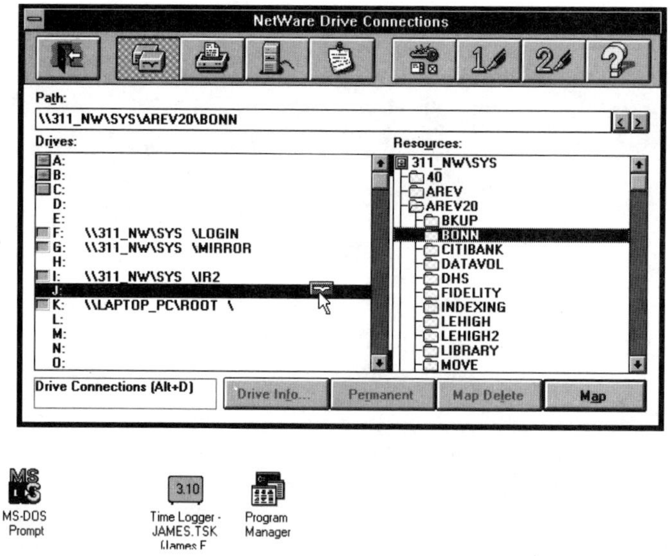

Getting Around the Workgroup with MS Windows

Once you have logged in to the workgroup, either with DOS commands or through the Personal NetWare program, you're in a new neighborhood. Luckily, it looks much like the NetWare file server neighborhood you're familiar with.

MS WINDOWS UTILITIES AND PERSONAL NETWARE

The MS Windows utilities you use when in stand-alone mode work perfectly well with your Universal NetWare Client software. Try using File Manager. The drive letters across the top of the active windows in File Manager show you the details of the drive that's highlighted by the surrounding blue box. Click on drive C:, and it will show you the files on your local hard disk. Click on drive F:, and it will show you the first network drive connection you have active.

With Personal NetWare, MS Windows doesn't care whether a drive is mapped to a NetWare file server or a PC workgroup server. It will show you the same level of detail either way.

Want to see how well Personal NetWare is integrated into MS Windows? Open File Manager, pull down the Disk menu, and choose Network Connections. Recognize the window that appears? It's the NetWare Drive Connections window from Personal NetWare. Not only did Personal NetWare pull up the NetWare Tools program for you, it opened it directly to the Drive Connections view.

Want to see more? Go back to the main Program Manager screen in MS Windows, then pull down the File menu. Choose Run, as if you were about to install a software package or run a MS Windows program that's not in a group. Click on the Browse button. When the Browse dialog box opens, click on the arrow pointing downward in the Drives box. You will see all the network drives you have available. All the same ones you saw with File Manager and Personal NetWare are available here as well.

What's the trick of getting around your workgroup using MS Windows? Do the same things you always do. The connections you have within the workgroup will be just as accessible as your own hard disk. But this brings up the case of what lies under the drive mappings we've been discussing.

YOU AND YOUR LOGICAL DRIVES

Your PC probably has either two or three physical drives. These are labeled A:, B: (if you have two floppy drives), and C: (if you have a hard disk). Some PCs have a second hard disk, labeled D:.

Some disk compression products (which are misnamed, because they really expand your disk as far as you're concerned; they compress the files) also give you a drive D:. However, that drive D: is not a physical drive—it's a *logical* drive, or it may be called a *virtual* drive. Either way, there is not a second physical hard disk in your computer, even though it's labeled drive D:, just as you would name a second hard disk. The same situation exists when you partition one disk into two or more sections. This was popular back when DOS could only address 32 MB of disk at a time. If you had a 40 MB disk, you either wasted 8 MB of it, or partitioned it into two disks: C: and D:.

So what is this virtual or logical disk? It's an easy and convenient way to refer to different sections of the same physical disk. In fact, there's nothing keeping you from partitioning a disk into a dozen sections and calling them drives C: through N:. The important thing to learn here is that logical disks are an illusion; they're not real disks. One physical disk can support dozens of logical disks.

That one physical disk can not only support a dozen NetWare logical disks, but those logical disks can move around the physical disk. When you change a directory on your C: drive, you're smart enough to realize that saving a file in the new directory means the file will be in a different place, and different path, than where you started from. For example, if you have a directory named \WP\MEMOS and another one named \WP\LETTERS, you know those are two separate and distinct directories. Files placed in one directory can't be found in the other directory, just like you can't find socks in your T-shirt drawer. Figure 2.13 shows this taken to ridiculous extremes: different drive letters for multiple subdirectories under one parent directory.

When you see your drive letters in the workgroup, realize that they are pointing at different subdirectories that may be on entirely different PCs. Drive G: isn't a physical drive G:; it's the logical drive that's really the \WP\MEMOS directory on Gus's PC workgroup server. If you change your directory to \WP\LETTERS with drive G:, it will still say drive G: but will be pointing to a different directory. If you ask Gus to help you find a memo, and tell him, "I put it on drive G:" instead of naming the directory that drive G: was pointing to at that time, Gus will probably laugh at you. And then he will tell you to reread this section again until you understand the difference between physical and logical disks.

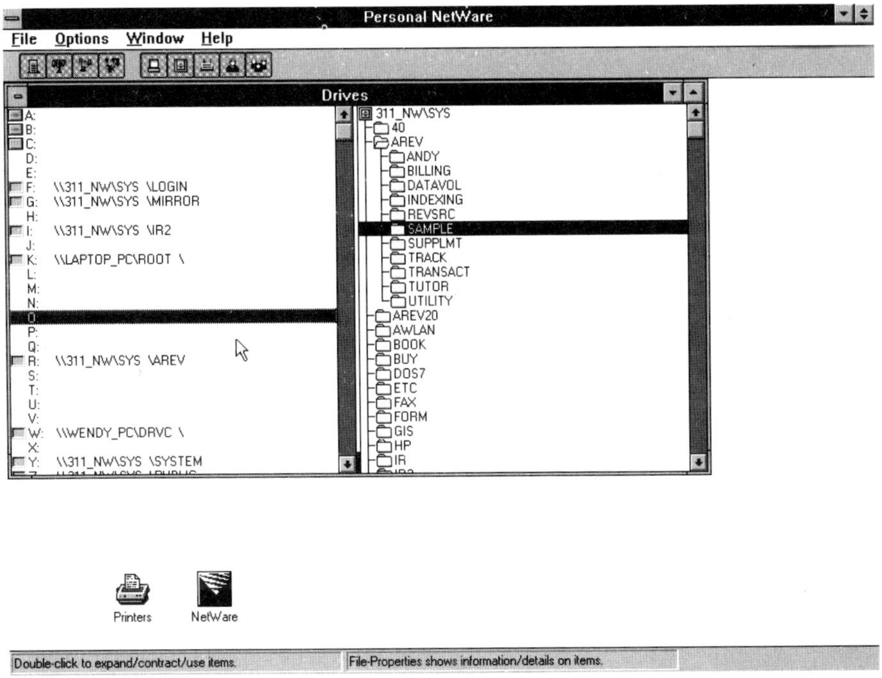

FIGURE 2.13

Logical drives configured illogically

Connecting to a NetWare 4.*x* Domain under MS Windows

2.11

THE FAST LANE

IN-A-HURRY? **Connect to a NetWare 4.*x* domain**

1. Press F6 to start NetWare Tools.
2. Double-click on the NetWare 4.*x* tree icon.
3. Fill in your name and password.

As mentioned in Chapter 1, with NetWare 4.*x*, you don't log in to a single server, you log in to the network, which may consist of many servers. Is this harder than logging in with NetWare 3.*x*? Not at all, especially if your administrator set up your NET.CFG file properly. That file should contain the line

NAME CONTEXT = *YOUR-NAME CONTEXT*

There may also be a line that says

PREFERRED SERVER = *SERVER-NAME*

But that's just there to confuse the issue. It's nice to have the name of the server you use most, but it's not necessary.

If you open the NetWare Tools program, one of the resources in the right window will be a NetWare 4.*x* server. In the Resources half of the window, you may see strange things such as

```
O=company_name
```

and

```
OU=department
```

and the like. The O and OU are for Organization and Organizational Unit, respectively. This should be a clue that NetWare 4.*x* is different from any other NetWare, and it is.

The symbol for the network is a tree. If the tree is black and white, you aren't connected. If the tree leaves turn green, you're connected. When you double-click on the tree on the left side of the window, it will tell you

```
Directory Services - Authenticated
```

and your name.

Double-click on the tree in the Resources box to start the login process. Once you do, the Login to NetWare dialog box will pop up. You can also drag and drop the tree icon from the right to the left, and the same Login to NetWare dialog box will appear.

CONNECTING TO NETWARE 4.*X* PRINTERS

IN-A-HURRY? **Connect to a NetWare 4.*x* printer**

2.12

THE FAST LANE

1. Press F6 to start NetWare Tools.
2. Click on the printer button.
3. Drag and drop the desired printer to the desired parallel port.

To connect to NetWare 4.*x* printers, in MS Windows, press F6 to bring up NetWare Tools. If the view that appears isn't NetWare Printer Connections, click once on the printer button at the top of the window to switch to that view.

This window appears the same as it does for any other NetWare system printers, as described earlier (see Figure 2.11). The printers serviced by NetWare 4.*x* servers look much like any other NetWare system printer. Unless the name of the printer or print queue gives it away, you won't be able to tell which is which.

The NetWare Printer Connections box shows only the printers that are active. If a printer you like is missing, the printer may have been reassigned, or you may not be connected to that organizational unit any longer. Either way, you won't be able to connect to that printer. You need to choose from the resources (printers) listed in the Resources box.

To check and see if you've somehow been dumped out of your organizational unit, click on the server button. Under Resources, you should see a tree icon. Under Connections, on the left side of the box, you should see that same tree icon with green leaves. This signifies you are connected and logged in to that domain. You may need to double-click on the tree on the right to log in to the domain again.

The procedures for connecting and disconnecting NetWare 4.*x* printers to parallel ports are the same as for other NetWare system printers. To make the connection between your parallel port and the printer of your choice, drag and drop the printer name onto the parallel port (usually LPT1:) you want to use to send jobs to that printer. Alternatively, click on the parallel port you want to connect to a printer, click on the printer you want connected, and then click on the Capture button at the bottom of the window.

To disconnect a printer, in the NetWare Printer Connections window, drag and drop the printer from the Ports box back to the Resources box. Alternatively, highlight the printer you want to disconnect and click on the End Capture button.

USING AND SAVING FILES IN A NETWARE 4.*X* DIRECTORY TREE

2.13 THE FAST LANE

IN-A-HURRY? **Connect to a NetWare 4.*x* drive**

1. Press F6 to pop up NetWare Tools.
2. Click on the drives button.
3. Click on the server and volume name you wish to map a drive to.
4. Drag and drop the server name onto the drive letter that will now access that drive.
5. Log in if prompted to do so.

Once again, the way you access files in a NetWare 4.*x* file system is the same as accessing files anywhere else in Personal NetWare. Drive letters can be mapped to the NetWare 4.*x* domain by using either NetWare Tools or the Personal NetWare program.

If you're using NetWare Tools, click on the drives button at the top of the window to see the familiar list boxes on the left and right (see Figure 2.12). The right side, Resources, shows what file systems and volumes are available to you. The left side, Drives, shows which drive letters are already pointing to server or workgroup files.

Again, if the resources you expect to find are not there, check the NetWare Connections window (by clicking on the server button), and log in to the proper places as necessary.

If you see the file system or volume you want listed under the Resources heading, you're ready to go. The quickest method of attachment is to drag and drop. If you're less mousy than some, you can easily connect without dragging and dropping. Click on the drive letter you want to attach. A blue highlight bar will appear on that drive letter, running all the way across the Drives portion of the box. You can also press the desired letter, and the bar will move there automatically. If it doesn't, move your cursor over to that side of the box and give your mouse a click. That will activate that window, and you should then be able to press the drive letter and have the cursor move there.

After the desired unused drive letter is highlighted, you will notice that the only button at the bottom of the window that's active is Map. On the right side, one of the Resources will also be highlighted. Using the mouse, move the highlight bar to the file system resource you want. Pressing Enter will then map the highlighted resource to the highlighted drive.

If you're still wondering if this really does work, feel free to close NetWare Tools and open up MS Windows File Manager. Click on the drive letter that you just mapped with NetWare Tools to see if it's the right place. Bet it is.

The Personal NetWare program will map the drives in almost exactly the same manner as NetWare Tools. Open the Personal NetWare program from the Program Manager group labeled Personal NetWare (there's no hotkey for this program) and click on the Drives choice in the Window menu. If the Drives window was open when you last closed the Personal NetWare program, it will be iconized (don't you love the way the computer business verbs every noun sooner or later?) as the same icon as in NetWare Tools. It will most likely be lurking across the bottom of the workspace. Figure 2.14 shows the Drives window, with icons for NetWare Connections and Printers at the bottom.

FIGURE 2.14

The Personal NetWare program, Drives view

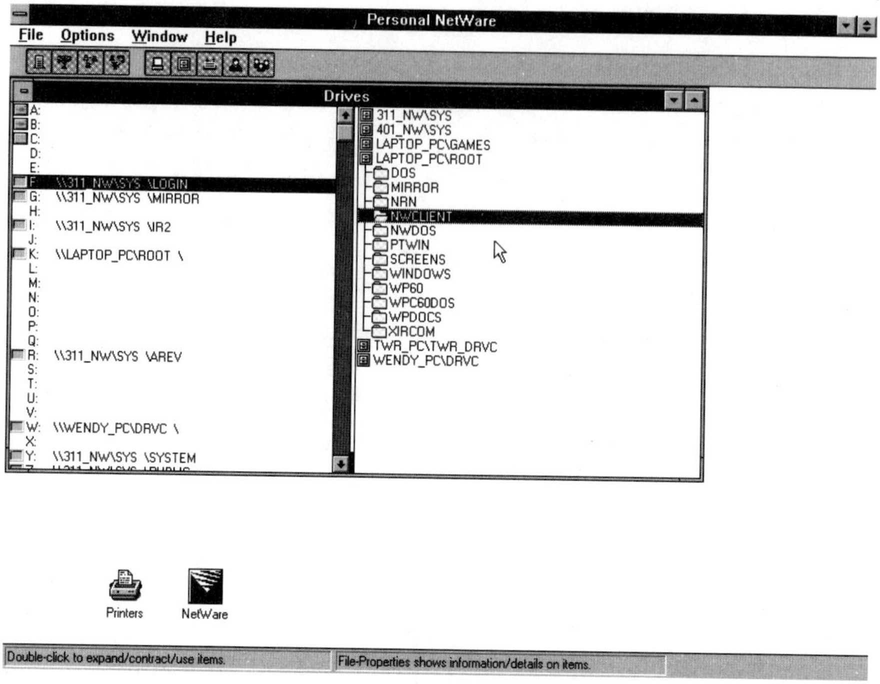

Once you get the Drives window open by double-clicking on the icon or choosing it from the Window menu, the same left and right format that's used in NetWare Tools will be shown. Although it doesn't say Resources and Drives above the right and left respectively, that's what they are. Dragging and dropping from right to left is the easiest method. If you prefer using the actual Connect command, you must highlight the drive letter of your choice, then highlight the resource of your choice. Next, pull down the File menu. The Connect option will already be highlighted. Press the Enter key, and the mapping will be done.

See the Properties option, the next command in dark letters on the File menu? Click on that and see what you get. Interesting? We'll get into these properties later. Look at this as a teaser for a later chapter.

Saving Your Setup and Connection Information in MS Windows

Although the drive mappings you set up for your workgroup may change, it's easy to configure your system to look the same every time you boot up. What must happen to make this a reality every time? Not much, just a mouse click or two. And it's just as easy to make the printer connections you've made remain.

MAKING DRIVE CONNECTIONS PERMANENT

IN-A-HURRY? **Make drive connections permanent** 2.14

1. Press F6 to pop up NetWare Tools.
2. Click on the drives button.
3. Highlight a current drive mapping you want to keep.
4. Click on the Permanent button at the bottom of the window.
5. Check that the highlighted drive icon has a red stripe.

When you get your drive mappings the way you like them, highlight one while in NetWare Tools. Once it's highlighted, notice that the large rectangular buttons (remember, these are technically referred to as command buttons) now have bold type. That means the command they represent is active, or at least can have an effect in this situation. To make the highlighted drive letter permanent, click on the Permanent button.

The drive icon beside the drive letter you have highlighted will now have a red stripe through it, like a big drive light. That means that the drive is permanent. The next time you log in to the network, that drive will be reset to point to the same directory it points to right now. If you log in and that server is not available, you will get a screen asking for instructions (changing workgroups can cause this).

The Permanent button is a toggle, meaning the same button turns the function on and off. If you click on the Permanent button again, the red line in the drive will go away. This signifies that the drive letter connection is not permanent, and you'll need to manually connect it again the next time you start the network. The only way to tell is by watching the red line in the drive icon. Red is permanent; plain is not.

You probably didn't notice, but each time you clicked on Permanent, your hard drive light flickered briefly. That's because NetWare Tools must write a line into a batch file each time you make or change a permanent listing of any kind. Try again while watching your drive light, and you'll see it.

In the Personal NetWare program, things work almost the same way. Open Personal NetWare and go to the Drives window. The highlighting part is the same, and the drive icon changes in the same way: red for permanent, blank for not. But since there are no command buttons across the bottom, you must use the File menu choice to find the Permanent option. There it is, the fourth one down. Click on Permanent, and the highlighted drive will become permanent, just as in NetWare Tools.

Again, this is a toggle, and you can turn it off if you're not careful. Another way to tell if a drive is permanent, as if the bright red line through the drive icon isn't enough, is to check the properties of a drive. Highlight one of your active drive letter connections, and then press Alt-Enter. A dialog box labeled NetWare Info will pop up. It shows some drive information, including whether the drive is permanent or not. Try it. The Properties choice often tells us interesting things. Figure 2.15 shows the Personal NetWare program and the dialog box telling you the highlighted drive status.

MAKING PRINTER CONNECTIONS PERMANENT

2.15

THE FAST LANE

IN-A-HURRY? **Make a printer connection permanent**

1. Press F6 to pop up NetWare Tools.
2. Click on the printer button.
3. Highlight a current printer connection you want to keep.
4. Click on the Permanent button at the bottom of the window.
5. Check that the highlighted blank box becomes a printer icon.

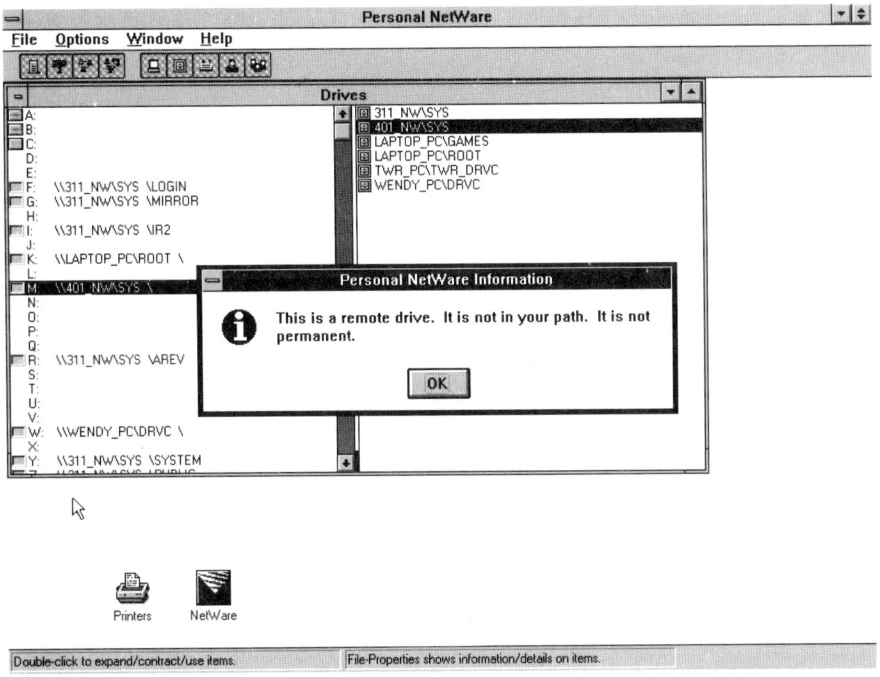

FIGURE 2.15
The NetWare Info dialog box with information about a permanent drive

The process of making printer connections permanent is much like that for the drives. Once you have NetWare Tools started and opened to the NetWare Printer Connections window, you see the three parallel ports available under DOS. Although you can have different printers set for LPT1:, LPT2:, and LPT3:, few applications are able to use three different printers without a lot of trouble. Most applications do well with one printer on LPT1:, which is why it's good that Personal NetWare makes it easy to change printers.

But if change is not your style today, feel free to make a printer permanent. Highlight the printer connection you want to keep, and the Permanent button, at the bottom of the window, will be active. Click on this button. Your hard disk light will blink briefly as the instruction is written to the Personal NetWare configuration files.

Notice that the blank box beside the LPT1: port has now become a decent icon of a printer. It shows a dot-matrix printer with the paper spewing out the top, but that's just the picture. The icon is the same, even if you connect to a laser printer. The icon doesn't know what kind of printer you connect, it just knows whether the connection is permanent.

Using the Personal NetWare program, the process is once again similar to that in NetWare Tools. You must open the Printers window if it's not already on your screen. Pull down the Window menu and click on Printers to activate the window. If there's a picture of a printer at the bottom of the screen, you can double-click on the icon to open the Printers window.

Highlight the printer connection you desire, then click on the Permanent option on the File menu. This is another toggle, so the way to turn it on also is the way to turn it off.

If you're curious, press Alt-Enter, or click on the Properties option on the File menu. A box labeled NetWare Print Settings for LPT*x* (*x* = 1, 2, or 3) will pop up. This is an easy place to change how the network handles your printer and certain details.

Remember the distinction between printer queues and printers themselves. The queue describes how the network is dealing with the printer, while the Printer Setup windows deal with the specific physical printer you have attached to that queue. We'll get deep into printing and printers in Chapter 5. But with what you've just learned, you should certainly be able to somehow coax your memo onto paper.

CHAPTER 3

How Do I Log In and Get Connected under DOS?

The whole idea of a network is to share resources. You may have read this at the start of Chapter 2, but it's just as true when you're working in DOS as when you're using Microsoft (MS) Windows. These resources include, but are not limited to, programs, data files, hard disk space, printers, and messages. Other network resources include modems, fax machines, and host connections to larger computers such as UNIX systems or mainframes.

In some ways, using Personal NetWare with DOS is more valuable than using it with MS Windows. In MS Windows, the easy point-and-click method of changing your PC applications is common. In DOS, however, that's been impossible. Personal NetWare makes DOS much friendlier than ever for network users. The NET program performs multiple functions with an ease only available with MS Windows in the past. If you've taken advantage of Novell DOS 7 as part of your Personal NetWare package, you can run several programs at one time. In fact, the multitasking capabilities of Novell DOS outstrip MS Windows in several ways. Rather than being behind, as a MS Windows dealer might try to tell you, you're actually ahead. And, by using DOS and your keyboard, you make the statement that you know how to type. Rodents aren't part of your computer accessories.

Good Networking Manners

How do you find out what's available on your network? Where are things on this network? Be prepared for the network to be somewhat "dynamic," which is a polite way to say "never the same way twice." Networks with NetWare file servers, especially those with a majority of DOS clients, are fairly stable and consistent, because there is usually at least one person dedicated to making sure the system is available for everyone. Some parts of the system, such as a fax server or a mainframe connection, may be separate from the file server itself. That explains why sometimes the file server is up but some of the resources aren't available. The goal, and the reality in the vast majority of cases, is that all the network resources are available at all times.

Your workgroup is a different story. The servers that are sharing resources are other PCs like yours, run by other people just like you. If you feel this makes things a little less dependable than a NetWare file server, you're right. Ever see those bumper stickers that say, "Warning—I drive as badly as you do"? You might want to print some that say, "Warning—I treat my PC as badly as you treat yours."

Just as people that work together depend on each other, people in a workgroup depend on each person using good computer manners. Office politics and corporate infighting have no place in your computer network. The rules are simple: if you share some resources of your PC, the PC must be available at all times. When you leave, turn off the monitor, but not the PC. If you do this regularly, you can complain with a clean conscience when Rose forgets and turns her PC off.

Logging In to NetWare File Servers with DOS

If you are already using NetWare, the login method with Personal NetWare is exactly what you're used to. One note concerning the LOGIN command, however. Many networks use the AUTOEXEC.BAT file to start the login process. Often, the commands to connect to a server and start the login process are listed at the end of the AUTOEXEC.BAT file. If your PC boots to a point where the prompt is

```
login:
```

you only put in your login name at this point. If you type LOGIN *YOUR-NAME*, it will be wrong. You will get an error message, and then be at a DOS prompt. Then, strange as it may seem, typing LOGIN *YOUR-NAME* will work. That's because the error message stopped the execution (running) of LOGIN.EXE, which was started from your batch file. So you need to type the LOGIN command to start the LOGIN.EXE program again and feed it your login name.

YOUR LOGIN NAME AND PASSWORD

Your login name will be given to you by the system administrator for your NetWare file server. If you're using this to log in to your workgroup, you're in the wrong place. This section is about connecting to a NetWare file server. That's why I'm sure you have a system administrator to provide you with a login name.

The STARTNET.BAT file starts your login process. When it finishes, the NetWare file server will know your name. The server will then ask for your password. Type that in, just as your administrator told you. If you have not been given a password before, the system will probably ask you to give yourself one. The rules vary, but generally a password must be five characters long. Combinations of letters and numbers are encouraged. Sometimes, your login name will have been given a password when it was created, but the system is set to replace that with a new password of your own invention the first time you log in. This provides extra security, since the supervisor (or administrator depending on your company's nomenclature) won't know your password after you log in the first time.

STARTING NET

Once you have completed all this, you will be greeted with basically nothing unless your supervisor has provided a menu program. The contents of the standard NetWare login opening screen can range from quite a bit of information about your machine, the time of day, and the drive mappings you have available to nothing but a DOS prompt. Even if there's lots of information, you still wind up at a DOS prompt unless you have a menu system in place. What do you say to the DOS prompt to get going? Try entering

```
NET
```

Introduction to the NET Program

When you type NET on the DOS command line, you will see the opening NET screen, as shown in Figure 3.1.

The NET program has the same interface made popular by DR-DOS over the last several years. This is called the CXL interface, versus the C-Worthy NetWare utility interface. Now released by Novell as Novell DOS 7, this interface has been chosen because it supports a mouse, scroll bars, and the drop-down menus popular today. Novell's older C-Worthy interface used in NetWare and NetWare Lite can do none of those things.

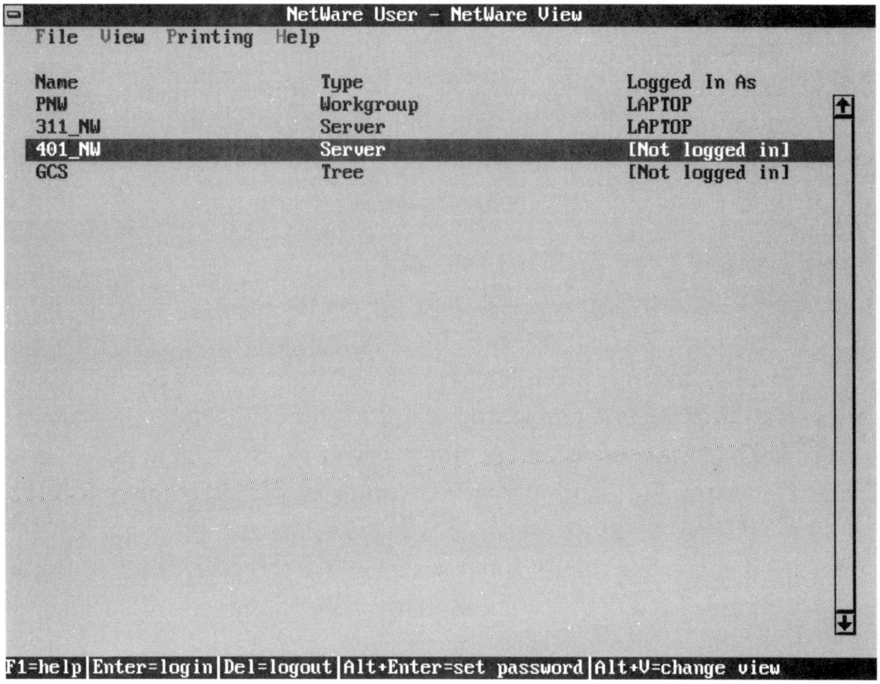

FIGURE 3.1

The NetWare View of the NET program

USING NET

If you're not familiar with NetWare under MS DOS or Novell DOS, don't worry. There are just a couple of rules to remember when you're using the NET utility:

- Context-sensitive help is available for every screen. Anywhere, anytime, pressing F1 brings up a Help screen. Often there are several pages of Help information, and the right side of the screen has a scroll bar if you're using a mouse under DOS. If you're not using a mouse, press Alt-N to go to the next page, or Alt-P for the previous page. Help on the Help function is available by pressing the F1 key twice.
- Descriptions of active keys are always listed across the bottom of the screen. Most of the keystrokes are consistent between the DOS and MS Windows versions of the programs. For example, Alt-X to exit and Alt-D for drives work in both programs. When in doubt, check out the bottom line of your monitor for a list of the active keystrokes.

NET VIEWS OF THE NETWORK

The NET program views of your network are the same ones available under MS Windows. If you press Alt-V for View, you will see NetWare, Drives, and Printers as menu choices. You will also see their Alt-key combinations, so you can skip the menu next time.

The last View menu option, Include, lets you select which network components to show. This helps if your network is large and you get screenfuls of users or servers—more than you want to see at any one time. On the other hand, if you don't think you're seeing all the servers that are available, choose Include from the View menu to list them on the screen. The default is to show only your workgroup servers.

The NetWare View screen shows each server resource in your network. If you press Enter with the highlight bar on the name of a server, you will be presented with the login window. Fill in your name and password, and you will then be attached to that server.

The Drives View screen shows drive letters A through Z in a window in the middle of the screen. Pressing Enter on any drive letter will cause the system to ask you what server resource you want to connect to that drive letter. Workgroup servers show the names for directories given them by the owners of those directories. This keeps you from needing to learn the names of the servers and the path to the directory you need. Just press Enter on the MEMOS directory on the server FRED, and you will be connected to Fred's PC at the directory he named MEMOS. That directory may really be something like C:\APPS\WP60\MEMOS, but you'll see the MEMOS subdirectory as your root directory for that drive letter. This keeps Fred's WP60 directory safe, and keeps you from needing to type the entire path just to get a few lousy memos when you need them.

Feel free to play around, try the Help screens, poke under some menus. You'll learn more about the program if you discover something you really like by being curious than you will by memorizing command strings.

SENDING MESSAGES

IN-A-HURRY? **Send a message**

3.1 THE FAST LANE

1. Pull down the File menu and choose Send Message.
2. Move the cursor through the Server/Workgroup list on the right until the user to receive the message appears in the Users list on the left.
3. Move the cursor to the Users list and highlight the user (press the spacebar or Enter key to mark multiple recipients).
4. Press Tab to move to the Message box, then type your message.
5. Press Tab to move the cursor to OK and press Enter.

The Send Message option is on the File menu. Press Alt-F, then S, and the message screen will appear, as shown in Figure 3.2.

FIGURE 3.2

The NET utility's message screen

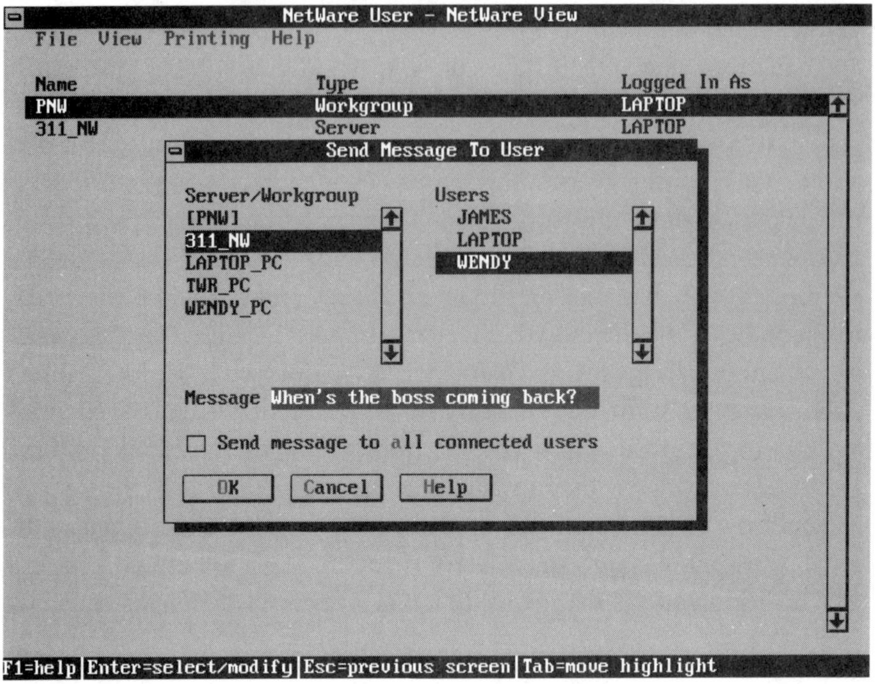

When you highlight one of the servers or workgroups listed on the left side of the screen, its users are listed on the right side of the screen. Move the cursor through the Server/Workgroup list until the user to receive the message appears on the right. Then move the cursor to the Users box and highlight the user. If you want to send your message to more than one user, press the spacebar or Enter key to mark each of them.

Press Tab to move to the Message line, then type your message. There is only room for 30 characters, since that's all the DOS version can display. This is not the place for memos; it's for quick notes. When you're ready to transmit your message, press Tab to move the cursor to OK and press Enter, or press Alt-O.

Connecting to NetWare File Servers under DOS

IN-A-HURRY? **Connect to a NetWare server** 3.2

THE FAST LANE

1. Type **NET** to start the NET program.
2. Highlight your server, then press Enter.
3. Provide your name and password, then press Enter.

Do you feel, as a DOS user, that computing is harder? More keystrokes to type? Feel that way no more, because Personal NetWare supports DOS users with perhaps more tools than available to MS Windows users. If you can type one or two letters in a row from a menu, you can get connected and running faster with DOS than with MS Windows. If you absolutely cannot type two letters in a row, go buy a Newton or some other pen computer and struggle to improve your handwriting.

The NET.EXE program for DOS provides all the information given by the NetWare Tools program under MS Windows and a little more. It is also the place where all the configuration is done (type NET ADMIN to get to the configuration functions, covered in Chapter 8). This part is the equivalent of the Personal NetWare program.

Using the same interface made popular by earlier versions of Novell DOS (then DR-DOS), the NET program supports a mouse and has drop-down menus. There are a variety of quick key combinations as well, such as Alt-P for print queue control and Alt-D for checking and changing your drive mappings.

You can connect to the NetWare file server of your choice from the NetWare View screen. This is the default screen when you start the NET program, so you may be there already. If not, pressing Alt-N will get you there quickly. If you prefer the long route, you can press Alt-V for View, then make sure the highlight bar is on the choice that says

```
NetWare Alt+N
```

Pressing Enter at that time will bring up the NetWare View screen.

The major portion of the NetWare View screen, on the left side, shows the name of the available servers, both NetWare file servers and workgroup servers. The second column tells you what kind of server each one is, and the third column shows whether you are logged in or not. If you are logged in under different names to different servers, not an uncommon event, the third column will show you that.

When you move the highlight bar onto a server to which you're not logged in and press Enter, a login window will appear in the middle of the screen, as shown in Figure 3.3. Fill in your name and password to get connected to that server. Pressing Escape at any time will cancel the operation.

FIGURE 3.3

The NET login window for connecting to any file server

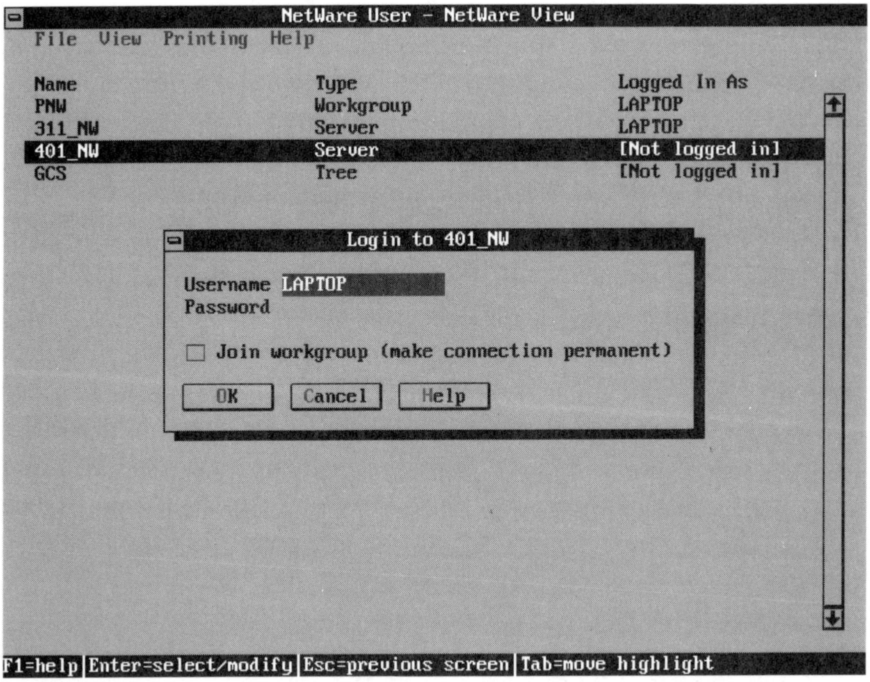

CONNECTING TO NETWARE SERVER PRINTERS

IN-A-HURRY? **Connect to a printer** 3.3

1 Type **NET** to start the NET program.
2 Press Alt-O.
3 Highlight LPT1, LPT2, or LPT3, then press Enter.
4 Highlight the desired printer, then press Enter.

To get to your printer information, press Alt-P from any of the other NetWare View screens. Oops, that shows you the print queues available. When you press Enter on a queue, you see a screen detailing what jobs are waiting in that particular print queue. Often, there is nothing waiting, and this screen is a bit boring.

So now try pressing Alt-O. Aha, this shows what we need. The three parallel printer ports available under DOS appear in a small window toward the top of the screen. If all three of the LPT listings show no attached printer and no server that owns that printer, just press Enter with the highlight bar on LPT1. A new window pops up just below the LPT listings, showing the printers available and their servers. Move the highlight bar to the printer of your choice and press Enter again to tie that printer to your primary parallel printer port. Figure 3.4 shows a connection to a network printer for LPT2, leaving LPT1 to print to the locally attached printer.

Disconnecting Network Printers

IN-A-HURRY? **Disconnect a network printer** 3.4

1 Type **NET** to start the NET program.
2 Press Alt-O.
3 Highlight LPT1, LPT2, or LPT3.
4 Press the Delete key.

If you want to use your local printer again, you must delete the connection between the network printer and your parallel port. Press Alt-0 to go

FIGURE 3.4

The NET Printers View screen for connecting a network printer to your PC

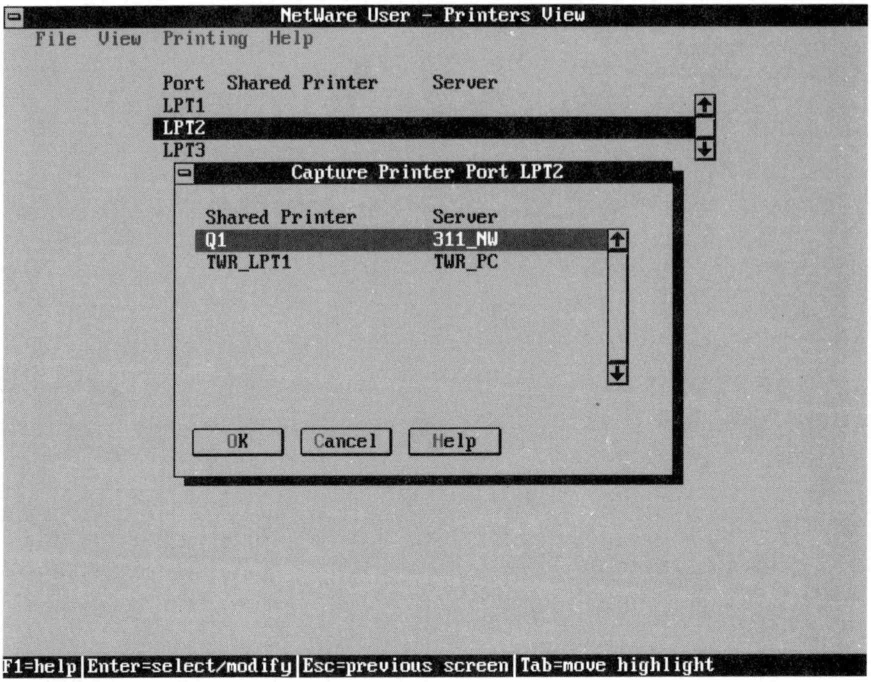

to the Printers View screen, highlight that LPT port, and press the Delete key. The NET program will politely ask if you really want to disconnect the port (parallel) from your printer. Pressing the Enter key answers that question, and once again your parallel port is connected to any physical printer you have attached to your PC.

Warning: if you have shared your printer with others in the workgroup, don't do this. You must access your printer through the workgroup, even though it's physically attached to your PC. Sounds strange, but it's not your printer any more; it belongs to the workgroup. You access it the same way everyone else in the workgroup does.

Changing a Printer Assignment

If you highlight a parallel port that has a printer assignment and press Enter, NET will assume you wish to change to a new printer. You will see a message box, asking you to verify that you really want to change printers. If you answer in the affirmative, the Capture Printer Port window appears again. Choose the printer you want now, you fickle thing, and it will be attached to that printer port.

USING AND SAVING FILES ON NETWARE SERVERS

IN-A-HURRY? Map drives to a NetWare server 3.5

1. Type **NET** to start the NET program.
2. Press Alt-D.
3. Highlight the drive you want to connect to a NetWare server, then press Enter.
4. Highlight the server that you want to map the drive to, then press Enter. The server must be one you're already connected to.
5. Log in if you're prompted to do so.

The NET program makes easy work of mapping drives from various servers to your PC's drive letters. Press Alt-D and a new window will fill the screen. Since there's not enough room for 26 drive letters in the window, some poor drives hang off the bottom. You can see all the way to Z when you press the Page Down (PgDn) key or scroll the highlight bar all the way to the bottom. If you're in a hurry, press the drive letter you want to configure, and you will jump directly there.

Pressing Enter on a drive letter with nothing attached to it brings up a window labeled Map Drive *YOUR-DRIVE* to Shared Directory. The program will put the highlighted drive letter in the window heading automatically. For the sake of demonstration, let's use drive G:. Figure 3.5 shows the drive connection process underway.

Once again, all the servers you have access to display their wares for your perusal. This time, of course, they're offering directories. You can only see those servers you're attached to in this screen. If you can't see the one that you need, press Alt-N to get to the NetWare View screen and connect to that server, as described earlier. Then go back to the Drives View screen.

FIGURE 3.5

The NET drive mapping process

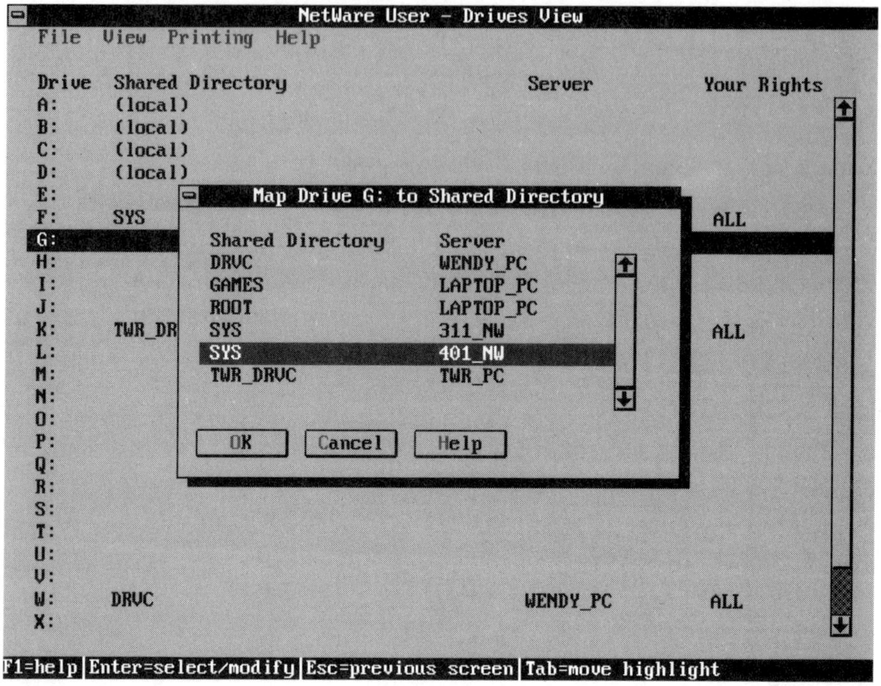

Highlight drive G: again for our demonstration and press Enter. With no fanfare, you will be in the Drives View screen. Highlight the server and drive connection you want for drive G: and press Enter (or Alt-O). Drive G: will now point to that server and the directory you chose.

DISCONNECTING DRIVE MAPPINGS

3.6 THE FAST LANE

IN-A-HURRY? Disconnect a drive mapping

1. Type **NET** to start the NET program.
2. Press Alt-D.

3 Highlight the drive mapping to disconnect.

4 Press the Delete key.

If you want to disconnect a drive mapping, just start NET, press Alt-D, and highlight the connection. Then press the Delete key. Your drive connection will be removed. The directory will not be deleted, of course, just your connection to that directory. But the idea of hitting the Delete key on a directory should prompt you to back up your files. Consider yourself warned.

LEAVING NET

Exiting the NET program by pressing the Escape key puts you back in DOS. Type G:, and your PC will present you with your connection to the server you chose. If you're not in the directory you wanted, type NET again. Go back to the Drives View screen by pressing Alt-D, and press G again. When the G: drive connection is highlighted, press Alt-Enter.

This brings up the Change Directory window, shown in Figure 3.6. From here, you can move around the directory tree as far as your security profile will allow. Once you have the directory you want, press the Tab key to move the highlight bar down to the OK button at the bottom of that box. Pressing Enter there will tie that drive letter to that server at that exact directory. You can also use the normal Change Directory (CD) commands under DOS, but what fun is that?

Once you exit back to DOS, using a mapped directory is no different than using drive A:, B:, or C:. All the files are available for you to read, write, or change. You can copy files to and from that directory, or delete everything. This is assuming you have the proper network security privileges. If you make a habit of deleting files in directories you share with others, your security profile may become more restrictive. Keep it up, and the nasty memos will fly. If you work with a particularly rough crowd, you might wake to find a computer monitor in your bed.

FIGURE 3.6

The NET Drives View showing available subdirectories

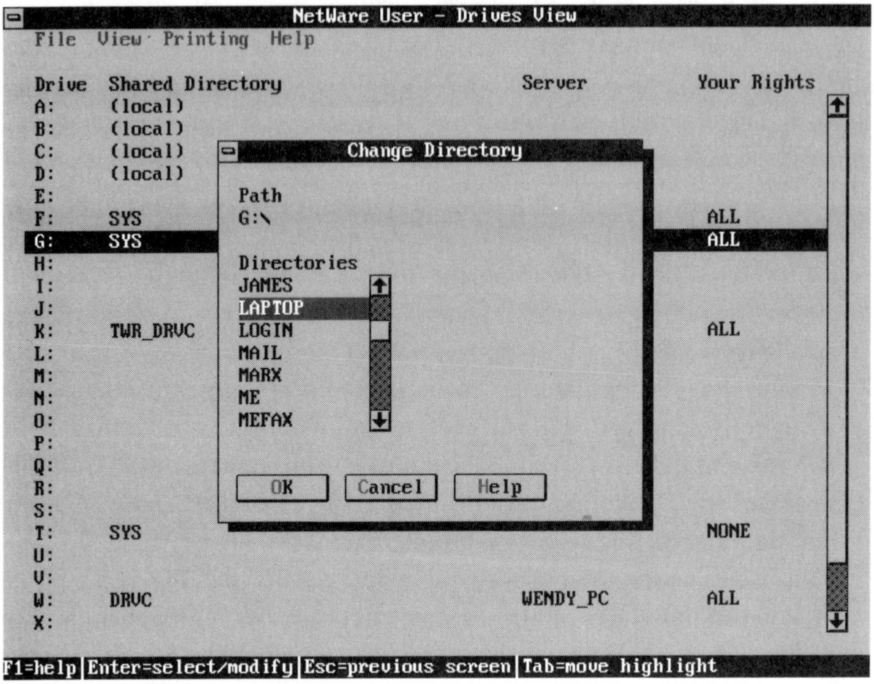

Getting Around the Workgroup with DOS

Have the MS Windows users gotten lots of extra functionality at the expense of the DOS users? Can a DOS PC, whether running Novell DOS 7 or Microsoft DOS 6, get the same information and flexibility in controlling its network resources? Absolutely. DOS users are not second-class citizens with Personal NetWare.

As we start, let me say that NetWare under DOS is built to look exactly like DOS. Is that strange? Not really, since the whole idea of NetWare is to support what you're doing on your PC, and your PC is doing DOS. So NetWare will support DOS in a manner you find comfortable and familiar.

There is one thing that is an extension beyond what you're used to with DOS. Once you get this under control, you'll be in good shape.

The extension in question is drive mappings. Your PC probably has either two or three physical drives. These are labeled A:, B: (if you have two floppy drives), and C: (if you have a hard disk). Some PCs have a second hard disk, labeled D:.

Some disk compression products also give you a drive D:. However, that drive D: is not a physical drive; it's a *logical* drive, or it may be called a *virtual* drive. Either way, there is not a second physical hard disk in your computer, even though it's labeled drive D:, just as you would label a second hard disk.

So what is this logical or virtual disk? It's an easy and convenient way to refer to different sections of the same physical disk. In fact, there's nothing keeping you from partitioning a disk into a dozen sections and calling them drives C: through N:. The important thing to learn here is that logical disks are an illusion; they are not real disks. One physical disk can support dozens of logical disks.

That one physical disk can not only support a dozen NetWare logical disks, but those logical disks can move around the physical disk. When you change a directory on your C: drive, you're smart enough to realize that saving a file in the new directory means the file will be in a different place, and different path, than where you started from. For example, if you have a directory named \WP\MEMOS, and one named \WP\LETTERS, you know those are two separate and distinct directories. Files placed in one directory can not be found in the other directory, just like you can't find socks in your T-shirt drawer at home. Figure 2.14 in the last chapter goes overboard to show silly drive mappings. Figure 3.7 here illustrates the magical changing drive G: that points to many different directories on the same disk.

When you see your drive letters, realize that they are pointing at different subdirectories that may be on entirely different file servers. Drive G: isn't a physical drive G:; it's the logical drive that's really the \WP60\MEMOS directory on one file server's hard disk. If you change directory to

FIGURE 3.7

Don't trust drive G: to stay put

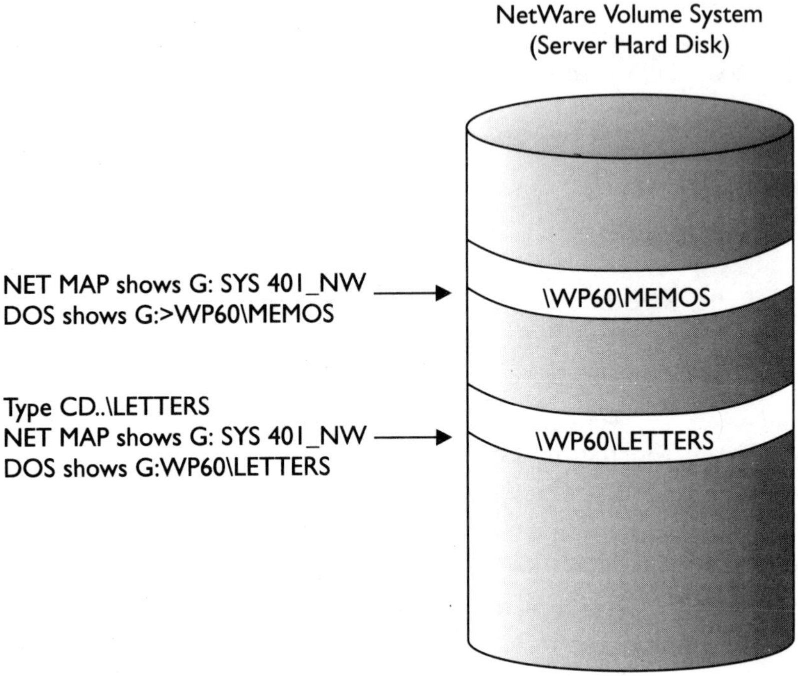

\WP60\LETTERS with drive G:, it will still say drive G: but will be pointing to a different directory. If you ask the network administrator to help you find a memo, and tell him, "I put it on drive G:" instead of naming the directory that drive G: was pointing to at that time, you will probably hear laughter. And that's why this section is repeated almost verbatim from Chapter 2: you need to understand the difference between physical and logical disks. Once you do, you'll be ahead of almost all other casual network users. Pat yourself on the back.

Connecting to a NetWare 4.x Domain under DOS

Although this isn't the time or book for a dissertation on the differences between the Novell 3.*x* Bindery method of security versus the NetWare Directory Services (NDS) of the new NetWare 4.*x*, let's touch on a couple of points. You'll find that the NetWare 4.*x*, and the idea of domains, has a lot in common with the workgroup for Personal NetWare. In fact, this idea of domains with resources and services (such as printers and disk drives) referred to only by name, not server location, is one of the more difficult for traditional NetWare users to comprehend. Pat yourself on the back again, because that's what we've been talking about for the workgroup all this time. What we've been calling services and resources are labeled *objects* in NetWare 4.*x*. You're ahead of most NetWare users without even breaking a sweat.

If you have at least one NetWare 4.*x* server running, you will see two entries for that server (if you're already connected to the 4.*x* server) when you start the NET program. One will be the server name, and the other will most likely be the organization. Every directory tree must have at least one organization container.

Don't let the word *container* fool you; we're not talking Tupperware here—it's still NetWare. The NDS syntax needed to find some way to refer to a directory structure that spans multiple servers. The containers, such as country (optional), organization, and organizational unit, hold objects, called *leaf objects*. Examples of leaf objects are the actual NetWare servers, print servers, printers, profiles (login scripts), users, and volumes (yep, physical disk volumes on the network).

All this sounds much more difficult than it is. If you have your NET.CFG file set up properly, there should be a line saying

```
NAME CONTEXT = YOUR-NAME-CONTEXT
```

This was filled in when your network software was installed on your PC. If you installed it yourself, you should have been given this information by your network administrator. Even if you didn't understand it, you were supposed to type it in at the appropriate spot.

Enough background, let's log in.

CONNECTING TO NETWARE 4.X SERVERS

3.7

IN-A-HURRY? **Connect to a NetWare 4.x server**

1. Type **NET** to start the NET program.
2. Pick your 4.*x* server and press Enter.
3. Provide your name and password, then press Enter.

Start up the NET program, and the opening screen will show the available servers. That's the default view (NET doesn't remember the last view like the NetWare Tools pop-up for MS Windows does). But it happens that this is the view we want, so we're one step ahead.

If the NET screen shows that you are already logged in to the NetWare 4.*x* server or the NetWare Directory Services tree, you're in good shape. If the far-right column, labeled Logged In As, says [Not logged in] for the NetWare 4.*x* server, log in you must. So use the cursor keys to move the highlight bar over that server and press Enter.

The traditional login window pops up, asking for your login name, password, and if this is a workgroup server, whether you want to join. Since this is not a workgroup server, the check box for Join workgroup will be automatically skipped.

Once logged in, everything functions the same here for NetWare 4.*x* as it does for other NetWare systems and the workgroup. When you move to the Drives View screen, the volumes available to you on the NetWare 4.*x* domain will be listed along with all the other volumes. Printers from the 4.*x* domain will show up when you check the Printers View screen. This should be old hat by now. Personal NetWare provides the same tools for the same jobs no matter what NetWare host system you reference. Do you think that's how it got labeled the Universal Client, or does NASA use it on their deep space probes?

CONNECTING TO NETWARE 4.X PRINTERS

3.8 THE FAST LANE

IN-A-HURRY? **Connect to a NetWare 4.x printer**

1 Type **NET** to start the NET program.
2 Press Alt-O (remember, O for Output).
3 Highlight LPT1 and press Enter.
4 Highlight the desired printer and press Enter.

Connecting to a printer supported by a NetWare 4.*x* server and domain is not much different than connecting to any other printer. That's the idea, remember: one method to perform the same job. That way, you can concentrate on your work, not spend time trying to outguess the programmers of your software.

Pressing Alt-O shows what we need. Not Alt-P, but Alt-O for Output. The three parallel printer ports available under DOS show up. If all three of the LPT listings show no attached printer and no server that owns that printer, just press Enter with the highlight bar on LPT1. A new window pops up just below the LPT listings, showing the printers available and their servers. Move the highlight bar to the printer of your choice and press Enter again to tie that printer to your primary parallel printer port.

When you want to use your local printer again, you must delete the connection between the network printer and your parallel port. Press Alt-O, highlight that LPT port, and press the Delete key. The NET program will ask if you really want to disconnect the port (parallel) from your printer. Press the Enter key to respond affirmatively, and once again your parallel port is connected to any physical printer you have attached to your PC. But remember, if you have shared your printer with others in the workgroup, you must access your printer through the workgroup, even though it's physically attached to your PC, just like everyone else in the workgroup does.

If you highlight a parallel port that has a printer assignment and press Enter, NET will assume you wish to change to a new printer. You will be asked to verify that you really want to change printers. If you answer in the affirmative, the Capture Printer Port window will appear again. Choose the printer you want, and it will be attached to that printer port.

USING AND SAVING FILES IN A NETWARE 4.X DIRECTORY TREE

3.9 THE FAST LANE

IN-A-HURRY? Map a drive to a NetWare 4.*x* directory tree

1. Type **NET** to start the NET program.
2. Press Alt-D.
3. Highlight the drive you want to connect to a NetWare directory tree, then press Enter.
4. Highlight the volume you want connected, then press Enter.

When you're ready to map a drive to the file system in a NetWare 4.*x* directory tree, start the NET program. Press Alt-D to get to the Drives View screen once again. The same list of drive letters appears on the left, with the shared directory name next, the server name, and your rights to each file system.

Press Enter on a drive letter, say G: for consistency's sake, to pop up the Map Drive G: to Shared Directory window. In that window are the servers and file systems you are logged in to and to which you have access. Do you see anything different about the NetWare 4.*x* servers as opposed to the workgroup servers and NetWare 3.*x* servers? Neither do I.

Although it doesn't say so across the bottom of the Drives View screen, pressing Alt-Enter pops up the Change Directory window (see Figure 3.6, earlier in the chapter). The same window pops up if you go into the File menu and pick Properties. This shows the subdirectories, if any, under the point where you have access to the volume. You can't see any parent directories; wherever you attach to the file system, no matter how many subdirectories down, appears to be your root directory for that drive.

When you press Enter on a subdirectory you like, don't make the mistake of hitting Escape to exit. You must press the Tab key to move the highlight bar down to OK and press Enter there for the change of directory to become effective.

Once you exit the NET program and are back in DOS, the drive letters you have defined will work just as your drive C: or any other drive. You can read, write, create, and delete files on these drive letters just as you can on your local hard disk. At least you can if you have the authority to do so. Check the column labeled Your Rights in the Drives View screen within the NET program.

Saving Your Setup and Connection Information in PNWLOGIN.SCR

IN-A-HURRY? **Save your setup**

3.10 THE FAST LANE

1. Type **NET** to start the NET program.
2. Press Alt-F to pull down the File menu.
3. Press V to choose Save Script.

Even though the nature of the workgroup is a bit transitory, with network resources being at the whim of other PC owners in your workgroup, you may still want to reuse the same setup tomorrow that you have today. In other words, you want a "network bookmark" to hold your place. Tomorrow, you want to pick up that book, or network, and be back at the same place.

Welcome to the PNWLOGIN.SCR file. Blame the lousy name limitations of DOS (eight characters, the period, and three more characters) for this obtuse label. If DOS were smarter, this file would probably be called the Personal NetWare Login Script.

Anywhere in the NET program, you can save or edit this script file. We won't go deep into editing now, since we have a nice space at the end of the book for this subject. But saving your configuration takes only a couple of quick steps.

After you are comfortable with the server connections, drive mappings, and printers you have configured for yourself, go into the NET program. From anywhere in the NET program, you can save your setup. Press Alt-F to drop down the File menu. Toward the bottom will be the Save Script option. Either move the highlight down to that line and press Enter or press

V. It would make sense to use S to Save, but that was already used for Send. Sorry.

Below Save Script is Edit Script. The script file itself is held three subdirectories down. The Path is something like

```
C:\NWCNTL\MAIL\000713A9\PNWLOGIN.SCR
```

So it's easier to let the NET program's Edit feature find it for you. Figure 3.8 shows the NET screen for editing PNWLOGIN.SCR.

If you're curious, the first directory is shorthand for NetWare CoNTroL, the second is Mail, the third directory is given a unique identifier number for a name. In my case, the number is 000713A9. The A is not a misprint; this is a hexadecimal number. Remember high school math? This is Base 16, meaning after 9 but before 10 you have the numbers A, B, C, D, E, and F representing numbers. Hexadecimal, often called just *hex* or represented after a number by an *h*, as in 713A9h, is a big deal inside your computer.

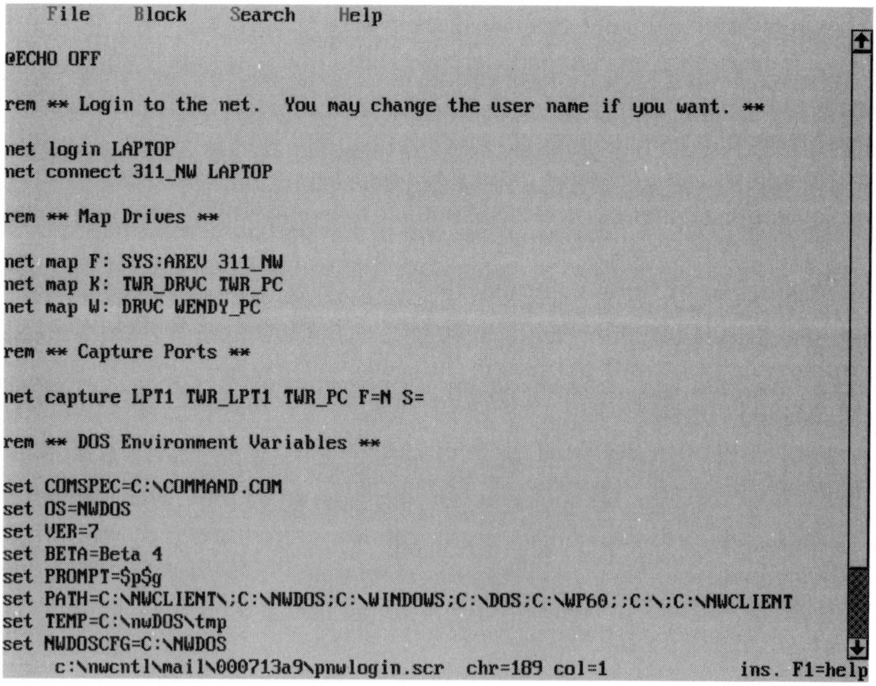

FIGURE 3.8

Editing your PNWLOGIN.SCR file through NET

Saving Your Setup and Connections with NET SAVE

IN-A-HURRY? **Save your setup with the NET SAVE command**

3.11

THE FAST LANE

1. Configure your connections as you want them.
2. Change to the \NWCLIENT directory.
3. Type **NET SAVE**.

Software design requires choices, and these choices are not always easy to make. Personal NetWare provides two different methods for saving your connection information. One works best for regular users of the NET program. The other works best for DOS command line users. The rub comes for those people that use both. The two methods of saving information conflict with each other.

If you're satisfied with the NET program, don't read this. The PNWLOGIN.BAT program that's created by the NET SAVE command performs the same job as the PNWLOGIN.SCR file described in the previous section. It makes the same connections and hooks your PC to the same printers. There is no advantage gained by using one over the other. However, a problem arises if you use both systems.

The first line of both PNWLOGIN.BAT and PNWLOGIN.SCR that actually does anything says

```
NET LOGIN WORKGROUP\YOUR-NAME
```

Looks innocent enough, doesn't it?

When you run NET LOGIN from the DOS prompt or log in through the NET program, the system looks to see if the PNWLOGIN.SCR exists. If it does, that's the script that is executed. All the commands that you put in the PNWLOGIN.BAT file by using NET SAVE are bypassed.

If you prefer having the login connection information in a place you can easily reach with your favorite text editor, PNWLOGIN.BAT may be for you. The file is placed in your current directory, which is why I suggest changing to the \NWCLIENT directory before running NET SAVE. Since

\NWCLIENT is placed in your DOS PATH statement by the installation program, typing PNWLOGIN anywhere on your system will start the login and connection process.

Boiled down, here's the scoop: use NET SAVE only if you have never selected the Save Script option within NET. Once you save your configuration within NET, your PNWLOGIN.BAT file created by NET SAVE will be ignored.

CHAPTER 4

Managing Files under MS Windows and DOS

Since you've made it to Chapter 4, obviously using files now and then is not enough. You've come here to learn how to manage and control those files. That we shall do.

Anything on Disk Is a File

Let's be sure we're talking about the same things here. Files are "A collection of bytes, representing a program or data, organized into records and stored as a named group on a disk." This is according to *Mastering DOS 6, Special Edition* by Judd Robbins, published by SYBEX.

That's the official definition, and we won't argue with that. However, the easy way is to think of anything on a disk as a file. Program files are those that have an extension of .COM or .EXE, or those files supporting the execution of the program. Files ending in .BAT are special, since they execute a batch file process, replacing keystrokes with written instructions. In MS Windows, files ending in .DLL are executable files of sorts, and those files ending in .INI are configuration files. There are lots more program files than just those that specifically end in .COM or .EXE.

A data file, again according to Judd Robbins, is "A named storage area, used by applications to store a group of related information, such as a spreadsheet. Also called a *document*." In other words, a data file is full of information created with the help of one or more program files. Any time a program asks you to name a file before you save it, such as in your word processor, you have created a data file. A program that asks for names for folders, or projects, or any other collection of information, is using the name you give it to make more data files.

All this is fine, but makes little difference in the management and control of your files. Data and program files both work exactly the same way when copied, moved, deleted, sorted, packed into a directory, undeleted, folded, stapled, and mutilated.

Finding and Using Files under MS Windows

Personal NetWare doesn't do operations on a file-by-file basis. The hard disk resources that Personal NetWare can control are limited to directories; no file operations are available. In MS Windows, using File Manager for all your file operations keeps things logical. After all, Personal NetWare wants to make remote file systems just as available to you as the file system on your own PC. What better way to do that than to use your normal MS Windows utilities on all remote volumes?

Remember earlier where we looked at remote volumes of other PCs just as easily as we looked at our own local hard disk? That's the plan here as well. We're going to use MS Windows exactly the same on the remote volumes as on our local hard disk.

For finding directories and mapping drives, both the DOS and MS Windows versions of Personal NetWare utilities work just fine. When you want to get down to specific files, that's where you'll switch to using your regular MS Windows or DOS utilities.

The manual goes to great lengths to name things like THISSERVER and THISDIR and THISAPP. Let's do this a bit more realistically. Let's take the example of a small Personal NetWare network of two machines, along with a few other NetWare servers available in case we need them.

There are two computers here. One is TWR_PC, for a large, deskbound PC in a tower case. The other is LAPTOP_PC, a laptop (not quite small enough to be called a notebook) computer that is certainly not deskbound. Both of these are running the Personal NetWare server software, so they can share their resources with each other, and anyone else running the Personal NetWare client software in the network. They are also clients, both to each other and to the NetWare 3.*x* and NetWare 4.*x* servers in the network.

It's not uncommon to have a desktop system and a portable. What is uncommon is the ease in which we can shift files around between the two. And if we need a file, but don't want to spread copies of it all over the place, we can use that file directly on the remote PC.

So let's get to work. User JAMES (I know, not terribly clever here, but I was named James before we needed to make this example) is on the TWR_PC. User LAPTOP is on the LAPTOP_PC machine, although that's really me again. I can be user JAMES on both systems at one time, but having the same name show up all over the place muddles our demonstration.

USING THE FILE MANAGER IN MS WINDOWS

The File Manager in MS Windows is not great, but it's functional. Using File Manager, you can see the contents of directories, print files, run program files from within File Manager, and mess things up by deleting the wrong files. So be careful when you delete files.

Let's take a tour. Open File Manager by clicking on the file cabinet in Program Manager, Main group. Things will churn a bit, for two reasons. First, File Manager is a fairly big program and may take a few seconds to load. Second, before it displays anything, it needs to get a grip on the current active directory. This is determined by the last directory displayed, if it's still available. Often it comes up showing drive C: and the MS Windows directory, which has well over a hundred files and five or more megabytes of files to get organized. That's why things churn a bit.

Once the churning stops, the typical File Manager screen appears. The displayed drive is identified across the top of the window, with the directory tree on the left and the actual directory contents on the right. Between the blue bar showing the drive letter and the white boxes showing the directory and file contents are several little boxes portraying different drive letters.

These are arranged in alphabetical order, so your floppy drive A: is first. Notice the icon; it looks much like your floppy drive, especially if you have a 3.5-inch drive. If you have two floppies, as does TWR_PC, and the second one is a 5.25-inch drive, the picture is the same for both. MS Windows isn't that smart. Figure 4.1 shows the File Manager screen.

The third drive icon shows a local hard drive, and it looks like many hard disk drives, back before they got so small it was easy to hide them

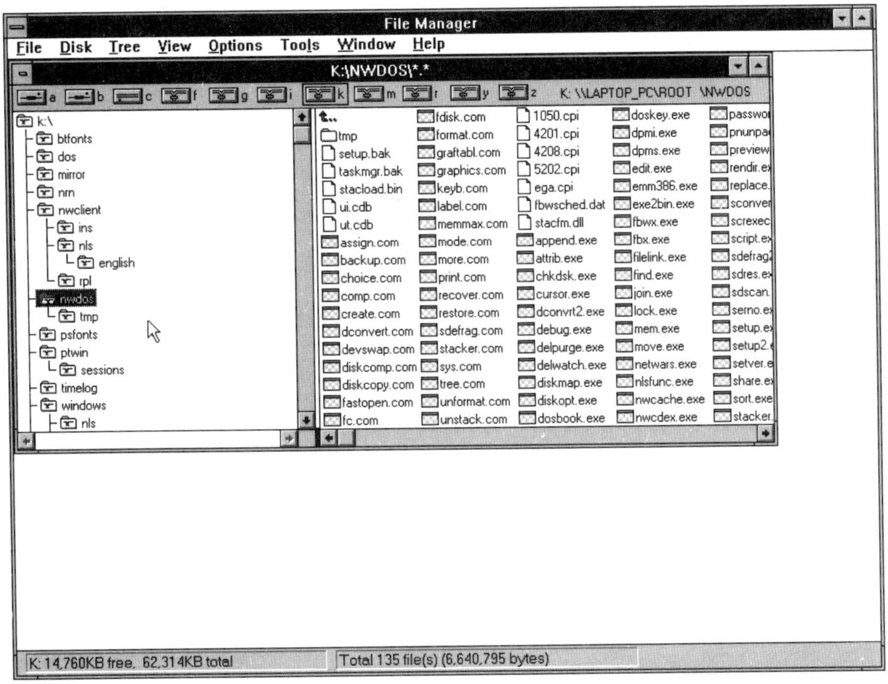

FIGURE 4.1

The File Manager screen showing the \NWDOS directory of LAPTOP_PC

somewhere inside the PC. You can see the horizontal vents and the drive light on the bottom left.

The next eight drive letters have an icon indicating remote drives. See the little cable that runs horizontally, but dips down to the small crossing connector? That's the hieroglyphic for remote drives. If you're interested, drive K: is connected to the LAPTOP_PC; drives F:, G:, I:, R:, Y:, and Z: are connected to a NetWare 3.11 server named 311_NW; and drive M: is connected to a NetWare 4.01 server named 401_NW. We did say this was a Universal NetWare Client, didn't we? There are more connections here than at a dating service.

The files showing in the directory are mostly executable, or program, files. Their icon is the horizontal rectangle with the dark band on the top, and their extension is .COM or .EXE. Double-clicking on these files will execute the program. You can also choose Run from the File menu, and the file you have highlighted on the right side will start running.

Checking File Properties

File properties, which are accessed from the File menu in the Personal NetWare program, can be seen here in File Manager as well. Although File Manager doesn't know about all the extended properties used by NetWare, it does show some file information. Figure 4.2 shows the same directory as Figure 4.1 after Properties was chosen from the File menu. The highlighted file, NETWARS.EXE, is the game included with both Personal NetWare and Novell DOS 7. Played it yet?

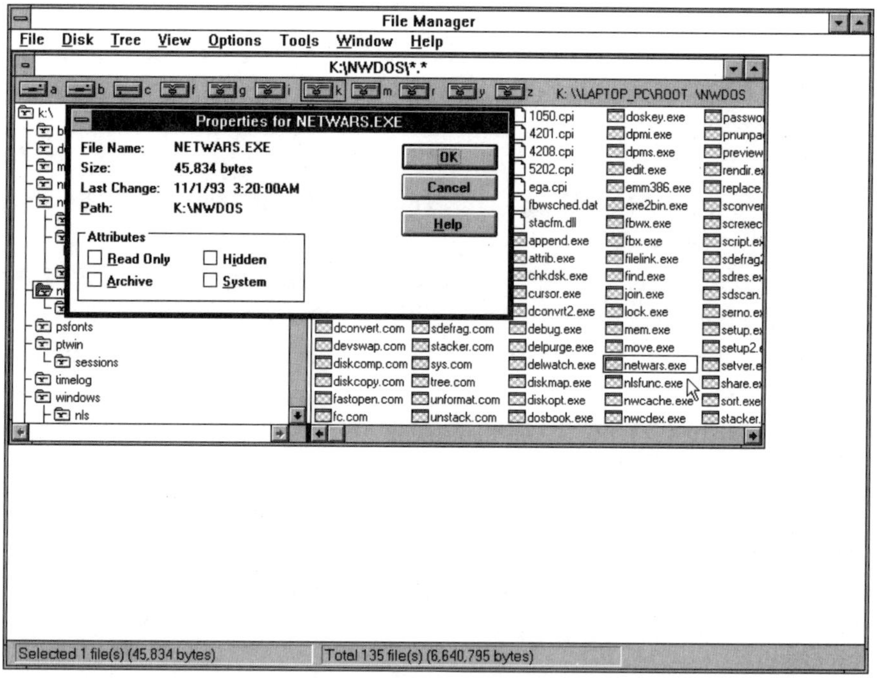

FIGURE 4.2

File properties seen by File Manager

Deleting Directories

IN-A-HURRY? **Delete a directory with File Manager**

4.1

THE FAST LANE

1. Open File Manager (through Program Manager, then Main group).
2. Click on the drive letter where the directory resides.
3. Highlight the directory in the directory tree display in the left box.
4. Press the Delete key.
5. Confirm your intentions to delete the directory.

One advantage of File Manager over DOS is the ability to delete an entire directory with one click of the mouse. In DOS, you must first delete all the files, then move up one directory level, then delete the directory. (Unlike MS DOS, Novell DOS 7 has the XDEL command, which allows you to delete a whole directory; see Chapter 9 for details.)

Let's delete a directory with File Manager, but not just any directory. Let's delete a directory over on the LAPTOP_PC computer, using our Personal NetWare connection.

This is both a good and bad example I'm setting here. It's a good example of the power of Personal NetWare, showing that your PC can use all your traditional utilities on remote volumes as easily as on your own local hard disk. It's a bad example because it's considered rude to delete directories on other people's computers.

We have a directory named TEST, which we're assuming is a directory on the remote LAPTOP_PC server that belongs to you and you alone. It's showing in Figure 4.3 as being on the LAPTOP_PC Personal NetWare server, and File Manager is running on TWR_PC.

I'm guessing you've already loaded File Manager and have your targeted directory in your sights. You can press either the Delete key or choose Delete from the File menu. Pressing the Delete key is faster, and your mouse won't get too lonely if you leave it for a few seconds.

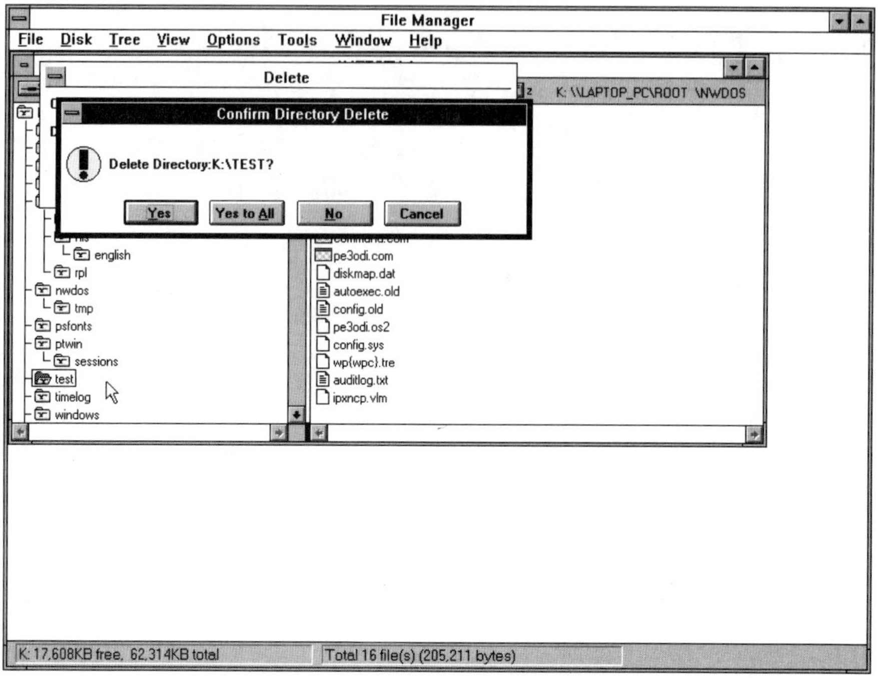

FIGURE 4.3

Deleting a directory on a Personal NetWare server

First, File Manager will show you the directory to delete and ask you to confirm that choice. Then File Manager will ask if you really do want to delete this directory. If you wrongly pick Yes, rather than Yes to All, you will need to confirm every file to be deleted. But before you blithely choose Yes to All, take a second to make sure this is the directory you want to trash. You will need to pick Yes to All again for the first file to convince MS Windows you really do want this deletion to happen.

There's one small difference when deleting a directory shared by a Personal NetWare server: if someone is using a file from there, you can't delete it. If someone merely has his or her current directory set in the directory you want to trash, the directory can't be deleted. If you delete a directory that is in your PATH statement or someone else's, there will be problems. Remember, you've got to be more polite now that you're sharing resources with others in your group. Deleting a directory that someone is using may result in hurt feelings, lost work, and a vow of revenge.

SEARCHING FOR DIRECTORIES WITH FILE MANAGER

IN-A-HURRY? **Get a full directory listing with File Manager**

4.2 THE FAST LANE

1 Open File Manager.
2 Pull down the Tree menu.
3 Click on Expand All.

It's a common occurrence to lose a file on your disk. It's also frustrating, and the fact that other people make the same mistake at times doesn't lower your blood pressure. With more places to put your files in the workgroup or on a NetWare server, there are more places to lose them as well.

First, you need to find the directory. Personal NetWare, as we've seen, allows all your MS Windows utilities to work on the remote volumes exactly as if they were local hard disks. The same goes for your directory searches.

In File Manager, the default is simply to show as little directory information as possible. But we can fix this. Click once on the Tree menu choice in File Manager, or press Alt-T if your fingers haven't withered from prolonged mouse use.

The quickest way to see all the directories is to pick the third option down, Expand All. There are actually three ways to make this happen. You can mouse and click it, you can press A, or you can press Ctrl-* anytime. Note that the * is the asterisk on the numeric keypad, not the shifted 8 key on the keyboard. This setting will last until you close MS Windows or switch to another disk to view.

The reason this expanded view resets to showing only the top layer of directories is the time it takes to display everything. If you watch the bottom-left corner of the main window when you expand the directory listing, you'll see that MS Windows has to go find and digest file and directory information for every nook and cranny of the disk. You can see on the right all the file information is displayed for the directory you highlight on the left side. This takes time. Since MS Windows is slow enough as it is, someone at Microsoft obviously decided to make the quickest view the default view.

Can you tell on your screen that the directory icons on the left side of the File Manager window have the little cable and connector drawing? This shows the displayed drive is remote, just as the larger icons across the top tell you the same information. If your screen isn't clear enough, or you're reading this in bed in search of slumber, look at Figure 4.4.

Once you have the full expanded tree on display, you can quickly reach the directory of your choice by typing the first letter of the directory name. This will speed your highlight bar there faster than any mouse. If several directories start with the same letter, each keypress will jump to the next appropriate directory. See, there are tricks to make MS Windows faster.

FIGURE 4.4

The File Manager screen showing the expanded root directory of LAPTOP_PC across a Personal NetWare connection

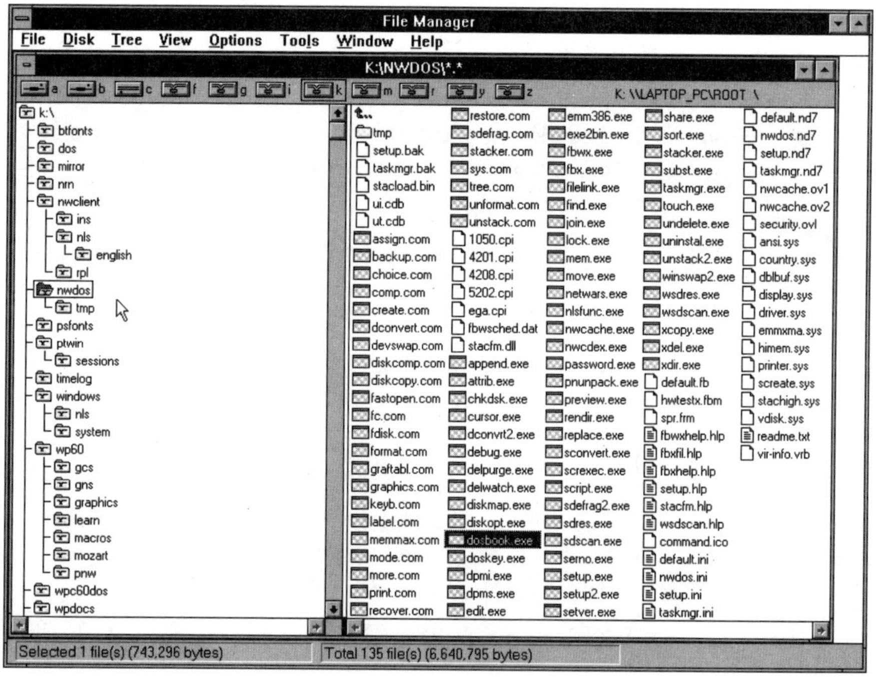

USING NETWARE TOOLS TO FIND DIRECTORIES

Since File Manager is a sizable application, it takes time to load. You also must leave the window you're in and go back to Program Manager to start File Manager. What if you want a quick view of some directories? How about NetWare Tools?

A quick press of the F6 key summons NetWare Tools, and you can find directories here similar to the way you find them in File Manager. Even more fun, this will pop up over any MS Windows program, anywhere. Look at Figure 4.5 to see what I mean.

The figure shows the current mapped drives on the left, and the disk resources on the right. We're cheating a little bit, using the drive mapping procedure to look for directories, but we'll just consider this creative usage.

On the right, we've highlighted the subdirectory of the \NWDOS directory we saw in Figure 4.4. Notice that some of the directory folders are open

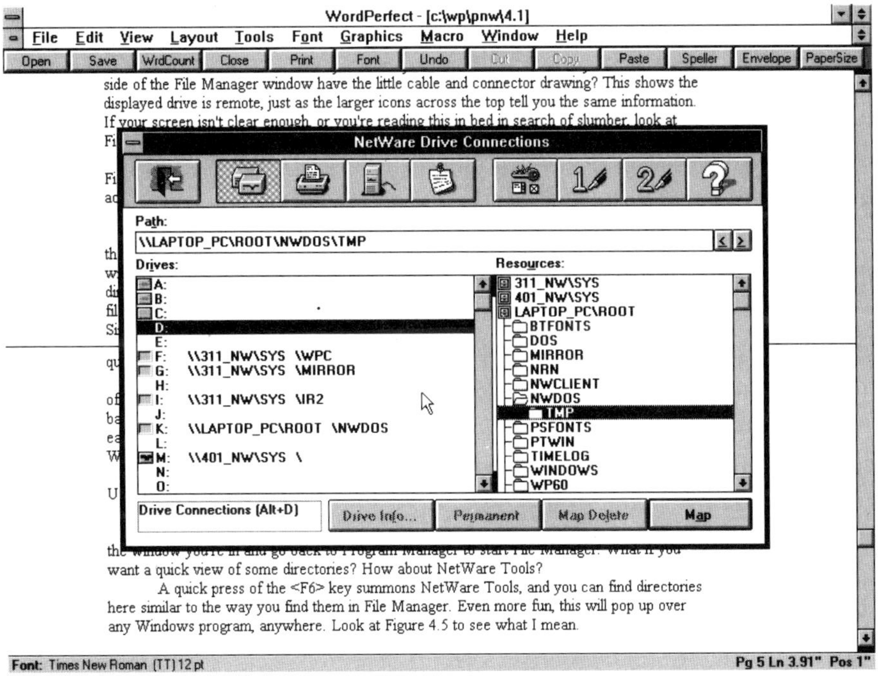

FIGURE 4.5
NetWare Tools popping up over WordPerfect

and some are closed. The open ones indicate we can see everything they have for us. The closed ones either don't have a subdirectory or they haven't yet been opened.

Once you find the directory you want, NetWare Tools has an advantage over File Manager. See the command button on the bottom right with Map in dark letters? Clicking that Map button will immediately map the highlighted directory on the right to the highlighted drive letter on the left.

The Path text box, just under the row of icons along the top, shows the official path. The \\ on the front just tells us that this is a network resource and not local. You can also drag and drop the directory to the drive letter of your choice. If you drop the directory on a mapped drive, you can replace the current mapping with the directory you're dragging all over the screen. The new mapped drive D: will start its directory tree at the \LAPTOP-_PC\ROOT\NWDOS\TMP directory.

Handy? You bet. The ability to quickly pop open the NetWare Tools program for directory searching is a good tool to have. And since there's little reason to look for a directory if you're not going to use it, the ability to map a drive to your directory of choice saves time as well.

USING PERSONAL NETWARE TO FIND DIRECTORIES

Using the Personal NetWare program to find directories is much like using the NetWare Tools pop-up for this task. You must call the Personal NetWare program from the Personal NetWare group since there is no hotkey available.

The view in Figure 4.6 is again the directory on LAPTOP_PC we've looked at before. The same disk resources are on the right, with the current drive mapping information on the left. Click on the icons at the bottom of the screen to see your NetWare and printer connections.

In the top left of the window, you can see the File menu has been pulled down. The items in dark letters are those that are available to you in this situation. You can't use the items in gray letters. For instance, the Disconnect command is not available, so it's in gray letters. The highlighted option, Connect, tells you that you can map your highlighted directory to any

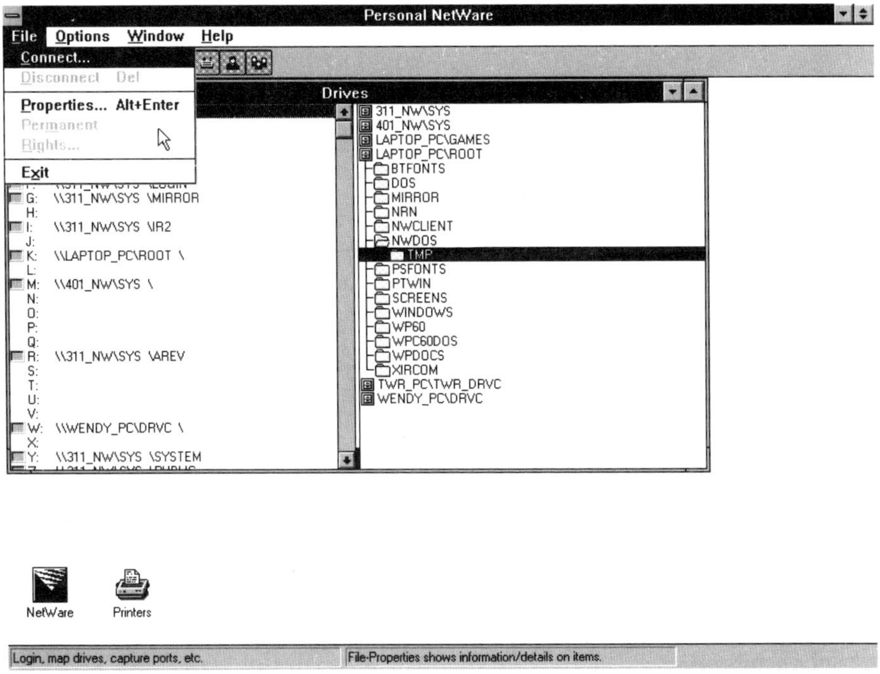

FIGURE 4.6

Looking at the same Personal NetWare remote volume through the Personal NetWare program

drive letter you wish. If you click on Connect, you will be asked to log in if you haven't already.

The same drag and drop capabilities are available here, just as in NetWare Tools. You might also want to see what happens when you choose Rights or Properties in the File menu. There are hints for you on the bottom line of the window as well.

SEARCHING FOR FILES WITH FILE MANAGER

IN-A-HURRY? Search for a file with File Manager

4.3

THE FAST LANE

1 Open File Manager.
2 Choose Search from the File menu.

3. Type the name of the file you want to find, then press Enter. You can include wildcards.
4. Read the results in the Search Results window.

Sometimes, even seeing the directory can't activate those gray cells between your ears enough to remember if that's the directory hiding the file you want. Then it's time to look for a particular file. Back to File Manager.

Let's say you want to find all the .BAT files on a particular drive. In this case, we'll once again attack the Personal NetWare K: drive on the LAPTOP_PC computer.

Open File Manager, then pull down the File menu. Toward the bottom is Search, with the *h* underlined as the activation letter rather than *S*. The MS Windows programmers assumed we would spend more time using Select than Search, so Select got the most natural activation letter. Oh well, you can always use the mouse to click on Search, so the activation letters don't matter all that much.

There's not an easy way to search for files across multiple drives, so you must still pick a drive letter. The default is to search through all subdirectories of the drive in question, so our search for all the *.BAT files on drive K: will search the entire file system of LAPTOP_PC.

The results are shown in Figure 4.7, all neatly corralled into a single Search Results window that pops up in the foreground. If you want to execute one of these files, either press Enter when it's highlighted or double-click on the name. Clicking on the down arrow in the upper-right corner, officially called the Minimize button, will iconize the Search Results window. Since this window will disappear when you close File Manager, you will need to iconize it if you want to see this list of files later.

Any typical MS Windows file operation can be performed on the files listed in the Search Results window. Once again, more information is lurking in the bottom corners of the window. In this case, MS Windows tells us it found three files. You can see in the Search Results window that each file was in a different subdirectory.

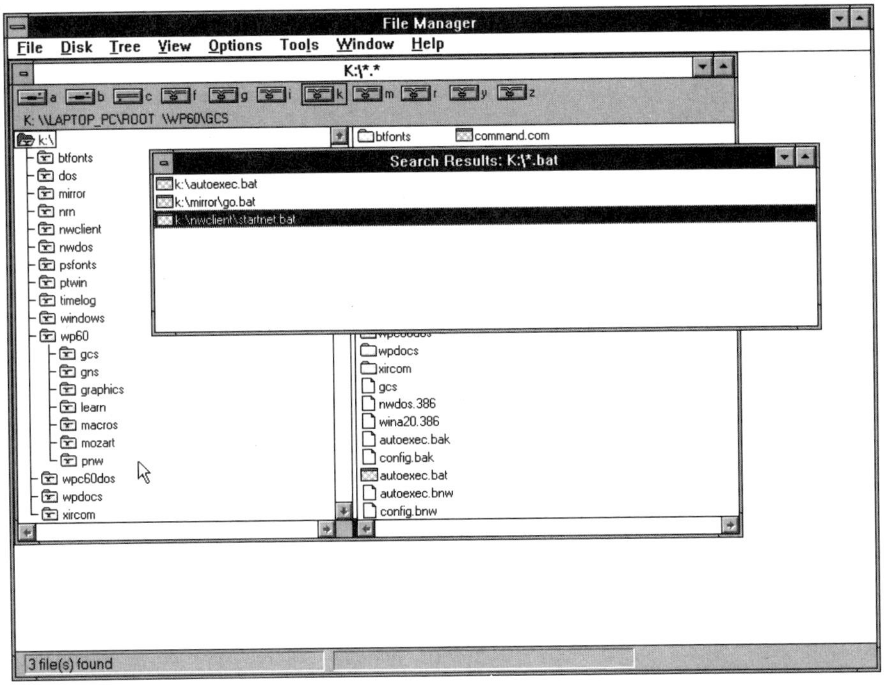

FIGURE 4.7
The results of a search for all files with the .BAT extension

Of course, if I was smart, I would search for all the files with a .BAK extension. Those are left over from editing ASCII files, since the Edit program and most other text processors leave the original in place with that .BAK extension. They take up disk space for no good reason, once you're sure the editing went fine. So your homework is to search for all your .BAK files and delete them through the Search Results window.

When you've found the files you want to delete, here's a quick MS Windows tip: use both your mouse and the Ctrl key to choose multiple files. Click on the first file, then press Ctrl and hold it while clicking on more files. Each file you click will stay highlighted. Press the Delete key to get rid of them.

Controlling File Access on a Server under MS Windows

Here we bump into a sometimes unpleasant reality in networking: just because you can see a file doesn't mean you can use it. There are plenty of situations when you can see files but have only limited access to those same files. There are also plenty of situations when you can't even see files unless you have permission. So if someone tells you to get a copy of a certain file and you can't find it, it may not be your fault. You may need more access privileges to that particular area.

YOU AND YOUR TRUSTEE RIGHTS

On a NetWare server, the system administrator sets the file rights. You, as a user, have no control over setting these rights. Traditionally, the shared areas of the server have somewhat restrictive rights, while your private areas allow you full rights. So we see three levels of rights for you on a typical server:

- Full control and rights in your private areas
- Some rights in shared areas
- No rights in the private areas of other users

The rights given to users and groups are called *trustee* rights. It is more efficient for the network supervisor to grant rights to groups rather than to individual users. If you're a member of the group, you get the same rights as the group. You might say you *inherit* those rights. They are as follows:

TRUSTEE RIGHT	DESCRIPTION
Read	Allows you to read files
Write	Allows you to write files
Create	Allows you to create files and subdirectories
Erase	Allows you to delete files and subdirectories

TRUSTEE RIGHT	DESCRIPTION
Modify	Allows you to modify files and subdirectories
File Scan	Allows you to see the file and subdirectory names
Access Control	Allows you to change the rights to the files and directories
Supervisory	You have all rights in this directory
None	Allows you no rights

To keep the system administrator from going crazy while setting rights in each directory, NetWare uses the idea of inherited rights. Like many things in life, some of which are not pleasant, rights roll downhill. By that, I mean that rights in a directory are inherited by all subdirectories.

This works quite well, actually. By granting you the rights to read, write, change, erase, and scan all files in a parent directory, the supervisor also allows you to perform all those same functions in every subdirectory of that directory. An example would be giving you rights to the \BUDGET directory, so you will have rights to the subdirectories labeled \JAN, \FEB, \MAR, and so on.

Since there are times when a user shouldn't have access to a subdirectory, NetWare has a way to change the inherited rights. This mechanism is called the Inherited Rights Mask in NetWare 3.*x*, but renamed the Inherited Rights Filter in NetWare 4.*x*. Filter may be a better description for the concept, since some of the rights are "filtered out" when you're moving down to some files or directories.

In our \BUDGET example two paragraphs ago, it's quite likely that more subdirectories than just the monthly ones mentioned exist. What if there's a subdirectory named \BUDGET\PAYROLL? Your boss may be happy for you to place monthly update files in the appropriate directories, but not to snoop around and see how underpaid you are. This would be an excellent reason for the directory to be hidden, or all the files in the directory to be specifically tagged with restrictions. This brings up the topic of file and directory attributes.

YOUR ACCESS AND FILE AND DIRECTORY ATTRIBUTES

Your trustee rights can be overridden by directory and file attributes. These are rights both for files and the directories that hold them. These expand on the DOS file attributes you may be familiar with. DOS file attributes are limited to System, Read Only, Hidden, and Archive (as shown in Figure 4.2). The file attribute applies to all users, and supersedes the user's rights, and in some cases overrides the rights of the supervisor. The following are the most common ones you need to be concerned with:

DIRECTORY OR FILE ATTRIBUTE	DESCRIPTION
Read Write	Allows you to read and change the contents of the file
Read Only	Prevents you from modifying the file
Shareable	Allows several users access to the file at the same time
Delete Inhibit	Prevents you from deleting the file or subdirectory
Execute Only	Prevents you from copying or backing up executable files
Hidden	Prevents DIR and NDIR commands from showing the file
Rename	Prevents you from renaming the file or subdirectory

Remember, these are not all the attributes, just the ones that may affect your work.

The supervisor will set these file attributes. The most common settings are combinations such as Shareable/Read Write, to allow multiple users to access database files, and Shareable/Read Only, for utilities and programs many people need to use but never modify. If you're interested in the supervisory details, pick up *Novell's Guide to NetWare 4.x Networks* or *Novell's Guide to NetWare 3.12 Networks*, both by Novell Press.

If you ever need to restore network files from a tape backup system, you may find that you've got the files themselves, but not these extended NetWare file attributes. Different tape backup systems mean different things by "NetWare-Aware." The marketing department may say NetWare-Aware if the tape software can get the DOS files from a mapped network drive. That is not the kind of NetWare-Aware you want. If your tape backup system is like this, upgrading is strongly recommended. If your boss is not convinced, explain how losing these file attributes will make the \BUDGET\PAYROLL directory available to everyone after being restored from tape. Then present your upgrade request.

CHECKING YOUR RIGHTS TO USE FILES UNDER MS WINDOWS

IN-A-HURRY? **View your rights to a mapped drive**

4.4 THE FAST LANE

1. Press F6 from an MS Windows program to pop up NetWare Tools.
2. Click on the drives button.
3. Highlight the mapped drive letter.
4. Click on Drive Info.

The obvious question here is, "How can I tell what access rights I have?" That is a good question. The answer depends on whether you want to check with the Personal NetWare program or the NetWare Tools pop-up. The DOS users will get their answer in just a bit.

With Personal NetWare, the utilities show only your rights as a user to files, as you can see in Figure 4.8. Any file and directory attributes that exist modify your assigned trustee rights.

Where did this screen come from? It's been there all the time, we just didn't need it yet. It's been hiding right there in NetWare Tools, under the Drive Info command button. You'll notice if you move the highlight bar up and down over the drive letters that the Drive Info button only becomes available when you highlight a mapped drive.

Once NetWare Tools is open, just place the highlight bar on a mapped drive. Click on the Drive Info button, and the screen in Figure 4.8 will pop up. Since this is my personal directory (see the Path item at the top showing SYS:JAMES?), I have all rights to this directory.

This same information is available in the Personal NetWare program as well. When you're in the Drives window in Personal NetWare, highlight a drive just as you did in NetWare Tools. Since there's no command button, you must open the File menu and choose Rights. The exact same Drive Info window will appear, giving you the same information. Isn't consistency refreshing in a computer?

FIGURE 4.8

The NetWare Tools pop-up showing all rights to a home directory

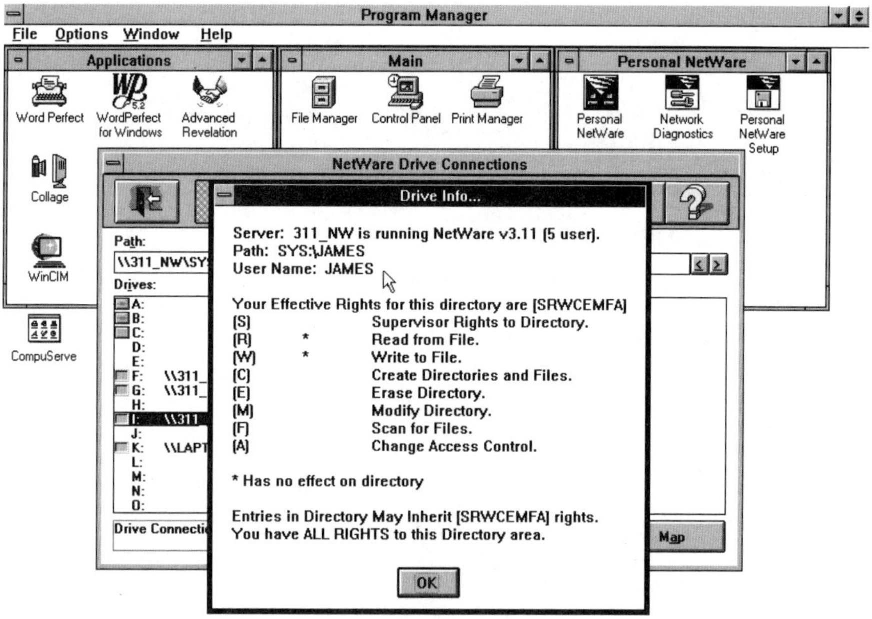

There are only a few differences in the file access rights a user has under NetWare 3.*x* and 4.*x*. None make a difference in your use and management of your files, so let's keep going.

Controlling Workgroup File Access under MS Windows

The same type of access rights and controls that we've discussed so far are implemented by Personal NetWare. The security control is based on that for NetWare servers, so the \BUDGET\PAYROLL directory on your boss's computer will still be safe from your snooping. But while the security procedures are just as tight, there are fewer access rights in Personal NetWare.

PERSONAL NETWARE ACCESS RIGHTS

The Personal NetWare access rights are as follows:

PERSONAL NETWARE ACCESS RIGHT	DESCRIPTION
All	Allows you full access
None	Allows you no access
Read	Allows you to read and execute files
Write	Allows you to write, modify, create, and delete files

You should recognize that many of these rights combine several of the NetWare server rights into one for ease of administration. Remember, every user is a network administrator with Personal NetWare, so the emphasis is on getting work done, not messing with the network all day.

There is no Inherited Rights Filter as with a NetWare file server, for a good reason. With a NetWare dedicated server, the entire directory structure is potentially available to all users. With Personal NetWare, each user makes only certain directories shareable on his or her computer. Since the entire directory structure isn't available to other users, we don't need to worry as much about easy ways to lock people out. Just don't share a directory with sensitive subdirectories, and everything will be fine.

It's easy to allow only certain users access to a shared directory. The best way to do this in a workgroup is to set a directory's default access to None. Then, assign nondefault rights for that directory only to the users that have a legitimate need for using that directory. As you'll see in Chapter 8, it's easy to control access to your computer and your files.

CHECKING YOUR WORKGROUP FILE RIGHTS

4.5 THE FAST LANE

IN-A-HURRY? View your rights to a Personal NetWare volume

1 Press F6 to pop up NetWare Tools.
2 Click on the drives button.
3 Highlight the drive letter mapped to the Personal NetWare volume.
4 Click on Drive Info.

The same method that is used to see your access to files on NetWare servers is used in Personal NetWare. Let's look at both a directory where we have full access and one where we have no access. Rejection is a fact of life, so you might as well see it here before it catches you by surprise in your workgroup.

Figure 4.9 shows the same NetWare Tool's Drive Info window that we saw in Figure 4.8, but this time it's looking at a Personal NetWare volume. We get there the same way, however, so here goes.

Press F6 to open the NetWare Tools program, and move to the NetWare Drive Connections window either by clicking on the drives button or by pressing Alt-D if your mouse is getting tired. Highlight a drive letter that is pointing to a Personal NetWare shared volume, then click on the Drive Info command button.

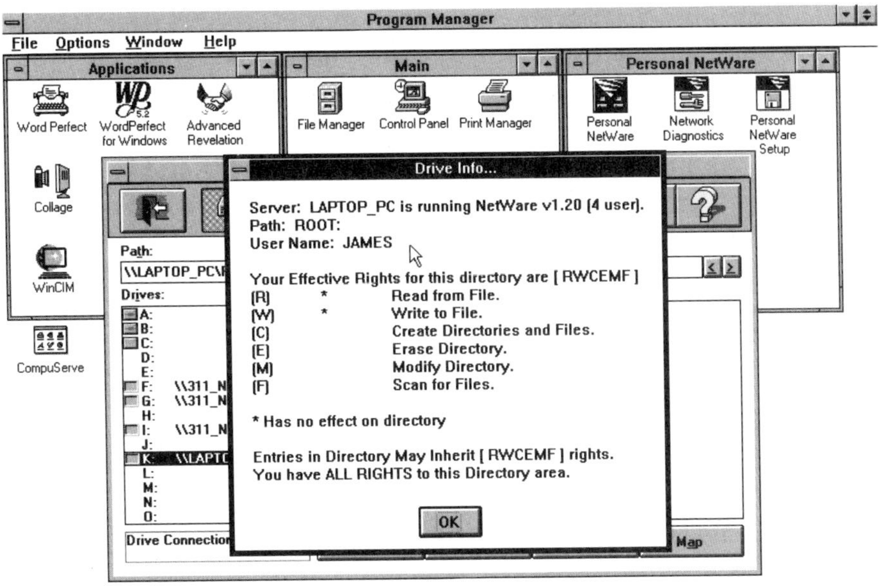

FIGURE 4.9

Full rights to a Personal NetWare volume

This display looks exactly like the earlier figure of the NetWare server drive, doesn't it? Oops, not quite. The first and last lines, Supervisor and Access Control, are missing. In the bracketed rights abbreviation description you can even see the spaces where the *S* and the *A* were in Figure 4.8. These two rights don't have exact equivalents in Personal NetWare, so they aren't included. But it's nice to see again how closely information for a Personal NetWare server matches that for a NetWare dedicated server, isn't it?

Now for that rejection I warned you about: Figure 4.10 shows the results of a rights query where you have no rights. Pretty bleak, don't you think? If there's any doubt about your access privileges, the NO RIGHTS statement in capital letters ends all speculation.

Notice that the Path item in the Drive Info window does not give a path as it did in Figures 4.9 and 4.10. Here, it gives only the name GAMES. As you'll see in Chapter 8, the shared directories in Personal NetWare are given names for a point of reference. And, no matter how far down in the directory

FIGURE 4.10

The Drive Info window showing a Personal NetWare volume where you are not welcome

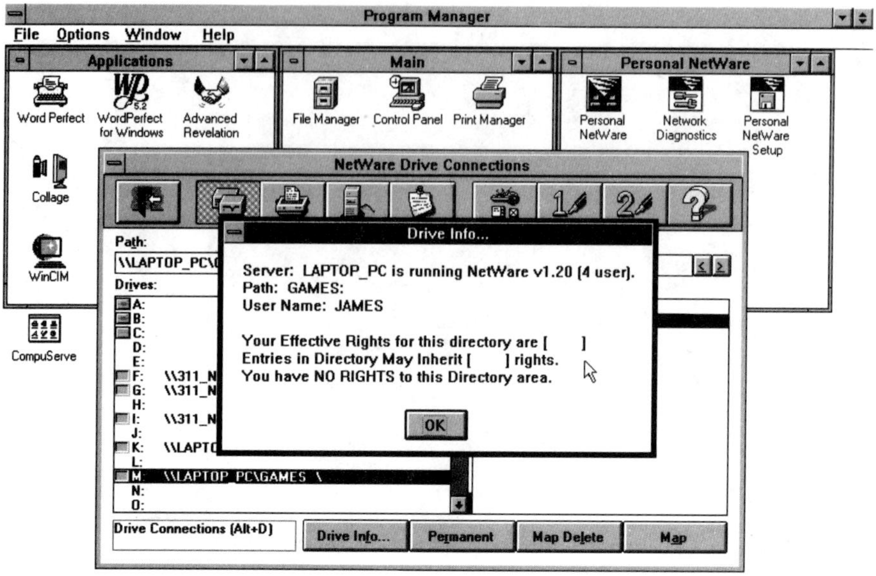

tree the shared directory is located, it looks like the root directory to all Personal NetWare users sharing that drive.

Copying and Moving Files from Here to There and Back under MS Windows

Files are all over your hard disk, but at least a few are probably not where you want them. This feeling is familiar to those of you that live where there is more than one story. When you're upstairs, something you need is always downstairs. Often it's something heavy, like your vacuum cleaner.

In a case like this, you have a choice. You can either move files (carry the vacuum cleaner upstairs) or copy files (buy a second vacuum cleaner).

Copying files tends to be the most common option, but remember what we said earlier about limiting the number of file copies but allowing more people access to those files. If you want to keep only a single file, you will want to move files rather than copy them. If it's more efficient and productive for everyone to have a copy of particular files, you will want to copy those files.

This question of moving versus copying is separate from making copies of important files for safety's sake. Even if you have a regular file backup schedule, there will be files you must have copies of to sleep better. Your budget in progress, your schedule, your insults file with your boss's name plugged in, and your resume are examples of files definitely worth copying. In some cases, they're even worth hiding.

COPYING A FILE WITH FILE MANAGER

IN-A-HURRY? **Copy a single file with File Manager** 4.6

THE FAST LANE

1. Open File Manager.
2. Double-click on the network drive icon.
3. Arrange the screen to see some of both drive windows.
4. Click on the file you want to copy.
5. Drag and drop the file to the desired directory.

All the earlier file finding and drive mapping information serves as the foundation for this section. I'm assuming you have identified some file that needs to be copied from one drive to another. Since this is a networking book, let's look at copying a file from a network drive onto your local hard disk.

Let's use Figure 4.11 as the example here. Drive C: is my local PC, while drive K: is LAPTOP_PC. Copying files between a portable computer and your desktop machine is a common operation. Using Personal NetWare makes it easier than flipping floppies all over the place.

Open the MS Windows File Manager program by double-clicking on the file cabinet icon in the Main group of the Program Manager. This will display the top window you see in Figure 4.11, which is now open to the TEMP directory. You can tell by the banner on the window that says

FIGURE 4.11

Copying a file from a remote Personal NetWare directory to a local hard disk

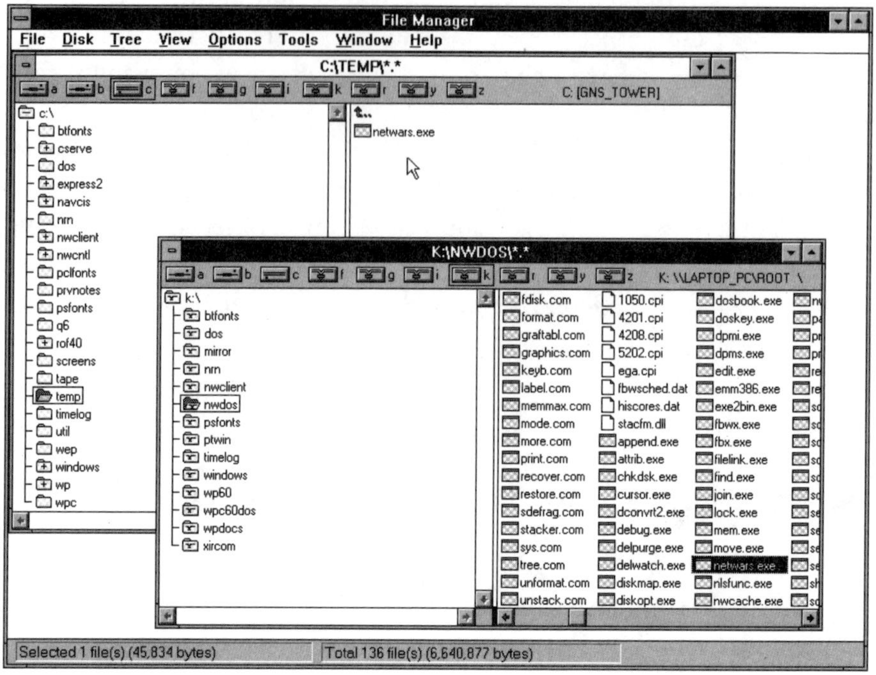

C:\TEMP*.*, as well as by the fact that the TEMP directory is boxed in the directory display on the left side of the screen.

If you click once on the drive K: icon, the existing window will change to show you that directory information. If you want both windows open at once, you must double-click on the drive icon of your choice. In this case, my choice is drive K:. Once you open that view by double-clicking on the drive icon, you'll need to move the window. The second window always opens right on top of the existing window, which doesn't help for a file copy operation.

The banner for that second window indicates drive K: is just another drive letter, and it is displayed just like drive C: in the top window. However, you can see the full path statement just to the right of the drive icons. It says

```
K: \\LAPTOP_PC\ROOT \
```

indicating I'm displaying the information for a remote drive K: on server LAPTOP_PC, volume name ROOT. The directory name that's highlighted in the left window is \NWDOS, and so the right side of the windows is showing all the files in that directory. Down toward the bottom you can see the highlighted file NETWARS.EXE.

Click on the file, then drag it by holding down the left mouse button and sliding up to the first window, C:\TEMP. When the file outline you're dragging is anywhere in the right side of the C:\TEMP window, release the left button. MS Windows will ask if you really want to copy that file, so press Enter to affirm you know what you're doing. The copy will be made immediately. Did you notice that there was a little plus sign (+) on the file outline? That's MS Windows' way to tell us we are copying this file rather than moving it.

Check the status line (the bottom line at the far left), which shows the size of the file you selected. This is important if you're copying files to a floppy disk with limited capacity. If you try to cram a large file into a small space, it won't work. The status line will be trying to warn you; remember to check there now and then.

COPYING MORE THAN ONE FILE WITH FILE MANAGER

IN-A-HURRY? Copy multiple files 4.7

THE FAST LANE

1. Open File Manager.
2. Double-click on the network drive icon.
3. Arrange the screen to see some of both drive windows.
4. Shift-click or Ctrl-click on the files that you want to copy.
5. Drag and drop the files to the desired directory.

Copying several files at one time is much like copying just one file. The trick here is to discover an easy way to tag multiple files.

If you want to copy a group of contiguous files (ones that are listed next to each other), the Shift key is the ticket. After you click on one file, press and hold down the Shift key. Move the mouse down to the last file you want to select, and click there. All the files in between will be highlighted as well.

And if you want to select multiple, but noncontiguous, files? Click on the first file, then press the Ctrl key. Mouse about and click on as many other files as you desire, and as long as you hold down that Ctrl key, each one will be highlighted. When you've picked your fill, release the Ctrl key and start dragging and dropping.

With multiple files selected, MS Windows assumes you want all of them to be copied. Position the cursor on any of the selected files, press the left mouse button, and drag them over to the destination directory. When you release the mouse button, MS Windows will ask if you want all these files copied, in the little Confirm Mouse Operation dialog box that will pop up, as shown in Figure 4.12. Just say yes, and all the selected files will do their duty and duplicate themselves.

FIGURE 4.12

The Confirm Mouse Operation dialog box for multiple copies

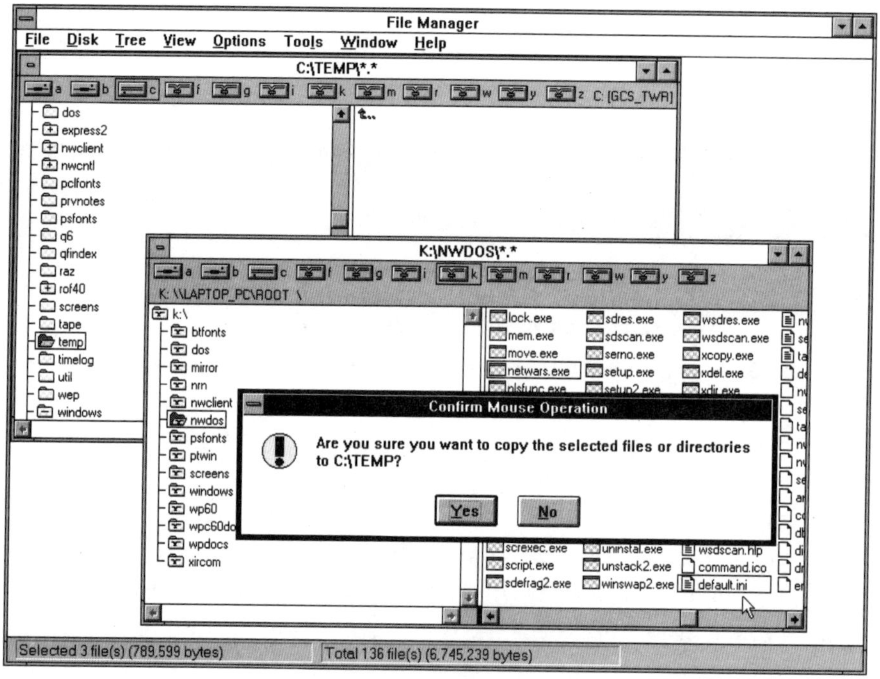

When copying multiple files, the status line information is even more important. If you're copying files from one hard disk to another, as in our example, space can still become a problem. Copying multiple files to a floppy is guaranteed to mess you up one day. Try to postpone that day by remembering to check that status line for the collective size of your selected files.

You can avoid mousing about by choosing Copy from the File menu, or press F8 anytime in File Manager. The Copy dialog box will have the name of the file to copy filled in if one is highlighted. You can then type in the destination for that file or files. This is one time the mouse saves quite a bit of time. If you wanted to type everything, you should have done this in DOS.

By the way, did you notice that the Confirm Mouse Operation dialog box mentioned moving files *or directories* each time? Yes, you can copy entire directories this way, but be careful. The chance of overloading your destination floppy or hard drive when moving a directory is even greater than when working with multiple files. Definitely do not copy or make major changes in directories used by others in your workgroup.

MOVING A FILE WITH FILE MANAGER

IN-A-HURRY? **Move a single file with File Manager**

4.8 THE FAST LANE

1. Open File Manager.
2. Double-click on the network drive icon.
3. Arrange the screen to see some of both drive windows.
4. Click on the file that you want to copy.
5. Press and hold down the Alt key.
6. Drag and drop the file to the desired directory.

The other option besides copying a file is to move it where you want it. This is like dragging that vacuum cleaner upstairs. This is also more in line with our networking idea of "one file, many users." Consistency may be the hobgoblin of small minds, but it certainly makes for better networking.

When you move files between two destinations on the same disk, you don't actually move anything. The move operation just tells your directory structure that the file BUDGET is now here rather than there. The file itself stays put.

When you move files between two different drives, however, things do move. The BUDGET file is first copied to its new location, verified, then deleted from its old location. There is a tiny chance of mishap, since actual bits on your disk get rewritten and deleted. If the moved copy somehow develops an error, or the power stops during the operation, your system may get confused and the old copy may get deleted. Then you're stuck with a bad moved file, because the new one is damaged, and the old one is deleted.

This is similar to a transporter accident on Star Trek. It's extremely rare, but makes for high drama when it does happen.

The instructions for moving files are amazingly similar to the instructions for copying files, with one important difference: you must hold down the Alt key while dragging your file to its new location. Technically, we're supposed to hold down the Ctrl key while copying files. But since copying is done more than moving, its operation became the default. If you don't tell MS Windows otherwise, it will copy files. To move files (and directories), you must remember to use the Alt key.

Open the File Manager and select your file's source drive letter. If you aren't moving the file between drives, just drag the file from the right side of the window to the directory icon on the left side and drop it. Remember that Alt key. But our instructions assume we're moving this file between drives, so let's do that.

Arrange the screen so you can see some areas of both windows. Click on the drive icon for the destination. Highlight your file just like you did for the copy procedure. Before you click on that left mouse button to drag the file, remember to press and hold down the Alt key. With the Alt key depressed, click and hold the left mouse button. Scoot the file over to its new home, and release the left mouse button.

You should notice that the file outline does not have a plus sign inside. This is MS Windows' way of telling you the file is moving. If you see a plus sign, you didn't hold down the Alt key at the right time. Try again.

MOVING MORE THAN ONE FILE WITH FILE MANAGER

IN-A-HURRY? Move multiple files with File Manager

4.9

THE FAST LANE

1. Open File Manager.
2. Double-click on the network drive icon.
3. Arrange the screen to see some of both drive windows.
4. Shift-click or Ctrl-click on the files that you want to move.
5. Press and hold down the Alt key.
6. Drag and drop the files to the desired directory.

Moving multiple files works similarly to moving a single file. Select the files in the same manner you did to copy them: hold either the Ctrl key for random files or the Shift key for consecutive files.

Once these are selected, press and hold down that Alt key before starting to drag one of the selected files to its new home. When you drag one, all the other selected files will go as well. If you see that plus sign in the file outline, try again. That indicates a copy operation, not a move operation.

Directories can be moved, just as files are moved. Everything works the same way. Drag your selected directory and drop it one level above where it will live. In other words, if you want to move that \BUDGET\PAYROLL directory we spoke of earlier to \PRIVATE\PAYROLL, drop the PAYROLL directory icon directly on the \PRIVATE directory.

Finding and Using Files under DOS

Don't expect some miraculous new DOS techniques for finding and using files while using Personal NetWare. The whole idea of the product is to share the resources of a remote PC or file server, without changing the way you work. Every program you use to handle files on your PC today will work just the same.

The DOS commands used the most when moving around your file system are CD (Change Directory) and DIR (DIRectory). Those work exactly the same way on the Personal NetWare shared directories. To DOS, the remote Personal NetWare volumes (shared directories) look exactly like a local disk volume.

USING THE DOSSHELL PROGRAM

Microsoft, trying to push DOS users into a graphical world before MS Windows was ready for prime time, included DOSSHELL starting in MS DOS 4.0. Although DOSSHELL is technically a nongraphics program and runs on monochrome monitors, it emulates a graphical interface. It has multiple windows, supports a mouse, and offers several lurid color schemes, as does MS Windows.

Figure 4.13 shows a view of the \NWDOS directory of LAPTOP_PC, acting again as a server to the workgroup. Doesn't this look similar to Figure 4.1?

We can guess that DOSSHELL is not as smart as MS Windows, because it doesn't show us the name of the remote server that's sharing this directory. But remember that Novell provided parts of the original MS Windows 3.0 code and included several utilities that work with MS Windows. There is no option for outside vendors to add additional features in DOSSHELL.

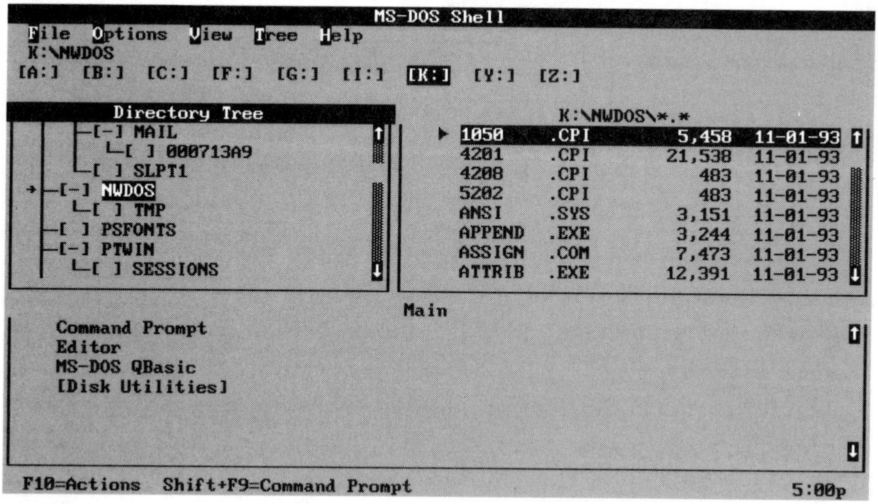

FIGURE 4.13

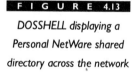

DOSSHELL displaying a Personal NetWare shared directory across the network

In spite of the limitations of DOSSHELL, it does have one feature that File Manager in MS Windows does not: the ability to view files. The sixth option on the File menu is View File Contents. The hotkey for that function is the F9 key.

As with File Manager, you can see the contents of directories, print files, run program files from within DOSSHELL, and mess things up by deleting the wrong files. At least DOSSHELL won't let you delete entire directories. You must delete all the files, then delete the directory, just like with DOS.

Getting a Directory Listing

IN-A-HURRY? **List a full directory with DOSSHELL**

4.10 THE FAST LANE

1. Open DOSSHELL (type **DOSSHELL** at the prompt).
2. If you're not in a network drive, choose one from the top of the screen.
3. Press Alt-T to pull down the Tree menu.
4. Press A to choose Expand All.

DOSSHELL takes longer to start than File Manager because it checks every directory and every file. This default makes it seem slow, which is probably why MS Windows chose not to start that way. The good part of this is the speed in showing the full directory tree if you choose to see it.

Once DOSSHELL is open, press Alt-T to pull down the Tree menu. If you're more interested in the roundabout method, press F10 to activate the menu options, then press T for Tree.

Whichever way you get there, once the Tree menu is displayed, you can see your options. Pressing A tells DOSSHELL to Expand All, so all the directories will be displayed. There is no delay in showing these expanded directories, because DOSSHELL already read every potential directory when it started.

Notice the shortcut: pressing Ctrl-* (the asterisk on the numeric keypad, not the shifted 8 key) performs the same job as dropping the Tree menu and pressing A. Isn't it nice that Microsoft makes these keystrokes consistent across both DOSSHELL and File Manager?

Using DOSSHELL to Find Files

4.11 THE FAST LANE

IN-A-HURRY? Search for a file with DOSSHELL

1. Open DOSSHELL.
2. Choose Search from the File menu (press Alt-F, then H).
3. Type the name of the file you want to find, then press Enter. The file name can include wildcards.
4. Read the results in the Results box.

The speed advantage of having the file information loaded before the search starts is obvious when you want to find a file. The DOSSHELL file search goes much faster than the one in MS Windows. This is not just because DOS doesn't need to paint all the graphics on the screen; this speed is because the files are already in the computer's memory. There's no delay to read the disk, since the disk was read and the information gathered when DOSSHELL started.

Open DOSSHELL by typing DOSSHELL at the command prompt; you don't need to type it in the \DOS directory. Pull down the File menu by pressing Alt-F or F10, then F. If you're a mousy person even in DOS, you can click on File to open that menu. Once it's open, press H for searcH. The Search File dialog box will appear, waiting for you to supply the name of the file or the wildcards you think will help you find your file. Unfortunately, there's no date option, so you can't look for the files you did last Thursday. For that, get a document management program or learn to use the DIR /od command (*DIR*ectory with the *o*rder set to *d*ate).

The results will appear in the Results box. Did you try searching for all the *.BAK files using the MS Windows search feature? Didn't think so. Now is a good time to do the same here. Search for all the files that have a .BAK extension, then go through and delete them.

USING NET TO SEARCH FOR DIRECTORIES

4.12 THE FAST LANE

IN-A-HURRY? **Find a directory with NET**

1. Open the NET program (type **NET** at the DOS prompt).
2. Press Alt-D to open the Drives View screen.
3. Place the highlight bar on the desired drive mapping.
4. Press Alt-F, then P to see subdirectories.
5. Press Enter on the directory name to search through.
6. Press Alt-O to map that new directory.

The NET program will help you find directories but not files. Like the NetWare Tools program in MS Windows, there is one big advantage when using NET instead of File Manager: it can map a drive to the directory you find.

Figure 4.14 shows the same view as Figure 4.5, except using the NET program rather than NetWare Tools. Drive K: on the TWR_PC is again mapped to the root directory of LAPTOP_PC, and we're again looking at the \NWDOS\TMP directory. Figure 4.14 shows this in splendid black and white.

Since the Personal NetWare installation procedure places the \NWCLIENT directory in your PATH statement, typing NET at the DOS prompt will call the program. Since the default view is your available NetWare servers, you'll need to press Alt-D to open the Drives View screen. On that screen, move the highlight bar down to the drive letter of your choice. For our purposes here, it must be a drive letter already mapped to a server, either a Personal NetWare workgroup server or any dedicated NetWare file server. The Universal NetWare Client approach provides the same tool for the same job, regardless of the server involved.

To see the subdirectories, the official way is to press Alt-F to open the File menu, then P to choose Properties. Yeah, Properties may not be the most intuitive name choice, but it's all we have. Each time you press Enter on a directory name, you will drill down and see all the subdirectories inside that directory. When the display box is empty, you've hit the bottom of your directory drill.

FIGURE 4.14

Searching for directories with the NET program

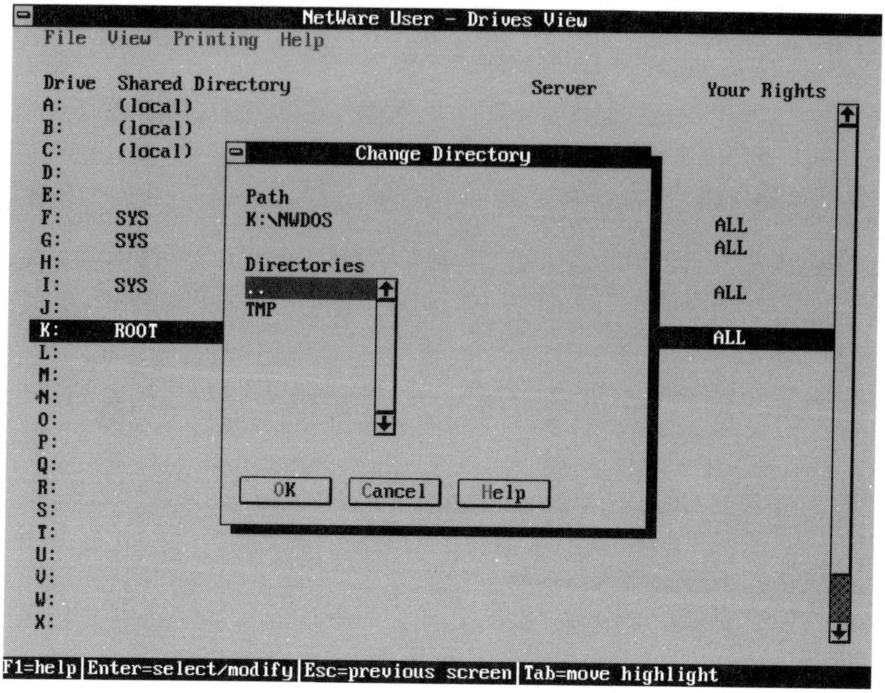

Two quick hints:

- Type the drive letter you want. The highlight will move to it immediately.
- Press Alt-Enter to see the subdirectories, even though the program doesn't tell you about that key combination on the status line across the bottom. It does tell you beside the Properties option in the File menu, but it's not clear that it works even without the File menu being open. Try it, it does.

While the Change Directory dialog box is open, you must take one more step to make your chosen subdirectory the current directory for that mapped drive. You must press Alt-O for OK to make the new drive mapping. If you just press Escape, you will find that the listed drive did not change directories. Just a warning to remember to take that extra step and avoid the frustration that will arise otherwise. You will not see the changed directory location until you exit NET and change to that drive letter.

Controlling File Access on a Server under DOS

Here again is that ugly situation that disappoints the inner child: you can't always get what you want. Files on a NetWare file server have security controls. For the full discussion, refer to the section about controlling file access on a NetWare server under MS Windows, earlier in this chapter.

Now we need to figure out how to tell our rights in a directory on a NetWare file server under DOS. It's not hard: at the DOS prompt on a network drive type

```
RIGHTS
```

You are actually running a program named RIGHTS.EXE that lives in the \PUBLIC directory on every NetWare file server. If you don't have a drive mapped to the \PUBLIC directory, you can also use Personal NetWare's NET RIGHTS command. It gives a simplified report of your rights, since the security in Personal NetWare is less complex than that for a NetWare file server.

Figure 4.15 shows the same RIGHTS command result as shown in Figure 4.8. The only difference is that this one is done in DOS, not MS Windows. This is just another example of how DOS and MS Windows often do the same thing. One is less cluttered, but also less colorful.

The displayed rights are more extensive than you will probably see, since I appointed myself supervisor (hey, it's my network). In your own directory, you will probably have all these rights except for Supervisory and Access Control.

FIGURE 4.15

My rights to my own directory on a NetWare file server

```
I:\JAMES>rights
311_NW\SYS:JAMES
Your Effective Rights for this directory are [SRWCEMFA]
    You have Supervisor Rights to Directory.    (S)
  * May Read from File.                         (R)
  * May Write to File.                          (W)
    May Create Subdirectories and Files.        (C)
    May Erase Directory.                        (E)
    May Modify Directory.                       (M)
    May Scan for Files.                         (F)
    May Change Access Control.                  (A)

* Has no effect on directory.

    Entries in Directory May Inherit [SRWCEMFA] rights.
    You have ALL RIGHTS to Directory Entry.

I:\JAMES>
```

How do you know if you have enough rights to do your job? Most application software needs the ability to Read, Write, Create, Erase, and Scan to perform properly. Some overzealous supervisors try to take away the Erase rights, but not for long. Software often creates temporary files, which are deleted either when some functions are finished or the program is closed. If the program can't delete those temporary files, the disk will get full one day and no one will know why except you.

Controlling Workgroup File Access under DOS

Even though the rights report in Personal NetWare is less complex than from a NetWare file server, the rights are still solid and will lock you out. One major difference is that with Personal NetWare, each PC owner sets the rights for the shared resources on his or her own machine. Because of this, many of these rights combine several of the NetWare server rights into one for ease of administration. The rights are as follows:

PERSONAL NETWARE ACCESS RIGHTS	DESCRIPTION
All	Allows you full access
None	Allows you no access
Read	Allows you to read and execute files
Write	Allows you to write, modify, create, and delete files

Figure 4.16 shows the DOS version of Figure 4.9, at least as far as the rights are concerned. The highlight bar is covering my drive mapping to LAPTOP_PC. The far-right column tells me what rights I have. Since this screen does lots of other things, not much time is spent explaining the

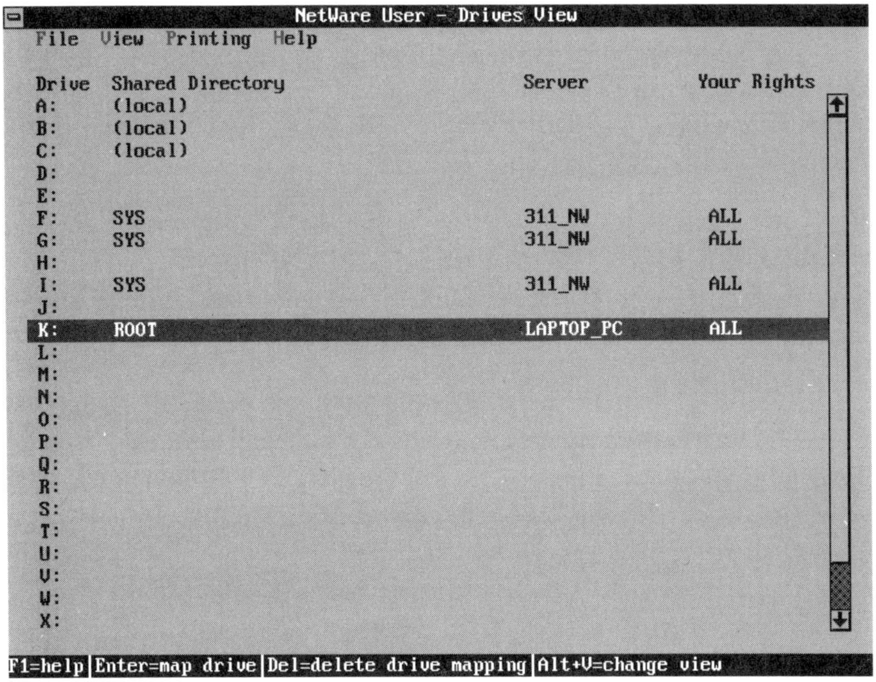

FIGURE 4.16

The NET program main screen, showing my rights to the LAPTOP_PC workgroup server

rights. It tells me I have ALL rights, which is all I need to know.

Personal NetWare doesn't have the same kind of file attributes that a NetWare server does. Why? Because Personal NetWare doesn't control those files; DOS does. Remember that a Personal NetWare volume is really a DOS directory on somebody's PC (maybe yours). Putting a bunch of extra file information in the form of extended attributes would cause your DOS programs to crash in confusion. Since Personal NetWare can't modify the file attributes, it controls access through the user rights that you grant to your shared directories.

Copying and Moving Files from Here to There and Back with DOS

Before you begin copying files and moving them about with DOS, read the opening paragraphs about performing these operations with MS Windows. The vacuum cleaner analogy applies here as well.

In MS Windows, you can use File Manager to move and copy files. In DOS, you can use DOSSHELL, but few people do. We'll focus on using the simple command line options you have, since they're easy to remember and much quicker than DOSSHELL.

COPYING FILES FROM THE COMMAND LINE

If you use DOS, you've used the COPY command. The format is easy to remember:

COPY *FILENAME FILENAME*

where the first file name is where it is, and the second is where you want the copy. If you want to make a copy of the file \BUDGET\PAYROLL from your hard disk to drive A:, here's the command:

```
COPY C:\BUDGET\PAYROLL A:
```

This puts the file \BUDGET\PAYROLL onto your floppy disk in drive A:. If you use subdirectories on your floppies, the command would more likely be like this:

```
COPY C:\BUDGET\PAYROLL A:\BUDGET\PAYROLL
```

You can, while copying a file, change the name of that file. All you need to do is type a different name as the destination, and the new copy will be renamed to the given name. Nothing about the original changes.

Wildcards make copying more efficient. Do you have a common extension for some files, such as those that contain letters? If all your letters end in .LTR for the extension, copying all those letters at one time is as simple as:

```
COPY C:\WP\*.LTR A:
```

Before you do that command, be sure there's enough room on the floppy in drive A:. First type

```
DIR C:\WP\*.LTR
```

to see how many bytes those letters add up to. It's embarrassing to copy 12 of 13 files, then need to start over because the disk was full.

Want to go faster? Use the XCOPY command, which is quicker because it reads several files at one time, then copies them all at once. The COPY command reads then copies one file at a time, so there is more overhead to the copy process, which slows it down.

When copying an entire directory and one or more subdirectories, you must use the XCOPY command. You must also use a *switch*, or extra instruction to DOS, along with the command. To copy our \BUDGET directory along with the PAYROLL and JAN, FEB, MAR, and all other subdirectories, the command would be:

```
XCOPY C:\BUDGET /S K:
```

This command will copy the \BUDGET directory and all subdirectories (that's what the /S is for) to drive K:. Since drive K: has been mapped to the LAPTOP_PC server, it looks like we're ready to take the budget files on the road.

If you use Compaq DOS, try this command:

```
XCOPY C:\BUDGET /S /L K:
```

The /L is for Long display, which shows you the status of your copy operation.

MOVING FILES FROM THE COMMAND LINE

The MOVE command does just what it says: moves files from one place to another, rather than copying them. Not all versions of DOS have a MOVE command, so if this doesn't work on your PC, get upgraded. One advantage of MOVE is its ability to specify several files to move without using wildcards.

If the boss is truly paranoid, he might want to move the \BUDGET\PAYROLL file rather than just copy it. The command he would use is:

```
MOVE C:\BUDGET\PAYROLL A:
```

The file is actually copied to drive A: then deleted from drive C:, but the result is a move. If he wanted to study just three particular files while on the road, he might use this command to move certain files to his laptop:

```
MOVE ED.PAY,CHRIS.PAY,MARILYN.PAY K:\BUDGET\RAISES
```

It seems the boss is moving payroll information for Ed, Chris, and Marilyn to the \BUDGET\RAISES directory on LAPTOP_PC server. Now, the only file concerning raises for Ed, Chris, and Marilyn will be on the laptop. I hope for their sake that the laptop doesn't get misplaced.

CHAPTER 5

How Do I Print, and Where?

If the question is printing, the answer is NOT. People print entirely too much. Save some trees by cutting down your paper consumption. And in this case, being nice to the environment actually saves you money. That's right; if your office prints less, it will become more efficient and productive. You will not only save money, you will save time.

Paper was the best storage method for information 500 years ago. Things have changed. Compared with the options we have with computers today, paper stores less, costs more, takes more physical space, and is more prone to errors. Copies of paper documents are so common that it's impossible to be sure if the information you hold in your hand is unique. Even worse, it's impossible to know if the information you hold is current. Chances are, it isn't up to date, and the most current copy is filed away. So you're working hard with old information, doing jobs that may well be rendered useless once the current information is found.

Avoiding Printing

Since your computer is now linked to the other computers in your workgroup, there are many ways to share information without putting it onto paper. Need to see Fred's sales guesstimate for next quarter? Look at his spreadsheet—use Personal NetWare to connect your spreadsheet application to view his data file. Need to send a memo? Dozens of electronic mail programs offer quick and inexpensive software to send memos, mail, and anything else on your computer to other computers. Some of them offer full group scheduling modules, allowing you to check Fred's schedule for a time to review his inflated sales forecast with him personally.

Take a stand and save a tree (and your sanity). Remember, you don't get sympathy for a mistake if you blame the file cabinet. Keep information on your computer, and everyone understands when you tell them that the computer messed up. Even if you messed up the computer by typing information from an old copy of an "important" paper.

Printing from MS Windows

You've seen how ingeniously Personal NetWare becomes a part of MS Windows, offering more functionality with no more effort on your part. Printing is part of that easily available functionality.

THE NEW AGE OF DISTANT PRINTING

It used to be, in the Dark Ages of Computing (about 1985), that printing was real straightforward. Your application sent its print output to the address on the PC motherboard that was connected to the parallel printer port. The address was always the same in every computer, brand name or clone. If you were unlucky, you had a serial printer. It was harder to set up and slower than a parallel printer connected to the parallel port, but you suffered through. Either way, the printer wasn't very smart, which was okay because your application used a total of two fonts if you were a power user. Underlining was a big deal.

Today, nobody prints directly to their printer port anymore. Using MS Windows means the applications are physically separated from the hardware address on the motherboard and must print through MS Windows. Even more distance between application and printer is created because many MS Windows users turn on Print Manager, hoping it will keep MS Windows from bogging down when printing a long job. It doesn't get rid of all printing headaches, but hope springs eternal.

When you print to a network, network print queues buffer your print job yet again. If you're using a NetWare 3.*x* or 4.*x* network, you may have Print Manager turned off, so only one print buffer stands between your application and the printer.

What's the point of all this explanation? Just to let you know that you never print from your application directly to the printer anymore. Or at least hardly ever. And if you did in the past, you will probably change now that you have Personal NetWare to connect your workgroup.

PRINTING TO A LOCAL PRINTER WITH MS WINDOWS

Perhaps you have a local printer, which is physically connected to your PC. Even in today's world of NetWare Everywhere, that happens. Often it happens for good reasons, such as because you need to print a lot or on unusual forms. Often the printer's just left over from before you got your network. Either way, you have it and want to print to it.

Figure 5.1 shows the MS Windows Print Manager screen showing a local printer attached to LPT1:. See the lonely printer. It may seem contradictory, but although I hate to see lots of printing done, I also hate to see unshared resources on a network.

With a local printer set up in this manner, your application will have no problem printing to the attached printer. And you won't have any problems changing that designation later. It will be easy to share your printer or direct your output to a different printer located elsewhere on the network (which is what this networking business is all about).

When you do redirect your printing, your application will be none the wiser. We've already seen that MS Windows puts several layers between

FIGURE 5.1

A local printer, not being shared with the workgroup

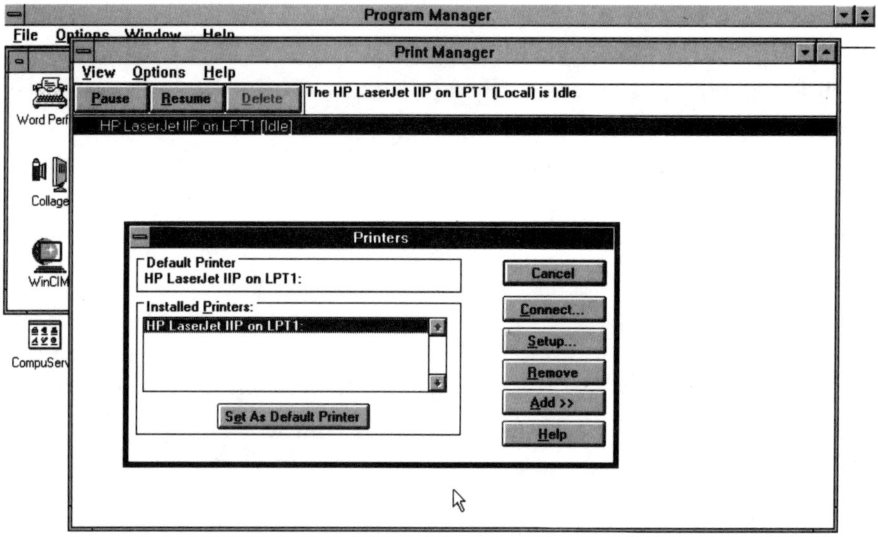

your application and your printer. Having a network involved will make no difference to the application, believe me.

Even after installing Personal NetWare, your personal printer can stay your personal printer. Nothing forces you to share that printer, and nothing in the installation of Personal NetWare interferes with the physical printer. If you say your parallel port belongs to you, your wishes will be respected. But if you have a nice printer, be prepared for your colleagues to whine as they pass your office heading way down the hall for their printouts.

PRINTING TO NETWARE SYSTEM PRINTERS WITH MS WINDOWS

IN-A-HURRY? Connect to a NetWare printer with MS Windows 5.1

THE FAST LANE

1 In MS Windows, press F6 to open NetWare Tools.
2 Click on the printer button.
3 Highlight an available print queue in the Resources box.
4 Drag and drop the print queue to LPT1:.

Most NetWare users depend on one or more NetWare system printers. There's nothing magic about a system printer; it's just one that is controlled by the NetWare file server. Even the lowliest 10-year old, dot-matrix printer can be a NetWare system printer.

A system printer can be physically connected to the NetWare file server, to a NetWare client, to a dedicated print server, or directly to the network cabling. The location is not important; the controlling system is.

In NetWare, you print to a print queue, which is connected to the printer you want to use. Your network administrator has set up all the printing details, including what form to use (the default on 99 percent of all NetWare printers is blank, white paper, but you can get fancy if you want). Figure 5.2 shows the same LPT1: port that was pointing at a physically connected printer in the earlier figure now sending print jobs to a NetWare system printer.

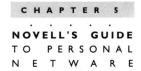

FIGURE 5.2

Your LPT1: port redirected to a NetWare system printer

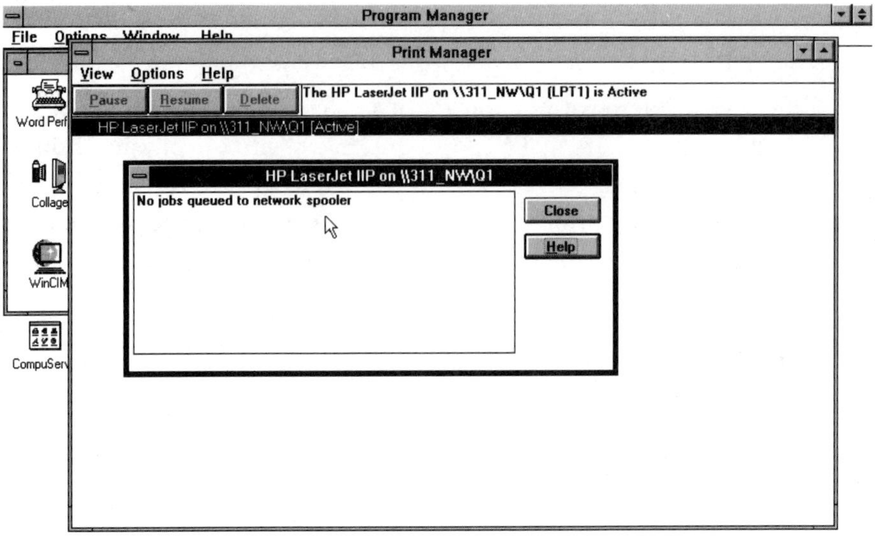

Notice the banner of the Print Manager screen shows that we are now pointing to a remote printer, \\311_NW\Q1, and that the printer is active. The two slashes (\\) at the beginning show that this is a remote resource. Remember that *remote* only means not directly connected, not necessarily far away. It could be attached to the PC in the next office.

All print jobs your local applications send to LPT1: will go from your PC, across the network, to the NetWare file server, then to the printer. Your application won't know this, nor will it care. MS Windows will know this, but it won't care either. Print Manager will send the print stream to the NetWare system printer.

When you log in to a NetWare file server, your login script often makes your printer connection automatically. The command will be something like

```
CAPTURE Q=Q1 NB NFF TI=5
```

This translates into CAPTURE the print output and send it to queue number one (Q=Q1). NB means No Banner (the page that has your name in big letters, used to separate print jobs on shared printers). NFF means No Form Feed (which keeps the system from putting a blank page after every page of output). TI=5 means TImeout in 5 seconds, telling the NetWare print queue to consider the print job finished if there's a 5-second gap in the print stream. The result of all this is simple: when you print, it automatically arrives at your assigned network printer.

Yes, you can have LPT1: connected to a local printer, and then send print output to the LPT2: port, which is connected to a network printer. This is entirely possible, but not often done. The problem is not with the network connections but with your local applications. Most people find it's more trouble than it's worth to configure two or three different printers within one application. Some programs also make it difficult to change printer ports for printer output. With the ease the NetWare Tools pop-up gives you to change printer connections, it's easy to leave all your applications pointing to LPT1: only.

How easy, you ask? No sweat. Here's how to connect a Personal NetWare client to a NetWare file server printer: while in any MS Windows program, open the ubiquitous NetWare Tools pop-up by pressing F6. It will be showing the view that was open when you last closed the program, so you have a one-in-four chance of seeing the NetWare Printer Connections banner. Assuming your luck runs like mine, either click on the printer button or press Alt-P to bring up the printer view.

On the left side will be your three parallel printer ports. All three can be configured. In fact, you can have a local printer, a Personal NetWare workgroup printer, and a NetWare system printer all connected at one time. However, wretched excess is no longer in style, so let's just connect LPT1: to the NetWare system printer controlled by the 311_NW server and be done with it. See Figure 5.3 for the picture worth a thousand words.

The right side of the box shows those printer resources available to you. If you think printers are missing, you probably need to log in to the servers that control them for access. But even if you're logged in to a server, the printer may still be unavailable.

You can either highlight the print queue desired and drag and drop it to the LPT1: port, or highlight the printer resource and click once on the Capture command button. *Capture* is Novell's term for capturing the print output of a parallel port.

FIGURE 5.3

One click on the Capture button, and LPT1: is connected to 311_NW\Q1

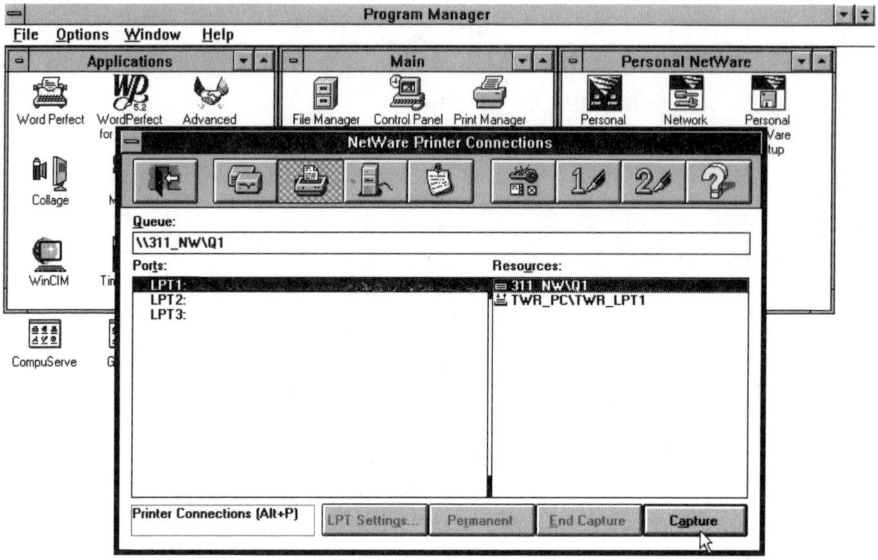

Since printers can be connected to multiple ports on the same client, the captured printer does not disappear as many connected resources do. The name of each printer stays in the Resources box on the right side of the screen. No harm comes from capturing a printer again to the same port it's already connected to or to a different port. The Help system is full of good ideas here. Press F1 or click on the question mark to see information about printing.

Once a printer is connected to a port, the other command buttons across the bottom of the window become active. End Capture disconnects the printer from its currently attached parallel port. Clicking on Permanent is the way to keep the connection. It adds a line in your PNWLOGIN.SCR file so that you always reconnect to that print queue when starting Personal NetWare. When you make a printer connection permanent, the icon beside the LPT listing changes from blank to a little printer. Clicking on the LPT Settings button displays a dialog box full of options for changing printing settings, as explained in the next section.

You can reach the Network Printer Connections window from Print Manager by choosing Network Connections from the Options menu, but pressing F6 is easier and quicker. This same NetWare Printer Connections window is also available in the Personal NetWare program. Start the program, then click on the printer icon if the Printers window is not already open. Highlight a connected printer, then press Alt-Enter (or choose Properties from the File menu). You'll see the NetWare Printer Connections window. It looks and works exactly the same way as it does when called from within NetWare Tools.

CHANGING PRINTING SETTINGS UNDER MS WINDOWS

IN-A-HURRY? Change printing settings with NetWare Tools

5.2

THE FAST LANE

1. Press F6 to open NetWare Tools.
2. Click on the printer button.
3. Highlight a connected printer.
4. Click on LPT Settings.
5. Make your changes, then click OK.

The LPT Settings command button in the NetWare Printer Connections window allows you to set all the print stream information from within NetWare Tools rather than through DOS command line options. When you click on this button, the NetWare Settings for LPTx: dialog box appears, as shown in Figure 5.4. As you can see, it offers quite a few options.

Here's what the check boxes on the left side of the dialog box do:

- Hold plugs up the printer, keeping your print jobs from being printed until you release them. You might use this if you're printing tons of little print jobs and don't want to walk down the hall time after time to fetch them. Check this box, choose to print your jobs from your application, then release them so they all print together.

FIGURE 5.4

The NetWare Settings LPTx: dialog box in NetWare Tools

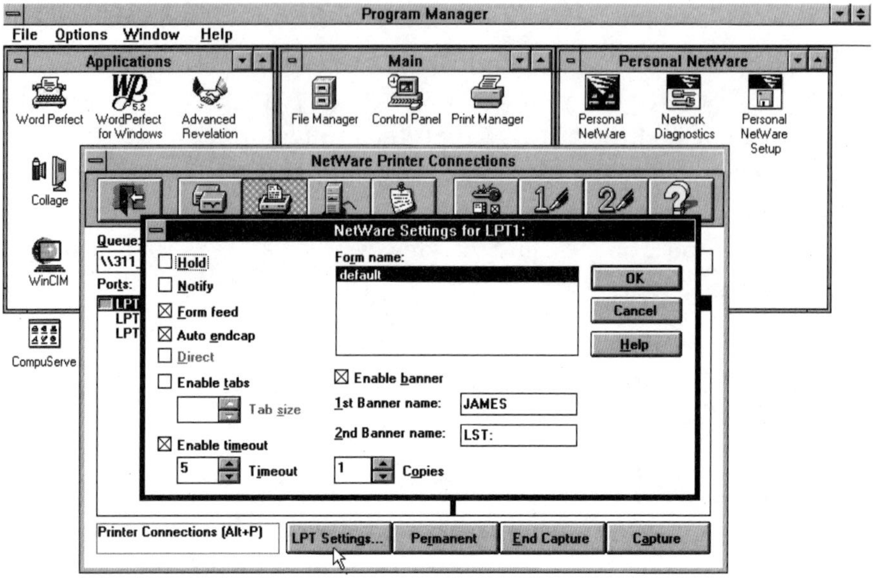

- Notify tells the print server to send you a message when your print job is finished. This allows you to kill time at your desk, rather than getting to the printer too soon and being forced to kill time at the printer. Wait until the NetWare SEND command hits your PC telling you the print job is finished. Of course, if you want to flirt with someone near the printer, you won't need to be notified.

- Form feed pushes the last page of your print job out of the printer. Some applications used to have trouble ejecting the last page of a job, especially from page-oriented printers like the ubiquitous laser printer. With Form feed checked, an eject command is sent to the printer at the end of each of your print jobs. Since applications are much better at dealing with laser printers today, this is rarely needed and only wastes paper.

- Auto endcap sets the timeout value discussed earlier. Each print job is spooled to a file on the server, and that file stays open until all the information is captured. Since applications don't send a clear "close the spooler and print" message, there must be a mechanism to tell the spool file to close and print the job. The ways to do this are to close the application or to send a second print job flushing out the first. With Auto endcap activated, the spool file will close when a certain amount of time goes by without new print information. The time is set in the Enable timeout box.

- Direct sends the job directly to the printer, or as directly as possible. MS Windows still gets in the way, and the jobs go to the spooler, but choosing Direct makes things happen faster with Personal NetWare printers.
- Enable tabs allows you to set the number of spaces in a tab stop. If you have a program so old it can't specify its own tabs, I feel for you. I've never seen this feature used.
- The Enable timeout check box sets the time interval to wait for print information, if you checked the Auto endcap option. The default is 5 seconds. If your application pauses for longer than the amount of time shown here, then starts printing again, the second batch will appear as a second print job.
- Enable banner places a banner page at the beginning of each print job. With heavily loaded shared printers, this is necessary so you can find your stuff in the stack. You can choose the banner wording. The default is your login name.

The Form name box allows you to choose which of the defined forms you wish to use for the upcoming print jobs. Default, the choice here, is most often the only choice, since most NetWare users don't define many forms.

The Copies box lets you set how many copies of a print job you want to print. The default is 1 for a single copy.

Any changes must be saved by clicking on the OK button. Pressing Escape will not get the job done.

MANAGING THE PRINT QUEUE WITH PERSONAL NETWARE

The Personal NetWare program provides one feature that NetWare Tools lacks: the ability to view the print queue. Since management is the domain of the Personal NetWare program, it contains a superset of features from NetWare Tools. You can do everything in Personal NetWare you can do in NetWare Tools. The NetWare Tools program is better suited to making network changes quickly and easily, but the Personal NetWare program is where you go to administer and maintain the network.

Figure 5.5 shows the print queue window within the Personal NetWare program. With the printer turned off, we can see the queue holding a file to print. Unless something unusual happens, you'll rarely catch files in the queue. The queue accepts print streams much faster than a printer does,

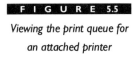

FIGURE 5.5

Viewing the print queue for an attached printer

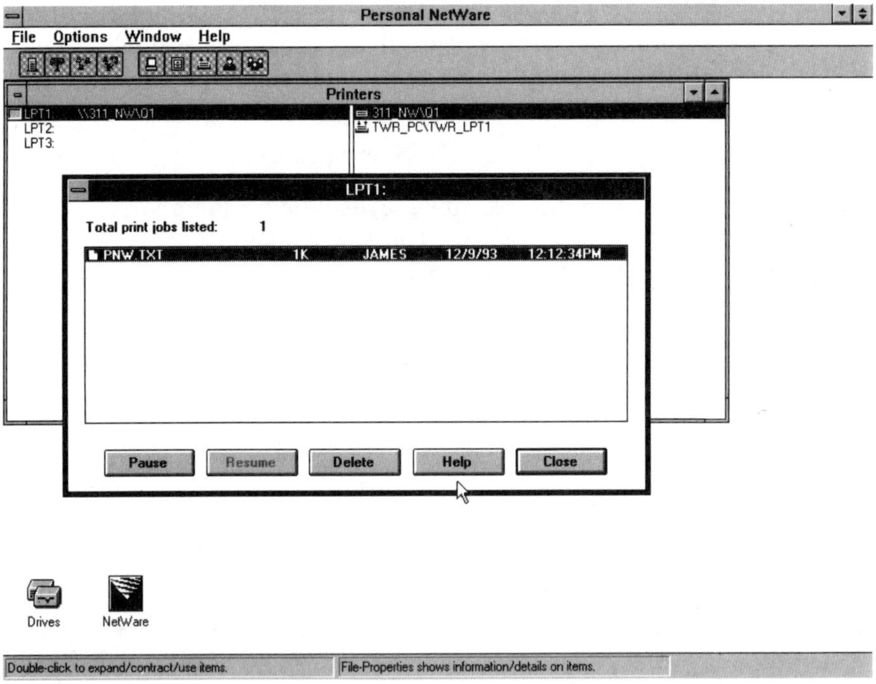

and it allows your application to return to work sooner. Then the queue doles the print job out to the printer in the background. If your printer is available, the delay in the print queue is minimal. That's why I turned off the printer so I could be sure a file would be waiting in the queue.

More details about the printer itself and its communication with the network are described in Chapter 8. If you're going to set up a few printers for the workgroup to share, you'll need to read that section of Chapter 8. If you're just interested in getting prose onto paper on a printer someone else configured and manages, we've done plenty for now.

PRINTING TO WORKGROUP PRINTERS WITH MS WINDOWS

With workgroup printers, we experience the joy of an object-oriented program, which treats all available printers exactly the same way. You don't need to worry whether they are NetWare system printers attached to a file server or workgroup printers hanging off the PCs of your office mates. Once you get into the NetWare Printer Connections window of NetWare Tools, the process is the same for any available printer.

WHICH SYSTEM CONTROLS THE PRINTER?

The major difference between types of printers in Personal NetWare is the naming conventions used. In the NetWare Tools pop-up shown back in Figure 5.3, the two printer names are your only clues about which system controls the printers. Since the default naming convention for Personal NetWare servers is the user name plus *PC*, it's easy for even upper management personnel to figure this out.

One note: your printer, if you have shared it with the workgroup, is no longer physically attached to your PC as far as Personal NetWare is concerned. Personal NetWare clients print to objects called printers, not to your PC and to your specific parallel printer port. No clients need reference your PC when sending print jobs to your printer, especially if the printer name has been changed to something descriptive like Laser4. That means you must also reference Laser4 for your print output, not your parallel port.

You must assign Laser4 to your LPT1: port to gain access. Leaving the port designation blank doesn't mean you just access your parallel port directly like the old days. It means you don't have a printer available.

CONNECTING TO WORKGROUP PRINTERS

5.3 THE FAST LANE

IN-A-HURRY? Connect to a workgroup printer under Windows

1. From MS Windows, press F6 to open NetWare Tools.
2. Click on the printer button.
3. Highlight an available printer in the Resources box.
4. Drag and drop the print queue to LPT1:.

After you share your printer with your workgroup, remember to connect the printer as an available network resource to your parallel port. But tell your applications you have the printer attached to the LPT1: port. Let Personal NetWare handle the details.

This procedure is as close to the procedure for connecting to a NetWare system printer as can be. The single difference occurs when you choose a printer controlled by the workgroup rather than by a NetWare file server.

From any MS Windows screen or application, pop open the NetWare Tools program by pressing F6. Open the NetWare Printer Connection window either by pressing Alt-P or by clicking on the printer button. The regular printer window appears, with the parallel ports listed on the left and the available printer resources on the right. Figure 5.3, a few pages back, shows this screen. In Figure 5.3, we were about to connect a printer to an empty parallel port, using the Capture command button. Dragging and dropping works just as well.

What if a printer is already attached to the parallel port you want to use? Nothing changes in any of the instructions, but NetWare Tools will want to make sure you plan to reassign that printer connection. Figure 5.6 shows the NetWare Warning dialog box that appears when printer connections are changed. In fact, let's change the printer setup in Figure 5.3 right over the top of an open MS Windows application.

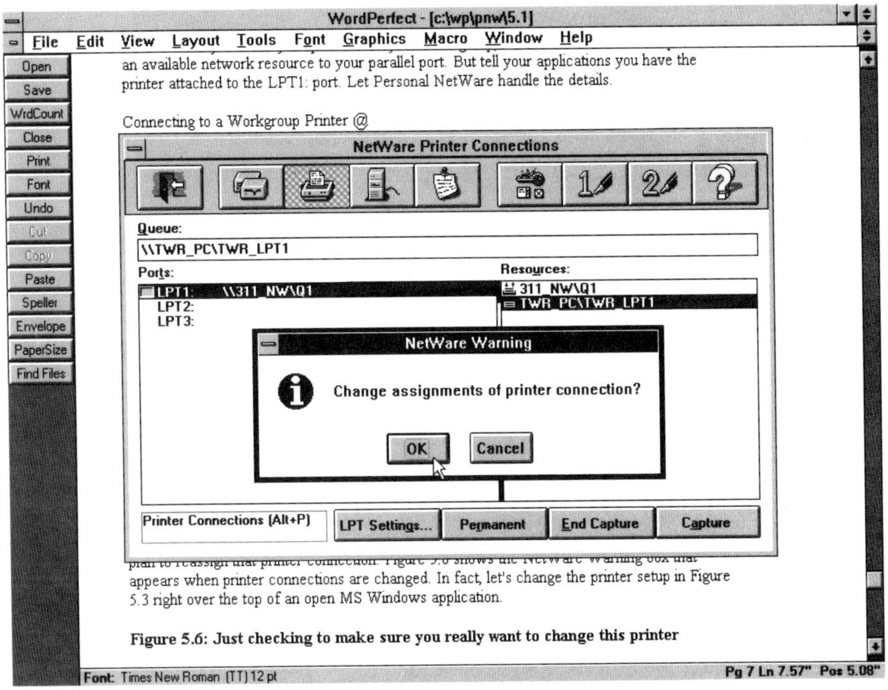

FIGURE 5.6

Just checking to make sure you really want to change this printer

Printing from DOS

Will there be trouble switching between printers in DOS, as just illustrated in MS Windows? Not if you remember to choose your printer before you start your application.

Since there is another layer or two of software between your application and the computer in MS Windows, it's easier to change printer assignments while running an application. One might argue that MS Windows makes it easier for people who don't know what they want until they're in the middle of work, while DOS is great for those who know what they're doing.

There are two ways to arrange your printer connections while in DOS:

- Use the NET program to help make your arrangements. This is similar to using the NetWare Tools pop-up in MS Windows, and it's the easiest method. Then save this connection in your PNWLOGIN.SCR file by using the Save Script option on the File menu.
- Type commands at the DOS prompt. This method is only slightly faster, and it's much more likely to generate errors.

DOS doesn't stick several layers of extra software between the application and the printer, as does MS Windows. While you might think having a few extra layers of stuff in the way makes it easier to intercept the print output and route it to a network printer, that's not the case. The mechanisms for printing between an application and the PC hardware under DOS are well known and easily redirected. There used to be some applications that went to the trouble to send output directly to the address on the PC motherboard that connected to the printer, but thankfully those are all gone.

The bottom line is simple: redirecting print output is just as easy under DOS as under MS Windows.

PRINTING TO LOCAL PRINTERS UNDER DOS

Just as under MS Windows, it's easy to keep a local printer completely local under DOS. If you choose not to share your printer port when you set up Personal NetWare on your system, your local printer will not be affected.

It may be considered rude and unfriendly to keep your local printer all to yourself. If the comments of those around you cause you to rethink your need to monopolize a printer, Chapter 8 tells you how to share that printer with the workgroup.

Unfortunately, there's no nice screen to show us a particular printer attached to a DOS computer. One reason for that is the inability of DOS to communicate with anything attached to the parallel port. Applications must do the work of discovering and controlling printers and other devices attached to any of the three parallel ports supported by DOS.

PRINTING TO NETWARE SYSTEM PRINTERS WITH DOS

IN-A-HURRY? **Connect to a NetWare system printer under DOS** **5.4**

1. Type **NET** at the DOS prompt to start the NET program.
2. Press Alt-O to see your LPT settings.
3. Highlight the parallel port of your choice and press Enter.
4. Choose the printer you want to connect and press Enter.
5. Exit NET and start your application.

A NetWare system printer can be connected to your parallel port using either Personal NetWare's NET program or the CAPTURE program on the NetWare file server. There are no important differences between the results of the two, once the printer is connected. Getting that printer connected is different between the two options, however. The CAPTURE program must either be in your NetWare login script or run from the command line in DOS. The NET program is easier and just about as fast.

Everything can be done through NET, which corresponds closely to the NetWare Tools program under MS Windows. NET ADMIN is the DOS version of the Personal NetWare program that controls and manages your PC server and other network resources.

The application doing the printing must know what kind of printer you have. Routing the print stream across the network doesn't change that requirement. Each application will have its own printer setup screens. Just remember that the application does not care that the printer is physically located away from your PC. Personal NetWare will take care of the details of routing the print output where it belongs.

Figure 5.7 shows the NET program displaying a NetWare system printer attached to LPT1:, along with the settings needed to control that printer connection. These are the same settings a non-Personal NetWare client has, but DOS is not as neat or as changeable.

FIGURE 5.7

Configuring printer redirection with NET

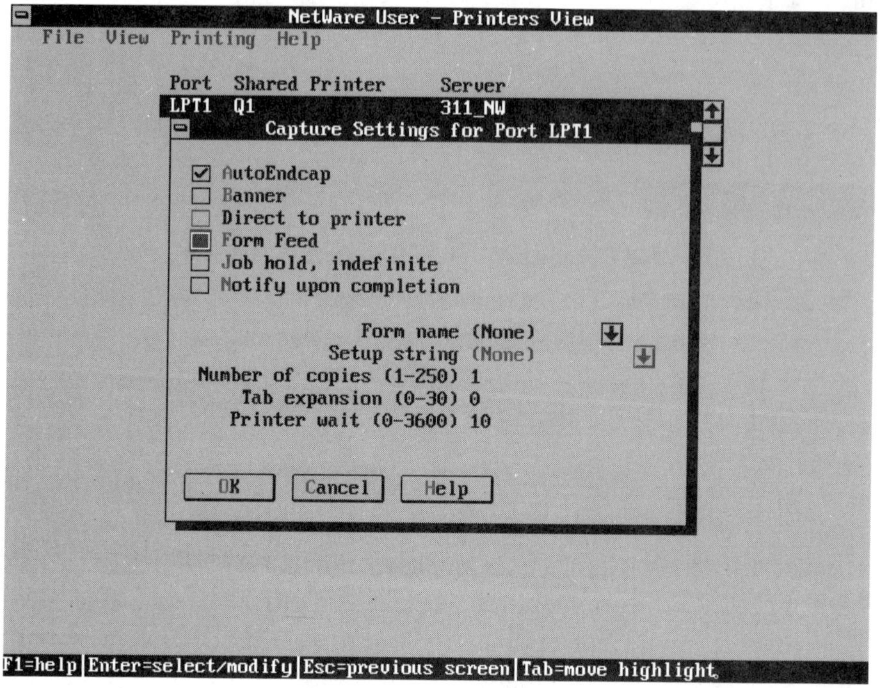

The NET program is located in the \NWCLIENT subdirectory (at least, that's its default location). The Personal NetWare installation program puts the \NWCLIENT directory in your PATH statement. Because of this, you can type NET at any DOS prompt, and the program will start. To see a list of all available printers, type NET PLIST at the DOS prompt.

NET opens with a view of the network. To see your printer options, press Alt-O (for Output). The dialog box that appears shows your current assignments for each of your parallel ports. Since you haven't connected any printers yet, all three lines are probably blank. Let's fix that.

Move the highlight bar to the parallel port you want to use (normally LPT1:) and press Enter. A dialog box labeled Capture Printer Port LPT1 pops up, showing each printer available to you. This should be the same list you see under NetWare Tools. If there's a printer missing, you probably haven't logged into that server, so it's not yet available to you. Figure 5.8 shows exactly what I'm talking about.

Once you highlight the printer you want, press Enter on that printer name. The OK button will be automatically selected for you, and the printer name will jump up to the LPT line you chose. Once you exit the NET program, that printer will be available to you and your applications.

If you want to save that printer connection and make it permanent, so that it is automatically connected when you start up, press Alt-F to pull down the File menu, then choose V for Save. The PNWLOGIN.SCR file will be modified, and the next time you log in, that printer connection will be made for you.

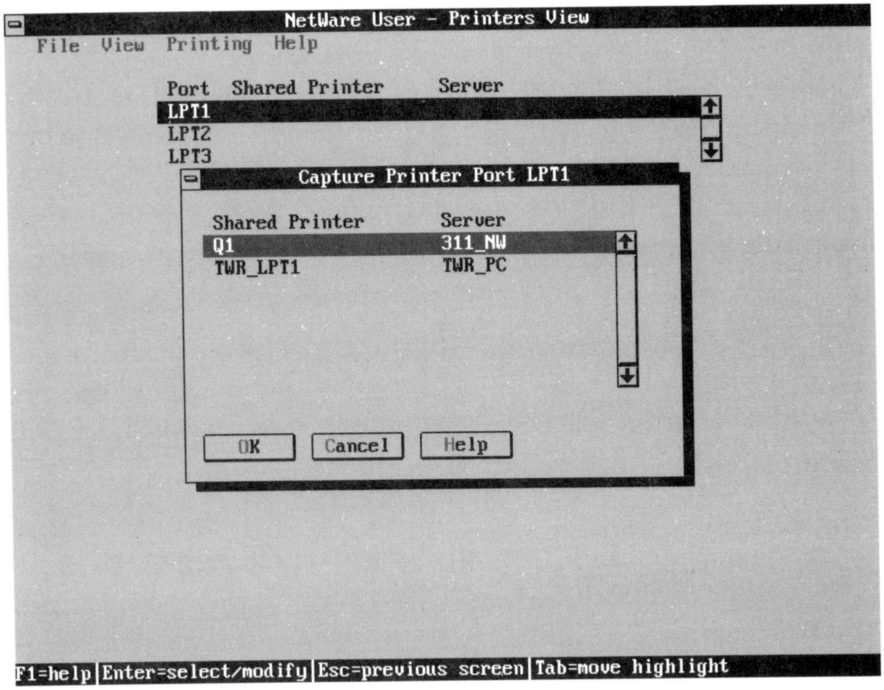

FIGURE 5.8

Connecting a printer to a printer port under NET

USING CAPTURE FROM THE COMMAND LINE

If you are at the DOS command line and want to see which printers you have available, type

```
NET CAPTURE
```

The resulting text will show you all connected printers.

If doing things from the DOS command line is more fun than using the NET program, the command you must type to recreate the printer configuration shown in Figure 5.7 is

```
NET CAPTURE LPT1 Q1 311_NW F=N W=10
```

This tells the Personal NetWare network you want to attach to print queue Q1 on NetWare file server 311_NW, with no form feed, and wait 10 seconds before assuming the application is finished printing. The Auto endcap default is on, so we need to specify how many seconds to wait before closing the printer spool file.

I told you the NET program was easier and quicker. Take a look again at all the other options in Figure 5.7 that we didn't need to specify under NET. That should give you an idea how long this command line could have been if we wanted to get fancy.

If you want to use a command string but don't think you really want to type that much every time, entering

```
NET SAVE
```

will write this information to the PNWLOGIN.BAT file in your current directory. Next time you log in to the workgroup, this printer configuration will return. If you use the NET program at all, don't use the NET SAVE command; use the Save command on NET's File menu instead.

PRINTING TO A WORKGROUP PRINTER UNDER DOS

Now, we've done this before, so you need to start paying attention. There is no difference between printing to a workgroup printer and printing to a NetWare system printer. Your application won't know and DOS won't know.

No one will know except your hairdresser, and she might not know for sure. Are you old enough to remember that commercial?

When the NET program presents available printers to you in the Printers View screen, no differentiation is made between NetWare system printers and Personal NetWare workgroup printers. The names are your only clues. Well, if you send a huge print file full of graphics to a workgroup printer, you might hear the owner scream as his PC slows down trying to digest the print request. Unfortunately, your name is attached to the print job. While you're waiting for your printing, perhaps you should lie low. If it's a really nasty, long print job with extensive graphics, perhaps you should leave town. Figure 5.9 shows the print queue from within the NET program (press Alt-P from any screen to see this information).

The procedure for connecting to a workgroup printer is the same as connecting to any other printer using the NET program. But if you have a

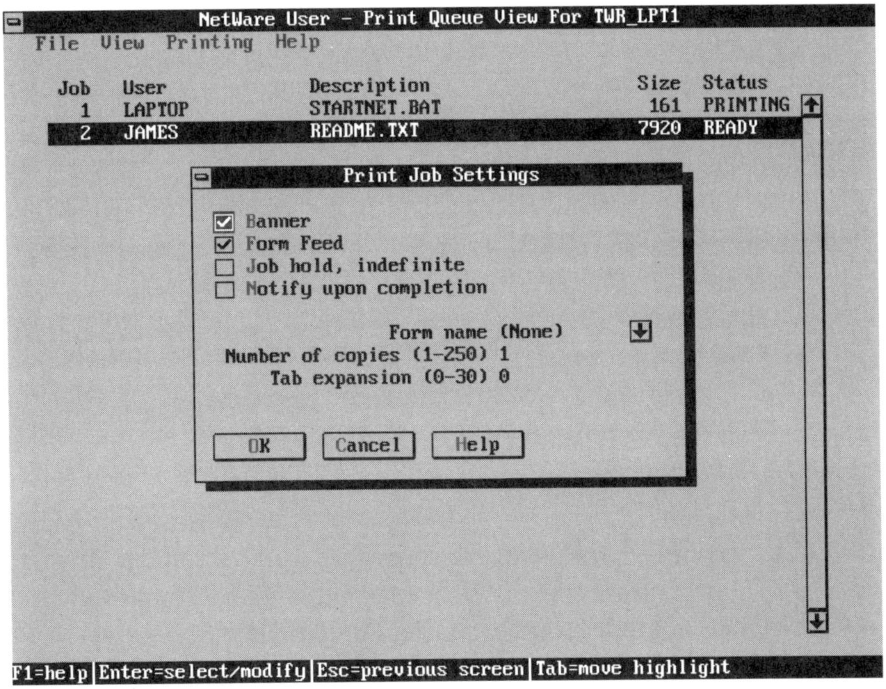

FIGURE 5.9

Managing the Personal NetWare print queue

choice of using a NetWare system printer or a workgroup printer, wouldn't you use the NetWare system printer automatically?

Not at all. There are more specialized printers now than ever before—color printers and ink-jet printers and plotters and transparency printers and so on. These have usually been tied to the computer of the person who used the application that required that printer. Most of the specialized printers require special care and feeding, so someone needs to have the printer close at hand. Putting it out in a common area just guarantees that everyone will assume someone else is taking care of that printer. So, of course, no one takes care of that printer.

Using Personal NetWare makes it easy for the few people that need specialized printers to share them with each other, but not everyone in the building. Only Personal NetWare clients can see Personal NetWare printers; they are not available to NetWare file server clients. Consider a workgroup printer a departmental shared resource.

CHAPTER 6

How Do I Use Applications across the Network?

You've already learned about the general methods for mapping drives and using files on different workgroup PCs spread across the network. Now it's time to get specific. In this chapter, we'll go over some examples that show every step necessary to use application resources across the network.

We'll focus on the workgroup, but remember that, with the Universal NetWare Client, these examples will work the same way when the applications are on a NetWare file server. But there are plenty of books around for that, so our time will be spent with real-world examples on a sample Personal NetWare workgroup.

The Copyright Laws and Your Workgroup

First, we must bring up an important aspect of computing in the age of networking. Since programs are not "physical," in the sense that a book like this is physical, many users are confused concerning the legal aspects of software. Once software is installed, it becomes just bits on a hard disk and is easily manipulated and copied. Some mistaken users feel that software is theirs, period—they can use it and copy it and share it to their hearts' content. This is not only wrong, it's expensive. The penalties for illegal software use are stiff, ranging up to a $100,000 fine per instance of illegal use.

Some confusion among users can be blamed on the software companies themselves. Most companies have done a poor job of explaining the rules for using their software products. So let's take an example of a good software license arrangement.

From the early days, the people at Borland, Inc., based their software licensing on the idea of a book. If you buy a book, you can use that book anywhere, anytime, and give it away. The important concept to remember is that a book can only be in one place at one time. If you give a book to a friend, you can't use the book at the same time as your friend. If you give Borland software to a friend, you can't keep it on your own PC and continue using it at the same time your friend is using it on his own PC. That's cheating.

A physical book, such as this, can easily be copied using an office copy machine, and then distributed to your friends. That would be just as illegal as copying software, and it has always been that way. But copying software is much easier and quicker than standing at the copy machine and making 500 different copies, so book copyrights have been upheld more by laziness than strong moral values. Unfortunately, this laziness factor doesn't come into play with software, so the problem of illegal software is much more prevalent than that of illegal, best-selling computer tomes.

Since you probably don't read the legal mumbo jumbo placed on every software package you open, just remember the book example. This will work for the vast majority of software; only the most greedy are more restrictive. You can generally use software in two different places (on a desktop PC and your laptop PC), as long as you use only one copy at a time.

An important point to make is that networking complicates this software copying situation. Just because you can use the software on the PC down the hall doesn't mean you have the legal authority to do so. Smart software vendors have special versions of their products to be shared on a traditional NetWare file server and a licensing arrangement in place. With peer-to-peer networking such as Personal NetWare, those arrangements are most likely not in place. So we'll concentrate on sharing data and sharing applications under legal circumstances.

Sharing New CD ROM Drives under MS Windows

IN-A-HURRY? **Share the CD ROM drive with the workgroup** **6.1**

THE FAST LANE

1 Start the Personal NetWare program in the Personal NetWare group.
2 Open the NetWare view, then double-click on the server name.
3 Highlight drive D:, the CD ROM drive.

4. Choose Share from the File menu, provide a workgroup name for the shared CD ROM, and then click on OK.
5. In the next screen, configure rights to the CD ROM drive.

A common computer peripheral today is a CD ROM (Compact Disk, Read-Only Memory) drive. This device plays the same type of CD ROM disks that your stereo CD player does, but instead of music, there's data on the disk.

Sharing these with a NetWare 2.*x* or 3.*x* server has been difficult in the past. The new NetWare 4.*x* now has support for a CD ROM as part of the file server itself. That CD ROM is presented to the NetWare clients as another NetWare volume.

None of these situations help share a CD ROM on a desktop computer. This is becoming a common situation, as the PCs offered for sale in many retail outlets have a CD ROM drive as part of the original equipment. In the UNIX world, some companies ship software only on CD ROM, especially for Sun computers. In the PC world, NetWare 4.*x* is delivered only on a CD ROM; floppies cost extra. So sharing a CD ROM among the workgroup has become a hot topic.

To investigate how a CD ROM can be shared, I installed a CD ROM kit from ATI Technologies of Thornhill, Ontario, Canada. The kit comes with an internal CD ROM drive and a stereo sound card and CD ROM controller combination, under the name of CD Sound Dimension. Two CD ROM disks came along, one for MS Windows and one for DOS. Both are collections of shareware programs and utilities, along with some demonstrations and free software.

Figure 6.1 shows the Personal NetWare screen (Drives view) on the TWR_PC detailing the rights to drive D:, the one with the CD ROM installed. If you look closely, you can see that the icon for drive D: shows a CD ROM drive, although it looks a bit like the drive is sticking its tongue out at you. Choosing Rights from the File menu brings up the Personal NetWare Information dialog box, also shown in Figure 6.1.

This dialog box says it all for us. Drive D: is now a CD ROM drive, and Personal NetWare knows that. The program knows this because a file named

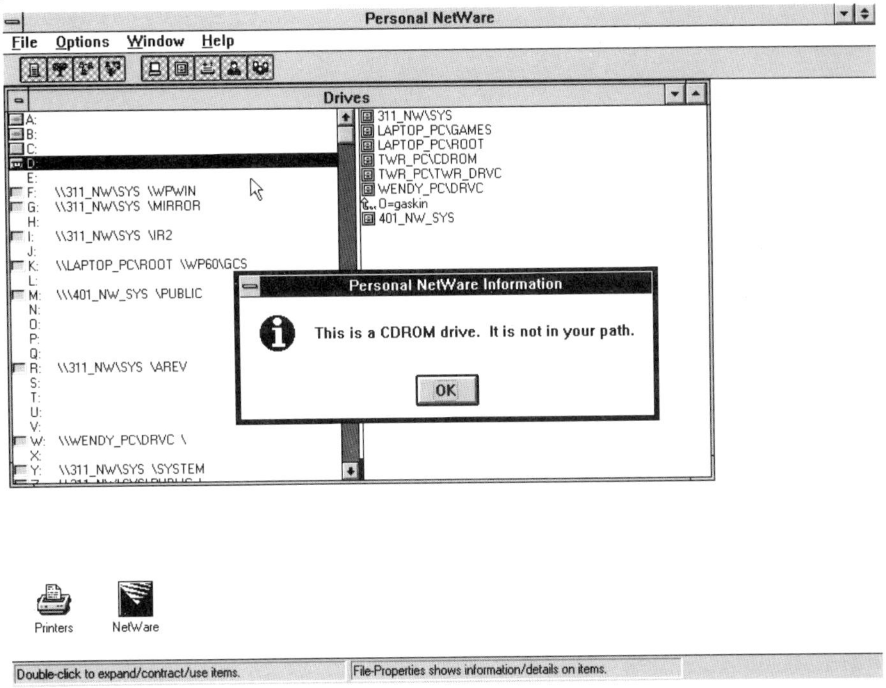

FIGURE 6.1

The local drive D: on TWR_PC is now a CD ROM drive

MSCDEX.EXE is loaded in the AUTOEXEC.BAT file. Short for MicroSoft CD EXtensions, this file is found in the \DOS directory of every MS DOS 6.0 computer. Novell DOS 7 has a comparable file named NWCDEX.EXE in the \NWDOS directory. The Novell DOS file takes less RAM but otherwise offers the same functions as MSCDEX.EXE.

All the CD ROM setup on TWR_PC happens separately from the network. However, once the installation is complete, the device must be shared for others in the workgroup to have access. How do you do that?

This will be covered in more detail in Chapter 8, but here's a quick version of sharing a resource, in this case the CD ROM just added to TWR_PC:

1 • Open the Personal NetWare program from within the Personal NetWare group in MS Windows. (The NetWare Tools pop-up

only works with existing shared resources; Personal NetWare is the program that configures shared resources.)

2. Once the Personal NetWare program is open, make sure you're in the NetWare view by double-clicking on the red Novell icon if it appears on the screen.

3. Once the NetWare view is open, check to see if the server containing your resource shows up on the left side of the screen. If it doesn't, it should be on the right awaiting your log in. If you have more than one workgroup on your system, make sure you're in the correct one.

4. Double-click on the server to see the resources of that server. In our case, that means drive D:, the CD ROM.

5. Place the highlight bar on that drive, and choose Share from the File menu. The NetWare Share dialog box opens, as shown in Figure 6.2. In the example, I've typed the name CDROM for the Shared Resource Alias.

The new name of this shared resource will be CDROM on TWR_PC, and it will show up in all Personal NetWare utility screens. Sharp-eyed readers might notice that there already is a TWR_PC\CDROM device listed. Yes, it's the same thing, I just didn't want to delete the device and recreate it again for the screenshot. If I choose OK in the NetWare Share dialog box, I will get an error message telling me I already have a resource named TWR_PC\CDROM.

This doesn't mean I can't have a device named CDROM on WENDY_PC or LAPTOP_PC. As long as the entire name isn't the same, I can have the same name for the resource. That makes things easy if Wendy gets a CD ROM next week.

We're almost finished, but not quite. A CD ROM disk is, by definition, a read-only device. There is no way you can actually write data back to that

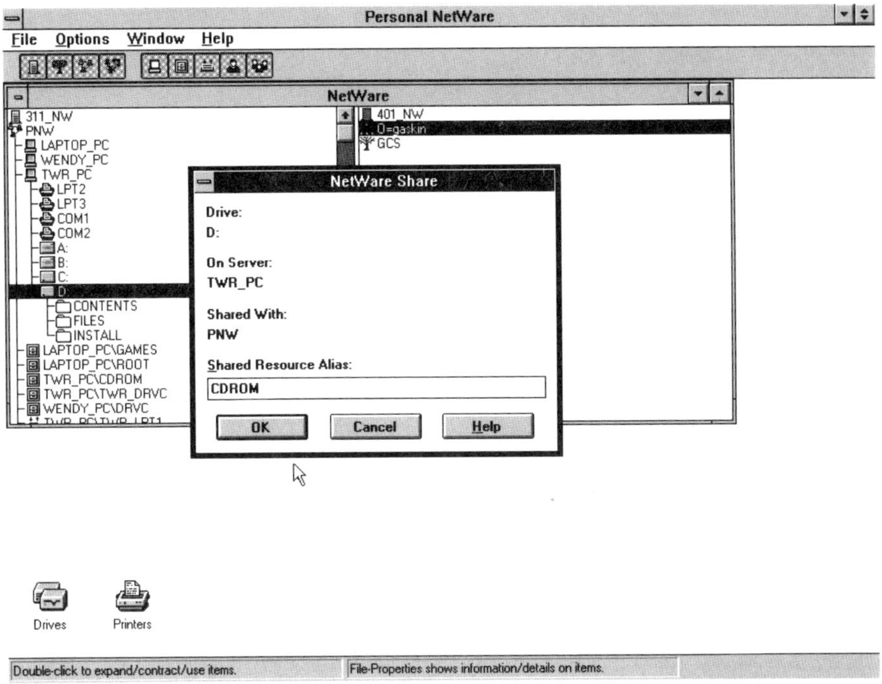

FIGURE 6.2
The NetWare Share dialog box

disk. But just to make sure no one locks up an application by trying to write to the CD ROM, let's make this Personal NetWare resource read-only.

The next screen that pops up after you say OK to the name of the new shared directory is the Personal NetWare Rights dialog box, shown in Figure 6.3. The default is for everyone to have the same access. You can see that the group icon is highlighted on the left side of the dialog box. The object name is listed across the top left. That name must be unique to get this far.

The Rights display is on the right, showing read-only access to this resource. When you're finished assigning rights in this dialog box, click on Close to save the information. The new resource will become available immediately. There's no need to reboot either this server or any client to be able to use this newly defined resource. If you wait just a second, the new resource will show up in the Personal NetWare display.

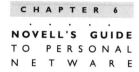

FIGURE 6.3

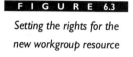

Setting the rights for the new workgroup resource

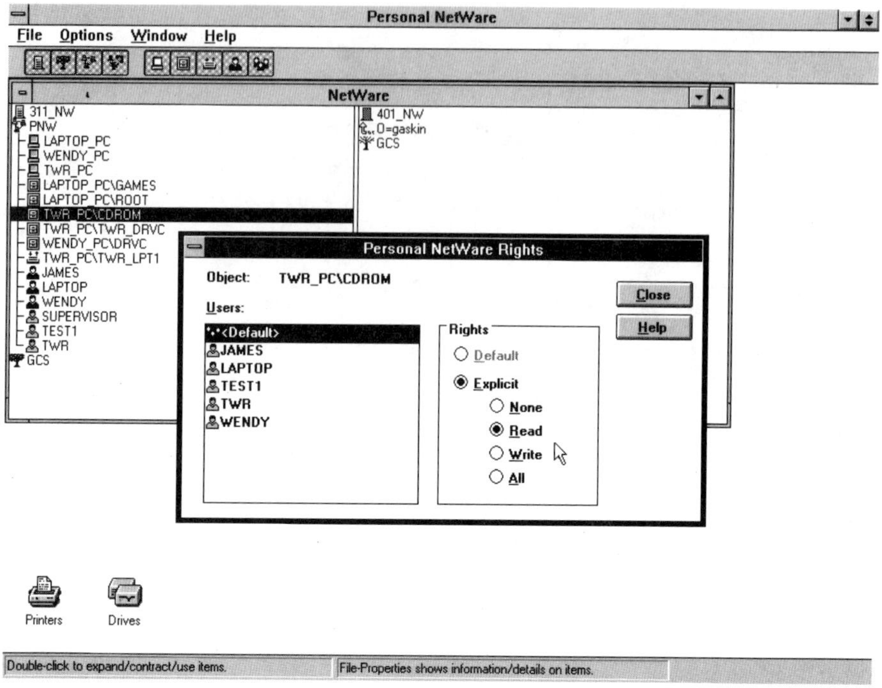

Using Workgroup Server Applications under MS Windows

Let's pretend all the stuff just described in this chapter so far didn't happen, or at least pretend we didn't need to do it. The word comes down: there's a new CD ROM drive on TWR_PC. The disk loaded in the drive is 500 MB of MS Windows utilities and programs. For the next week, peruse to your heart's content, and try out all the shareware you wish. Anything in use after the week is over must be either paid for or deleted.

This is the case with shareware: try it and pay for it if you keep using it. It's common to include disks like this with new CD ROM drives, as ATI did with our drive. So there aren't any copyright concerns in this example.

Shareware authors generally ask that you copy and share their programs with as many people as possible.

FINDING APPLICATIONS

How do you find that new resource on the network? One way is for the owner of the resource to send everyone a message advertising the new CD ROM drive. Another way is to simply notice that there is a new available resource in the NetWare Tools pop-up window. That's the way LAPTOP found out about the new CD ROM.

Figure 6.4 shows that LAPTOP has found the CD ROM drive and is interested in checking it out. The new item was seen in the Resource list box and dragged and dropped on drive R: (for ROM). The actual dragging motion was caught for this figure. This procedure is nothing unusual, since we've been dragging and dropping all over the place since Chapter 1.

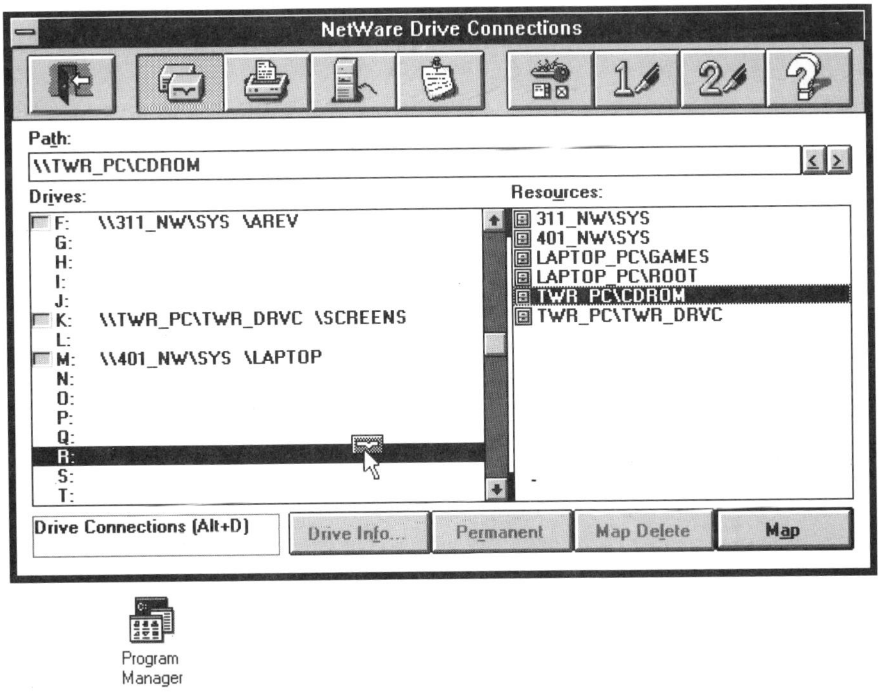

FIGURE 6.4
Connecting the CD ROM resource to drive R:

ACCESS CONTROLS ON THE WORKGROUP SERVER UNDER MS WINDOWS

One thing about the CD ROM resource shown in Figure 6.4 is unusual: its access rights. Remember when we set up the CD ROM on TWR_PC as a read-only resource, just so people wouldn't get confused about what kind of drive this was? Take a look at Figure 6.5, which shows the Drive Info window, giving the access rights user LAPTOP has on \\TWR_PC\CDROM.

Of course, any hard disk drive resource and directory can be shared as read-only, not just a CD ROM drive. For example, it's common to have budget templates or contract boilerplate documents available to everyone on a network, but in read-only mode. This forces users to save the budget template with their own expense figures (a Famous Hypothetical Example) under a unique name on their own PCs. If they try to save the budget file back under the same name, NetWare will give them an error message, especially if they try to write to a CD ROM.

FIGURE 6.5

Read and Scan rights on the CD ROM drive

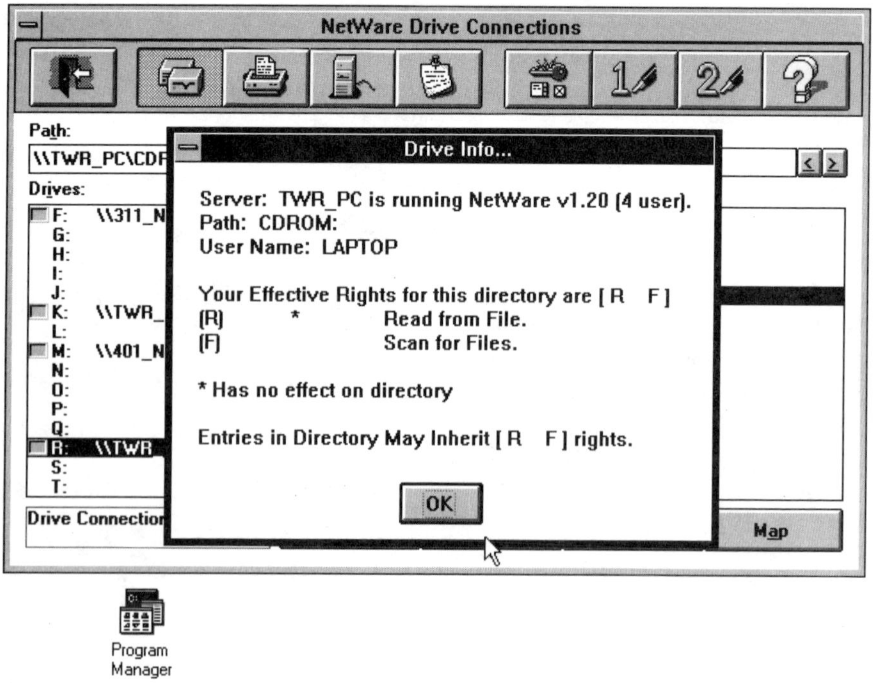

So now that LAPTOP has connected to this new CD ROM drive, what happens next? A program on the CD ROM disk installs on the hard disk of the machine holding the CD ROM drive, in this case TWR_PC. The program helps speed performance when searching and using the CD ROM.

But LAPTOP doesn't have the CD ROM drive attached physically, and it won't use the CD ROM that much anyway. All LAPTOP wants is a chance to play with a few files and download some to examine in more depth. The trick is to find the program that starts the CD ROM access and run that program across the network.

Figure 6.6 shows trusty old File Manager at work. Drive R: was selected, and the contents of the CD ROM disk are shown on the right side of the screen. Notice that our remote drive is shown in the upper-right corner of the File Manager window, in this case R:\\TWR_PC\CDROM.

Only seven files appear in the root directory of the CD ROM, and only two of those are program files. README.EXE looks important, but not for

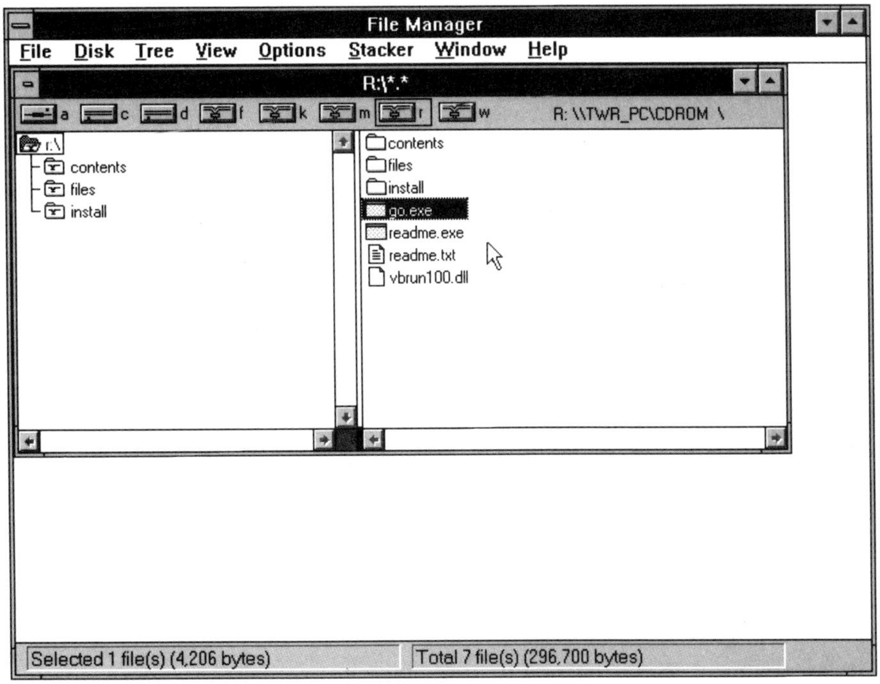

FIGURE 6.6

Starting to access the CD ROM drive across the network

examining the disk in detail. For that, GO.EXE seems to be a much better choice. You can see that the GO.EXE program is highlighted in Figure 6.6, and we're just about to double-click and see what happens.

What happens is Figure 6.7, showing the main program for the ATI Technologies Windows Master disk included with the CD ROM drive. This software is kept on the CD ROM drive, available for anyone on the network to test and examine. Click on the categories on the left to see detailed descriptions on the right. Since multi-media and sound to jazz up presentations are hot topics lately, LAPTOP clicked on the Audio Video category.

From this screen, LAPTOP can peruse and test any or all of the programs on the CD ROM, without having a CD ROM physically attached. Any program can be run directly from the CD ROM disk; however, regularly used programs will be copied to the local hard disk for convenience and performance. And any programs that are "keepers" will be registered and paid for, as should be done with all shareware.

FIGURE 6.7

Accessing the CD ROM software from LAPTOP

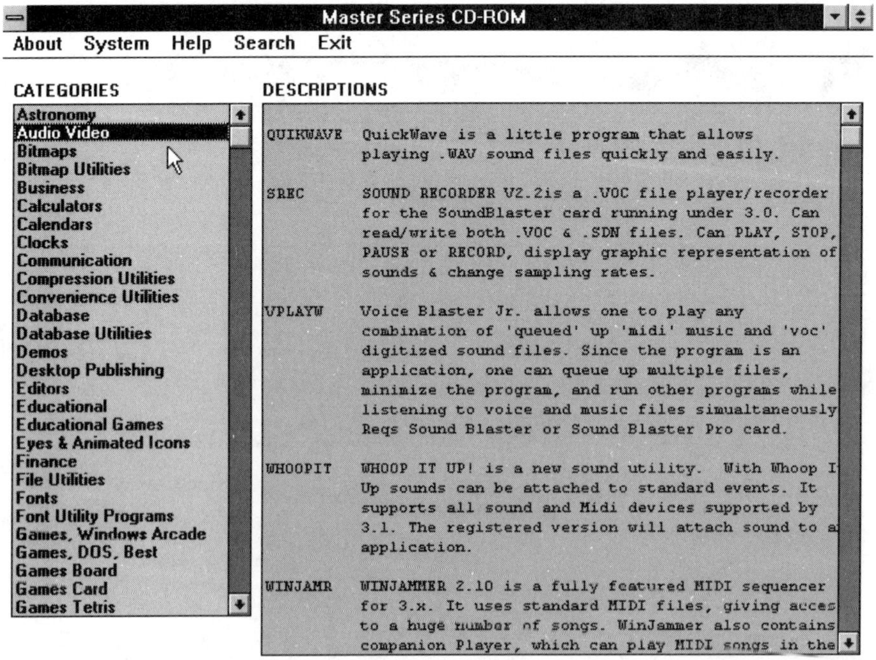

You can see there are 28 categories listed, and we're not through the G's yet. A lot can be loaded onto CD ROM disks, which is another reason they're starting to be so popular. The multi-media we spoke of two paragraphs back generally includes sound and video, and those types of files take lots of space.

Using Multiuser Applications and Data Files under MS Windows

Multiuser applications are built to be used in a networked environment. The software is able to provide file access control beyond that of DOS. This allows several users at one time to run the executable files and access the data files for the multiuser software.

The most popular multiuser applications are databases, which include specialized programs such as accounting databases. As you can imagine, it's handy to adjust inventory, accept payments, and report on backordered items all at the same time. Multiuser networked accounting programs can do this.

One of the advantages of Personal NetWare over the earlier NetWare Lite is the closeness of Personal NetWare to regular NetWare. All the programs that run on regular NetWare run on Personal NetWare as well.

If you start loading several programs on a server, its performance levels may degrade. The user of the server with the multiuser software loaded and running will constantly complain that the network service load is impacting the time available for local PC functions. That user will be right.

When you have more than one multiuser program loaded onto Personal NetWare servers, especially one that is used a lot, it's time to look at upgrading to a NetWare file server. All your client configuration and software will remain exactly the same, and the workgroup will function in the same manner it always has.

Sharing New CD ROM Drives under DOS

6.2

THE FAST LANE

IN-A-HURRY? Share the CD ROM drive with the workgroup

1. Type **NET ADMIN** from the DOS prompt.
2. Press Alt-D, then press the Ins key to set up a new shared directory.
3. Name the new directory for the workgroup.
4. Highlight the server that's sharing this new resource, then press Alt-O.
5. Set the directory path and rights to this new shared directory.
6. Press Alt-O to accept the configuration and set up the new shared directory.

As we've seen before, everything you can do under MS Windows you can do with DOS. In fact, tying such things as CD ROM drives to older PCs running DOS is one of the advantages of Personal NetWare. Do you have some old AT computers that don't have enough memory management to run the new programs? Hang printers and CD ROM drives from them, and bravely volunteer to donate your AT in exchange for a new 486 fire-breather.

Taking the same ATI CD ROM kit described earlier, let's show how to share that new CD ROM using NET ADMIN rather than the Personal NetWare program.

The NET ADMIN program can be run from any PC on the network and still configure any Personal NetWare desktop server. Although the \NWCLIENT directory is in your DOS PATH statement, I'm cautious enough to still change to that directory before starting NET ADMIN.

The NET ADMIN program always opens with the available servers display for your current workgroup. To get to the screen showing the shared directories, press Alt-D. All the directory resources shared across your workgroup are displayed here, which is why it takes a few seconds to display this screen. If you're curious, try running the Personal NetWare diagnostics program on one PC while performing some of these functions, and you'll see your network at work. (See Chapter 7 for more information about Personal NetWare diagnostics.)

When you press the Insert key in the Shared Directories View screen, the Add Shared Directory dialog box pops up, as shown in Figure 6.8. There are two items of information needed:

- A name this resource will present to the workgroup
- The Personal NetWare server that owns this resource

In our case, the name is CDROM and the server is TWR_PC. One note about the name: it can't be longer than 15 characters.

When you press Alt-O for OK to exit the Add Shared Directory dialog box, the Properties for Shared Directory: CDROM dialog box pops up. This is shown in Figure 6.9. Does this remind you of Figure 6.3? It should, since it's the same information in DOS rather than MS Windows. Here again, the

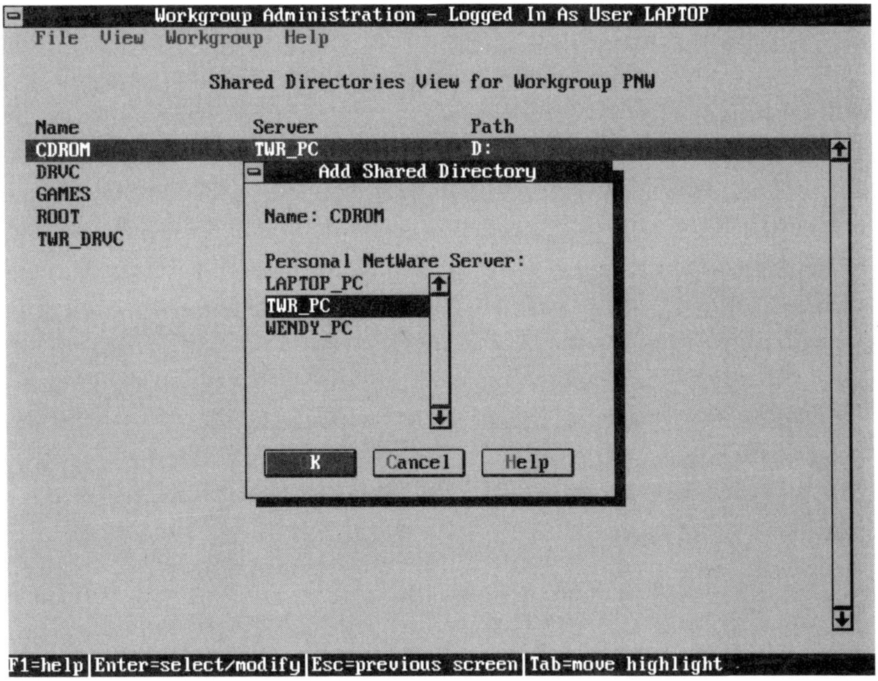

FIGURE 6.8

Adding a shared directory

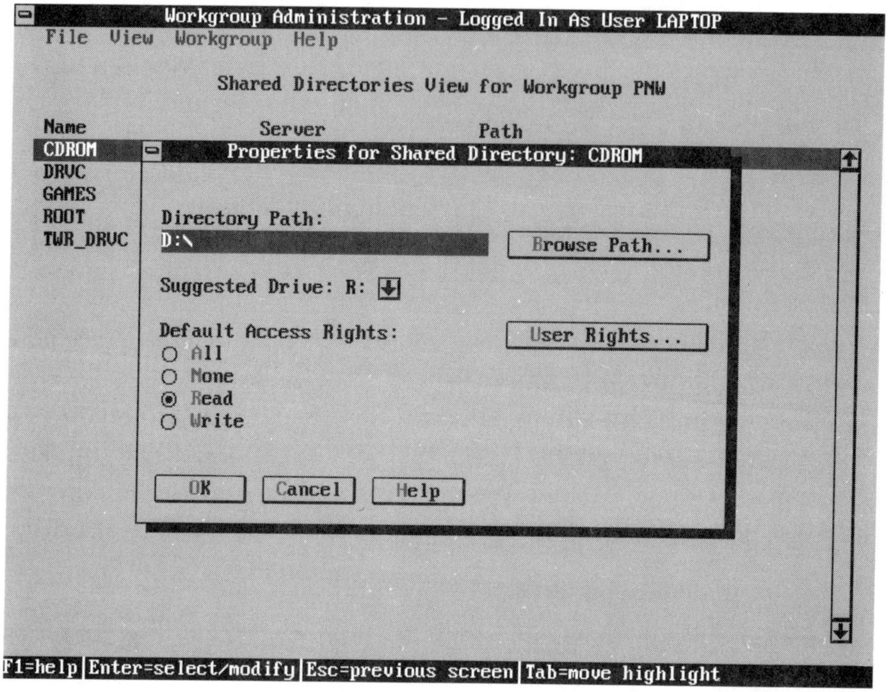

FIGURE 6.9

Setting access rights for a shared directory

rights are set to read-only, because a CD ROM drive cannot be written on. The default setting is for everyone to have these rights to this resource, so we'll leave that alone.

Pressing Alt-O tells this screen OK, and the CD ROM is available to the network almost immediately. There's no need to restart the server or client software in any PC to use the new CD ROM resource on server TWR_PC.

Using Workgroup Server Applications under DOS

If you skipped the first part of this chapter concerning copyright laws, go back. The meat of the matter is simple: just because you now can allow several people to share a program doesn't mean it's legal. It's not. Keep your thumb on this page as you go back to the start of the chapter to learn about the legalities of networking. Okay, let's go on.

LOCATING APPLICATIONS

Rather than redoing the CD ROM exercise under DOS, I thought another example would be more fun. On my laptop computer lives a program called the Humor Processor, by Responsive Software in Berkeley, California. It's a program that helps people write jokes by increasing brainstorming efficiency, using the same techniques professional joke writers use. It includes more than 500 jokes as examples and the start of your own joke database. Several chapters of the manual talk about ways to write jokes, according to proven formulas used successfully for years.

Since traveling is not much fun if I'm not in a good mood, having the Humor Processor on my laptop makes it easy to keep busy during airport layovers doing something that looks like work but isn't. I leave the program and joke database on the laptop, even when I'm not traveling. Using Personal NetWare, it's easy to run the Humor Processor from my desktop machine, since my laptop is configured as a Personal NetWare server.

Figure 6.10 shows the NET ADMIN program running on LAPTOP_PC, and I'm logged in as user LAPTOP. You should recognize the Shared Directories View screen and the Properties for Shared Directory: ROOT dialog box. This is just like the earlier figure showing the CD ROM setup, isn't it?

ACCESS CONTROLS ON THE WORKGROUP SERVER DRIVES

Notice in Figure 6.10 that all directories of my laptop are open to the workgroup. In the dialog box, the shared resource is named ROOT, the name for the highest directory level on a hard disk. The root directory is where the initial startup files such as AUTOEXEC.BAT and CONFIG.SYS are. All subdirectories are below the root directory, so if you have access to the root directory, you have access to everything.

FIGURE 6.10

Making the server LAPTOP_PC available to the workgroup

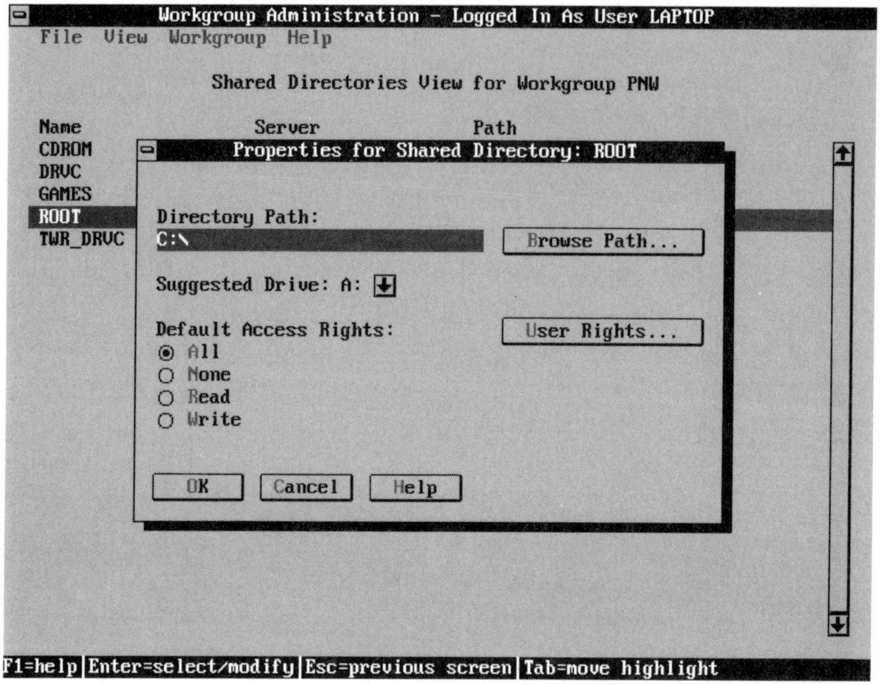

The Directory Path text box has only C:\ listed, specifying the root directory. The Default Access Rights option is set to All, meaning everyone not specifically locked out has access to LAPTOP_PC.

Now we know that LAPTOP_PC is available and also that the Humor Processor is on that system. Time for the NET program, run from the TWR computer.

Figure 6.11 shows the NET program Drives View screen with the Change Directory dialog box. NET always opens with the NetWare View screen, showing all the available servers. Pressing Alt-D brings up the Drives View screen.

The drive letter highlighted, K:, has previously been mapped to the LAPTOP_PC server. The name of the server is hidden behind the Change

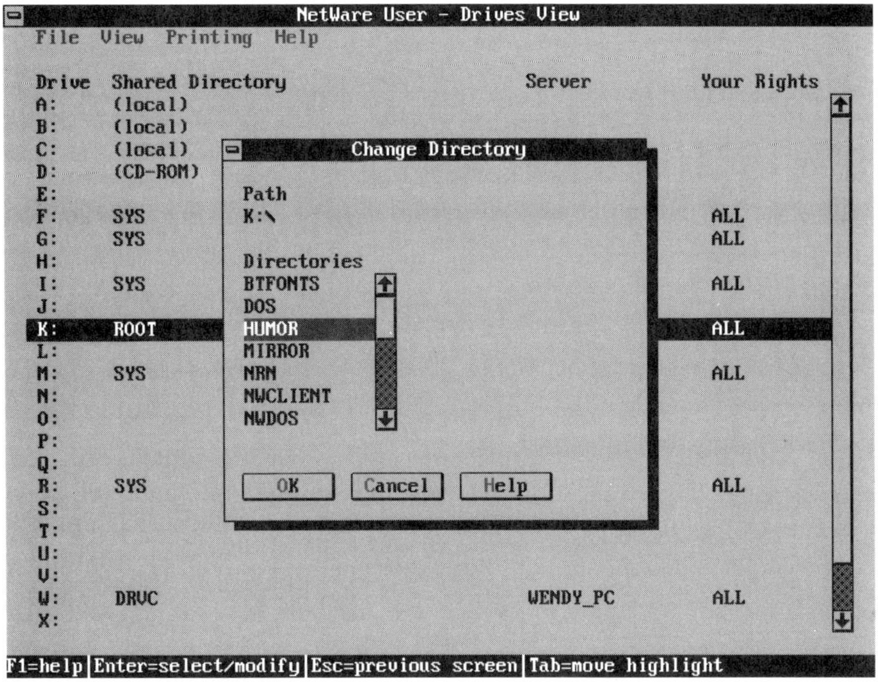

FIGURE 6.11
Finding some HUMOR on a workgroup server

Directory dialog box right now. The Change Directory dialog box is retrieved by pressing Alt-Enter on a mapped drive letter, or by choosing the Properties option on the File menu. We know that the program we want, the Humor Processor, is a subdirectory of the root directory.

While scanning the directories available on LAPTOP_PC, one seems a likely candidate to hold the Humor Processor: the directory labeled HUMOR. Moving the highlight bar to the HUMOR directory and pressing Enter, then Alt-O for OK, changes the directory referenced by drive K: from ROOT to HUMOR. Exit the NET program and let's see what we have.

When we change to drive K:, we see that the DOS prompt says

```
K:\HUMOR
```

Do we have the rights to run this program? Typing

```
NET RIGHTS
```

will tell us. The result of the NET RIGHTS command is

```
NetWare Volume: ROOT
 Server: LAPTOP_PC
 Path: HUMOR

Your rights: ALL
Default rights: ALL
```

This tells us everything we need to know. First of all, we are mapped to volume ROOT on server LAPTOP_PC. The DOS path has been changed to HUMOR, just as shown in Figure 6.11. And our rights are ALL, as are the default rights. The only operation left is to type

```
HUMOR
```

and see the first joke, shown in Figure 6.12.

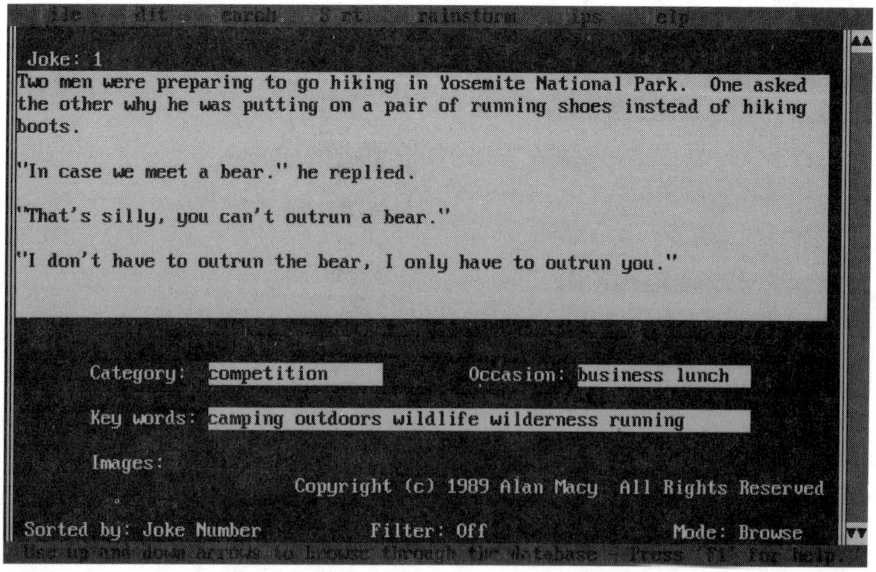

FIGURE 6.12

The opening screen of the Humor Processor

Using Multiuser Applications and Data Files under DOS

The rules for multiuser applications are the same under DOS and MS Windows. The Personal NetWare software will support these multiuser programs, but performance becomes an issue. If one workgroup server is supporting several users running several different multiuser programs, such as accounting software or databases, that's probably too much work. The actual user of that PC will complain, and with good reason.

When one server is supporting several of these multiuser programs, it's time to do one of two things:

- Dedicate that workgroup server to nothing except servicing the workgroup, and give that user a different PC to use as his or her workstation.
- Start pricing a regular NetWare file server. You will get considerably better performance and have lots of new options for other programs and features.

Playing NETWARS

The ultimate shared application for Personal NetWare is the game NETWARS. This is an arcade style, galactic, shoot-the-bad-guys game. The fact that the bad guys are often your co-workers just adds that much extra excitement. Talk one, two, or three of your office mates into being targets for your lasers, and let's get started.

This is virtual reality, of sorts. Pretend you are looking out the front window of your spaceship, and the keyboard is your control panel. Your radar screen, the grid on the bottom right of your screen, shows everything surrounding you. As with real radar, no blip displays as your ship. Your location is smack in the middle of the grid, at the intersection of the two central lines.

It isn't necessary to have everyone connected to the same copy of NETWARS.EXE to play in the same game. If you choose the Multi Player Mode on the opening screen, the program will find any other players active in your workgroup. Just type

```
NETWARS
```

from the \NWCLIENT directory in Personal NetWare or the \NWDOS directory in Novell DOS 7, and you're on your way.

It's important to type in your name when asked by the multiplayer version. When you zap an opponent, that player's screen displays

You were killed by *username*

This makes them want to play at least one more game to get even with you.

There are two major differences between the single and multiple player modes. In single player mode, you protect purple pods from the pirates. The pirates and their friends shoot you every chance they get, so shoot them first. The other difference is that in single player mode, you have smart missiles. If you see your crosshairs change from lines to large triangles, as shown in Figure 6.13, you can fire one of your missiles by pressing the Enter key.

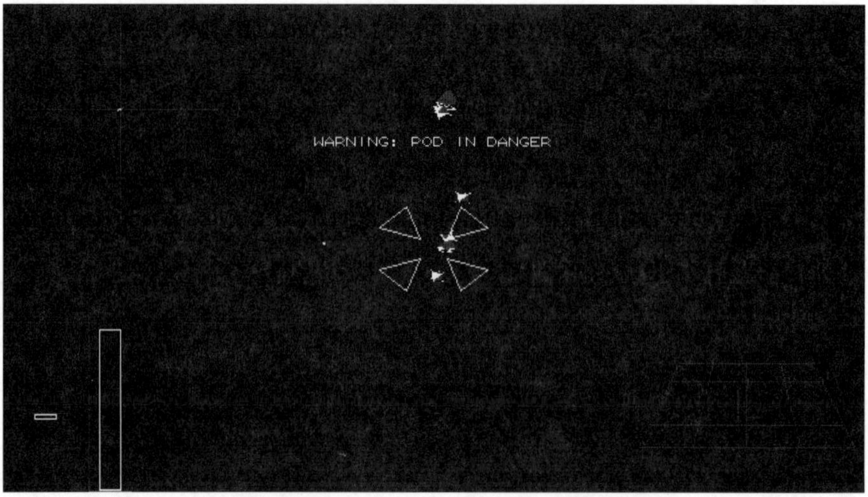

FIGURE 6.13
Playing NETWARS

THE SCREEN DISPLAY AND CONTROLS

Each corner of the screen holds important information for us. The radar part in the bottom right is the most important, because that tells you where everyone else is located. Other players show up as green or blue dots (arrows when they're farther away from you). White indicates a satellite carrying extra shields, missiles (in the single player game), thrust, or firepower. All of these are good, so capture them by running into them.

The + (plus) and – (minus) keys on the keypad act as range adjusters for the radar. Plus makes the radar grids smaller, so things are more spread out. You can tell, because on the single player game, using + opens up the view so you can see the space between your purple pods. Minus makes the grids larger, clumping things together in the middle of the grid.

The next most important display is in the lower left. The two vertical gauges represent shield strength (s) and velocity (v). When shield strength gets down to zero, you're history, so watch that. The velocity indicator is anchored in the middle. The farther up the bar, the faster forward you're going; the farther down, the faster backward.

Oh, yes, you can scoot around backwards. It's a good trick at times. The direction and velocity are controlled by the Shift (forward) and Ctrl (backward) key. It works easily for me to use my left hand to control the Shift and Ctrl keys, with my left thumb pressing the spacebar to fire my laser pulses.

The upper-left display is difficult to understand, because it's representing three dimensions on a two-dimensional computer screen. It shows which direction you're traveling, with speed either forward or backward indicated by the green lines superimposed on the red indicator. Right and left and up and down don't make much sense in space, but that's what the other indicator lines show.

The last information, in the upper-right corner, shows the score in both single and multiple player versions, and the number of remaining missiles in the single player mode. The score doesn't matter during the game, at least not on our network. Here, the last one alive is the winner, regardless of the score.

STRATEGY FOR THE SINGLE PLAYER GAME

The first pirate comes from due east, the second from due west, third from the south, and fourth from the north. Each will zoom toward you, fire a missile, then swoop away. You should shoot the missiles before they hit you if you can. Save your own missiles for the faster enemies in higher levels. I try not to fire a missile at a pirate ship, just at the fighters, guardians, and commanders.

The only time I fire a missile at pirate ships is after they hook onto one of my pods. It's difficult to hit the enemy with a laser pulse without hitting your pod when they're hooked together. The missiles will hit only the pirate ship. It's great fun to watch a missile follow an enemy and swoop around to miss the pod but still get the enemy ship.

The radar screen display should tell you one important thing: how to draw a bead on your enemy. By pressing the cursor keys (more than one cursor key at a time can be held down) in the direction the arrows point on the radar screen, you can catch what you're chasing.

There's no limit to your laser pulses, so feel free to hold down that spacebar. You'll learn after a few games to stop shooting your own pods.

STRATEGY FOR THE MULTIPLAYER GAME

The controls work the same in both games, so there's nothing new to learn. Unfortunately, your enemy co-workers don't come from predictable places.

Don't sit still. Get moving forward and use your cursor keys to swoop around. It's more important in the multiple player version to follow your enemies to catch them. In the single player game, the enemies will come to get you, don't worry. But your co-workers may not be so dedicated to your destruction, so you'll need to chase them.

Using the radar screen will make your chase easier. Remember to push the cursor keys in the direction the arrows on the radar screen point. If you're quick on the cursor keys, you'll be able to follow exactly behind a ship. Then blast it. And keep blasting; it's tough to destroy each other.

If you pick up the satellite that gives you extra firepower, shoot sparingly. The yellow laser pulses don't last forever. An indicator for this will appear under the score in the upper-right corner of the screen.

One last, underhanded trick is to blast the satellites if you can't get to them before other players do. It's best for you to get every one of them you can, but the second best thing is not to allow anyone else to get any.

WARNING: THIS IS ADDICTIVE

NETWARS, especially the multiplayer version, is great fun. I've had three preadolescent boys bypass Sega Genesis to play NETWARS together. They played for about an hour until I threw them out.

I was worried about this being too much a man's type of game for women to enjoy, but I was wrong. About half the women whom I've introduced to the game like it, a much better average than most arcade games. Evidently, the idea of sneaking up on your husband and blasting him into bits holds a certain amount of appeal to certain women. Hmmm...

CHAPTER 7

What Other Utilities Are Included to Help Me?

Utilities are programs that perform some utilitarian function, such as cleaning up your hard disk, increasing your available computer memory, and generally making your computer easier to manage and maintain. Most of the DOS programs you use are utilities. For example, the DOS BACKUP and RESTORE functions are actually utilities. Personal NetWare includes utilities as well. Many of them are integrated into the NET, NetWare Tools, or Personal NetWare programs, but there are a few extra programs that seemed to need a chapter to call their own, so here we are.

An Overview of the Personal NetWare Utilities

Help systems are somewhat of a gray area for where they belong in a book like this. So they're in here as utilities, as are the Personal NetWare Tutorial programs. Diagnostic programs can easily be called utilities, so they belong here as well. To better learn who's using your PC for what nefarious purposes, you can use the Personal NetWare auditing and connection monitoring utilities. You'll also find coverage of memory management programs, including the NWCACHE disk-caching program that comes with Personal NetWare.

Three utilities that you probably won't use are mentioned at the end of the chapter. These utilities are for booting diskless PCs from a Personal NetWare server (diskless PCs are not a good idea anymore), handling programs when using a task-switching program such as MS Windows, and setting up your PC to be monitored by network management console systems. They are all included in Personal NetWare, so they deserve mention. But try to avoid doing these things yourself if at all possible.

Getting Help

According to the old song, we all need a little help from our friends. In this case, the "friends" are Personal NetWare Help utilities. These are much more legal than the original "friends" mentioned in the song.

Help screens are available in the places you expect, and through the usual methods. Pressing F1 in the NET program, for instance, opens specific help information based on what you're doing at that moment. This is called *context-sensitive* help. In MS Windows, clicking on a Help button or menu option provides context-sensitive help. Help for all of the NET commands is available from the DOS command line.

GETTING HELP IN MS WINDOWS

7.1 THE FAST LANE

IN-A-HURRY? Get context-sensitive help in NetWare Tools

1. Press F6 to pop up NetWare Tools.
2. Open the screen that pertains to the topic about which you want to see help information.
3. Press Alt-H.

The easiest and quickest place to get help while in MS Windows is by using the NetWare Tools pop-up. Inside NetWare Tools is an entire series of Help screens. The help information pertains to the network view you have open at the moment. For example, if you open NetWare Tools to the NetWare Drive Connections screen and press Alt-H for help (or click on the big yellow question mark in the upper-right corner), you get information about drives, such as how to connect drives, check your rights, and disconnect drives. Figure 7.1 shows this Help screen.

A handy tool is the ability to print the Help topics within MS Windows. On the File menu, Print Topic is one of the four choices available. When you select Print Topic, the resulting page will look almost exactly like the help information on your monitor. If you're more organized than most people, including me, you can print many of these screens and save them in a

FIGURE 7.1

NetWare Tools drive connection help of all kinds

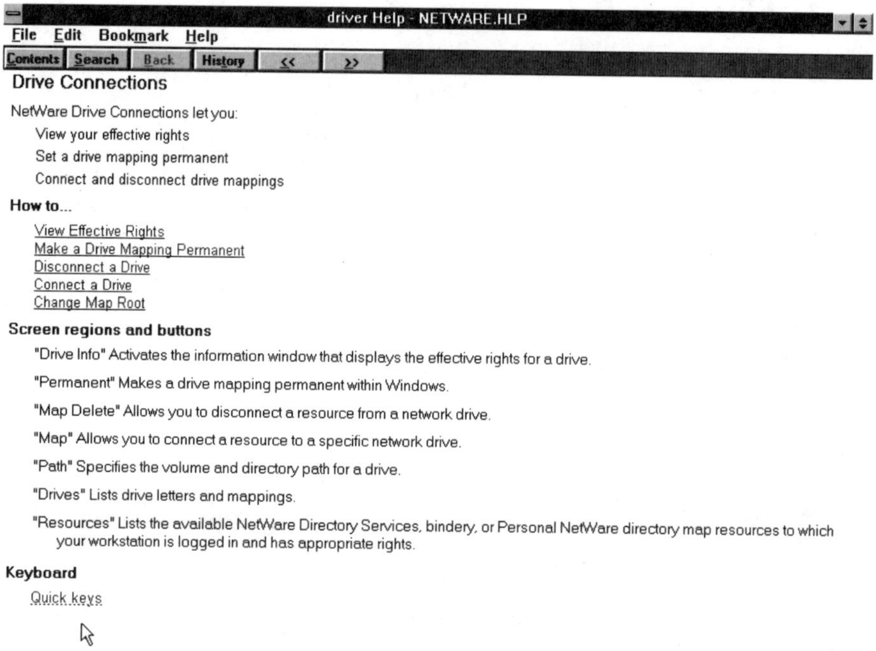

notebook. If you prefer, you can copy the Help screen to the MS Windows Clipboard and paste it wherever you want, including into other Help screens. Use the Copy command on the Edit menu.

You can even add your own two-cents worth to the Help screen itself. The Edit menu includes a choice called Annotate, which lets you add an electronic sticky-note. You can add one annotation per Help screen, but the note can be as long as you want. The indicator for the additional information is a paper clip icon beside the title. When you click on the paper clip, the annotation pops up. It first appears in the upper-left corner, so it's always in the way. In Figure 7.2, I moved my pop-up note out of the way of the help text. Do you see what I mean by making direct and personal comments on the Help screen?

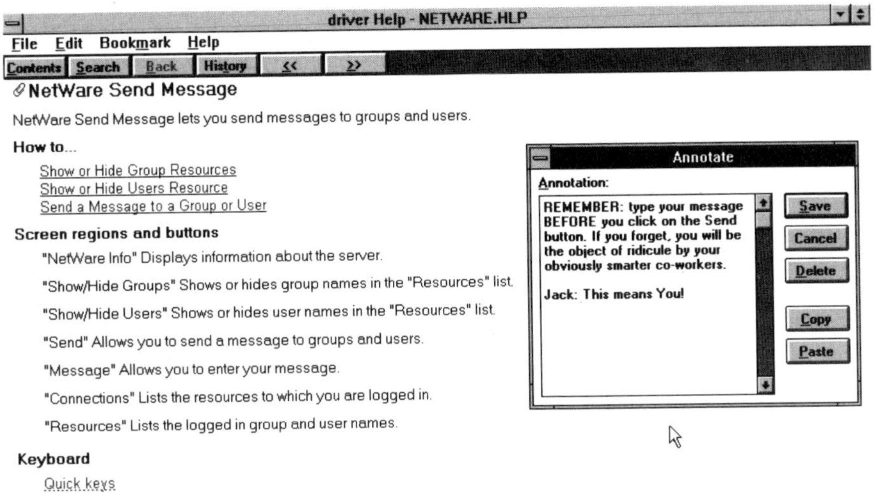

FIGURE 7.2

My annotation to the NetWare Send Messages Help screen

MS Windows Help system works as a *hypertext* application, which means that the underlined topics are linked directly to the page of the Help system that describes that topic. When the arrow cursor gets close to the underlined topics to activate the hypertext link, it turns into a pointing hand. Click on the topic where your cursor/hand is to see that Help screen. To return, click on Back on the menu bar at the top of the screen. Through the Back button, you can follow your trail all the way back to the first Help screen you activated.

One last detail about the Help system: if you see a topic underlined with a dashed line rather than a solid underline, clicking on that topic will pop up an explanation field called a *hotspot*. In Figure 7.2, the Quick keys topic is underlined with a dashed line. Try clicking on it. You'll see a pop-up window that tells you all the key combinations you can use to bypass the menus, such as Alt-X to exit.

The Help system works the same way in all the Personal NetWare program screens, including the hotspots and annotations. Much of the information for daily network usage is the same in the Personal NetWare and NetWare Tools programs.

GETTING HELP IN THE NET PROGRAM

7.2 THE FAST LANE

IN A HURRY? **Get help in NET**

1. Type **NET** from the DOS command line.
2. Move to the screen that pertains to the topic you want to see information about.
3. Press function key F1.

Don't think that clever Help systems are only available for MS Windows programs. The Personal NetWare DOS programs do a good job, offering the same hypertext type of help information as Personal NetWare under MS Windows.

NET's Help function has color phrases that are linked directly to other topic screens, just as in MS Windows. The red words and phrases indicate these links. You may also notice some green words, which work just like the hotspots in MS Windows. Press F1 to bring up the Help screen. Then press Enter on a green word, and a note will pop up and stay as long as you hold down that Enter key. With a mouse, the message stays as long as the mouse button is depressed. See Figure 7.3 for an example of a Help screen in NET.

You can see the highlighted topic, Drives View, just about in the middle of the Help screen. Pressing Enter on this topic will bring up that topic's Help screen. You can see the buttons across the bottom for Back, Next, Prev (for Previous), and Exit. By pressing the Tab key to reach your option of choice or pressing Alt and a key combination, you can maneuver around the Help system in NET, just as you can in MS Windows. You can even use your mouse here in the Help screens, if you're so inclined and your mouse driver is set up to work in DOS.

Give yourself permission to poke around the Help system in both DOS and MS Windows. Eat lunch at your desk one day (keep the crumbs out of your keyboard, please) and spend that hour exploring the Help system. You'll see interesting information that later will be important to you. Then you'll be frustrated because you remember the information you need is available, you just don't remember where. Ah, the joys of computing.

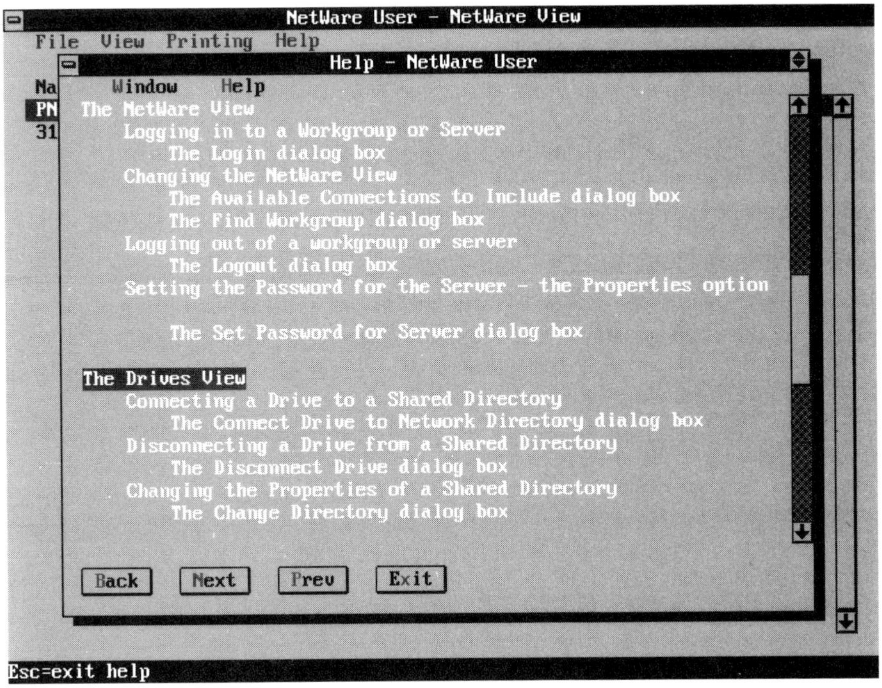

FIGURE 7.3

A Help screen in the NET program

GETTING HELP FROM THE DOS COMMAND LINE

IN-A-HURRY? **Get help on NET commands**

7.3 THE FAST LANE

1. Type **NET HELP** from the DOS command line.
2. Type **NET**, the name of the command you want to see information about, followed by **/ ?**.

If you use DOS, you probably spend lots of time on the command line. There are 30 or so NET commands that can be run directly from that same command line. These command line versions will do many of the same things the NET interactive program will do, but they have the convenience of speed. If you just want to see which drives are mapped to which servers, for instance, there's no reason to run NET and wait for the program to load and then press Alt-D to reach the Drives View screen. Just type the command line option to show that exact information.

But is that command NET SHOW? Or is it NET DRIVES? Give up? Type

```
NET HELP
```

to get the full listing of all commands. Figure 7.4 shows the results of typing NET HELP.

The full screen may be a bit overwhelming at first glance, since so many commands are listed. But there's no reason to panic. Just because the commands exist in no way obligates you to use them all. The few you do use, however, are available for a quick review whenever you need. Many of the commands have several option switches. Remembering those switches is difficult at times, especially for the commands you seldom use. So when in doubt, check it out with the NET HELP command.

There are some commands in Figure 7.4 that intrigue you, right? What in the world is NET SETDOG and why are dogs messing around in your computer network? Go ahead, type NET SETDOG / ? and see what dogs are involved.

FIGURE 7.4

The main Help screen for the NET commands

```
NET                        NET Command-line Help                        1.00

  Purpose: To display online help for commands.
  Syntax:  NET [command] /?

  Commands:
     ADMIN          INFO           RECEIVE        TIME
     AUDIT          JOIN           RIGHTS         ULIST
     CAPTURE        LINK           SAVE           USER
     CONNECT        LOGIN          SEND           VLIST
     CONSOLE        LOGOUT         SETDOG         WAIT
     CONTEXT        MAP            SETPASS        WGFIND
     DIAGS          NTIME          SHARE          WGLIST
     DOWN           PLIST          SLIST          XLIST
     HELP           PRINT          SYNC

  For example, to:                              Type:
   Display help for NET MAP                      NET MAP /?

C:\NWCLIENT>
```

The Personal NetWare Tutorial

Novell has a long history of providing CBT (Computer Based Training) programs for NetWare, and Personal NetWare is no exception. Although the Tutorial is not the same as an in-depth training class, it offers good information and a pop quiz. If you're one of those Type A competitive types, you can match scores against your workmates.

The Tutorial doesn't take too long, and it's well worth checking out. Bring another sack lunch to eat at your desk, and you'll have plenty of time to cover the entire Tutorial and play some NETWARS, too.

RUNNING THE TUTORIAL UNDER MS WINDOWS

IN-A-HURRY? **Run the Personal NetWare Tutorial** 7.4

THE FAST LANE

1. To install the Tutorial (if it isn't already), put Tutorial Disk 1 in a floppy drive, choose Run from the Program Manager File menu, and run WINTUTOR.EXE.
2. Open the Personal NetWare Tutorial group.
3. Double-click on the Personal NetWare Tutorial icon.

If you didn't install the Tutorial during installation of Personal NetWare, get your diskettes now. For MS Windows, choose the Run option on the File menu while in Program Manager. Put your Tutorial Disk 1 in a floppy drive, and run the program WINTUTOR.EXE. The installation program will take over from there, creating a Personal NetWare Tutorial group and placing the Personal NetWare Tutorial icon in that group.

The Personal NetWare Tutorial program provides quite a bit of information and background. This is the kind of information that's difficult to put in Help screens, for two reasons. First, people needing help may not care for the history of the command they can't remember how to use properly. It may be a case of good information coming at a bad time, like just when they're trying to print the report for the boss. Second, the more information packed into the program, the slower it runs. Since Tutorial information can easily be used outside the program itself, there's no reason to overload the program.

Figure 7.5 is a screen from the Tutorial showing an overview of Personal NetWare. This is one of 56 screens of the Tutorial, not counting help and the glossary.

You can see the command buttons across the bottom of the screen. They work as follows:

Exit	Leave the Tutorial
Help	See Help screens on the Tutorial itself
Topics	The opening screen, listing all Tutorial sections
Challenge	A multiple-choice question about the current Tutorial topic

FIGURE 7.5

A screen from the Personal NetWare Tutorial program

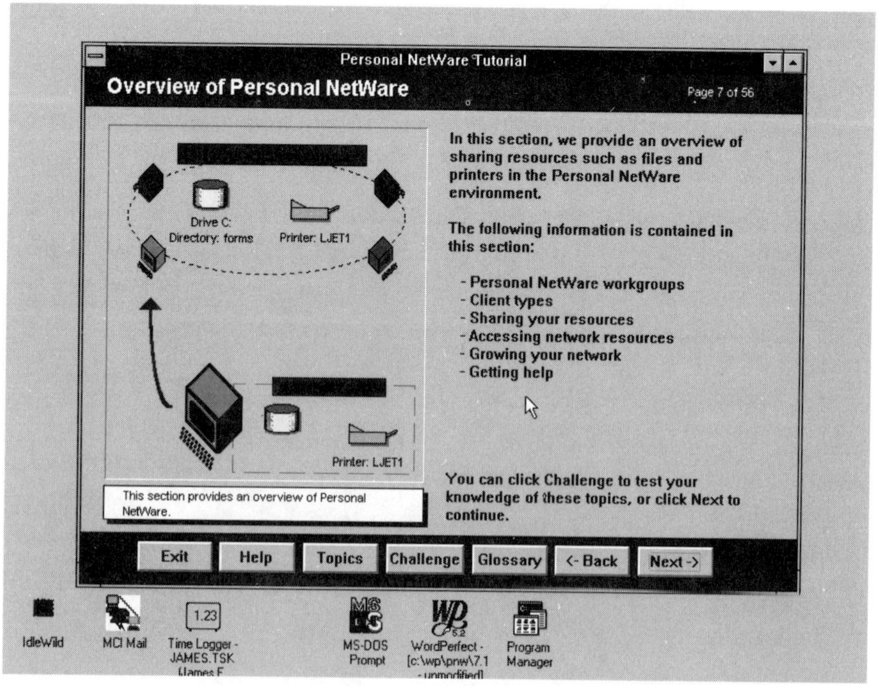

Glossary	More than 35 Personal NetWare terms defined
Back	Move back one screen
Next	Move forward one screen

RUNNING THE TUTORIAL UNDER DOS

IN-A-HURRY? **Run the Personal NetWare Tutorial under DOS**

7.5

1. To install the Tutorial (if it isn't already), put Tutorial Disk 1 in a floppy drive, change to that drive, and type **DOSTUTOR**.
2. Type **PNWTRAIN** from the DOS command line.

Don't think DOS users are second-class citizens with Personal NetWare. Every option that is available under MS Windows is available under DOS. The Personal NetWare Tutorial is certainly included in that statement. In fact, you actually get a bit more information in the DOS version than in the one for MS Windows.

To install the DOS version, take that same Tutorial Disk 1 and put it in your floppy drive. Change your current drive to that floppy diskette drive, and type

```
DOSTUTOR
```

to run the DOSTUTOR.EXE program. The program will install itself, placing the program in the \NWCLIENT directory (unless you tell it otherwise). After installation, type

```
PNWTRAIN
```

from the DOS command line to start the Tutorial.

If you installed the program somewhere other than \NWCLIENT, you'll need to change to that directory to run the program. This is because the \NWCLIENT directory is included in your DOS path during Personal NetWare installation; the drive you pick for the Tutorial may not be.

Figure 7.6 is the DOS version of the screen shown in Figure 7.5. Notice that the command buttons are activated by single keystrokes, as it tells us across the bottom of the screen:

```
Press 'N' (for Next) or 'ENTER' to continue.
```

It doesn't matter which version you play with, just be sure to take a few minutes and use one of the Tutorial programs.

Network Diagnostics

If you're at all curious, the network diagnostics programs are for you. Even if you wouldn't recognize a network packet if it floated in your soup, you still may want to know how many of them are created when you send those birthday party invitations to the laser printer.

There are more official reasons for using diagnostics. Do you want to know which server has the most hard disk space available? How about

FIGURE 7.6

The Overview of Personal NetWare screen in the DOS Tutorial

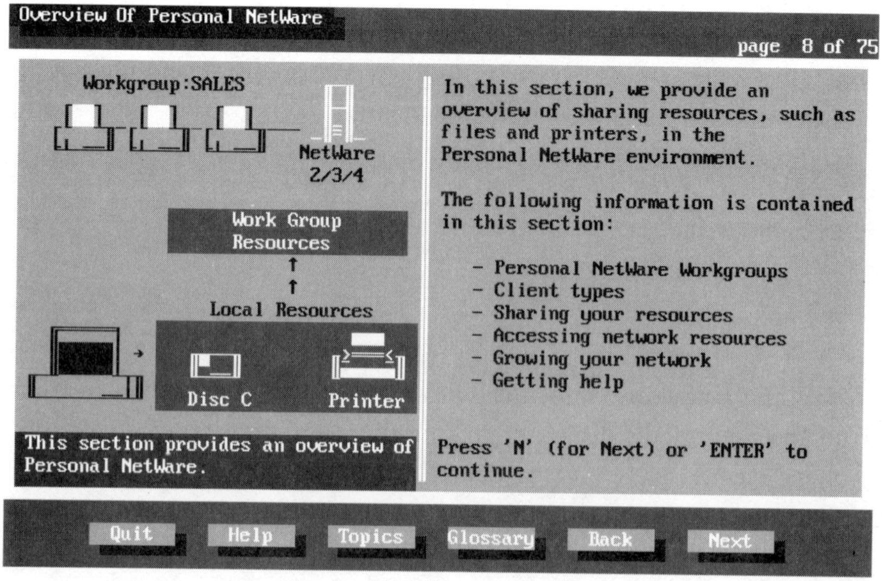

which server has the most users connected? All this information is available under both DOS and MS Windows. These programs show only Personal NetWare traffic, not traffic to and from dedicated NetWare file servers.

You must be logged in to the workgroup and have loaded the NMR.VLM during the PC network connection process before you can run the diagnostics programs. If you're not sure whether the NMR.VLM is loaded, run the SETUP.EXE program in the \NWCLIENT directory and check the Optimization/Network Management section. The check box for Load NMR Network Management module, under the Network Management heading, must be checked, as shown in Figure 7.7. If it isn't, please check it and save your new configuration. You must reboot your PC to allow the NMR.VLM program to load along with the other network client software.

A quick way to check if you're ready to run diagnostics is to take a look at the NET.CFG found in the \NWCLIENT directory. The SETUP

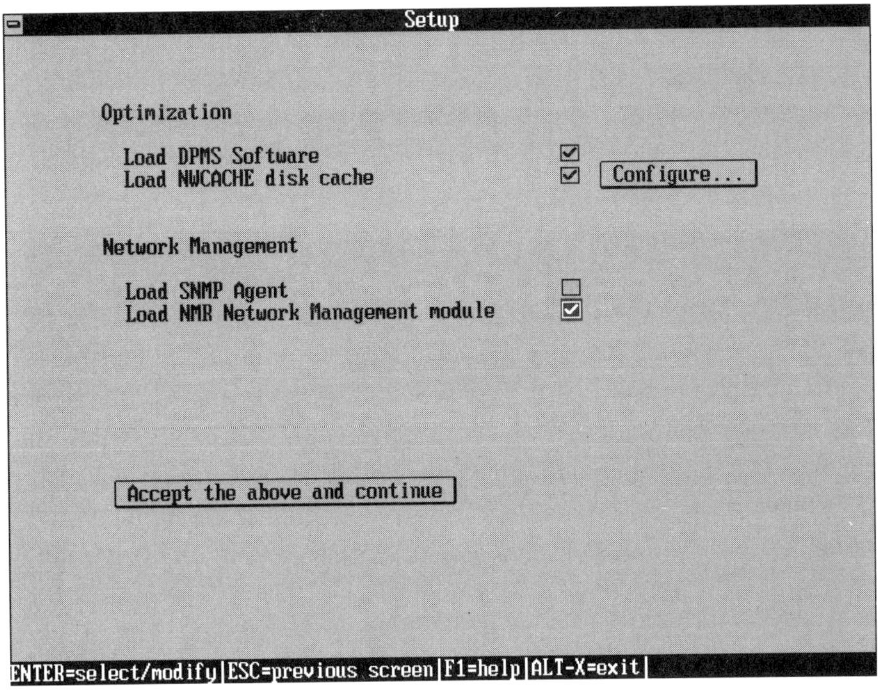

FIGURE 7.7
Checking that the NMR.VLM is loaded

program adds the line

```
VLM=NMR.VLM
```

to the NET.CFG file when the Load NMR check box is selected.

RUNNING THE NETWORK DIAGNOSTICS PROGRAM UNDER MS WINDOWS

In the Personal NetWare group is an icon showing a screwdriver and a wrench. It isn't NetWare Tools, although it would make a good icon for that program. It's the diagnostics program, PNWDIAG.EXE, hiding in the \NWCLIENT directory. The file placement and icon setup are all done by the Personal NetWare installation process. To start the diagnostic program, double-click on the NetWare Diagnostics icon. You'll see the diagnostics program's opening screen, as shown in Figure 7.8.

FIGURE 7.8

The opening screen of the diagnostics program under MS Windows

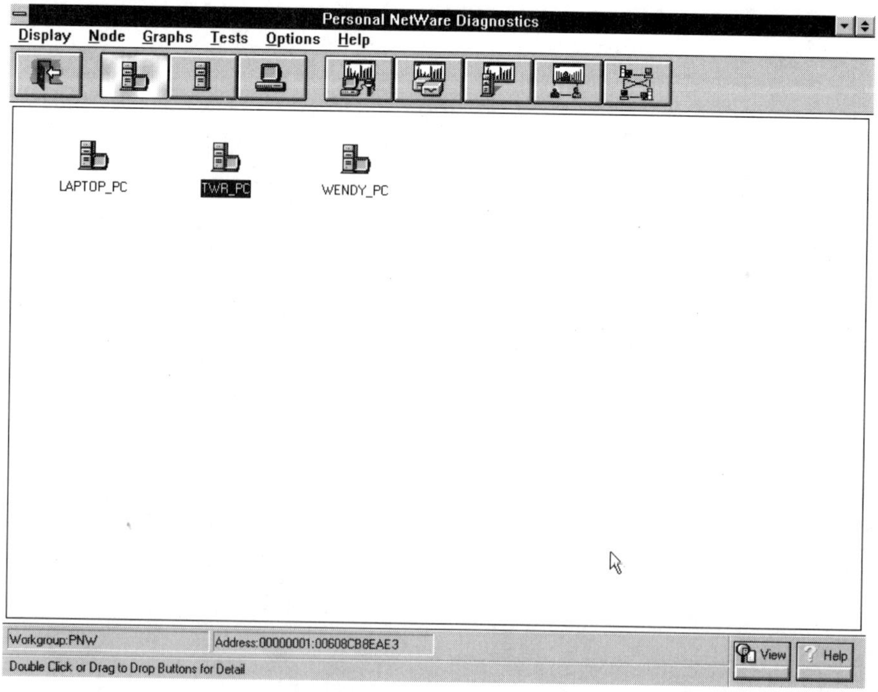

Turning on Diagnostics Help Information

IN-A-HURRY? **Activate Diagnostics Help display under Windows**

7.6 THE FAST LANE

1. Open the Personal NetWare group.
2. Double-click on the Network Diagnostics icon.
3. Choose the Status Bar option from the Options menu.
4. Check the Mouse Sensitive check box, then click on OK.
5. Drag your mouse across the icons to see descriptions in the bottom-left corner of the screen.

Once you start the diagnostics program, there will be a slight delay as all the different servers, clients, and PCs that are doing both are discovered and displayed. As soon as you regain control of your cursor, you should turn on a setting that will help you learn how to use the diagnostics program. Pull down the Options menu item, then click on Status Bar, the only choice in the menu.

The Status Bar Options dialog box opens in the middle of the screen, as shown in Figure 7.9. The bottom check box, Mouse Sensitive, needs to be checked. When you click on OK, your mouse is now much more intelligent than it was before. Slowly drag your mouse across all the icons on the button bar while watching the bottom-left corner of the screen. See it? The definitions for each button show up, giving you a quick Help screen. Figure 7.10 shows an example. As you drag your mouse across the different PCs shown, the network address for each shows up at the bottom of the screen.

Choosing the Stations to Display

The first group of icons on the button bar (bypassing the Exit icon) lets you choose what type of network stations will be displayed:

- The first icon, the tower case with the monitor beside it, is for nodes. This is for everything, including stations that are just Personal NetWare servers, just clients, or those PCs acting as both.

FIGURE 7.9

Making your mouse more intelligent

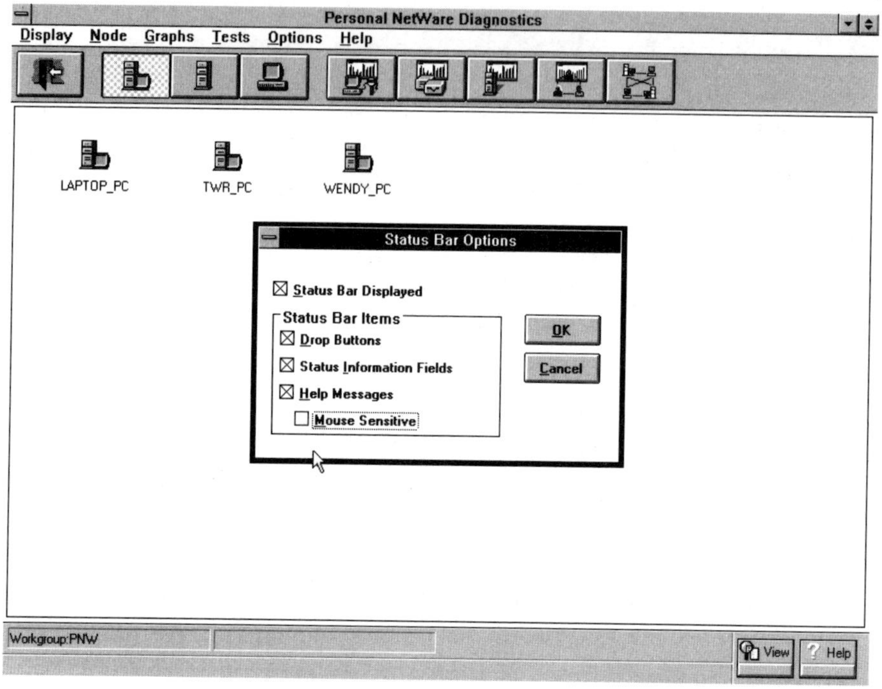

- The second icon, the tower case without the monitor, is for just server PCs. Many of the servers will also be clients, of course, but here the focus is just on those servers.
- The third icon, the desktop PC configuration, is for clients only. You'll notice that the names of the stations, even those that are both servers and clients, will change when this option is chosen. When the display option is either client/server or server, the server name is used to reference each machine. When the display option is for clients only, the server names are dropped and only the client names are used.

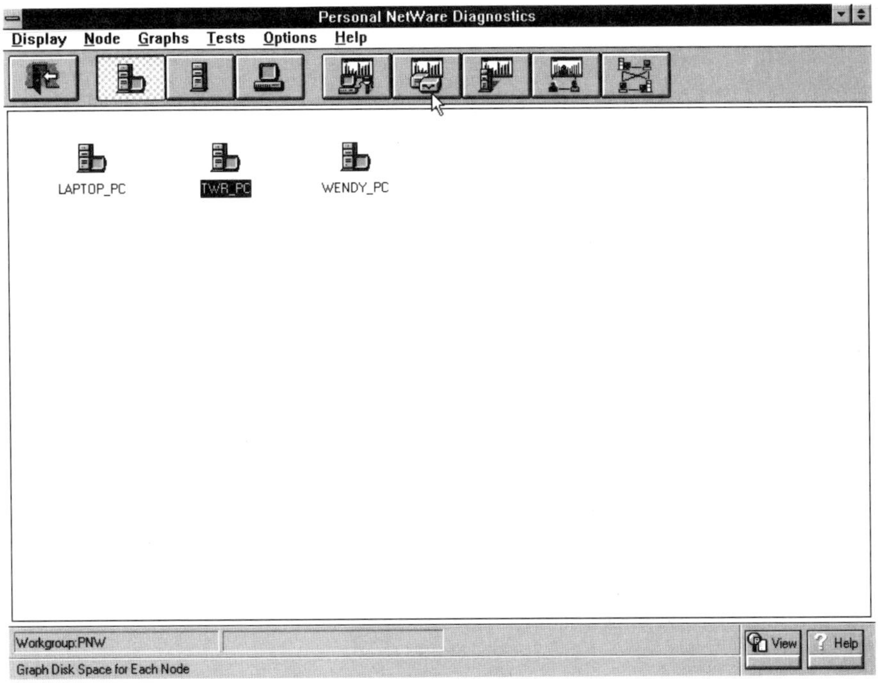

FIGURE 7.10
Notice the extra information in the bottom-left corner

If you prefer using the menus to clicking on icons, the three choices just described can also be selected from the Display menu. Click once on Display, then click on Nodes, Servers Only, or Clients Only. Using the mouse is probably quicker, and you have the advantage of information concerning each icon showing up on the status line in the bottom-left corner of the window. You won't see this information when you use the menu.

Performing Diagnostics

The next group of icons on the button bar represents the actual diagnostics to perform. From left to right, these icons offer the following choices:

- Graph traffic for each node
- Graph disk space for each node

- Graph server utilization
- Graph workgroup traffic
- Run an all points test

These choices are also available on the Graphs menu. One good reason for checking out the Graphs menu is the last option in that menu: All Graphs. This displays the four graphs at one time, each updating information as the totals change. Take a look at Figure 7.11 to see all four graphs up and running simultaneously.

Unfortunately, the black-and-white reproduction here hides some of the detail. Each of the two bars in the first three graphs use blue and maroon to differentiate between the options shown. Welcome to the world of gray scale confusion; dark blue and maroon look very different in color, but they have very similar gray scale values. Oh well.

FIGURE 7.11

A busy screen of diagnostics

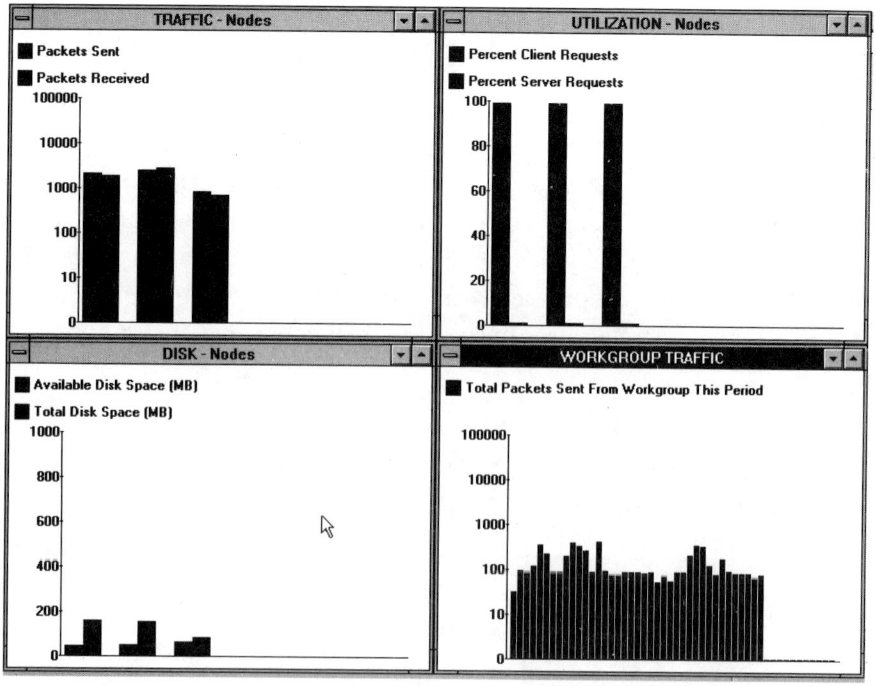

Each of these graphs work well in full size, or even collapsed down to icons to be checked now and then. My favorite display is the one for disk space. It provides a quick way to see how much disk space is available on any of the server machines. There is also an option to see the total hard disk space available all across the workgroup. Take a look at Figure 7.12 to see the Disk Space Totals dialog box popped up over the graph itself.

Having an easy way to look at disk space on servers is important. Strange things happen when a server runs out of disk space and someone sends a big print job to the printer attached to that server. As the print spooler fills up the last byte of available disk space and then needs more, the server crashes in confusion. You can't blame Personal NetWare for this. Every operating system from DOS through the largest mainframe goes crazy when the disk is full. Watching this graph now and then will help you avoid a

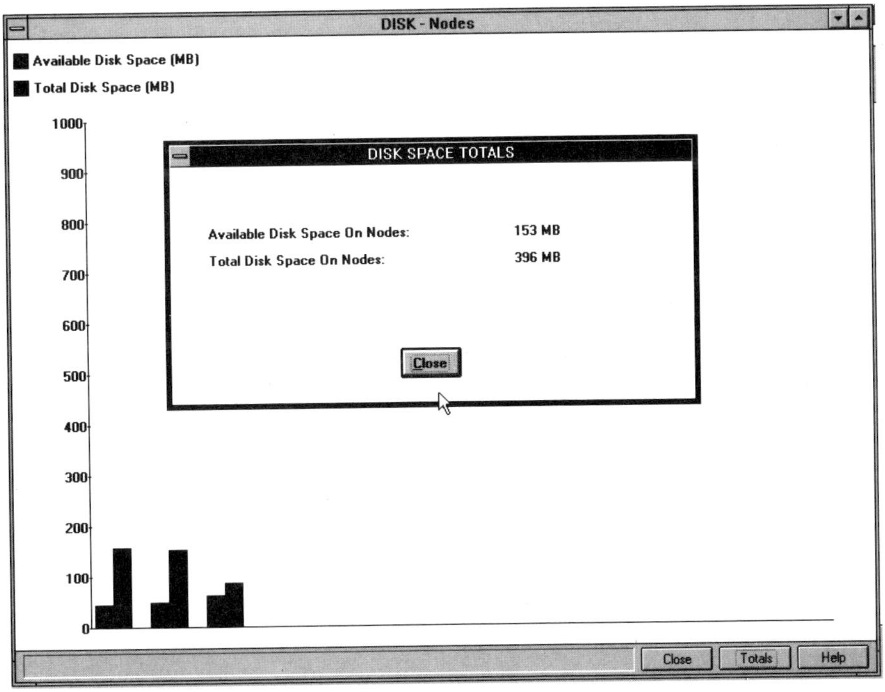

FIGURE 7.12
Graphing available disk space in the workgroup

nasty surprise some day. If you click on any of the vertical bars for a particular machine, another dialog box will pop up giving totals for that one PC. Click on the Totals button in the bottom-right corner to see the Disk Space Totals dialog box (as in Figure 7.12).

The all points test is a great help when you're setting up a new network. Even if the central computing group (or whatever they call it in your company) sets up the systems for you, there's bound to be a problem somewhere. The all points test sends packets to and from each of the active nodes in your workgroup. If you're having trouble with Marilyn's PC, and you suspect pilot (Marilyn) error, run the all points test. If Marilyn's PC passes the test, have a chat with Marilyn. If Marilyn's PC doesn't pass, you know to spend some time checking the cabling, the PC configuration, the network setup information, and everything else connected to that PC. Then apologize to Marilyn.

GOOD REASONS TO USE DIAGNOSTICS

Use the diagnostics programs to give you a quick overview of the network. With the graphs, it's easy to answer the standard questions, such as which server is overloaded. Taking our graphs in order, let's see what kinds of problems each of the graphs can solve in a typical network.

Graphing Node Traffic

7.7 THE FAST LANE

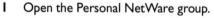

IN-A-HURRY? Graph traffic for each node

1. Open the Personal NetWare group.
2. Double-click on the Network Diagnostics icon.
3. Click on the Graph Traffic icon on the button bar.

When you graph traffic for each node (be sure and focus either on the server only or client/server display), you discover which system may be overloaded. Click on the Graph Traffic icon on the button bar (the first one in the second group of buttons), or choose Node Traffic from the Graphs menu to run this diagnostic.

Since each of the Personal NetWare servers also functions as a workstation for someone, overloading the server part of the machine may interfere with that user's work. There are no hard and fast rules, but if one server is considerably busier than every other server, check into it. You can do two things to keep this problem from getting out of hand. Number one, make sure the user of that particular PC server uses the computer as seldom as possible. A machine that's busy helping everyone else in the workgroup is not the best choice for churning big spreadsheets or compiling huge reports. Give that machine to a manager; they rarely understand computers anyway and are least likely to overwork one.

The other way to help balance the load is to spread around some of the programs on the busy server. Move one application to each of the least loaded PCs. This method keeps the information available but allows the user of the overloaded server to regain some performance.

Graphing Disk Space for Nodes

IN-A-HURRY? **Graph disk space for each node** 7.8

THE FAST LANE

1. Open the Personal NetWare group.
2. Double-click on the Network Diagnostics icon.
3. Click on the Graph Disk Space icon on the button bar.

Clicking on the Graph Disk Space icon (the second one in the second group of buttons) quickly shows how much disk space is available on each server. If you prefer, you can choose Disk Space from the Graphs menu instead.

This information is important for the reason given previously: full disks mean trouble. A quick glance at this graph now and then will give you some lead time before disaster strikes, so that you can move applications or data off that overloaded disk drive. Or you can start preparing management for a capital expense labeled "new disk drive." Click on the vertical bars to see information for that particular PC.

Graphing Server Utilization

7.9 THE FAST LANE **IN-A-HURRY? Graph local or remote utilization for each node**

1. Open the Personal NetWare group.
2. Double-click on the Network Diagnostics icon.
3. Click on the Server Utilization icon on the button bar.

The Server Utilization option shows exactly how much processing time for each server is spent supporting remote users and how much time is used to support the local user. You can either click on the Server Utilization icon (the third one in the second group of buttons) or choose Utilization from the Graphs menu to run this diagnostic.

There's no hard and fast rule of percentages for this one either, but the lower percentage of server requests, the better the local performance. The remedy for server overutilization is the same as that for disk space problems: move some functions off the server machine. The graph of server use will probably match the graph of disk space use fairly closely, although printing takes quite a few CPU cycles. Remote clients using a particular server heavily will start eating up the disk space as well as CPU time. For this problem, another faster PC may be the answer. Or you can again reapportion the common files to underworked servers.

Graphing Workgroup Traffic

7.10 THE FAST LANE **IN-A-HURRY? Graph traffic for each workgroup**

1. Open the Personal NetWare group.
2. Double-click on the Network Diagnostics icon.
3. Click on the Workgroup Traffic icon on the button bar.

To graph workgroup traffic, click on its icon (the fourth one in the second group of buttons on the button bar) or choose Workgroup Traffic from the Graphs menu.

The workgroup traffic diagnostic is less cut and dried, because we have no comparisons within this graph. Over time, you will realize what's busy for your network and what's overloaded. The only way to know what's abnormal is to check the normal traffic levels now and then.

UPGRADING OVERWORKED PERSONAL NETWARE NETWORKS

One of the natural laws of networking is that networks grow—always. Business people realize immediately that sharing information and resources is more cost effective than not sharing. You learned this fact in kindergarten: sharing is good. At least, sharing some things is good. Keep your toothbrush to yourself.

What should you do when the diagnostic programs tell you things are getting busier? When users complain their printer is constantly spitting out pages for everyone in the building? When every disk is full? When the traffic levels on your network regularly set new volume records?

You just hit the famous peer-to-peer network wall. Everything has a limit, and the Personal NetWare workgroup is no exception. It's time to grow.

This is no different than a small company or a department in a large company. With five employees, everyone knows everyone and people share the work and responsibility equally. With fifty people in that group, there must be more structure. Some must be more equal than others.

With Personal NetWare, you have an easy, two-step upgrade path. The first step is to take the workgroup server doing the most work and make it a dedicated Personal NetWare server. If David's PC has become the de facto server, give David another PC, leaving the workgroup server doing nothing but workgroup service. This costs more money in hardware but little in software. The only software expense will be the new Personal NetWare software on David's new PC.

When that option is outgrown, you need to step up to a dedicated NetWare file server. The hardware requirement is much like that of a workgroup server, although more RAM is needed. Full NetWare provides better performance than the Personal NetWare servers. You may also want to buy a huge disk drive to place in that PC, since it will be the focal point of all file activity. The rule of thumb is to buy a hard disk so big you'll never outgrow it. Buy one so big your management will complain. Then you'll have about six months before that huge disk is full. If you buy a disk to handle your current needs and a rational amount of growth, it will be full in only six weeks.

The software required for a dedicated NetWare file server is different than that for Personal NetWare. It is also more powerful and allows enhanced communications and processing power.

A good analogy for moving from Personal NetWare to a dedicated NetWare file server might be a pickup and a dump truck. If you want to haul enough dirt for your garden, the pickup does fine. If you want to haul enough dirt for a mountain, get the dump truck.

By the way, when you get a dedicated NetWare file server, not a single byte of a single program on any of the client PCs will need to change. That's the beauty of the Universal NetWare Client.

RUNNING THE NETWORK DIAGNOSTICS PROGRAM UNDER DOS

The DOS version of network diagnostics has several options that are not available in the MS Windows version:

- You can view another workgroup's information and manage the user information for that workgroup without leaving your own workgroup.
- You can save the user information created during the process of associating network names for use with Novell's LANalyzer for MS Windows product.
- A screen in the DOS version, Server Utilization, combines information that's scattered about on several MS Windows screens into one succinct display.

The option of using either DOS or MS Windows diagnostics is handy. Some users feel more comfortable with bar graphs, and some prefer real numbers.

Which you prefer doesn't matter, since you get both in the same box.

Starting the Diagnostics Program

Start the network diagnostics program from the DOS command line by typing

```
NET DIAGS
```

You can also start the program by typing

```
PNWDIAGS
```

However, since more than 30 other commands start with NET, using NET DIAGS keeps things consistent. If your workgroup has lots of PCs, don't get impatient. Gathering information on all the active network nodes may take a moment or two.

The user interface is different from the other NET utilities, because this program is inherited in large part from regular NetWare. This interface is commonly referred to as the *C-Worthy* interface, named after the programming library used to create this look in the early 1980's. It's a bit dated now, and it doesn't work with a mouse, but millions of NetWare users think of this as the official look of network utilities. Figure 7.13 shows the opening screen of the NET DIAGS program.

There is a keystroke you might like to use that's not mentioned on the status line at the bottom of the screen. No matter where you are, or how many menus deep, you can press Alt-F10 to bring up the Exit dialog box. This is a trick from the utilities on NetWare file servers. Use this and amaze your friends, at least those who have not used NetWare utilities.

To choose an item from a NET DIAGS menu, highlight your choice and press Enter. You can use the arrow keys to move up and down through the menu selections, or move directly to a menu choice by typing the first letter of the first word of the choice. If more than one menu starts with the same letter, each keypress moves to the next one.

FIGURE 7.13

NET DIAGS, the DOS version of the diagnostic program

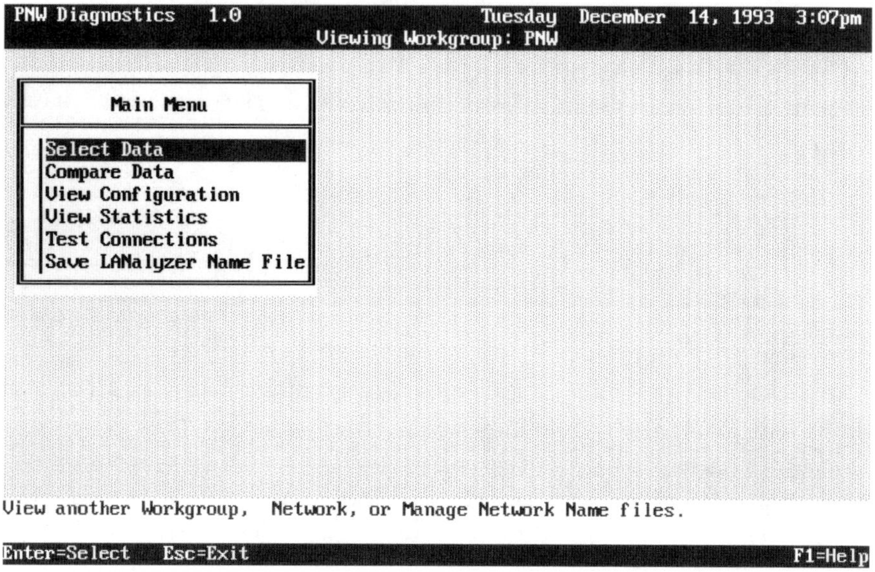

Viewing Other Workgroups

7.11 THE FAST LANE

IN-A-HURRY? **Select a different workgroup to monitor**

1. Type **NET DIAGS** from the DOS command line.
2. Highlight the Select Data option on the Main menu, then press Enter.
3. Highlight the Select a Workgroup option, then press Enter.
4. Highlight the workgroup of your choice, then press Enter.

If you plan to view other workgroups beside your default workgroup, make sure you run the WorkGroup FIND utility before starting NET DIAGS. To run this utility, from the DOS command line, type

```
NET WGFIND
```

This develops the working list of workgroups in your network and makes it available to the diagnostics program.

To view other workgroups, choose the Select Data choice, the one at the top of the Main menu. Highlight it and press Enter. A box entitled Data Selection Items pops up just to the right of the Main menu, as shown in Figure 7.14. The first entry is Select a Workgroup. Highlight this item and press Enter to see a list of the available workgroups in a box labeled Select Workgroup Name. Choose the workgroup by highlighting it and pressing Enter. Then you can go on to use whatever monitoring utility you had in mind.

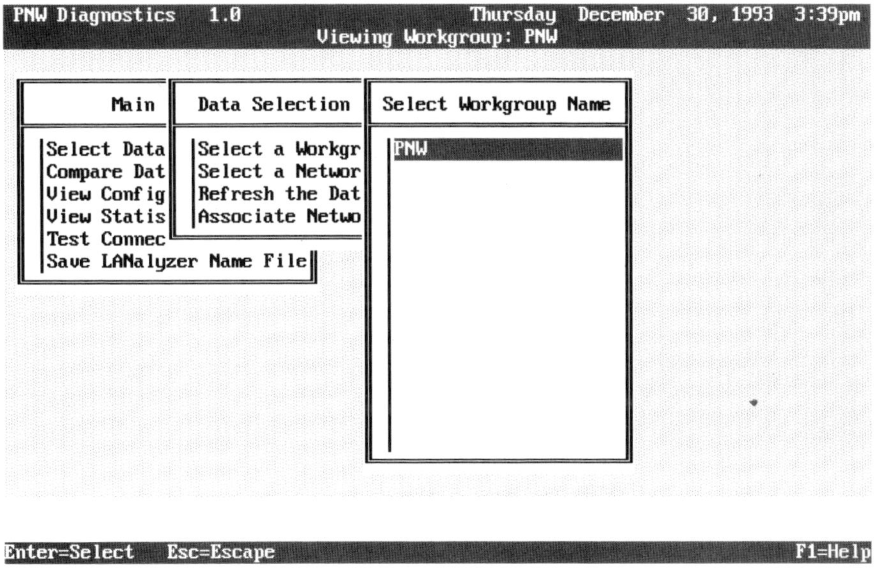

FIGURE 7.14
Selecting the data you want to view

Viewing Disk Space Available under DOS

IN-A-HURRY? **View available disk space**

7.12

THE FAST LANE

1. Type **NET DIAGS** from the DOS command line.
2. Highlight the Compare Data option on the Main menu, then press Enter.
3. Highlight Servers, then press Enter.
4. Highlight Resource Distribution, then press Enter.

Remember Figure 7.12 a few pages back? The one showing all the available disk space? You can recreate that same information in the DOS version with no trouble at all.

The second option on the Main menu is Compare Data. That's a good description, since all the screens offered by this option show comparisons between the active clients, servers, or all nodes in the workgroup. Once you choose which set of workgroup clients you want to view, choices abound.

For our purposes now, let's look at disk space. Start the NET DIAGS program and choose Compare Data from the Main menu by highlighting it and pressing Enter. The Select Nodes menu will pop up. You must choose whether you wish to see All Nodes, Servers, or Clients. Pick Servers for now. The Compare Options menu pops open. Choose Resource Distribution. This shows more than just disk space, as you can see in Figure 7.15. It also lets you see what kind of display monitor is used and the CPU inside each system.

The Resource Efficiency option on the Compare Options menu displays a screen similar to the one in Figure 7.15, with one added wrinkle. In place of the video display information, a measurement of how busy each node is appears under the heading Activity. The numbers displayed provide a quick way to check which servers are the busiest. In fact, if you could leave this screen up for an entire workday or two, you would have a listing in order of your busiest servers. Management will appreciate information like this when you request some more equipment. Numbers are always better when begging for capital expenditures.

The Compare Options menu leads to screens similar to the ones we saw in the MS Windows diagnostics section. The first option on the menu, Traffic, shows how many packets have gone between the various nodes in your workgroup. Let's take a look at that now.

PNW Diagnostics 1.0 Tuesday December 14, 1993 3:12pm
Viewing Workgroup: PNW

NAME	CPU	DISPLAY	AVAIL DISK	TOTAL DISK	
WENDY_PC	80386	VGA	60004 K	83112 K	
TWR_PC	80386	VGA	46388 K	149324 K	
LAPTOP_PC	80386	VGA	42762 K	155222 K	
					Elapsed Time: 0 hr. 2 min. 5 sec.
TOTALS			149154	387658	

Esc=Escape F1=Help

FIGURE 7.15 *The NET DIAGS screen showing available disk space in the workgroup*

Viewing Traffic Totals under DOS

IN-A-HURRY? View node traffic totals

7.13 THE FAST LANE

1. Type **NET DIAGS** from the DOS command line.
2. Highlight the Compare Data option on the Main menu, then press Enter.
3. Highlight All Nodes, then press Enter.
4. Highlight Traffic, then press Enter.

After NET DIAGS is started, highlight the second menu choice, Compare Data, and press Enter. Because we want to see all the traffic we can, press Enter on the All Nodes choice on the submenu. Traffic is the first option on the Compare Options menu, so press Enter there. Figure 7.16 shows the traffic totals displayed by the diagnostics program.

Although there are no pretty pictures as in the MS Windows version, it's easier to see how many packets are traversing the network over a given

FIGURE 7.16

Watching the packets go by

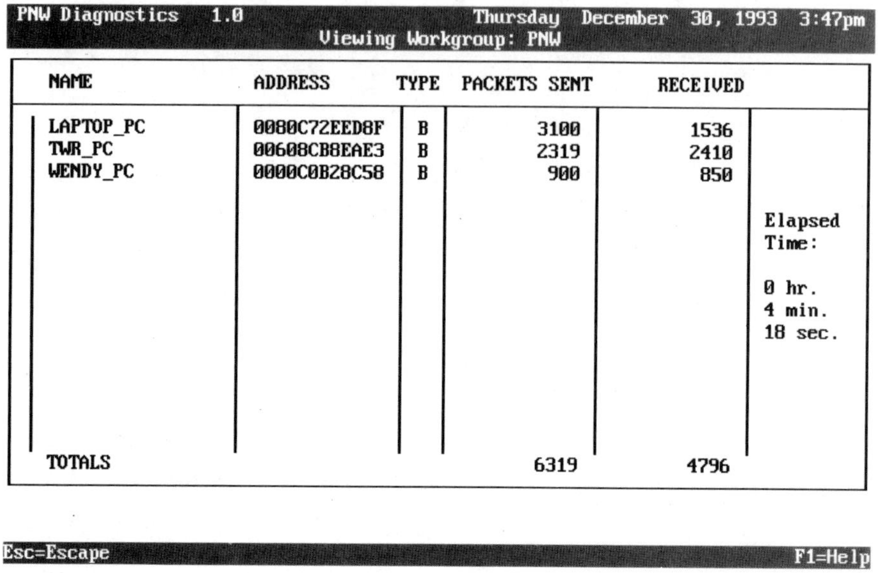

PNW Diagnostics 1.0 Thursday December 30, 1993 3:47pm
Viewing Workgroup: PNW

NAME	ADDRESS	TYPE	PACKETS SENT	RECEIVED	
LAPTOP_PC	0080C72EED8F	B	3100	1536	
TWR_PC	00608CB8EAE3	B	2319	2410	
WENDY_PC	0000C0B28C58	B	900	850	Elapsed Time: 0 hr. 4 min. 18 sec.
TOTALS			6319	4796	

Esc=Escape F1=Help

point of time. The traffic totals reset each time you start the traffic monitoring. This is a nice screen to leave on for an hour or so now and then. It's a good idea to write the totals down every few weeks on your calendar, so a busy network doesn't creep up on you. Okay, it may still creep up on you, but at least you'll have some comparison numbers over time to see how fast the traffic is growing.

Viewing Local and Remote Utilization under DOS

7.14 THE FAST LANE

IN-A-HURRY? View local and remote utilization

1. Type **NET DIAGS** from the DOS command line.
2. Highlight the Compare Data option on the Main menu, then press Enter.
3. Highlight All Nodes, then press Enter.
4. Highlight Local/Remote Utilization, then press Enter.

The ratio of local to remote utilization is shown, amazingly enough, by the Local/Remote Utilization option. After starting NET DIAGS, choose Compare Data, then All Nodes to bring up the Compare Options menu. Press Enter on Local/Remote Utilization to see the screen shown in Figure 7.17.

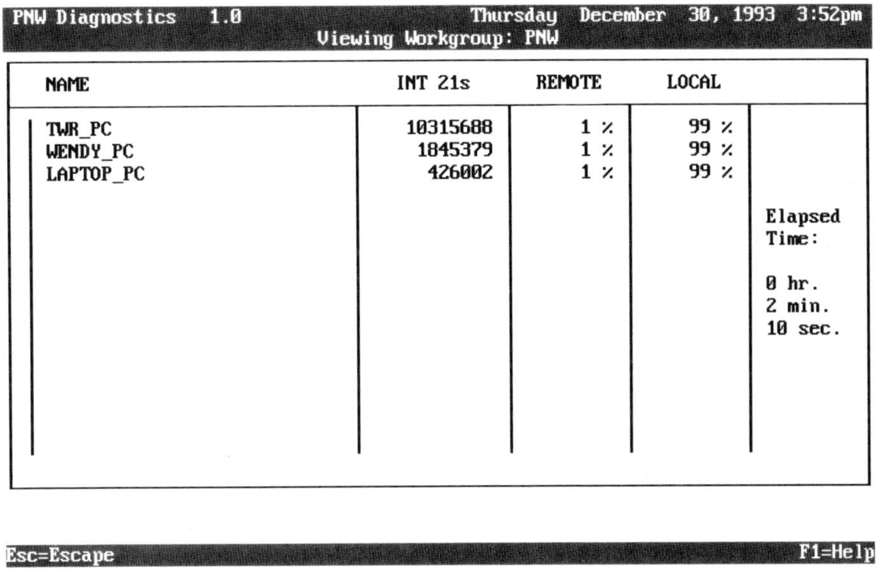

FIGURE 7.17

Three servers not overwhelmed with work

You'll see extra information here, along with the utilization percentages. The first column, Int 21s, shows the number of DOS requests made by each machine listed. These numbers are huge because each operation your computer performs is counted here. So, Rose may be playing Solitaire instead of maintaining her database, but the numbers will show she's been busy.

The important numbers here are the percentages of local to remote processes. Busy servers with high remote percentages will perform slower as workstations. Give these busy servers to people who don't depend on their PC's performance for their jobs. Management personnel come to mind; many of them are still scared of their PCs. Be sure and train them not to turn off their computer every day, or that server won't be available. Tell them the PC fan noise reminds you of the surf on the eighteenth hole of the Pebble Beach Golf Course.

Viewing Server Utilization under DOS

7.15 THE FAST LANE

IN-A-HURRY? View server utilization

1. Type **NET DIAGS** from the DOS command line.
2. Highlight the Compare Data option, then press Enter.
3. Highlight Servers, then press Enter.
4. Highlight Server Utilization, then press Enter.

The Server Utilization option is not available in the MS Windows version of the diagnostics program. This screen combines several measures of server activity in one spot.

Start the NET DIAGS program, then choose Compare Data. Select Servers from the submenu, then Server Utilization. The familiar table format of the Server Utilization screen displays four different measurements, as shown in Figure 7.18. These measurements are as follows:

MEASUREMENT	DEFINITION
Busys	Number of packets sent to a workstation indicating the server is busy
Packets	Total number of packets sent and received by that server
Connections	Number of active client connections to the server
Open Files	Current number of open files on that server maintained by connected clients

Viewing Server and Client Configuration and Statistics

7.16 THE FAST LANE

IN-A-HURRY? View node configurations

1. Type **NET DIAGS** from the DOS command line.
2. Highlight the View Configuration option, then press Enter.

3 Highlight All Nodes, then press Enter.

4 Press Enter on the node you wish to examine.

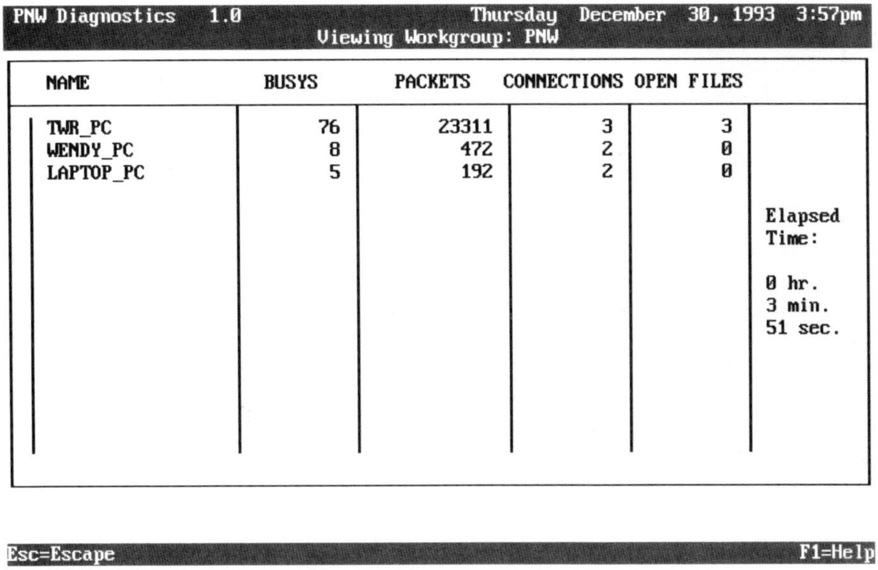

FIGURE 7.18

The Server Utilization screen in NET DIAGS

Let's move back to the opening screen of NET DIAGS and look at some of the options we skipped. View Configuration is a big help to network administrators, because it allows them to discover plenty of server and client configuration details without traipsing all over the office checking each PC manually.

Start NET DIAGS and choose View Configuration, the third option on the Main menu. Choose All Nodes, then select the station you wish to examine.

A screen similar to the one in Figure 7.19 will appear. It will show your network nodes, not mine, and list them by server name. If you chose Clients rather than All Nodes earlier, the same PCs would appear listed by their user names, such as James and Wendy and Laptop.

The small down arrow in the bottom-left corner of the screen indicates more information is listed. Press the Page Down key to see more of the information; there's quite a bit of it, much of which we don't currently need.

FIGURE 7.19

Some of the server details for LAPTOP_PC

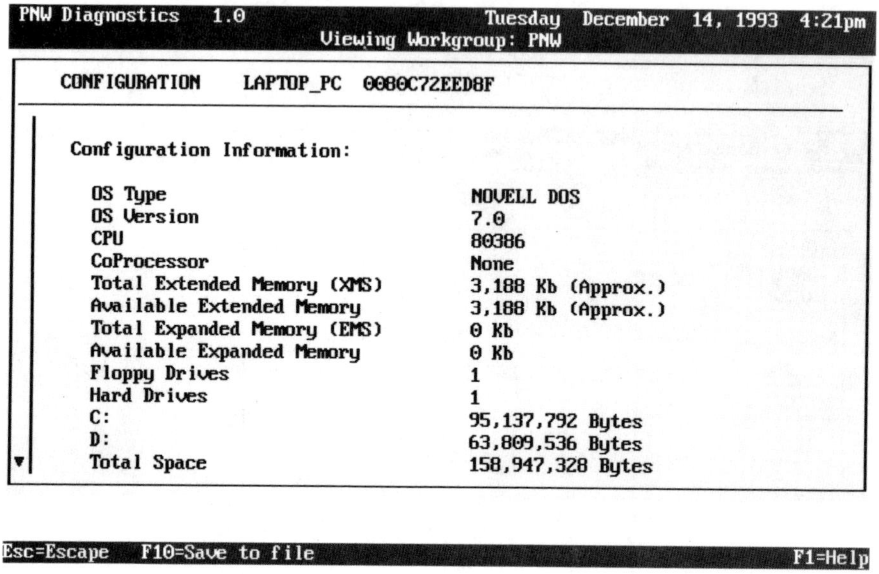

No, there are not two hard disks in the LAPTOP machine. What you see is the result of running the Novell DOS Stacker disk software. Included with Novell DOS, Stacker effectively doubles your disk space. It uses a false file masquerading as another disk to store your disk files in a compressed mode, giving you more space. Since Novell DOS 7 can be bought with Personal NetWare, Stacker might be worth checking out. See Chapter 9 for details on using Novell DOS 7.

The status line includes the option to press F10 and save this information to a file. It would be a good idea to do this once for every node on your network, preferably soon after the network is up and running. This type of information from when your network is running properly is valuable when your network is running poorly.

The View Statistics screen is similar to the View Configuration screen, but it focuses on the network mechanics. It also includes some information about the NWCACHE program. Mostly, however, the information here is of little use to casual Personal NetWare administrators. This screen actually provides more information than with regular NetWare file server administration utilities.

Testing Connections

IN-A-HURRY? Test network connections 7.17

THE FAST LANE

1. Type **NET DIAGS** from the DOS command line.
2. Highlight the Test Connections option, then press Enter.
3. Highlight either Point to Point Test or All Points Test, then press Enter.

The penultimate choice on the Main menu is Test Connections. This is great to use when new cables are installed, a new user joins the workgroup, or you start getting complaints about the network. You can test connections between just two nodes (great for testing that brand new user to the network) or test all points at once.

Start NET DIAGS, then highlight Test Connections and press Enter. On the Test Connections menu, choose either Point to Point Test or All Points Test. If you choose Point to Point Test, another menu appears with a list of the active nodes. Press Enter on the first node you wish to test to make it the Source node. Then press Enter on the node to be the Destination. You'll be given a time estimate for the test, along with a chance to cancel it. If you choose to continue, the test will take off, thoroughly checking the network between the two devices with 10,000 packets.

The All Points Test option takes much less time to execute and there are no choices to make. Simply press Enter and watch the details.

After you have played with all the options within NET DIAGS you can stand, back up to the MS Windows part of this chapter and read the section labeled Good Reasons to Use Diagnostics, as well as the one titled Upgrading Overworked Personal NetWare Networks. These sections apply to the network, whether you're a DOS or MS Windows user.

Better Memory Management through DPMS

Let's tell the truth: there are no free lunches. Networking provides some great advantages, but it does require some computer RAM. No one I've ever met has enough RAM or hard disk space, and you probably aren't the exception.

Although this Personal NetWare lunch isn't free, it's discounted. Several utilities are included to limit the amount of memory required for the Personal NetWare software. Starting at the top, the first helpful program is DPMS (DOS Protected Mode Services).

DPMS works with your existing memory manager in computers with 80386 and 80486 CPUs. You may be familiar with programs that can use extended memory for some of their program code, meaning they need a smaller amount of the precious 640 KB RAM that has been the DOS limit since 1981. DPMS goes one step further: certain DPMS-aware programs can load and run in the CPU's protected mode, outside the conventional 640 KB RAM area.

This ability is based on the fact that Intel's CPU versions 80286 and above have two modes of operation. Real mode emulates the 1981 processor and DOS limitations of 640 KB RAM. Protected mode enlarges the allowable RAM up to 4 GB (gigabytes, 1000 times larger than a megabyte). CPU versions 80386 and above also support a virtual 8086 mode, allowing programs to believe they are running in real mode while protected mode features are available. This is why the 80386 was such a leap forward over the 80286: memory control and management.

The bottom line? A program designed to use DPMS can run almost entirely above the 640 KB area. Very little of the lower 640 KB RAM is used for these programs, leaving more for your DOS and MS Windows programs to run better with more memory.

How NWCACHE Improves Performance

One of the best programs to take advantage of DPMS is NWCACHE.EXE (NetWare CACHE). DOS disk processing has a high degree of repetition built in. In other words, programs looking for a file may stop and start looking on the disk drive dozens of times before they find and read all of the file. NWCACHE provides a place in computer RAM to store everything read off the disk. So if your program needs to search the file again for something right away, that information will probably still be in RAM. And even though hard disks are getting faster, they're a hundred times slower than RAM. This allows NWCACHE to deliver information to your applications five to ten times faster than reading it from the hard disk.

Here are some of the features of NWCACHE:

- Caches data on all types of compressed drives, like Stacker, SuperStor, and Doubledisk
- Shares part of the cache memory with other applications (optional)
- Uses delayed write and buffered write options to help limit the number of times your applications write information to disk, speeding up disk-write operations
- Uses lookahead techniques to analyze disk activity to get the information your program needs before the program asks for it
- Installs easily
- Works with all types of noncompressed hard disk drives and diskettes

Installation instructions for NWCACHE are in Appendix A. There are two things to be said here, however.

First, use as much cache as you can. If you do not run MS Windows, make as much of your RAM as possible available to NWCACHE. If you do run MS Windows, use NWCACHE in place of SmartDrive. NWCACHE has been written by Novell engineers, people with more than a decade of experience writing cache programs for NetWare file servers. They know their business, and the solidity and performance of NWCACHE attest to that.

Second, use the delayed write options, but buy a battery backup for your computer. When your application sends information to be written to disk, NWCACHE intercepts that information and tells your application the data was written to disk. But it's lying; NWCACHE will wait for more data to come, so it can write a bunch at once and reduce the overhead needed for multiple writes to disk. If more data hasn't come in a certain amount of time (which you can set), the data will then be written to the disk. There is a lag when your application believes data has been safely stored on the disk, but it hasn't. If your computer loses power just at that second, the data waiting in the cache buffers will be lost. This is rare, but it can happen. So get that battery backup, okay?

Backup and Restore for Mental Health

What good timing—the section on backup and restore comes just after talking about how data can be lost. Does this tell you to develop a little healthy paranoia? If you're not paranoid about losing your data, you just haven't been playing with computers long enough.

The workgroup information kept and spread throughout the Personal NetWare network contains all the details about users, servers, printers, and shared directories. Network data is copied to each server, while some server-specific information is kept at each server separately from the network information. It doesn't make any difference to the backup utility which is which; it will get it all.

BACKING UP YOUR DATA

IN-A-HURRY? Back up the workgroup data

7.18

THE FAST LANE

1. Log in as a user with administrator privileges.
2. Type **NET ADMIN** from the DOS command line.
3. Highlight the server to backup.
4. Press Alt-Enter.
5. Press Alt-B.

To back up the workgroup related data, you must log in to the workgroup as a user with administrator privileges. From the DOS command line, type

```
NET ADMIN
```

to run the NET ADMIN program. Then highlight the server you wish to back up. Press Alt-Enter to open the Properties view, then press Alt-B to open the Backup Databases window.

Figure 7.20 shows this window, opened and ready to be told where to store the backup. It's a good idea to store the backup data on a different server than the one you're backing up. In the figure, you can see by the top of the screen that I'm logged in as LAPTOP, but I'm backing up TWR.

Just below the Backup Databases window, you can see the option to Restore Databases, something I hope you never need to do. But now you know where it is, so you have a chance to rebuild your network if something terrible happens.

BACKING UP YOUR PROGRAM AND DATA FILES

The NET ADMIN program ***does not*** backup any of the actual program and data files on any of these servers. Your memos, letters, spreadsheets, and databases must be backed up separately. Backing up your files should be done regularly, unless you have so much free time that recreating six months of work is no problem.

FIGURE 7.20

Backing up the workgroup data

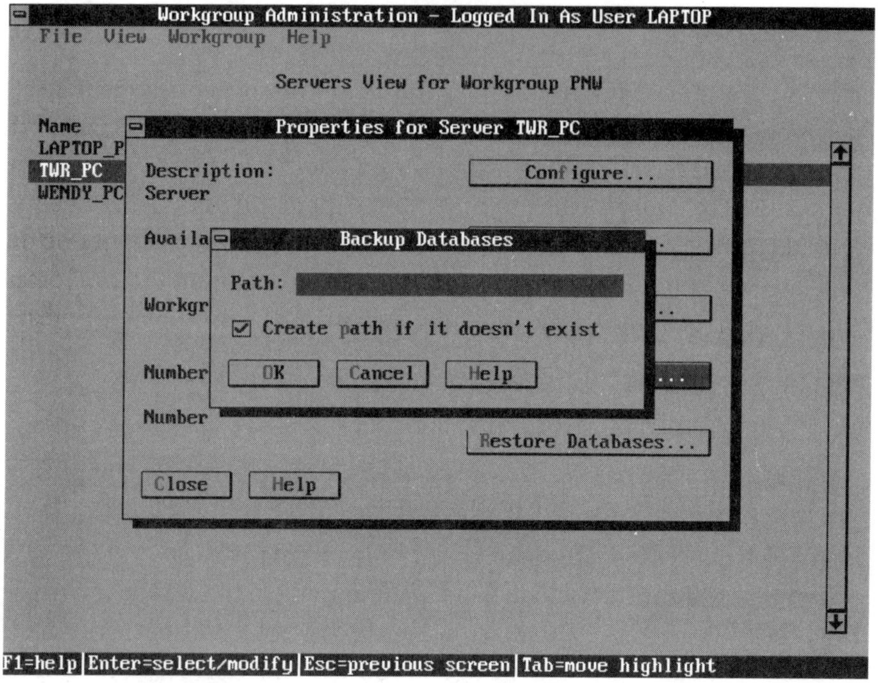

Many people believe that backups are used only when a disk crashes or something equally catastrophic occurs. Network administrators will tell you, however, that 99 percent of restoration operations are done to fix user mistakes on the network. Have you ever deleted the wrong file by accident? Ever formatted drive C: when you meant drive A:? Ever typed DEL *.BAT when you meant *.BAK? Multiply your number of mistakes by dozens more users, and you may start to appreciate the value of a good tape backup system.

While some cheap tape drives don't back up and restore NetWare file attributes and security files from NetWare file servers, that doesn't concern us. Remember, no NetWare file attributes are attached to Personal NetWare files, because these are DOS files being shared. Any tape backup unit that captures DOS files reliably will work, because the workgroup database backup utility we just discussed will take care of the Personal NetWare special files.

Since all DOS tape systems back up DOS drives, a tape machine on your PC will be able to back up all other Personal NetWare servers you are authorized to use. Make sure you have connected and mapped drives to the servers you intend to back up before starting the tape software. In the tape software program where you specify which drive to backup, you should see all the same drive letters listed as when you type NET MAP.

If your tape system software is smart, it will let you pick several drives to back up at one time. Even if it doesn't and you must back up each server separately, the extra work is worth it. Better to back up for an hour than re-create for a month.

One more word about the tapes: get plenty of them. Tapes are cheap and lost data is expensive. Keep a monthly full backup for at least a year, and try to get a tape system that allows you to back up a full server on one tape. It's much easier to find the file you want if you know every file is on the same tape. If you do lots of incremental tape backups, you will look through a dozen tapes before you find the file you want.

Auditing Activities on Your PC with NET CONSOLE

If your PC is being shared with the workgroup, you might be curious to see who is accessing your shared resources. The command that shows this information is

```
NET CONSOLE
```

NET CONSOLE is found in your \NWCLIENT directory, meaning it's in your DOS path, so you can run the command from any DOS prompt. You must have administrator privileges to use this command, but if you're sharing your PC as a server, you probably have those privileges.

Figure 7.21 shows the NET CONSOLE screen. Each connected user gets a separate block. This looks exactly like what NetWare file servers used to show on their console screens, but has a bit more functionality than the old version.

FIGURE 7.21

NET CONSOLE showing three users connected to the LAPTOP_PC server

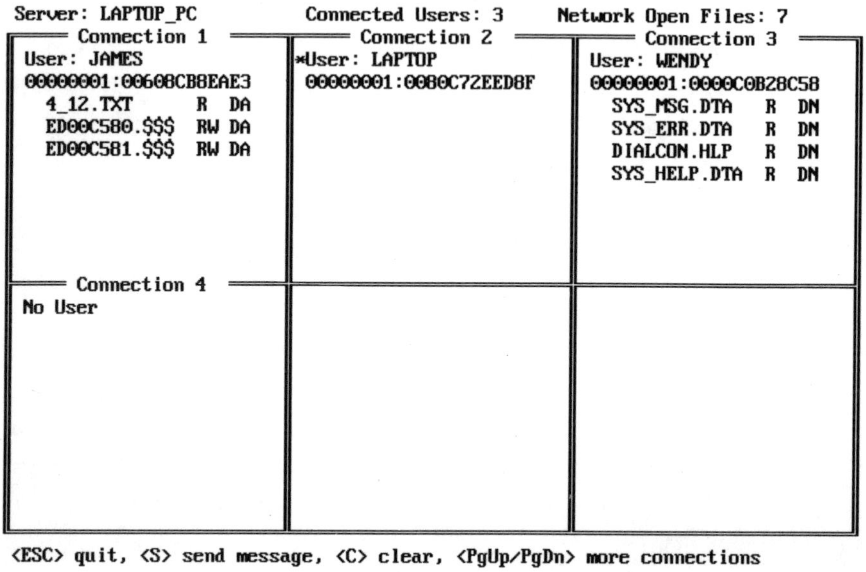

Both James and Wendy are connected to LAPTOP_PC, and both have some files open. The box in the center, LAPTOP, shows the user LAPTOP is logged in as well. The files that LAPTOP is using under DOS or MS Windows don't show up here; only network connections appear.

Two commands at the bottom of the screen are for dealing with users connected to your PC. First is S for Send Message, which broadcasts a message to all users. This is great to use when you need to shut down your PC. Although I prefer you to leave the PC server on and just turn off the monitor when you leave, the LAPTOP_PC has a good reason to shut down: it's going somewhere. So send a message to everyone telling them to clear out.

Yes, you can send the same message from other places in Personal NetWare, but sending it from NET CONSOLE provides an immediate look at those that do or do not disconnect as you ask. That's where C for CLEAR comes in. When you type C, a window opens and asks which connection number you want to clear. Then your server software closes those files that user has open. It does not log out that user, but it gracefully closes the files so no files will get scrambled.

As it says on the status line, use Page Down and Page Up to see more connections than will fit on one screen. You will see a neat screen saver if you leave the NET CONSOLE screen on for more than two minutes. Giant block letters PNW for Personal NetWare are gradually erased by a wandering snake (not a bad snake—it has a smiley face for a head) and rebuilt in another part of the screen. Try it and see. And here are some tricks for playing with that snake: control it with the cursor-movement keys, make it longer and shorter with the plus (+) and minus (–) keys, have it go faster and slower with the Insert and Delete keys, and switch between fill and erase with the P key.

Utilities You Shouldn't Need to Use

As in most computer products, there are more features in Personal NetWare than you will probably need. The three utilities we'll talk about next fit into that category. Unless you're the sole supervisor of the network, you shouldn't need to mess with these. One of them, the SNMP support, is rarely used unless large, expensive network management systems are in place. Another option, diskless PCs, was rarely used when it first became available and has been losing popularity.

The only ones you may need to work with provide support for task-switching programs. These are supplied by Novell to use with a few ill-behaved programs. Let's look at those first.

TASK-SWITCHING CONTROL FILES

A task-switching program allows several programs to be loaded on your computer at one time, but with only one program active at a time. Active, in this case, means the program is actually running and executing. The other programs are still loaded in your computer, but they are stopped. Think of this as a phone with call waiting. One conversation is active; the other conversation is on hold, doing nothing.

Just like you when you're put on call waiting, programs on hold sometimes get mad and hang up. This happens most often with programs that need to keep in contact with the network. When the network can't be reached, the program hangs and stops.

The programs TBMI2.COM and TASKID.COM get around this problem by allocating some data buffers needed to keep network connections alive for programs that aren't active at the moment. They're necessary when using programs that bypass the NetWare DOS Requester client files and write directly to the IPX/SPX protocol. There aren't many of these, luckily, but you may find a few still out there.

The most popular task-switching program is MS Windows running in real or standard mode. If you run MS Windows in enhanced mode, you have nothing to worry about. If you're running MS Windows 3.0, now is a good time to upgrade and avoid these problems. Actually, last year was a good time to upgrade, but it's not too late.

If MS Windows hangs for no apparent reason, try running the TBMI2.COM program before starting MS Windows. If you're running MS Windows 3.0, run the program TASKID.COM for every DOS session you open. Before closing that DOS session window, run the command

```
TASKID /U
```

to unload the TASKID program.

Be aware that MS Windows crashes somewhere between once a week and twice a day for 90 percent of the users out there. Using these files may help, but it may not. The only way to know is to try it.

SUPPORTING SNMP WITH PERSONAL NETWARE

SNMP stands for Simple Network Management Protocol, first cogitated over dinner in March of 1987. By early 1990, it was a recommended Internet protocol and a force in the networking industry. SNMP went from napkin sketches to functional products faster than any other Internet standard.

There are two pieces to the SNMP system: a management station, typically UNIX-driven, to monitor and control all the network devices, and agent software for each network device that responds to the management station. What Personal NetWare provides is that agent software for the PCs on your network.

Because SNMP is used to control devices for large networks, such as routers, bridges, and wiring concentrators, you're not likely to need it in a standard Personal NetWare installation. If SNMP is used in your company, there will be system engineers to help you set things up. A few questions won't make sense during the installation process unless you get some help.

SNMP is easy to install for Personal NetWare stations. Simply run the SETUP program, choose Optimization/Network Management, and check the box for Load SNMP Agent. When the changes are saved, your NET.CFG file is altered to include several new VLM files that provide the SNMP support.

If you have an SNMP management console in use, your Personal NetWare stations will be better managed than any other PC networking clients available from any other manufacturer. A big race is underway to provide management of networked PCs, and Personal NetWare is winning that race.

BOOTING DISKLESS PCS FROM A PERSONAL NETWARE SERVER

PCs without either a floppy or hard disk (diskless PCs; isn't that clever?) have never been popular. They started to appear in the early days of PC networking, the early 1980's. Part of the reason was security. Without a floppy drive, people couldn't copy secret files to a floppy disk and steal them. Part of the reason was expense. Even a floppy drive cost several hundred dollars, and the 10 MB hard disk that appeared in the IBM XT cost close to a thousand dollars. Part of the reason was some people missed the point of a PC. Mainframe computer managers said terminals don't need floppies, why should a PC?

All these reasons are rather lame today. Floppy drives are cheap, hard disks are cheap, and most important, many programs today demand hard disks. MS Windows can't run on a floppy-only PC without a lot of extra work and slow performance. Even run-of-the mill DOS programs expect to find plenty of hard disk megabytes available for installation.

For those that believe diskless PCs are the best deterrent to computer viruses, I must disagree. If only one PC has a floppy drive, or any of the PCs have modems attached, a virus can get into your system. The proper defense is good virus-checking software for PCs and your NetWare file server (if you have one). Don't allow users to bring floppy disks from home and put them into their work PC until they've been checked.

I may also be biased against diskless PCs because every time we used to get things set up right, either the version of DOS or NetWare changed, requiring us to configure everything all over again. Network interface cards have a place to put a PROM (Programmable Read Only Memory, a special chip that stores program information), which controls the diskless boot process. The expense of buying a new boot PROM every time a version changed quickly wiped out the savings earned by not buying a floppy drive.

There are two kinds of boot PROMs now: Old and Enhanced. Here we immediately get into a problem. The Enhanced PROMs don't work with the network packet frame type that's used by the vast majority of NetWare users. How do you tell if you have an Old or Enhanced PROM? Look at the information that came with the PROM. If the documentation doesn't mention being Enhanced, you can assume it's the Old type.

The process for supporting diskless PCs is spelled out in mind-numbing detail in Chapter 12 of the Personal NetWare documentation. This can work, but it's a lot more trouble than getting a floppy drive for each computer.

Life is hard enough without looking for more frustration. Don't start trying to set up a diskless PC without antacids in hand. Better yet, don't start at all.

CHAPTER 8

How Do I Share My PC with My Workgroup?

The time has come: you will share. You've been told this since you were three years old. This is one of the things you learned in kindergarten. Sharing is important in all aspects of life, and your computer is no exception. Besides all these noble things, if you don't share your computer, you'll never get Rose to share her new color printer.

There are many good reasons to share your computer resources with your office mates. The most important reason is that networking your computer systems is the first big step to sharing information. This peer-to-peer network, between your PC and the other PCs belonging to your compadres, can be the pipeline of higher productivity in your office.

Allowing Other Users Access to Resources on Your PC

Although sharing is necessary, it's often somewhat disconcerting at the start. Part of the problem is that many people still believe PC stands for Personal Computer, which it did in the early 1980's. Today, however, that PC on your desk staring back at you with the 14-inch eye becomes part of your company's Information Infrastructure. When you place a network interface card into a PC, it's no longer a personal item.

The rules change when you access other network resources and other people access your computer. Etiquette now becomes important, much like table manners become important when you go from eating alone in front of the television to a formal dinner party. Not only must you become a better guest than you have been in the past, you also must become a better host.

The people you work with are going to start relying on you and your PC. How you treat your PC is now important, because of this increased reliance. When you curse and reboot your computer, you will be inconveniencing people besides yourself. When you forget to add paper to your printer, other people will be delayed. When you skip backing up your data, other people may lose weeks of work.

These are not burdens beyond your capacity to bear; they are just the new facts of life. There will be times when sharing your PC will aggravate you. There will be many more times when it is more efficient. This will be the case more often than not. If networking didn't help, why would your genius managers buy it?

THE KIND OF RESOURCES YOUR PC SHOULD HAVE

Your PC needs more than good intentions to become a workgroup server in your new Personal NetWare network. Technically, it needs a hard disk with 8 MB of open space, 640 KB of RAM, a working network interface card and supporting cabling, DOS of some kind, and the Personal NetWare software. Realistically, it need dozens of megabytes of open hard disk space and as much memory as you can get. If you run MS Windows, the minimum RAM requirement is 2 MB of RAM. That's too little for even a stand-alone MS Windows PC, so figure at least 5 MB of RAM to be a server. More is better.

I'm assuming your PC will continue to be your PC after it's configured as a Personal NetWare server. This is why you need as much memory as possible and plenty of hard disk space. The more RAM available for the NWCACHE program, the higher performance from your PC. Files that are read from NWCACHE demand less from your PC.

Hard disk space is dropping in price, but it's rarely available where it's needed. Sharing available disk space among the workgroup will make life easier for everyone. If some of the workgroup members are working on a joint project, the shared disk space alone will save them enormous time and trouble exchanging information.

You need to seriously consider two important backup tools for your PC now. First, each PC acting as a server should definitely have a battery backup unit or UPS (uninterruptible power supply). This supplies power to your PC when the electricity is disrupted. Individual backup units are down around $100 and are well worth the cost. If your AC power doesn't stop completely but just fluctuates up and down, a UPS will smooth those disruptions so your PC doesn't get seasick. The basic surge suppressor you bought at the office supply store for a plug strip will not provide backup power; replace it with a system that will.

TAPE BACKUP OR CRY

The second item you must get, either for your PC or at least for the workgroup, is a tape backup unit. There is no excuse for not saving your information on a daily basis. As a network consultant, I have seen strong men weep when asked, "Where is your backup tape from yesterday? The network disk is dead." If you believe it's too much trouble to spend two minutes a day setting up your backup tape to run overnight, where are you going to find three weeks to recreate all the data you can lose?

The costs for tape backup units have fallen considerably the last few years. You can get gigabytes (more than 1,000,000,000 bytes), or probably one hundred times your hard disk space, of tape storage for around $3,000. You can get hundreds of megabytes (more than 1,000,000 bytes), or ten times your hard disk, of tape storage for $500 or so. Some computer vendors offer a built-in tape system for an extra few hundred dollars when you buy the PC. Take them up on the offer if no one else in the workgroup has a tape system already. Trust me, nobody backs up a hard disk to floppies more than once a month (usually just once). Tape backups need to be done every day if you want to sleep at night. I always say that if you haven't lost important files, you haven't been playing with computers long.

The most common type of restoration from tape is for a few files erased accidentally. Merrill doesn't pay attention, and types DEL *.* in the wrong directory. Then he comes crying to you, begging for salvation. If you have a tape from last night, Merrill is saved. If there is no tape backup, Merrill becomes another casualty in the corporate wars.

You may believe, as I do, that people should pay a "stupid penalty" when they do something stupid. However, this penalty is out of proportion to the stupid deed. Besides, your project may depend on some of those files Merrill deleted. You certainly don't want to pay a stupid penalty for Merrill's mistake, so get that tape backup system up and running today.

One last word about tape backups: get plenty of backup tapes. I recommend keeping a monthly backup tape for over a year, plus two weeks of daily backups. Rotate your 13 monthly tapes in order, as well as your 12 daily backup tapes. This assumes you can back up everything on a single backup tape, which is the best way to do a backup. And keep those monthly tapes off-site. In a catastrophe, if the server burns up, the box of backup tapes beside it will burn up as well.

Managing Workgroup Servers under MS Windows

All network administration under MS Windows is done with the Personal NetWare program, found in the Personal NetWare group. The NetWare Tools pop-up doesn't contain any facilities for administration. Everything we do in this chapter will be done with the Personal NetWare program unless otherwise noted.

BECOMING A WORKGROUP ADMINISTRATOR

IN-A-HURRY? Grant workgroup administrator rights

8.1 THE FAST LANE

1. Open the Personal NetWare group, then double-click on the Personal NetWare icon.
2. Double-click on the NetWare icon, then on the workgroup icon, then on the user name.
3. Click on Configure.
4. Check the Workgroup Administrator box, then click on OK.

To perform administrative functions, you must either be logged in as SUPERVISOR or have workgroup administrator rights. These rights are given when a user is created, or they can be granted later. As you might guess, workgroup administrator rights can only be granted by another workgroup administrator or by the SUPERVISOR.

To grant these rights through the Personal NetWare program, double-click on the workgroup, then double-click on the user name to bring up the NetWare User Information dialog box. Clicking on the Configure command button displays the Personal NetWare User Account Configuration dialog box. In Figure 8.1, the windows have been arranged to show the route taken to the dialog box. In this dialog box, check the Workgroup Administrator box, as shown in Figure 8.1. Then click on OK. Now that you're an administrator, we can continue.

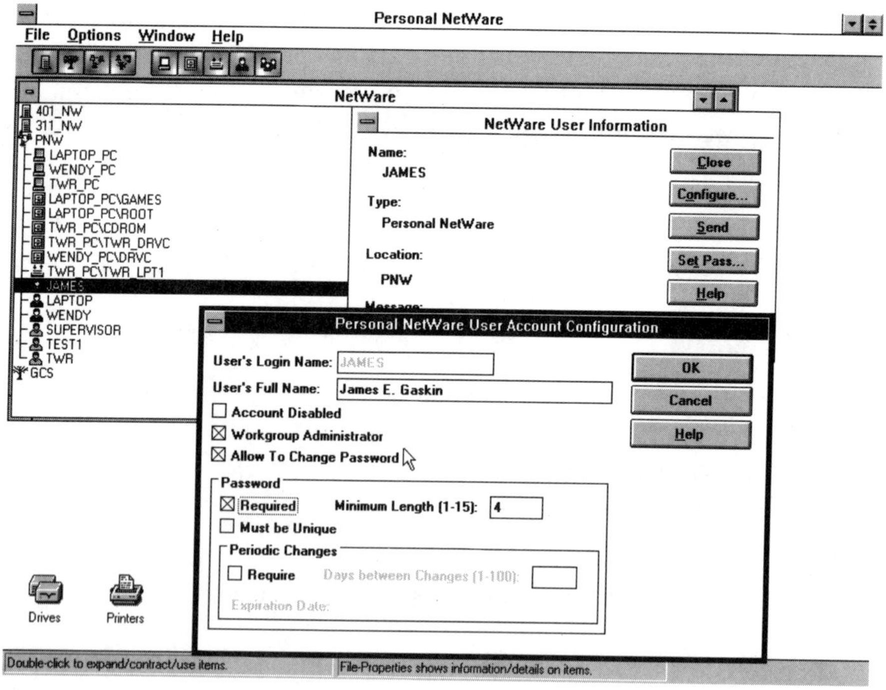

FIGURE 8.1 *The Personal NetWare dialog box for granting administrator authority*

In the world of networking, the SUPERVISOR (or equivalent, such as a workgroup administrator in Personal NetWare) is in complete control of everything. The creation (and deletion) of every network resource is the realm of the administrator.

Some have likened the administrator to God, to illustrate his or her power over the network. However, this is less the Judeo-Christian God of infinite wisdom than a Greco-Roman god. Full of whimsy, cunning, stupidity, and human weaknesses, the gods of mythology are the direct ancestors of network administrators. There is less reliance on a single network administrator with a peer-to-peer network like Personal NetWare, but beware. If the administrator shows up in a toga on a day that's not Halloween, you've been warned.

Any user with workgroup administrator privileges can perform the following operations (this is straight from the Personal NetWare Help screen, so everyone can discover this without working too hard):

- Create workgroups
- Create, modify, and delete user accounts
- Change any user's password (without needing to know the old password)
- Manage any server for which the workgroup administrator rights are set to All (this gives full access to hard disks)
- Synchronize servers in the workgroup (calibrate the times of all servers)
- View, save, and delete workgroup audit and error logs

You can see that a badly trained workgroup administrator is in a position to wreak havoc in a big way. Although training classes are not necessary to become productive with Personal NetWare, it's best to limit your administrators to those people that understand and like PCs in general.

MAKING YOUR PC A WORKGROUP SERVER

8.2 THE FAST LANE

IN-A-HURRY? **Make a PC a workgroup server under MS Windows**

1. Open the Personal NetWare group, then double-click on the Personal NetWare Setup icon.
2. Click on the check box labeled Share this computer's resources.
3. Provide a unique name in the text box.
4. Click on OK.

Your PC can be shared only if you told the Personal NetWare installation program to share the resources of your PC. This is usually done during the initial setup. However, you can make your PC a server anytime by going back into the Personal NetWare Setup program.

The check box to make your PC a server is not hard to find. In fact, it's on the opening screen of the Personal NetWare Setup program. The Novell people want you to share your resources, so they make it easy to do so.

When you click on the check box to share your computer, you must provide a unique name. The server portion of your computer will take the name you provide and add an underscore and *PC* to that name. Figure 8.2 shows this name already filled in (that's why the text is light and hard to see). Click on OK to save the new configuration. You can now configure the Optimization/Network Management options (see Appendix A for more details).

MANAGING WORKGROUP USERS

Here's where you start to feel in control of your workgroup. As administrator, you can create, modify, disable, or delete user accounts in the workgroup. Create, modify, and delete functions are easy to understand. Disable is handy when you want to close access to an account but aren't ready to delete that account. Is a user misbehaving? Disable her account, then wait for her to come complain because she can't log in. Then provide some quick training while you have her captive. When you enable the account again, everything will be the same as it was. Except, perhaps, this user will now behave.

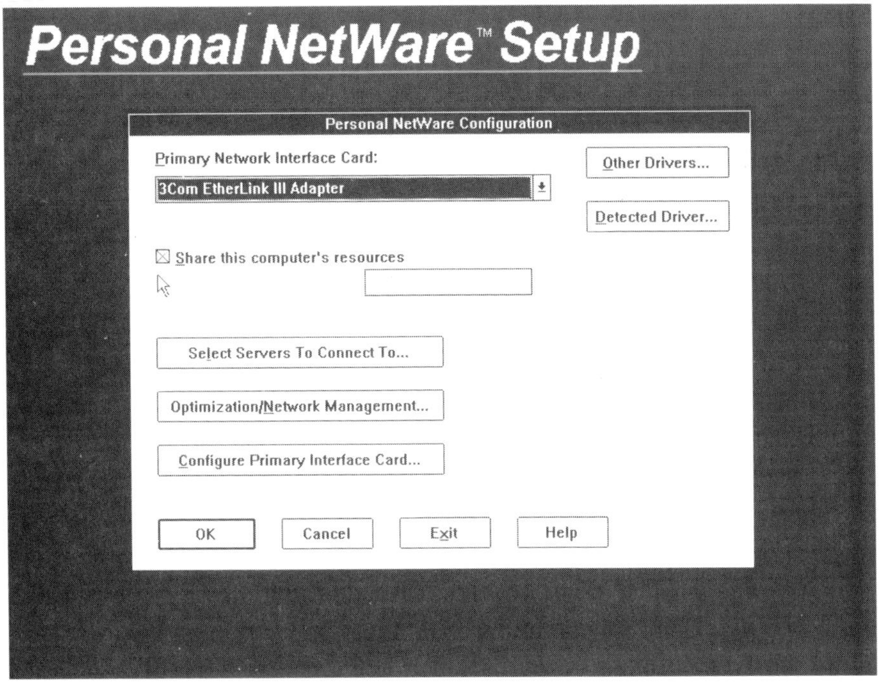

FIGURE 8.2
The initial Personal NetWare Setup screen, with the arrow pointing to the check box that turns your PC into a server

Creating Workgroup User Accounts

IN-A-HURRY? **Create a workgroup user account under MS Windows**

8.3

1 Open the Personal NetWare group, then double-click on the Personal NetWare icon.
2 Double-click on the NetWare icon, then on the workgroup icon.
3 Press the Insert key.
4 Highlight PNW User.
5 Type the user name, then click on OK.
6 Modify Personal NetWare User Account Configuration items as necessary, then click on OK.

Several steps are involved in creating user accounts, but they go quickly. Once you have the Personal NetWare program open and the NetWare view on your screen, it's a snap.

The manual says you must double-click on the workgroup name to display all the current network resources before pressing the Insert key. That's not necessary, although you may want to look at the names you already have so that you don't assign the same name twice.

In the Create New dialog box that appears after you press Insert, choose PNW User, then type the new user's name. After you click on OK, the Personal NetWare User Account Configuration dialog box pops up. In the example in Figure 8.3, we're setting up a new user named David.

The two text boxes at the top of the Personal NetWare User Account Configuration dialog box are for the user's name. In the User's Login Name box, enter the name for this user to provide when he or she logs in to the

FIGURE 8.3

Creating a new user account

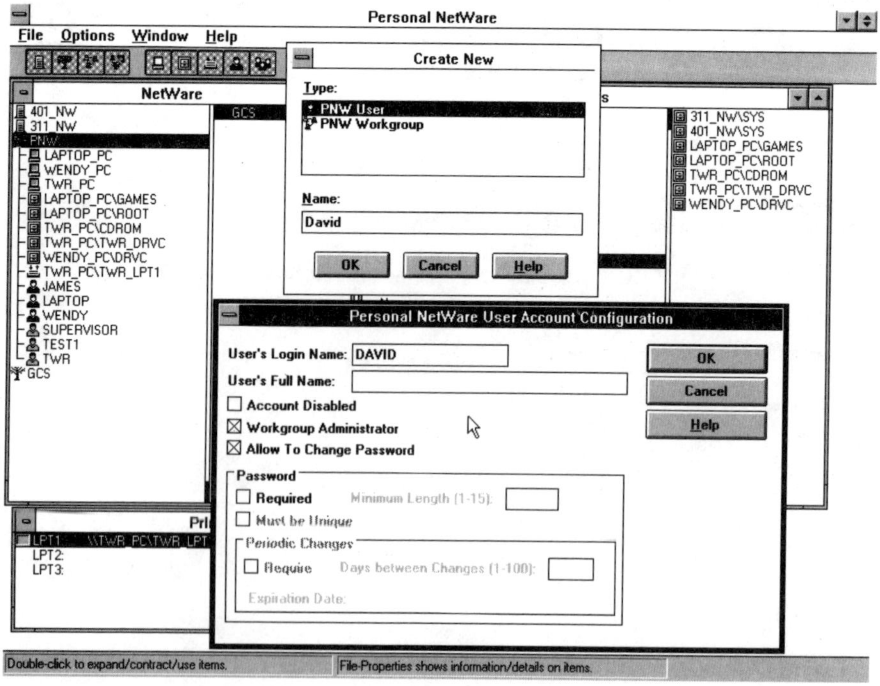

network. If it's the same on all other NetWare 2.*x*, 3.*x*, or 4.*x* servers, one log in will connect all network resources. Fifteen characters are allowed for the login name (although when you create users during initial setup, you can enter only up to ten characters). Then enter the user's full name in the next text box.

The three check boxes beneath the name work as follows:

- **Account Disabled**: Allows the administrator to temporarily disable an account. Checking this box will lock out the user.
- **Workgroup Administrator**: Gives this user workgroup administrator privileges.
- **Allow To Change Password**: Allows the user to change his or her own password at any time. Normally enabled.

Remember the warning about workgroup administrators earlier in the chapter. For most users, I suggest that you remove the check from the box for workgroup administrator. Save that for the people who have a good feel for networking. Owners can control and share their own PC resources without being administrators.

The other user account settings pertain to the user's password. Check the Required box to force this person to use a password for access to the network. Fill in the Minimum Length box to force passwords to be a certain length. The default is four characters. The Must Be Unique check box restricts this person from using one of his or her own previously used passwords. In the Periodic Changes section, check the Require box to force this person to change the password. Then you can set the time between password changes for this user by filling in the Days Between Changes box. Finally, the Expiration Date setting shows the date this password will expire if you chose to require periodic password changes.

You should decide how restrictive your security will be before you set up your network. It's common to have either strict security everywhere, with full passwords requiring regular changes, or a more relaxed attitude. People tend to one extreme or the other, without many in the middle.

If you're going to have strict security, you will fill out everything in the User Account Configuration dialog box. If you're more relaxed and share only printers and information that everyone in the office can use, you may not have any passwords at all. There is no right or wrong to the security question. It all boils down to what makes you comfortable.

Modifying Existing User Accounts

8.4 THE FAST LANE

IN-A-HURRY? Modify a workgroup user account under Windows

1. Open the Personal NetWare group, then double-click on the Personal NetWare icon.
2. Double-click on the NetWare icon, then on the workgroup icon.
3. Select the user whose account you want to modify.
4. Change Personal NetWare User Account Configuration items as necessary, then click on OK.

After a user account is created, you can easily change it, which you should rarely need to do. But when you must, return to the Personal NetWare User Account Configuration dialog box and make your changes there.

You can change the user's name, disable the account, give the user workgroup administrator status, or assign a new password to this user.

Deleting User Accounts

8.5 THE FAST LANE

IN-A-HURRY? Delete a workgroup user account

1. Open the Personal NetWare group, then double-click on the Personal NetWare icon.
2. Double-click on the NetWare icon, then on the workgroup icon.
3. Highlight the user's name, then press Alt-E.
4. Confirm that you want to delete this user.

Deleting a user is almost too simple: highlight the user's name in the list and press Alt-E for Erase. If you prefer using the menus, pull down the File menu, then choose Delete.

You must verify that you want to delete this user before the system will allow you to do so. None of the user's files are erased when the user name itself is deleted.

SHARING YOUR DIRECTORIES

IN-A-HURRY? Share a directory on a workgroup server 8.6

THE FAST LANE

1 Open the Personal NetWare group, then double-click on the Personal NetWare icon.
2 Double-click on the NetWare icon, then on the workgroup icon, then on the icon of the server with the directory to share.
3 Double-click on the drive icon, then on each subsequent directory until the desired directory is displayed.
4 Choose Share from the File menu.
5 Provide a unique name (unique within this server) for the directory, then click on OK.
6 Set the rights for the workgroup users.

Here we get to one of the biggest advantages of Personal NetWare: sharing information on disks scattered around the office. Sharing directories with your workgroup eliminates SneakerNet, which is the earliest form of networking. SneakerNet uses the physical connection medium of feet, as people carry diskettes of files and information from person to person. Those days are gone, at least in your office.

After the Personal NetWare program is open to the NetWare view, you can display all directories on all workgroup servers. This is done by "drilling down" the network, or stepping successively deeper into the directory structure with each double-click. The first double-click on the workgroup name displays all the workgroup servers. A double-click on the server of your choice displays all that server's resources, including hard disk drives. Double-clicking on the drive icon opens a display of the top-level directories on that drive. If one of those will be shared, you're ready to start. If a deeper directory is needed, keep on double-clicking until you reach it. Sorry, but there isn't a hotkey shortcut to display all the various directory levels, as there is in File Manager.

When you reach your directory to be shared, pull down the File menu and choose Share. This brings up a screen similar to Figure 8.4, showing the \HUMOR directory we spoke of in Chapter 6 preparing to get its own shared directory name.

FIGURE 8.4

Starting to share a directory on LAPTOP_PC

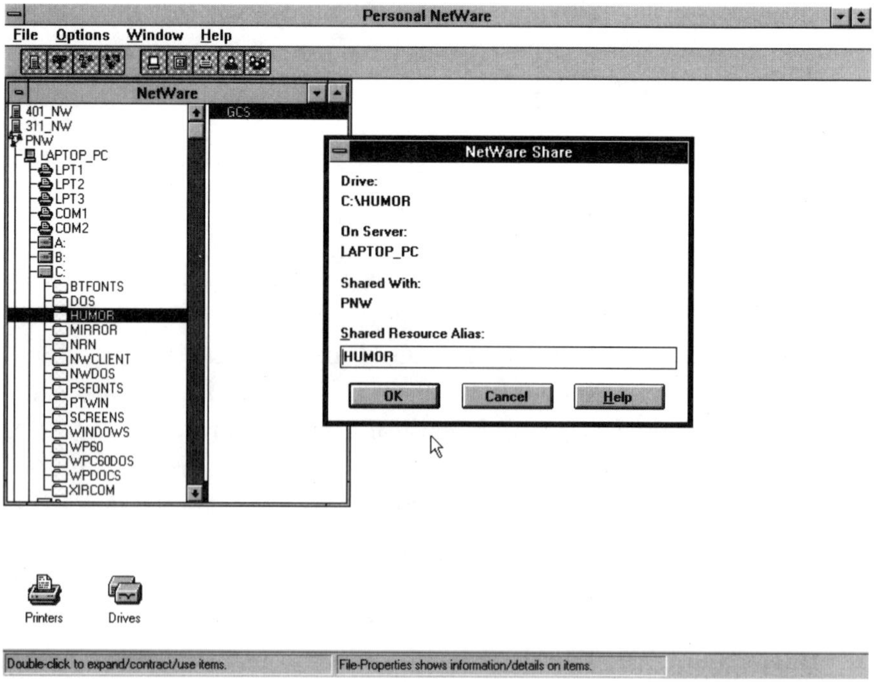

The only place you provide input is the Shared Resource Alias text box at the bottom of the NetWare Share dialog box. The name here need not correlate with the DOS name at all. Personal NetWare guessed I wanted to call this new resource HUMOR, which is a good choice. The DOS drive, server name, and current workgroup are all displayed in the NetWare Share dialog box, and they are determined by your current location and active workgroup.

The name format again allows up to 15 characters (but during initial setup, you can enter only up to 10 characters). No spaces or control characters are allowed. This name must be unique within this server only. When directories become shared resources, they're always listed with the server name. So if you have several PCs with CD ROM drives, you can legally have \\ALEX_PC\CDROM and \\LAURA_PC\CDROM in the same workgroup.

Clicking on the OK button brings up the Personal NetWare Rights dialog box, as shown in Figure 8.5. The important question here is whether to use Default or Explicit rights for the users listed in the Users box on the left side of the window.

Explicit rights grant specific rights to specific users. These may, or may not be, more restrictive than the Default rights granted to either users or administrators. Explicit rights override Default rights. Default rights define the access privileges of all users not specifically listed with Explicit rights.

Here in Figure 8.5, Personal NetWare offers to give everyone (the <Default> group) the Explicit rights level of All. This means everyone can read and write all files in the shared directory. This also means they can add new files and delete new or existing files as well. Everyone has the same level of access to this shared workgroup drive as you have to your own hard disk.

The new shared directory resource will become available to the workgroup within a few seconds. The PC where the workgroup administration is being performed will update all the other servers, and clients will have access to the new resources.

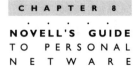

FIGURE 8.5

Assigning rights to the newly shared directory

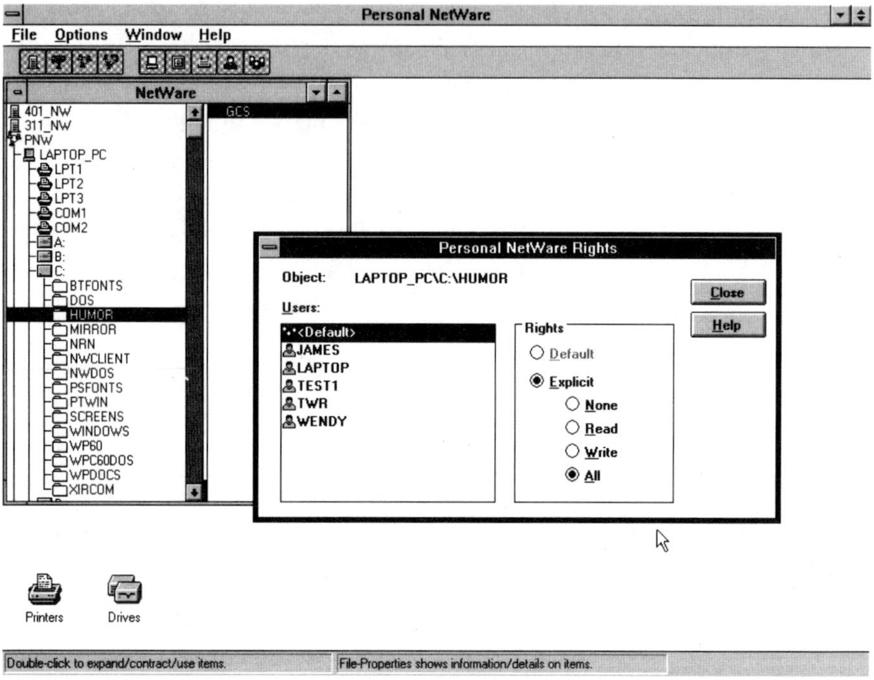

It's common practice to have some directories listed as read-only, but rare to have directories listed as write-only. Write-only means that users can create new files and write to existing ones, but can't read or execute those existing files. In fact, they can't even scan the directory and see which files are there. That's why write-only is not used often.

Rights flow down the directory hill. If \HUMOR had subdirectories \HUMOR\CLEAN and \HUMOR\DIRTY, users would have the same access rights to both directories as they had to \HUMOR. If you wanted to make \HUMOR\DIRTY a private directory, you would need to list it as a shared directory itself, separate from \HUMOR, with its own separate rights profile. This would block the downhill rights, and you could restrict access to \HUMOR\DIRTY in a different way. Or you could avoid potential trouble and keep your dirty jokes at home.

REMOVING SHARED DIRECTORIES

IN-A-HURRY? Delete a shared directory 8.7

THE FAST LANE

1. Open the Personal NetWare group, then double-click on the Personal NetWare icon.
2. Double-click on the NetWare icon, then on the workgroup icon.
3. Highlight the directory you no longer want to share, then press Alt-E.
4. Confirm the deletion.

The two previous figures show the screens used to both set up new shared directories. Any changes made in these screens will take effect immediately, although users logged in when the changes are made won't see a difference until they log in again. Deleting a shared directory is slightly different.

Let's pretend I decided sharing \HUMOR was a bad idea, because people spent too much time writing jokes and not enough time working. After I highlighted the \HUMOR directory and pressed Alt-E (I could have selected Delete from the File menu for the same result), I see the warning

```
Are you sure you want to delete the selected object?
```

Please note, clicking on OK *does not* delete the directory. It just removes the directory from the list of shared resources.

To modify a shared directory, first delete that directory. Then start over and share it again with your modifications.

SHARING YOUR PRINTER

IN-A-HURRY? Share a printer on a workgroup server 8.8

THE FAST LANE

1. Open the Personal NetWare group, then double-click on the Personal NetWare icon.
2. Double-click on the NetWare icon, then on the workgroup icon, then on the icon of the server with the printer to share.

3. Highlight the port where the printer is connected, then double-click on that port.
4. Provide a name, unique to that server, for the printer, then click on OK.
5. Change the rights profile for this printer as necessary, then click on Close.

Setting up shared printers is remarkably similar to setting up shared directories. You'll see that this consistency continues throughout Personal NetWare. If you understand how to share directories, you can probably set up a shared printer now without my help, but I'll explain it all just for good measure.

From the NetWare view in the Personal NetWare program, display the workgroup servers and all other resources by double-clicking on the workgroup icon. Choose the server that has the printer to share by double-clicking on the server name. You'll see the shareable resources of that server, which will consist of disk drives and printer ports. Choose the printer port where the printer is attached (LPT1, 99 percent of the time) and double-click there, or select Share from the File menu. Figure 8.6 shows the NetWare Share dialog box that pops up.

Doesn't this screen look amazingly similar to Figure 8.4, where a directory was shared? Printers, however, usually get more descriptive names than directories. The most common names are the printer type (such as Laser, LaserIIP, Dotmatrix, or Color). Although the use of forms is not popular, those companies that do have forms loaded often name the printer after the form (such as Invoices, Labels, or Envelopes). The 15-character name length restriction is still in effect. The name must be unique within the server, not the workgroup.

When you click on OK in the NetWare Share dialog box, the Personal NetWare Rights dialog box (Figure 8.5) appears again. Most networks provide all users access to all printers with few exceptions. There are problems with this occasionally, but not serious problems. Printers get confused when a user sends a print job to the wrong printer and the print control codes are not correct. This happens quite a bit where PostScript and non-PostScript printers are in use. The owner of the afflicted printer will need to reset the printer before it can be used again.

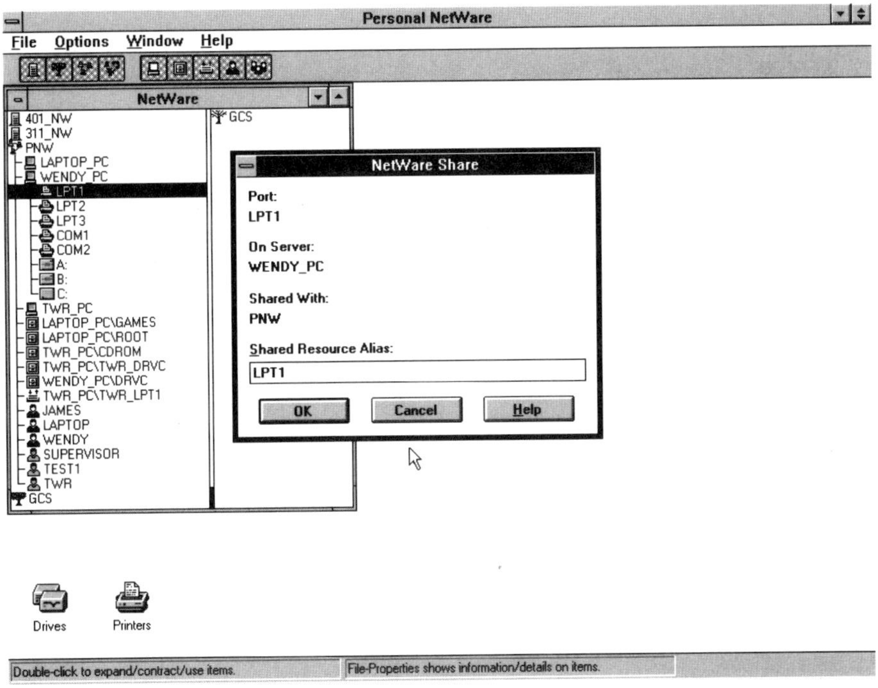

FIGURE 8.6

Naming your shared printer

After you set up a printer to be shared, you can optionally configure the print queue. Highlight the new shared printer name and press Alt-Enter to see the Print Queue Configuration dialog box, shown in Figure 8.7.

The dialog box settings work as follows:

Startup form name	If form types are used, the default form name is listed here. This box is blank if no forms are defined. (The Forms button opens the dialog box where forms are specified.)
Characters/ second	Specifies the maximum rate characters are sent to the printer. The number shown is the default and works well for parallel printers.

FIGURE 8.7

Controlling the print queue for a shared printer

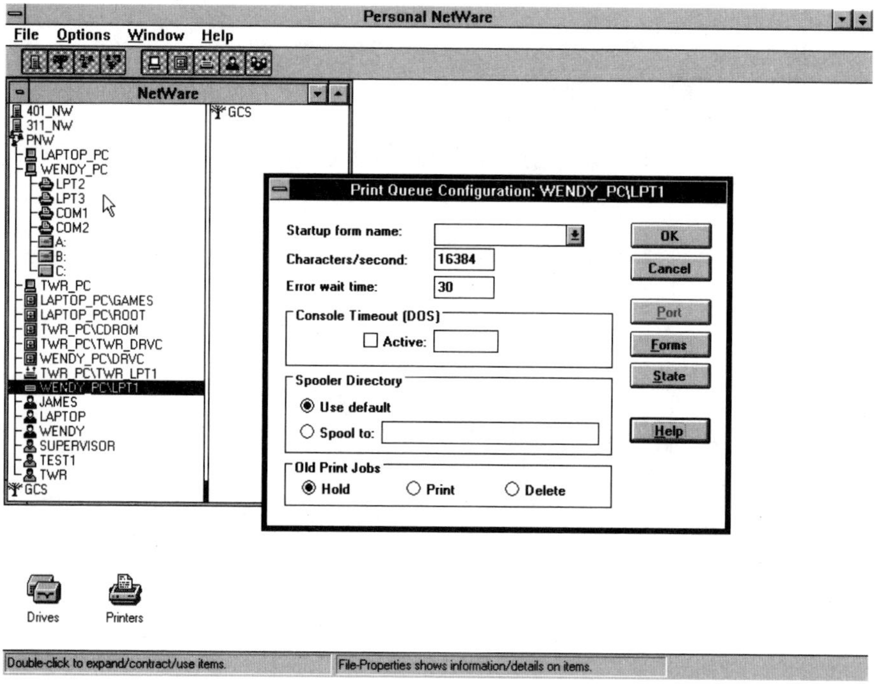

Error wait time	Specifies how long the server will wait for a nonfunctioning printer before alerting the server with an error message.
Console Timeout (DOS)	Specifies how long the error message should be displayed on the server screen. No number means forever.

Spooler Directory	Specifies where print output is written to disk before being sent to the printer. The default is \NWCNTL\SLPT1 for LPT1. Make sure the server disk has plenty of room to accept print job spooled output. If the output can't be written to disk, the server may crash. For the best printer performance with the least server impact, name a VDISK as your spooler directory.
Old Print Jobs	Specifies what to do with print jobs still in the spool queue from a previous session when the server starts again. You can choose to hold them, print them, or delete them.

Unless you have a strange printer, the default values will work fine. That's why this configuration is optional. If you don't change a thing here, all the defaults will be in effect from the minute you define the shared printer.

In Figure 8.7, notice the port connections where the arrow cursor is pointing. Since LPT1 is now shared, it no longer appears as an available shared resource on the server display.

If you share your printer on your PC, you can't address it directly. You must connect your LPT1 port to the printer queue through the network. If you try to print directly to the printer port rather than through Personal NetWare, your print output will seep into another dimension, never to be seen again. To avoid this, immediately connect your LPT1 port to the print queue and save your new configuration.

REMOVING SHARED PRINTERS

IN-A-HURRY? Delete a shared printer

8.9

THE FAST LANE

1. Open the Personal NetWare group, then double-click on the Personal NetWare icon.
2. Double-click on the NetWare icon, then on the workgroup icon.

3 Highlight the printer you no longer want to share, then press Alt-E.
4 Confirm the deletion.

Deleting a shared printer works the same way as deleting a shared directory. To delete (unshare) a printer, highlight the printer name and press Alt-E, or choose Delete from the File menu. Verify that you want to delete the shared object (delete the fact that it's shared, not the object itself). Then go back to being greedy with your personal, nonshared printer.

Be prepared to hear from the users that have been relying on that printer. When one of your co-workers logs in and tries to connect to that printer, especially if that connection is in the user's PNWLOGIN.SCR, that user will get an error message. You will then get a call.

BACKING UP AND RESTORING WORKGROUP-RELATED DATA

All the information we've been creating while sharing printers and directories is replicated (copied) around the network to all servers. But in case of disaster, a tape backup program won't get the information properly, so you won't be able to restore the information from the tape.

Personal NetWare provides special utilities provided for this backup and restore job. Unfortunately, these are not available under MS Windows with this version of the program. Refer to the section about backing up workgroup data under DOS, later in the chapter, for details.

Advanced Personal NetWare Administration under MS Windows

Network administration is not about managing your network as much as it is about managing changes to your network. If nothing in your network changes, there's no reason to do any administration.

For this reason, 80 percent of your network administration will be concerned with the 20 percent of the network commands we've discussed. Personal NetWare is built to share computer resources among a workgroup, and that's been covered. You can now set up user accounts and share hard disk directories and printers.

But that last bit of network administration does become important at times. For those occasions, you can use the more advanced administration functions in the Personal NetWare program.

FINE-TUNING WORKGROUP SERVERS

Personal NetWare servers have three standard levels of performance: minimum memory, maximum performance, and balanced. These levels are set in the NET ADMIN program under DOS, as described later in this chapter.

Within those three levels, however, there is room for fine-tuning, although this is rarely necessary. The indications that you need to fine-tune a server and the changes to make are as follows:

SYMPTOM	ACTION
Server response slows down	Increase the size and number of receive buffers.
Error messages indicating files cannot be opened	Increase directory buffers, increase the FILES statement in CONFIG.SYS.
Shared directories or printers are suddenly unavailable	Check the maximum number of connections and increase them if necessary.

Set the number of receive buffers to the number of concurrent connections plus two. It's not necessary to have more than 12 receive buffers. Set the size of the receive buffers at 4096 for Token Ring and 1432 for Ethernet to allow maximum packet performance on the network.

Don't change these settings until the network has been up and running for several weeks. In fact, don't be in a hurry to change these settings unless something goes downhill in a big way. It takes time to know how your network runs normally, so it follows that it takes time to know when it's running abnormally. That's why it's a good idea to turn on the network diagnostics now and then to have some basis of comparison. See Chapter 7 for details on running network diagnostics.

All the server configuration is done through the Personal NetWare program, the same one we've been using this whole chapter. To make changes, you must be logged in to the workgroup and be a workgroup administrator.

After opening the Personal NetWare program to the NetWare view, double-click on the name of the workgroup to display all the available resources. Pick the server you want to configure by highlighting its name, then press Alt-Enter to show its properties, or pull down the File menu and choose Properties. You'll see the Personal NetWare Server Information dialog box, shown in Figure 8.8 (in the figure, I've moved the dialog box so that it doesn't block the workgroup listing).

Since just about all the serious configuration happens here, let's go down the list and explain what everything is.

Server Name	The server name provided during server setup
Description	The description provided during server setup
Status	The location (Local or Remote) and operational status (Up or Down)
Workgroup	The server's current workgroup
Connected Users	List of users currently connected to this server

The command buttons in this dialog box work as follows:

Disconnect User	Disconnects the selected user and closes all files that user has open on this server
Open Files	Displays the names of all open files for the selected user

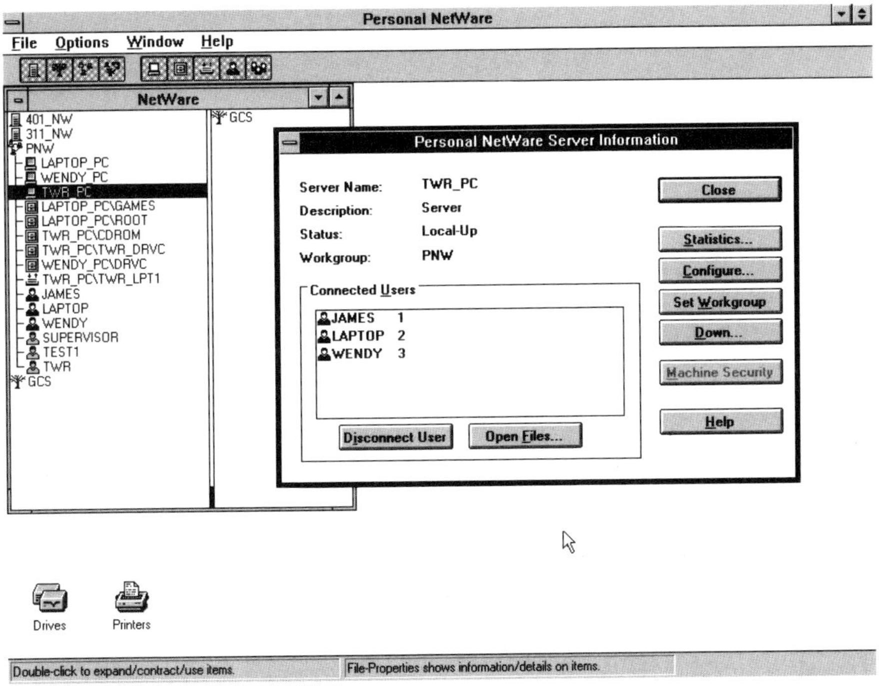

FIGURE 8.8

The Personal NetWare Server Information dialog box

Close	Saves the settings and closes the dialog box
Statistics	Displays the Personal NetWare Server Statistics screen
Configure	Displays the Personal NetWare Server Configuration screen
Set Work-group	Displays the Change Workgroup dialog box
Down	Closes all files, disconnects all users, and stops the SERVER.EXE program
Help	Displays a comprehensive, MS Windows-format Help screen

The server's name and description can't be changed from the Personal NetWare Server Information dialog box. You can disconnect users, but you can't change user information from here. What you can do is click on the command buttons to see and change server configuration details. Let's take the screens you can get to from this dialog box in order.

VIEWING SERVER STATISTICS

Click on the Statistics button in the Personal NetWare Server Information dialog box to see the Personal NetWare Server Statistics screen, which shows details of the current server. You can see details for both local and remote servers. In fact, all server operations except setting the workgroup and changing the owner can be performed remotely. Figure 8.9 shows an example of a Statistics screen.

FIGURE 8.9

The statistics for TWR_PC

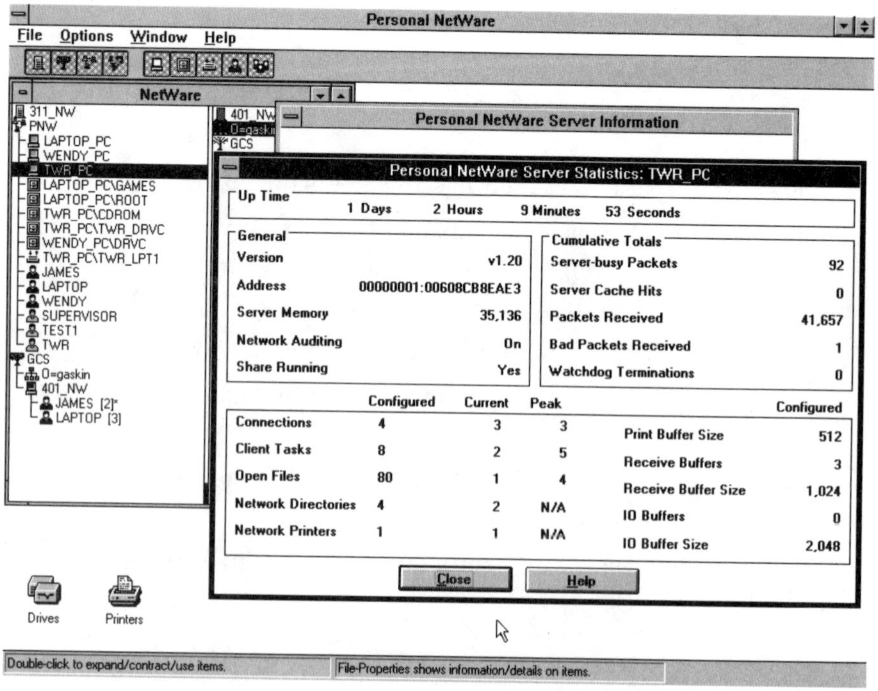

You can't change any of these values from this screen. Many of the settings can be adjusted from the Configuration screen, which is described in the next section. The rest are set during the initial setup of the server.

The Personal NetWare Server Statistics screen shows the following information:

Up Time	How long SERVER.EXE has been loaded.
Version	Current version of SERVER.EXE.
Address	Network address of the server PC, in the format *NETWORK:PC ADDRESS*.
Server Memory	Amount of memory SERVER.EXE is using. You can change this through the Configuration screen.
Network Auditing	Whether the auditing function is on or off.
Share Running	Whether DOS SHARE.EXE is loaded.
Server-busy Packets	Number of packets rejected because of server load.
Server Cache Hits	Percentage of server cache hits since SERVER.EXE was loaded (not the same as NWCACHE hits, which are shown by the NWCACHE /S command). IO buffers must be enabled to have the server cache.
Packets Received	Total number of packets received by this PC since SERVER.EXE was loaded.
Bad Packets Received	Total number of bad packets received since SERVER.EXE was loaded.
Watchdog Terminations	Number of client sessions disconnected for inactivity since SERVER.EXE was loaded.
Connections	Configured, current, and peak number of client connections since SERVER.EXE was loaded.

Client Tasks	Configured, current, and peak number of client tasks on this server since SERVER.EXE was loaded.
Open Files	Configured, current, and peak number of open files since SERVER.EXE was loaded.
Network Directories	Configured and current number of directories on this server defined as shared directories for use by workgroup clients.
Network Printers	Configured and current number of printers supported by this PC acting as a server.
Print Buffer Size	Size of the print buffer in kilobytes. You can change this through the Configuration screen.
Receive Buffers	Number of receive buffers. You can change this through the Configuration screen.
Receive Buffer Size	Size of each receive buffer in bytes. You can change this through the Configuration screen.
IO Buffers	Number of cache buffers. You can change this through the Configuration screen.
IO Buffer Size	Size of each cache buffers in bytes. You can change this through the Configuration screen.

It's a good idea to check this statistics display now and then, but not to leave it on your screen. Much of this information, along with traffic statistics that are more helpful, are available in one of the diagnostics programs (see Chapter 7).

VIEWING AND CHANGING SERVER CONFIGURATION

8.10

THE FAST LANE

IN-A-HURRY? Change workgroup server information

1. Open the Personal NetWare group and double-click on the Personal NetWare icon.
2. Double-click on the NetWare icon, then on the workgroup icon.

3 Highlight the name of the server, then press Alt-Enter.

4 Click on Configure.

5 Make changes as necessary, then click on OK.

We've been promising, and now we're here: the Personal NetWare Server Configuration screen. Click on the Configure button in the Personal NetWare Server Information dialog box to bring up this screen. Again, just because this gets a lot of pages to explain doesn't mean it's something you need to deal with often. It's quite likely you'll never need to adjust any of these values. Changing these should be a last resort, not the first thing to try.

Figure 8.10 shows the Configuration screen (again moved around so you can see parts of the earlier screens). Everything in text boxes can be changed by clicking on the box and typing a new entry. Everything, that is, except the

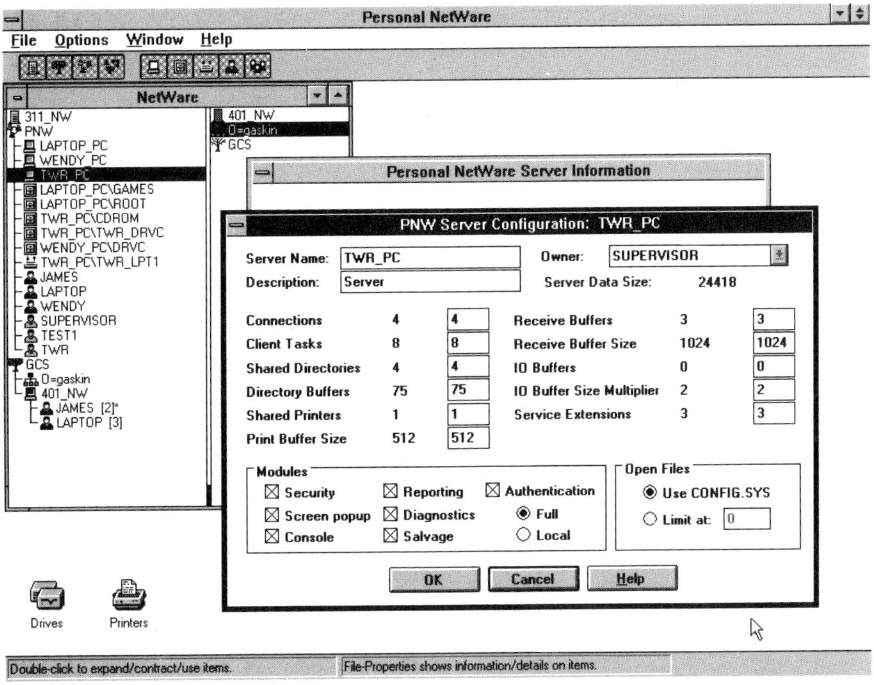

FIGURE 8.10

The Personal NetWare Server Configuration screen

owner unless you're logged in as that same person. During initial setup, the SUPERVISOR is the only one active, so the first workgroup server is always owned by SUPERVISOR. If I wanted to change that, I would need to log in as SUPERVISOR rather than JAMES.

The similar screen in NET ADMIN has more detail than the MS Windows version. That screen contains not only all the settings with their current values, as does this Configuration screen, but also the maximum and minimum values for each function.

But that's in a later section, so look at Figure 8.10 as we go over its contents:

Server Name	Changes to the server name or description will be in effect when the server is rebooted.
Description	Changes will show after the server is rebooted.
Owner	Can only be changed by the owner. Choose a user account name from the list box.
Server Data Size	Server's data segment, which is the amount of RAM used for servicing client requests.
Connections	Number of client connections configured.
Client Tasks	Number of client tasks that can run concurrently on the server.
Shared Directories	Number of server PC directories this server is configured to share as Personal NetWare volumes.
Directory Buffers	Amount of space used to store information for directory calls from clients.
Shared Printers	Number of printers this server is configured to share.
Print Buffer Size	Amount of memory used to service print jobs.
Receive Buffers	Number of receive buffers for sending and receiving client requests and information.
Receive Buffer Size	Number of bytes in each receive buffer.

IO Buffers	Amount of buffers used to send and receive data. With an external cache such as NWCACHE, keep this number low.
IO Buffer Size Multiplier	Number of buffers configured. Multiple it by the number of IO buffers to get the total buffer size.
Service Extensions	Number of slots available for custom programs written to use special features of the server.
Open Files	Number of open files allowed. This can be changed here or in CONFIG.SYS. If more than 255 open files are needed, that number must be set here, not in CONFIG.SYS.
Modules	Pieces of SERVER.EXE code that can be adjusted. See the section about fine-tuning your server's loadable modules, at the end of this chapter, for details.

Keep in mind, you don't want to play with these settings. If you do plan to make changes, it's important to copy down all the original numbers before starting. Change only one item at a time, and thoroughly check the results before getting frustrated and trashing everything in a fury. From experience, I can tell you that getting mad and changing several things at once guarantees a long night and much head scratching as you try to put things back the way they were. If you need to save memory on a particular server, see the section about advanced settings, later in this chapter, for suggestions on adjusting these values.

CHANGING YOUR SERVER'S WORKGROUP

If you have more than one workgroup, you may want to change the one your server belongs to. Click on the Set Workgroup button in the Personal NetWare Server Information dialog box to see the dialog box for changing the workgroup. This dialog box allows you to move your server from your current workgroup to another workgroup that has at least one active server.

There's no reason to have multiple local workgroups unless you're getting close to 50 people in your current workgroup (240 is the technical limit, but that's too many). But if your boss feels better with multiple workgroups for security or management reasons, there's nothing to limit the number of workgroups. One server can only support 50 concurrent users. If your workgroup gets close to this limit, it's getting too big.

Figure 8.11 shows the Change Workgroup dialog box, although it's a little dull with just one group. I personally prefer a single workgroup and suggest you stay with one as long as possible. If you have two, people will get lost between the two groups and ask you irritating questions at inconvenient times.

FIGURE 8.11

The Change Workgroup dialog box

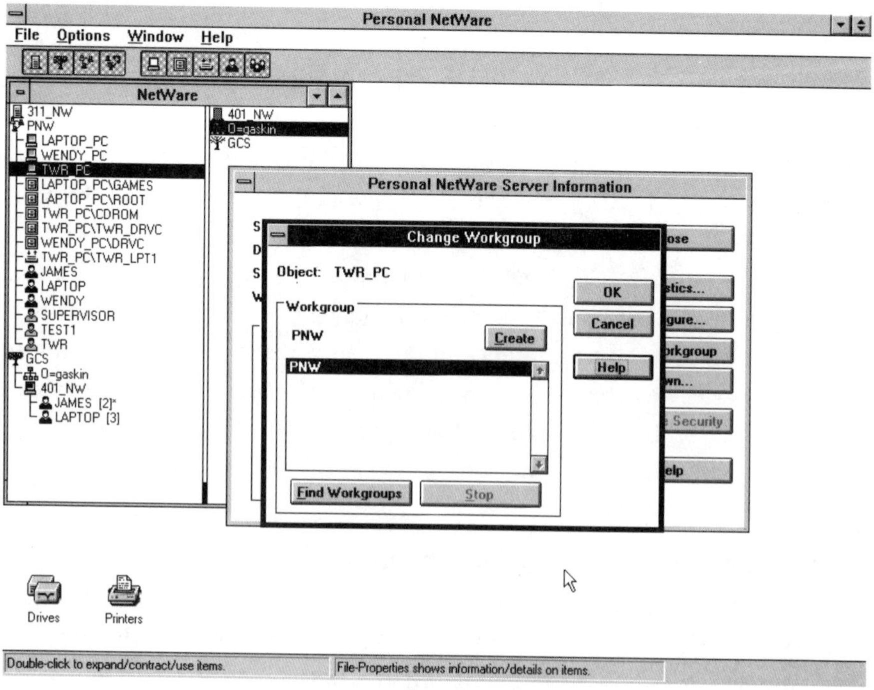

Another way you can change workgroups is through workgroup properties. Highlight the workgroup name from the NetWare view in the Personal NetWare program, then press Alt-Enter to display the properties. One of the options is to change the workgroup. If you click on Change, you'll see the same dialog box as the one that appears when you click on the Set Workgroup button in the Server Information dialog box.

DOWNING THE SERVER

"Downing" the server from the Personal NetWare Server Information dialog box is different from disconnecting a server from the main Personal NetWare screen. If you highlight a server name and pull down the File menu, you'll see a Disconnect option. When you choose that option, your client PC will be disconnected from that server. Any resources you shared from that server will no longer be available.

Downing is much more serious. This turns the server off, and any clients that are using the resources of that server are out of luck. They will most likely lose some data when the server goes down in this way.

Figure 8.12 shows the warning box that appears when you click on the Down button in the Server Information dialog box. Make sure you really, really know what you're doing before clicking on OK.

Managing the Workgroup as a Whole under MS Windows

Everything in this chapter so far has centered around a single server at a time. To get information about the entire workgroup through the Personal NetWare program, highlight the workgroup name, then press Alt-Enter. You'll see the Workgroup Connection Information dialog box shown in Figure 8.13. Each option in this dialog box shows information about all the workgroup clients and servers.

FIGURE 8.12

Are you sure you want to pull the plug?

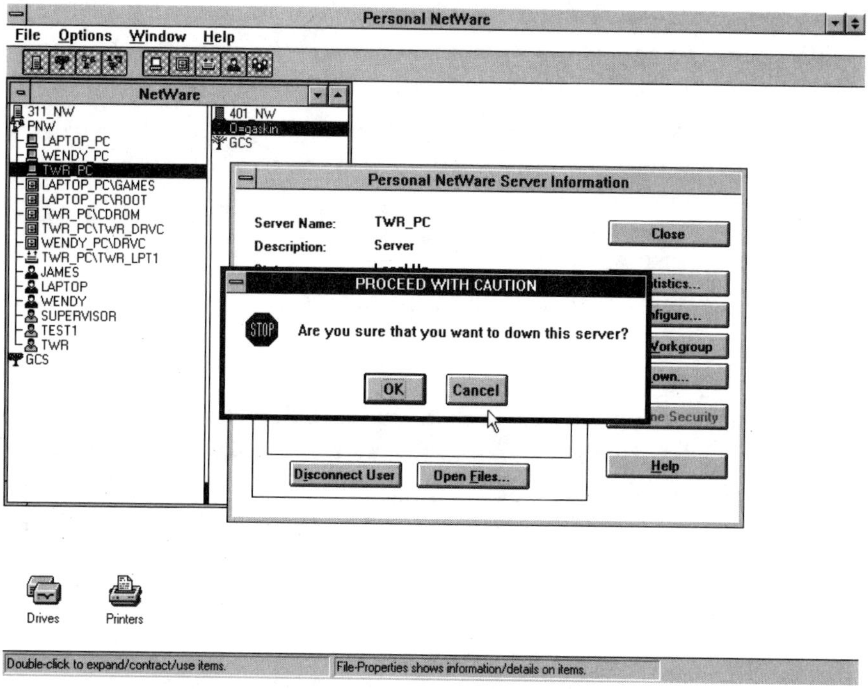

REVIEWING THE AUDIT OR ERROR LOG

8.11

IN-A-HURRY? Display the audit or error log

1. Open the Personal NetWare group, then double-click on the Personal NetWare icon.
2. Highlight the workgroup name, then press Alt-Enter.
3. Click on the Audit Log button or the Error Log button.

The audit log shows which servers started and stopped and which users logged in and out. Click on the Audit Log command button in the Workgroup Connection Information dialog box to see this log. The file can be saved as an ASCII file for manipulation in other report writers and the like. The audit log doesn't show a lot of information, but it does provide some

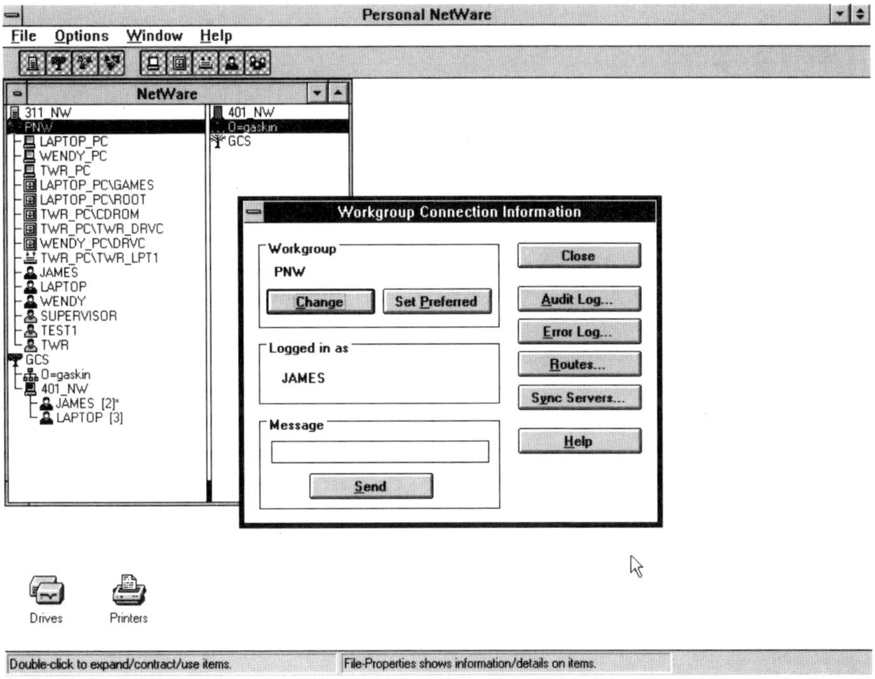

FIGURE 8.13

The Workgroup Connection Information dialog box

detail about user activity and server stability. Figure 8.14 shows the audit log for my little workgroup.

Since servers should stay turned on, scan the audit log now and then to make sure users aren't stopping their servers every night. If you take the offending user a printout from the log showing that server up and down like a Yo-Yo, you have a better chance of getting some cooperation.

Separate from the audit log, the error log cares little about servers going up and down. The only items tracked here are errors. Click on the Error Log button in the Workgroup Connection Information dialog box to display this log. As you can see from Figure 8.15, printing to a disconnected server causes network errors.

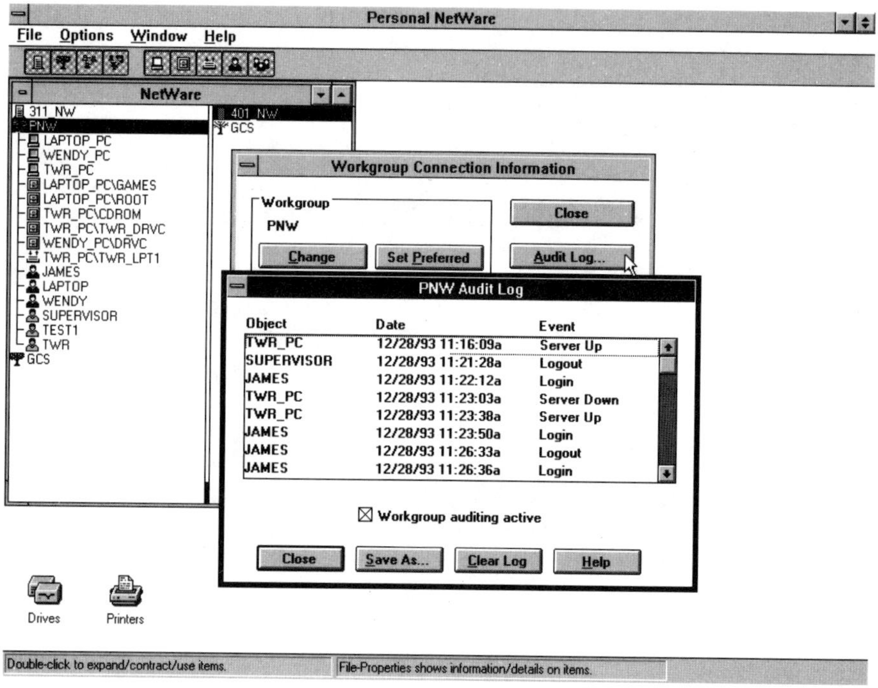

FIGURE 8.14

The type of detail provided by the audit log

Like the audit log, the error log can be saved and manipulated separately. If one station generates most of the errors, check that station over carefully. There is probably a configuration error somewhere, or a user that needs some extra training.

MANAGING ROUTES

If you have a single workgroup and a single network, route management won't mean anything to you. Routes are the highways you define to connect with other workgroup servers. The format is *NETWORK ADDRESS:MACHINE ADDRESS*. Your primary route is created for you during installation.

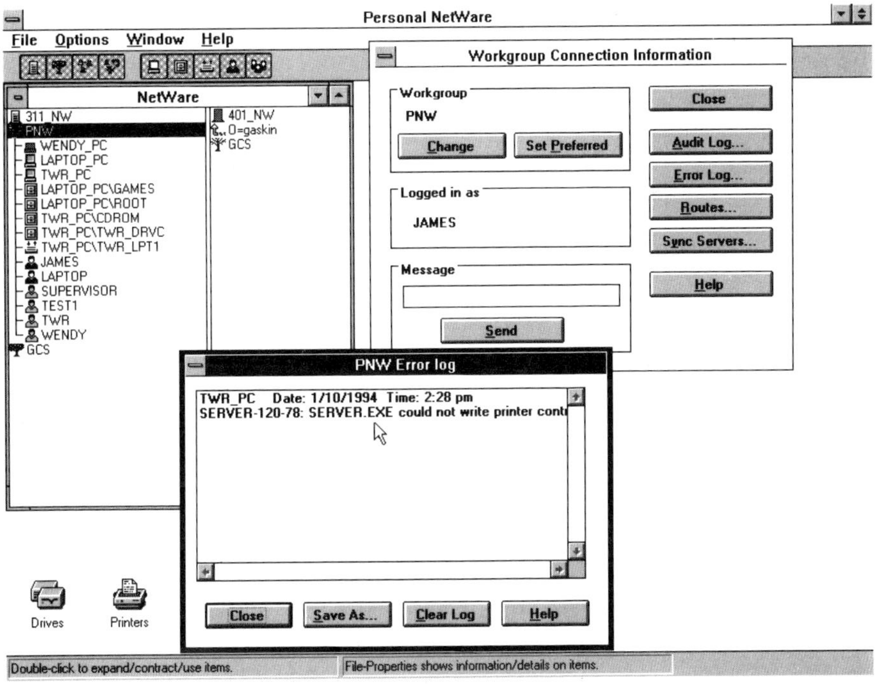

FIGURE 8.15

The result of shutting down the server with a print job pending

Take a look at Figure 8.16 for a display of routes. This dialog box appears when you click on the Routes button in the Workgroup Connections Information dialog box.

SYNCHRONIZING WORKGROUP TIME

Does anybody really know what time it is? If you have applications that care about time, the Sync Servers command button in the Workgroup Connection Information dialog box will help. With one quick command, all servers will synchronize their clocks, just like in spy movies. Figure 8.17 shows this about to happen.

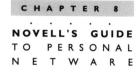

FIGURE 8.16

The Configure Workgroup Routes dialog box

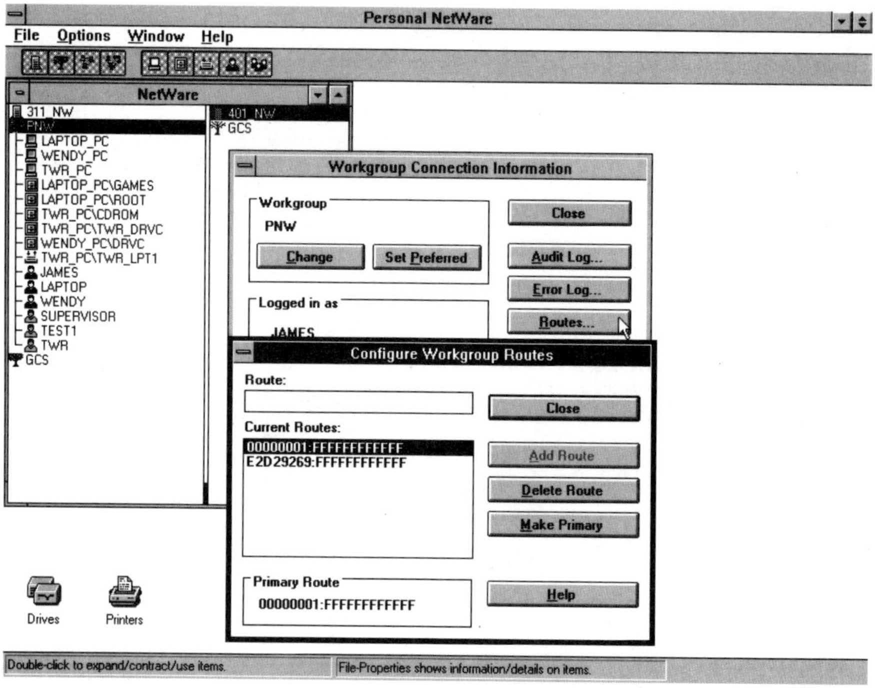

Managing Workgroup Servers under DOS

Personal NetWare is built to run on all computers, from original PCs with a maximum of 640 KB on up to the largest machine that can run MS Windows. This is in contrast to some of the peer-to-peer networks available today. Because of this coverage, Novell has gone to the time and expense to recreate every bit of the management control under DOS as well as under MS Windows. In fact, a few functions are available only under DOS.

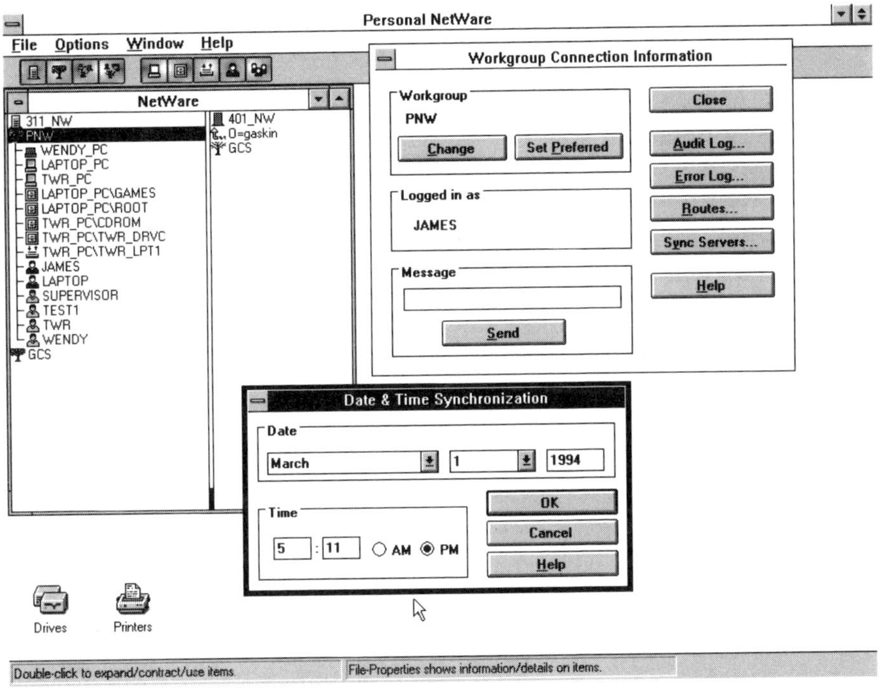

FIGURE 8.17

Synchronizing all workgroup servers' clocks

SETTING UP A WORKGROUP ADMINISTRATOR

IN-A-HURRY? Grant workgroup administrator rights under DOS

8.12

THE FAST LANE

1. Log in to the workgroup as SUPERVISOR or as someone with administrator privileges.
2. Type **NET ADMIN** from the DOS prompt.
3. Press Alt-U to display the Users View screen.
4. Highlight the user, then press Enter.
5. Check the box for Workgroup Administrator.
6. Press Alt-O to save and exit.

All the reasons to control who has administrator privileges discussed in the MS Windows section at the beginning of this chapter are still valid under DOS. The administrator has the same rights under DOS and under MS Windows.

Everything that we'll do in this and the following sections assumes you have logged in to the workgroup as either SUPERVISOR or a user with administrator privileges. There is no need to physically sit at the server you plan to configure, since NET ADMIN will perform all functions across the network to remote servers. In fact, notice in Figure 8.18 that I'm logged into the LAPTOP_PC as user LAPTOP while I'm configuring user JAMES on TWR_PC. This stuff saves shoe leather in a big way. It's not as fun as teleporting, but it's better than schlepping up and down stairs all day.

After typing NET ADMIN from any DOS prompt (the NET program is in the \NWCLIENT directory that was placed in your PATH statement by

FIGURE 8.18

The NET ADMIN screen for granting administrator privileges

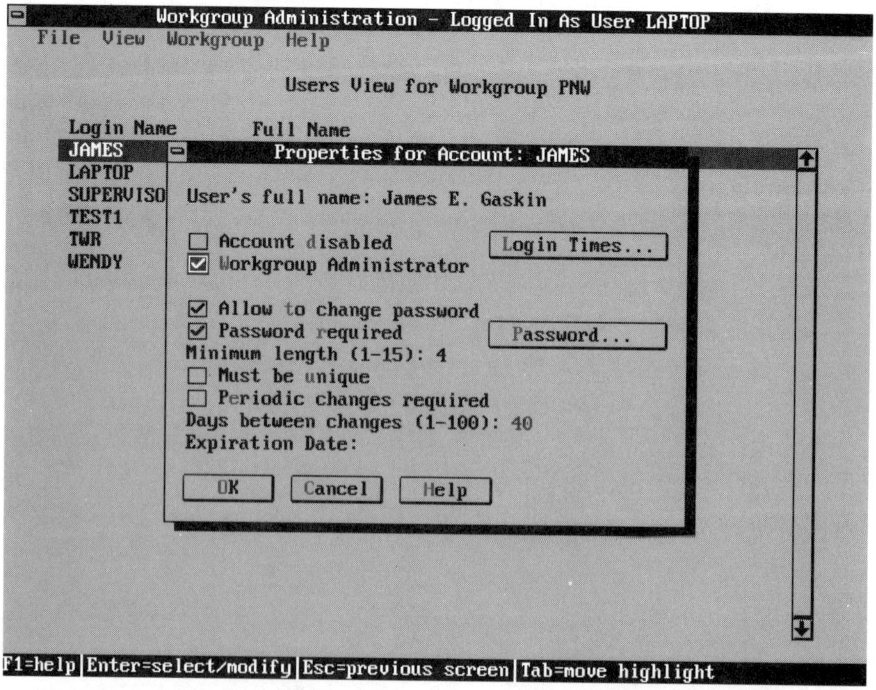

the installation process), you'll always see the Servers View screen. Press Alt-U to see the Users View screen. The longer route is to press Alt-V to open the View menu, then highlight Users, then press Enter. Either way, you'll see a listing of all workgroup users. Highlight the user you wish to configure and press Enter to see that user account's properties. A hint line across the bottom of the screen says the same thing.

The box that appears in our example is labeled Properties for Account: JAMES. The Tab key moves the cursor around to each check box or text box that is active. Pressing Shift-Tab moves the cursor in reverse. You can press Alt and the highlighted key for each check box to toggle the check mark on and off. A mouse works as well, but this is DOS, so we'll ignore that.

To check the box to make JAMES a workgroup administrator, press Tab to move down to that line and press either the spacebar or Enter to toggle the check mark. Alt-W toggles the check mark and moves the cursor to that line from anywhere on this screen. Pressing Alt-O for OK saves the new configuration and exits. James will have these new properties the next time he logs in.

Notice the command button labled Login Times? That wasn't in the MS Windows version, was it? Pressing Alt-L brings up the Login Time Restrictions dialog box, as shown in Figure 8.19.

Each 30-minute time increment has an asterisk that says this user is allowed to log in at that time. Pressing the spacebar toggles these asterisks on and off. As you can see in Figure 8.19, we allow this user no access on Saturday and Sunday, and access only between 8:00 and 5:30 on Monday through Thursday. On Friday, there are no access restrictions.

This is useful for security purposes and for preventing people from logging in to the system while you're doing your tape backup. If everyone is restricted at 2:00 am, starting the tape backup at 2:30 am guarantees no open files to miss because users left their system in the middle of some job. If you allow several people to use the GUEST login, set the time restrictions to normal workday hours so there's less chance of mischief.

FIGURE 8.19

Locking a user out of the system during different parts of the week

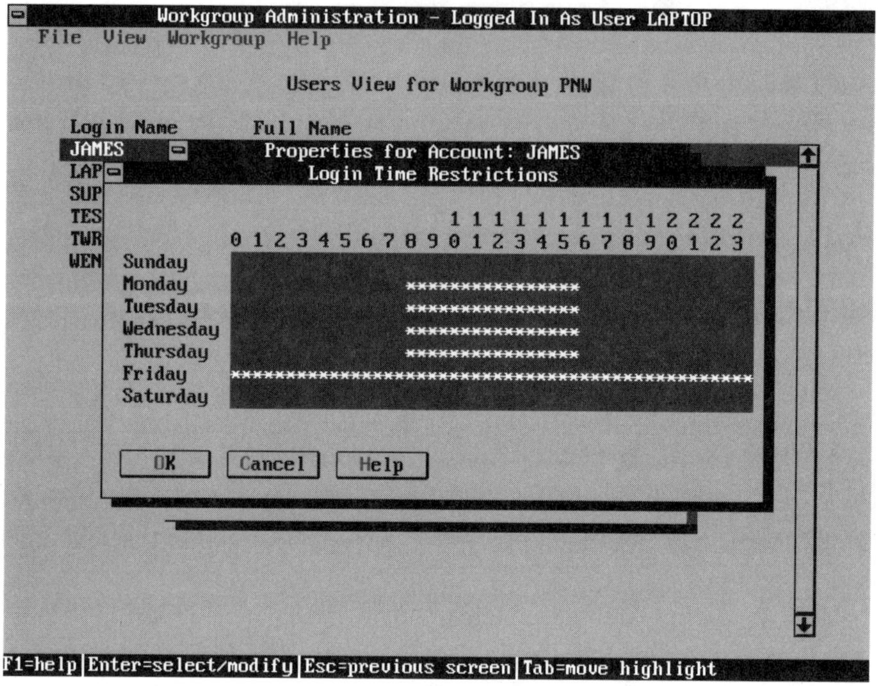

SETTING UP WORKGROUP SERVERS

8.13

THE FAST LANE

IN-A-HURRY? **Make a PC a server under DOS**

1. Type **SETUP** from within the \NWCLIENT directory.
2. Check the box labeled Share this computer's resources.
3. Select the Save Changes and Exit option.
4. Reboot the PC.

If you missed your chance to make your computer a server during installation, it's easy to change that. Figure 8.20 shows the initial DOS Setup screen. This is what you see after you type

```
SETUP
```

in the \NWCLIENT directory. Although this directory is in your path, many other programs that are also in your path may have a SETUP program. So change to the \NWCLIENT directory before you type the SETUP command.

The line that says

```
Share this computer's resources
```

has a check box. Since this computer is already set up, the name has been assigned. Making this PC a server is as easy as checking this box. When the PC is rebooted, it will start the SERVER.EXE program and be able to share any resources it has. I think even a manager can handle this, don't you?

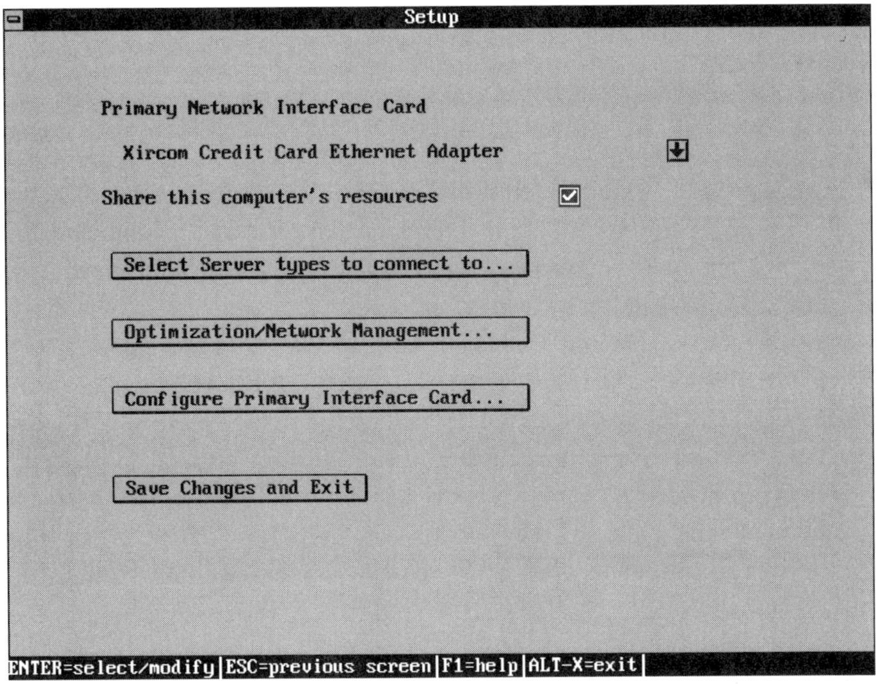

FIGURE 8.20
Making this PC a server under DOS

MANAGING WORKGROUP USERS

Creating and managing workgroup user accounts is one of the primary network administration jobs. If there is little turnover in your group, you probably won't need to create and delete too many user accounts, but you'll certainly need to create a few to start everything.

Setting Up User Accounts

8.14

IN-A-HURRY? Create a workgroup user account under DOS

1. Type **NET ADMIN** from the DOS prompt.
2. Press Alt-U to open the Users View screen.
3. Press Insert to create a new user.
4. Provide a user name in the text box.
5. Configure the new user's properties.
6. Press Alt-O to save and exit.

After starting NET ADMIN, press Alt-U to get to the User View screen. On the status line across the bottom of the screen, you'll see the hint that pressing the Insert key adds a user, and pressing the Delete key deletes the highlighted user. Figure 8.21 shows the text box where you assign the new user's login name.

Notice there is nothing here that assigns a user to a particular server. That's one of the advantages of Personal NetWare's object-oriented view: users are objects with properties, controlled by the network, not a particular server. That's why users can still log in even if their primary workgroup server is not available.

After assigning the name, the Properties for Account box from Figure 8.18 appears again. The default is to make each new user a workgroup administrator. I'm not sure that's smart, so be careful to remove the check for users who are liable to make mistakes. The login time restrictions for users may be applied anytime, using the Login Times command button, as described earlier. Once everything is the way you want, press Alt-O for OK to save and exit this screen. The new user can log in almost immediately (wait a few seconds for the user's information to be replicated across the network to all workgroup servers).

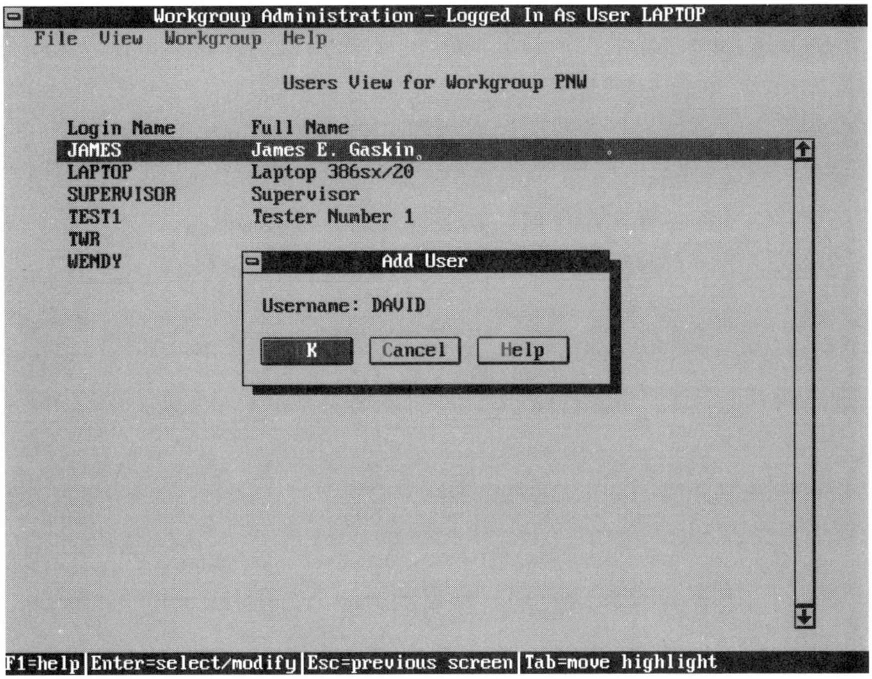

FIGURE 8.21
Adding a new user under NETADMIN

Deleting User Accounts

IN-A-HURRY? Delete a workgroup user account under DOS

8.15

THE FAST LANE

1. Type **NET ADMIN** from the DOS prompt.
2. Press Alt-U to open the Users View screen.
3. Highlight the name of the user, then press Delete.
4. Confirm the deletion.

Deleting users happens from the main Users View screen as well. It's almost too simple: highlight the user's name in the list and press the Delete key.

You must verify you want to delete this user before the system will allow you to do so. None of the user's files are erased when the user name itself is deleted.

SHARING DIRECTORIES

8.16

THE FAST LANE

IN-A-HURRY? Add a shared directory under DOS

1. Type **NET ADMIN** from any DOS prompt.
2. Press Alt-D to display the Shared Directories View screen.
3. Press Insert to add a shared directory.
4. Provide a name to be used by workgroup clients.
5. Highlight the workgroup server where the directory is located, then press Alt-O to save this information.
6. Configure the properties for the new shared directory.
7. Press Alt-O to save and exit.

The configuration of shared directories can be done from any PC in the workgroup. Once you have logged in as either SUPERVISOR or as a user with workgroup administrator privileges, start the NET ADMIN program.

The default view will be that of all the workgroup servers, so press Alt-D to go to the Shared Directories View screen. All the current workgroup shared directories will be listed here. As you might guess, this is where you modify existing shared directories as well.

Pressing the Insert key pops up a dialog box labeled Add Shared Directory, as shown in Figure 8.22. The name must be less than 15 characters, but shorter is safer. After typing the name, press Tab to move to the server selection box, and press Enter on the server of your choice. In the example, I'm sharing the network interface card drive directory from WENDY_PC, consisting of drivers for the SMC ElitePlus 10Base-T Ethernet card that's in that PC. Press either Tab again or Alt-O for OK to save this information and move to the next screen.

When you choose OK, the Properties for Shared Directory dialog box appears. Figure 8.23 shows this dialog box, set to allow everyone in the workgroup All access rights. The User Rights command button opens another dialog box where explicit rights can be set for particular users.

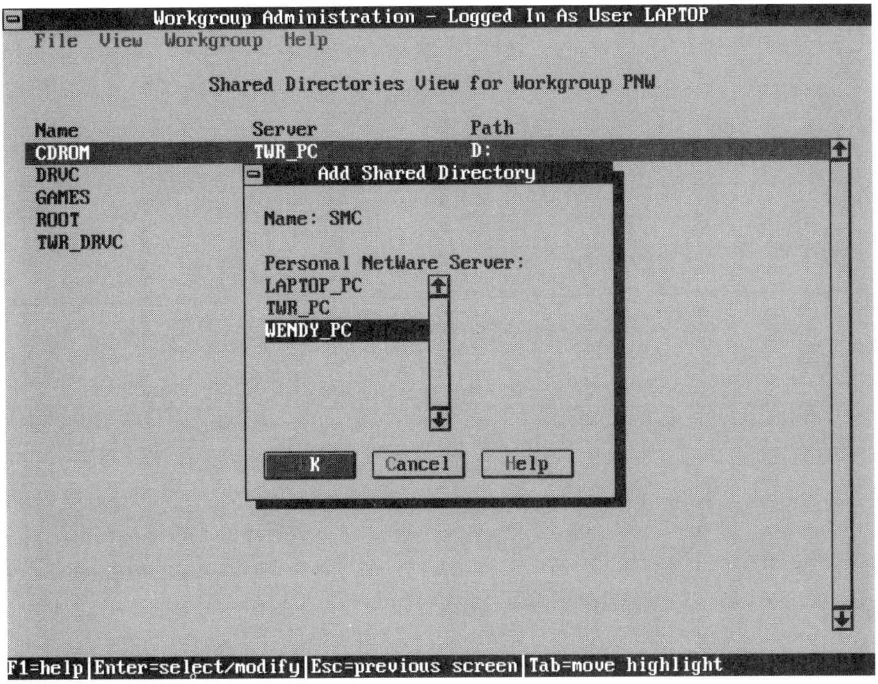

FIGURE 8.22

The first step in sharing a directory under NET ADMIN

REMOVING SHARED DIRECTORIES

IN-A-HURRY? **Remove a shared directory under DOS**

8.17

THE FAST LANE

1. Type **NET ADMIN** from any DOS prompt.
2. Press Alt-D to display the Shared Directories View screen.
3. Highlight the directory you no longer want to share, then press Delete.
4. Confirm the deletion.

The Shared Directories View screen is where shared directories can be unshared, as well. Across the bottom of the screen, the status line tells you that

```
Del=delete
```

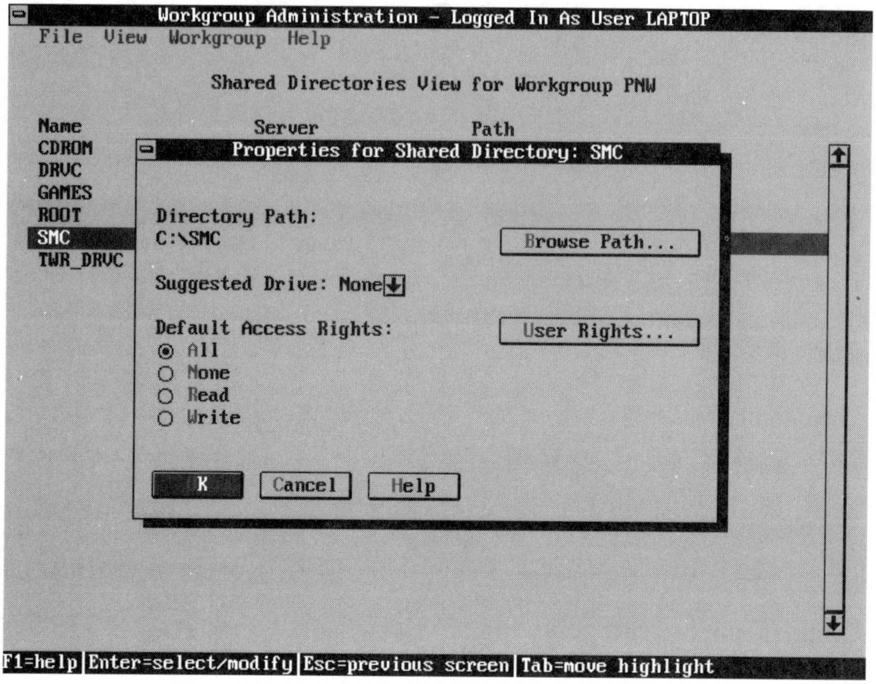

FIGURE 8.23

Assigning access rights for workgroup users to this new shared directory

Highlight the directory to be "deleted," which is confusing because the directory won't be deleted, only unshared. Pressing Delete brings up a dialog box asking you to verify that you actually want to delete this particular directory.

All these operations take a few seconds to ripple across all the servers in the workgroup. You will also have little luck removing a shared directories someone is using.

Since the PC owners can also share and unshare the directories on their machines, it's best to let them do so. After you initially set up the network, let the PC owners share what they feel is necessary for their jobs.

SHARING PRINTERS

IN-A-HURRY? **Share a printer on a workgroup server under DOS** 8.18

THE FAST LANE

1 Type **NET ADMIN** from any DOS prompt.
2 Press Alt-P to display the Shared Printers View screen.
3 Press Insert to add a new workgroup printer.
4 Name the printer, choose its server, then press Alt-O.
5 Modify the printer properties as necessary, then press Alt-O.

Again, you can share printers on a remote server without problems. To share a printer, the PC must be a server; there's no printer-only share status available. But see the end of the chapter for details on lowering the memory requirements for a PC to make it effectively a printer-only server.

In NET ADMIN, pressing Alt-P displays the Shared Printers View screen. All existing printers will be displayed here. Pressing Insert pops up a dialog box labeled Add Shared Printer, as you can see in Figure 8.24. You must type the name, press Tab to reach the server section, then highlight the server where the printer is located. In this example, the printer is named Invoices, indicating to everyone that invoice forms are loaded and ready on this printer at all times.

Pressing Alt-O for OK then moves you to the Properties dialog box, shown in Figure 8.25. This dialog box sets the default access rights and allows adjustments of some of the variables we spoke of in detail in the section about sharing printers under MS Windows, earlier in this chapter.

Choosing the Advanced Info button brings up the the dialog box shown in Figure 8.26. The information from Figures 8.5 and 8.7 shown earlier is arranged a bit differently in NET ADMIN, but all the same settings are available.

FIGURE 8.24

Naming the new shared printer

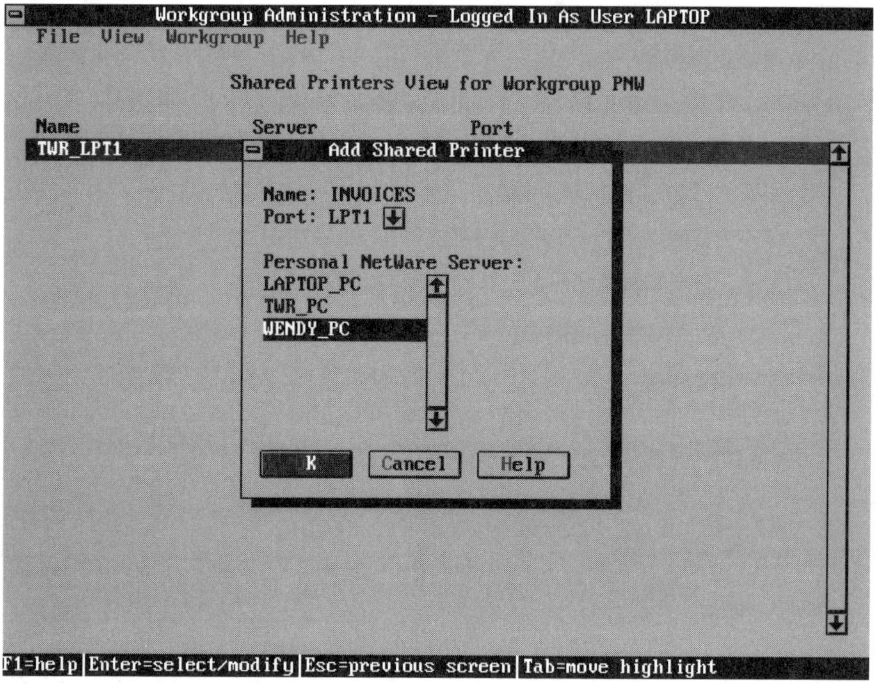

REMOVING A SHARED PRINTER

8.19

IN-A-HURRY? **Delete a shared printer under DOS**

1. Type **NET ADMIN** from the DOS prompt.
2. Press Alt-P to open the Shared Printers View screen.
3. Highlight the printer that you no longer want to share, then press Delete.
4. Confirm the deletion.

Deleting (unsharing) a printer is as easy as deleting a shared directory (described just a bit ago). From the Shared Printers View, highlight the printer to be deleted. Just as with the directory, press Delete and verify your decision to remove that printer from the list of shared resources. It will

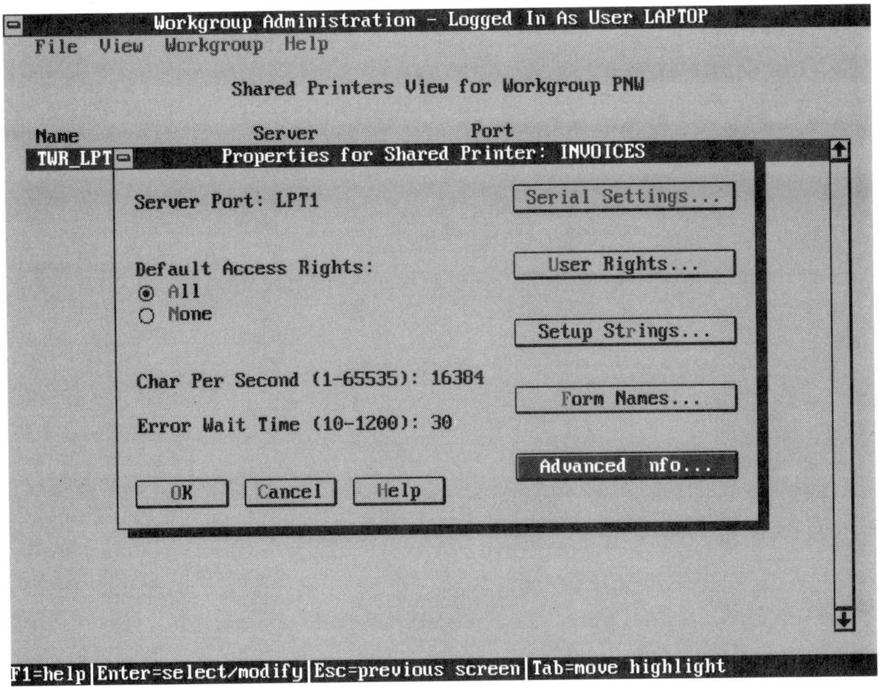

FIGURE 8.25

Setting rights for the new printer Invoices

again take a few seconds for all servers in the workgroup to be advised of the change.

Be prepared for users that have been relying on that printer to call you the next time they log in. When they try to connect to that printer, especially if that connection is in their PNWLOGIN.SCR, they will get an error message. You will then get those calls.

BACKING UP YOUR WORKGROUP-RELATED DATA

IN-A-HURRY? **Back up the workgroup databases**

8.20

THE FAST LANE

1 Type **NET ADMIN** from the DOS prompt.
2 Highlight the server to back up, then press Enter.
3 Press Alt-B to choose Backup Databases.

4 Provide a path to store the information.

5 Press Alt-O to begin the backup operation.

FIGURE 8.26

The Advanced Information dialog box for the new printer

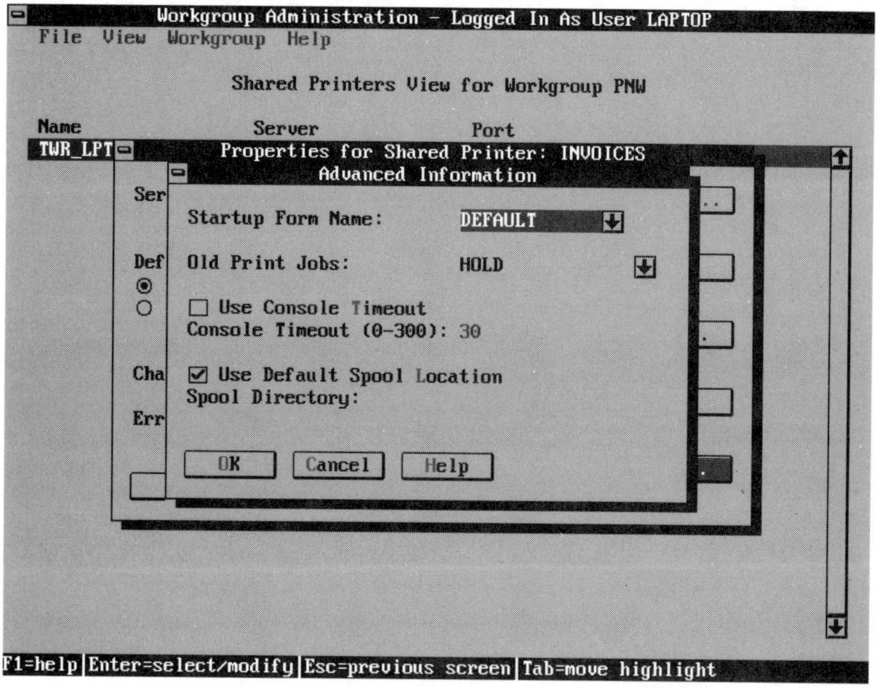

Three databases are kept by Personal NetWare, replicated across the network. One is for users, one for resources, and one is for server-specific information. These should be backed up regularly, separate from the tape backup system you're using (you are using one, aren't you?) to back up your data.

You can back up any server where you have administrator privileges from any other station in the workgroup. It takes little time to perform the backup operation, because not much information is involved. Unless you have many servers in your workgroup, this will take well less than a minute.

To begin, start the NET ADMIN program. From the Servers View screen (the default), highlight the server that you want to back up, and then press Enter. Next press Alt-B to bring up the dialog box shown in Figure 8.27

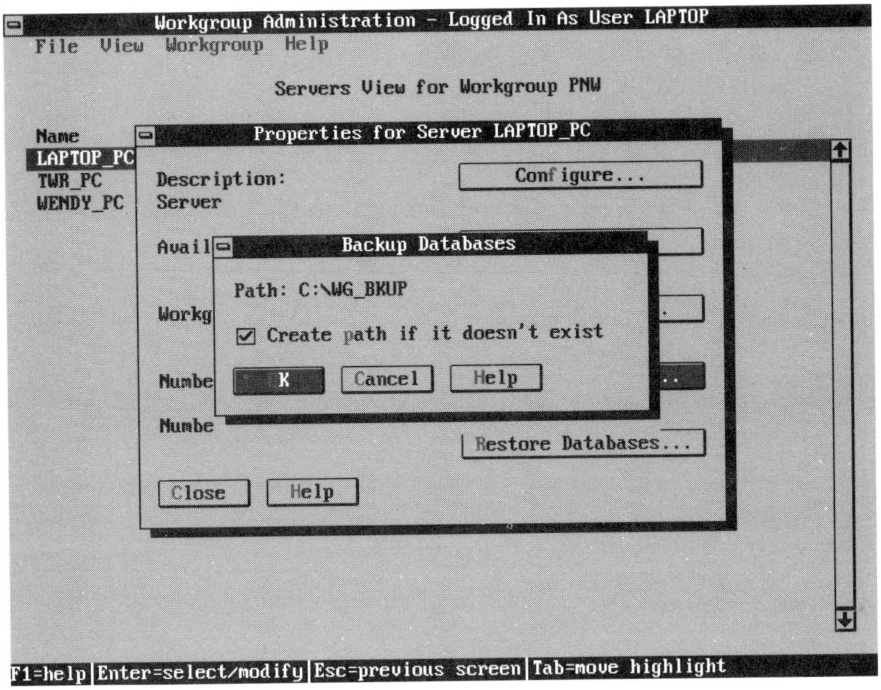

FIGURE 8.27

Backing up the information for LAPTOP_PC

(the example shows a path already typed in). In the Path field, type in the complete path of where you want to store the backup. Press Alt-O to choose OK, and the backup process will begin.

It's a good idea to store these backups on different PCs and even on floppies so it's easier to take the information off-site. It's also a good idea to floss your teeth. I hope you back up your data more often than most people floss.

RESTORING WORKGROUP DATA

IN-A-HURRY? **Restore the workgroup databases**

8.21 THE FAST LANE

1. Type **NET ADMIN** from the DOS prompt.
2. Highlight the server to restore, then press Enter.
3. Press Alt-R to choose Restore Databases.

4 Specify the path from your latest backup.
5 Choose which part of the backup to restore.
6 Press Alt-O to begin restoration.

If your workgroup control information gets corrupted, usually by a server crashing with lots of files open, two things must happen. First, you need to buy that battery backup unit I told you about for that server, to give it a fighting chance. Second, you need to restore the workgroup databases from one of your many, many backups.

To begin the restoration process, run NET ADMIN, highlight the name of the server, then press Enter. Select Restore Databases (by pressing Alt-R) to see the dialog box shown in Figure 8.28. In the dialog box, specify the path from your latest backup and select the part of the backup to restore.

FIGURE 8.28

Restoring workgroup databases

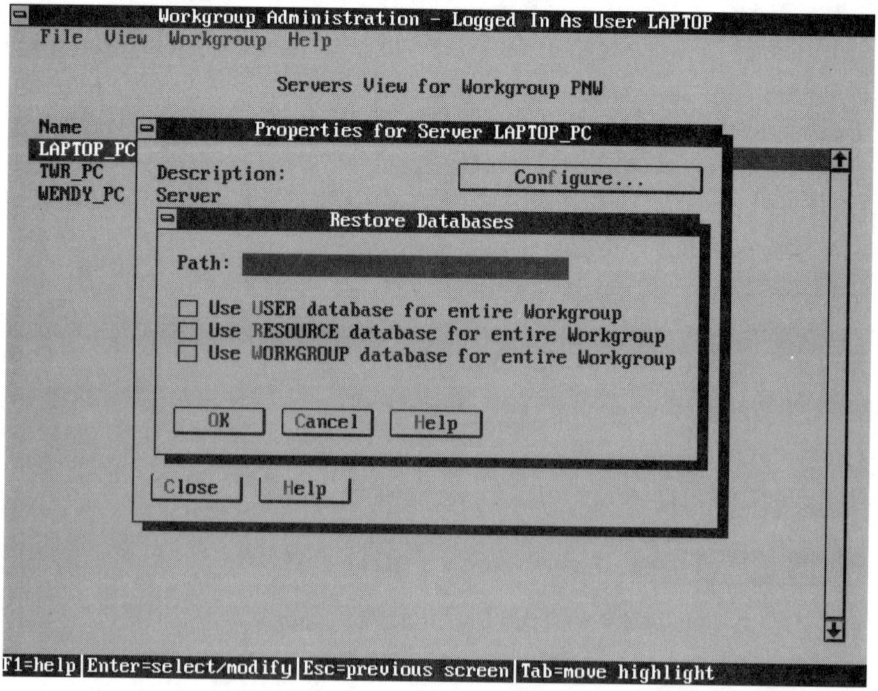

You can restore just one or two of the databases or all three. When you press Alt-O, the utility starts restoring the workgroup data.

If you restore all of your workgroup information, it will replace the existing information on all your servers. This will result in lost information of all workgroup details changed since your last backup. See why I tell you to backup regularly?

Advanced Use of the NET ADMIN Program

As with the MS Windows section, we come to the area of administration you will use least. This statement is based on experience. Networks tend to keep running once they get started. This network isn't an old car you need to push-start every day.

CONFIGURING WORKGROUP SERVERS

IN-A-HURRY? **Display server configuration information**

8.22 THE FAST LANE

1. Type **NET ADMIN** from the DOS prompt.
2. Highlight the server, then press Enter.
3. Press Alt-F to see the Configuration screen.
4. Press Alt-A to display the Advanced Settings screen.

From the Properties screen for any server, the screen that appears if you press Enter (or Alt-F) is the Server Configuration screen, shown in Figure 8.29. Choose the Advanced Settings command button to see the screen from which you can change configuration settings. The NET ADMIN Advanced Setting screen, shown in Figure 8.30, contains the same information as shown in the MS Windows version (Figure 8.10). These settings are discussed in more detail in the section about fine-tuning advanced settings, later in this chapter.

FIGURE 8.29

The NET ADMIN Server Configuration screen

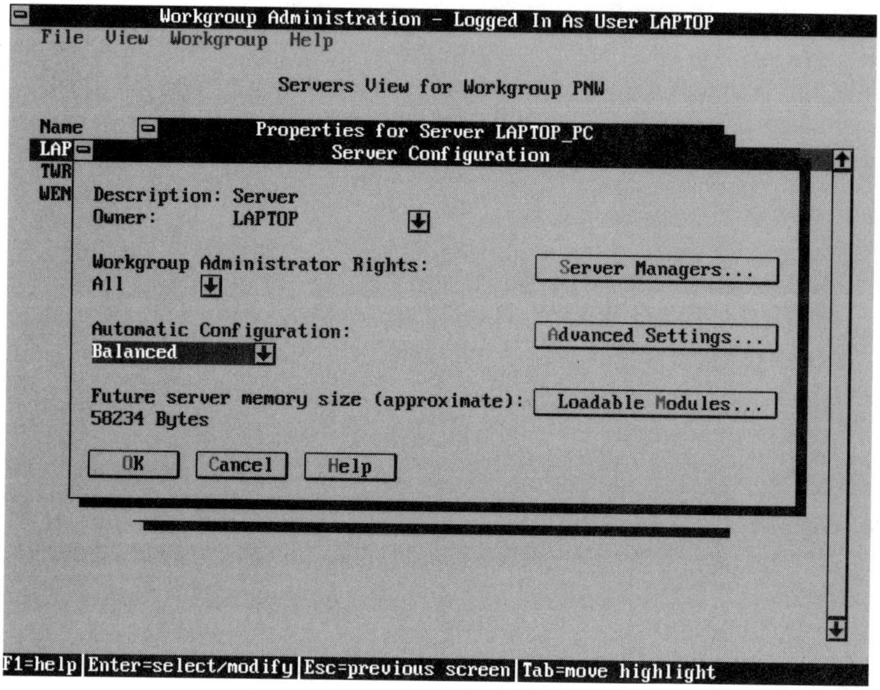

The only change you might want to make several weeks after setting up your network is to the Automatic Configuration field in the Server Configuration screen. The three choices are Balanced, Minimum Memory, and Maximum Performance. An estimate of needed RAM appears directly below the Automatic Configuration field. The actual RAM impact tends to be less than it shows here, but you can experiment with this yourself. When you choose another option in the Automatic Configuration field, the information in the Advanced Settings screen will be modified.

VIEWING SERVER STATISTICS

The rationalization for changing any of the configuration settings must come from the usage statistics kept by each server. From the Properties screen, press Alt-S for Statistics.

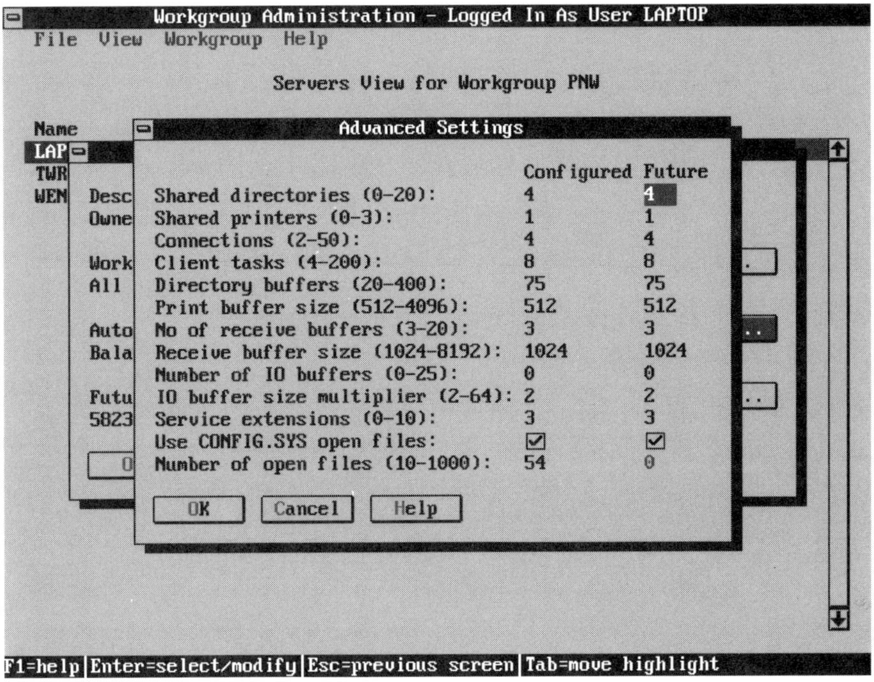

FIGURE 8.30

The NET ADMIN Advanced Settings screen

Here we are checking statistics of TWR_PC from LAPTOP_PC, another example of remote management. Since TWR_PC has emerged as the server of choice in my workgroup, there is more traffic here to see as well. Figures 8.31 and 8.32 show the two Statistics screens for TWR_PC.

CHANGING YOUR SERVER'S WORKGROUP

One of the few functions you can't perform remotely is changing a server's workgroup. That must be done from the server you want to reassign. If you try to change a remote server's workgroup, you will get a polite error message.

FIGURE 8.31

The first NET ADMIN Statistics screen

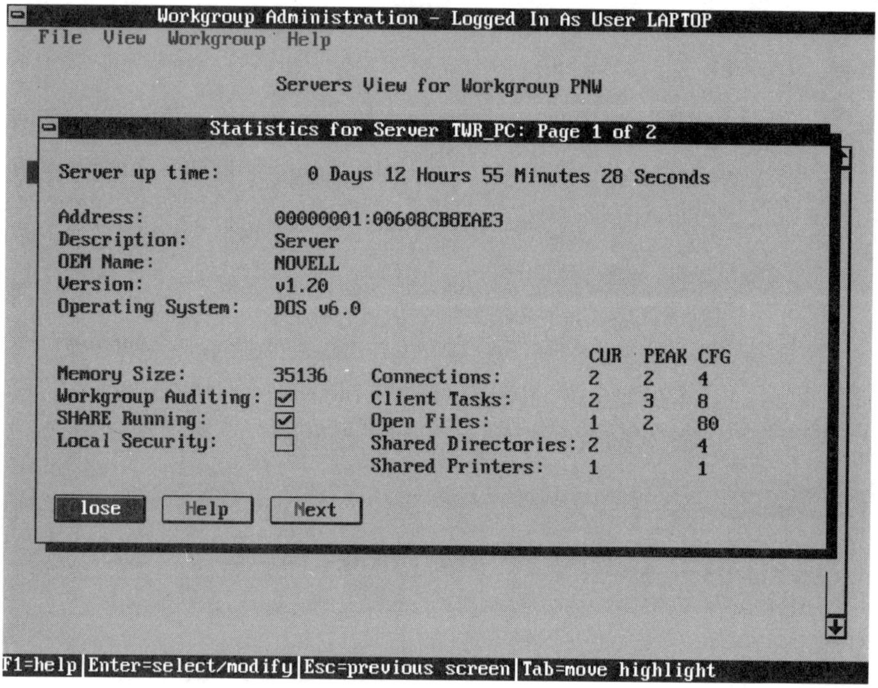

Figure 8.33 shows the Set Workgroup dialog box in NET ADMIN. To get to this dialog box, press Alt-W from the main Properties screen. It includes a check box to move the existing shared resources to the new workgroup.

If you're curious, check Figure 8.33 against Figure 8.11 for the MS Windows version. As I mentioned there, it's better to limit the number of workgroups unless you have an overriding need to add more. Life is complicated enough.

DOWNING THE SERVER

This is a trick section! You can't down the server from within NET ADMIN. This is about the only function you can do under MS Windows that you can't do under DOS.

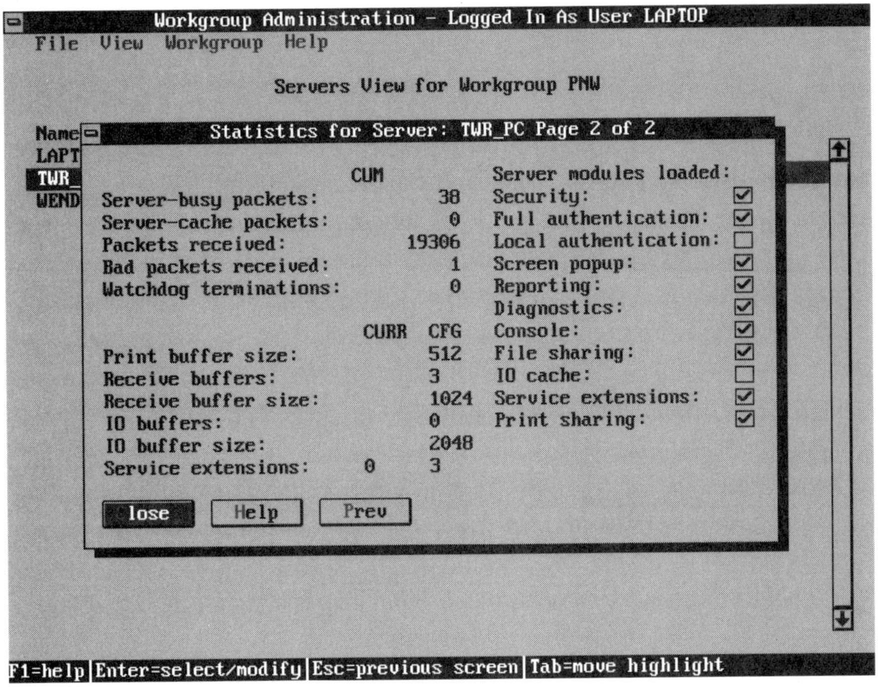

FIGURE 8.32
The second NET ADMIN Statistics screen

Rather than typing NET ADMIN then looking for a Down Server option, type

```
NET DOWN
```

to shut down your server. You'll have a chance to change your mind, and you'll be told how many current connections you have that will be inconvenienced if you persist in shutting down the server.

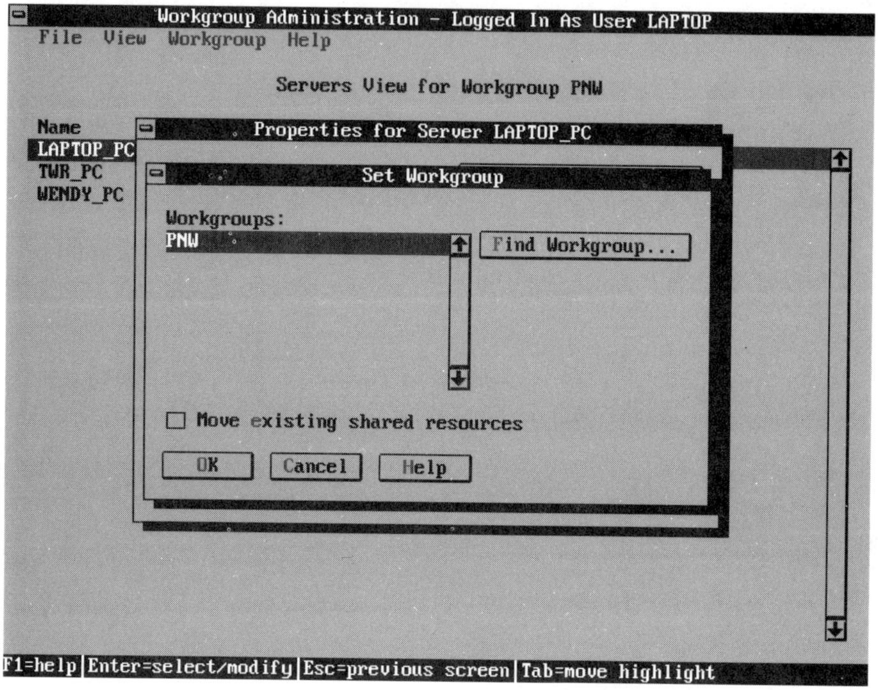

FIGURE 8.33

The Set Workgroup dialog box in NET ADMIN

Management of the Workgroup as a Whole through NET ADMIN

Everything so far has been aimed at particular servers. This section deals with the workgroup as a whole. After all, everyone in the group can generate an error, can't they?

Each of the following functions are accessed by pressing Alt-W from the main NET ADMIN screen. This drops down the Workgroup menu. From there, highlight your choice and press Enter.

DISPLAYING THE AUDIT AND ERROR LOGS

8.23

THE FAST LANE

IN-A-HURRY? **Display the audit or error log under NET ADMIN**

1. Type **NET ADMIN** from the DOS prompt.
2. Press Alt-W.
3. Highlight Audit Log or Error Log, then press Enter.

If you compare Figure 8.14 in the MS Windows section to Figure 8.34, you'll find that they look remarkably similar. The audit log is the same, no matter which computer or which utility displays it.

There seems to be a paucity of errors to my network here in the laboratory. I can mark that off to either natural talent or the clearing of the error log on a regular basis. Either way, the same error we saw in Figure 8.15 appears here in Figure 8.35.

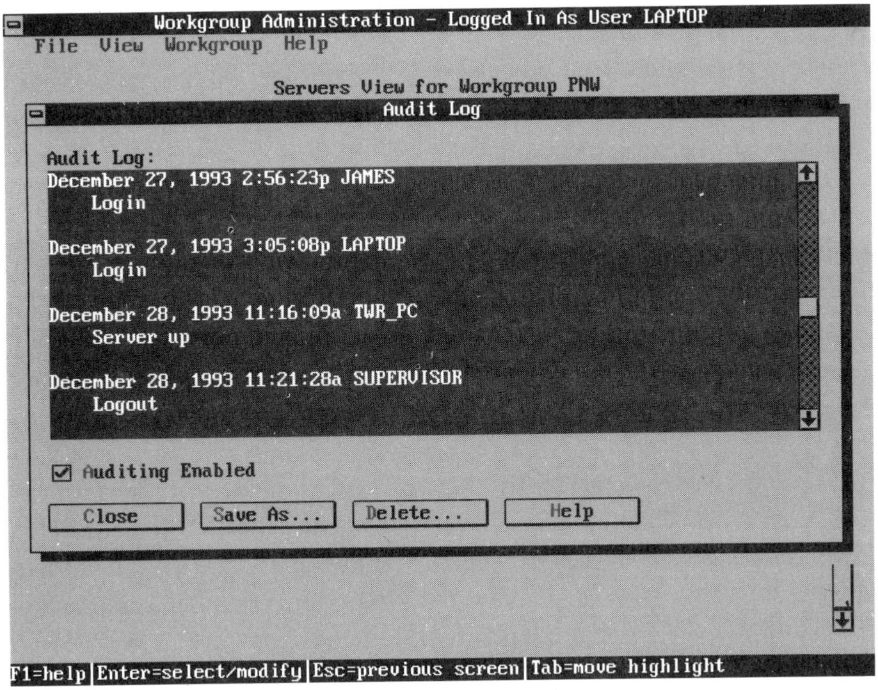

FIGURE 8.34

The audit log view from NET ADMIN

FIGURE 8.35

A printer error in the workgroup revealed by NET ADMIN

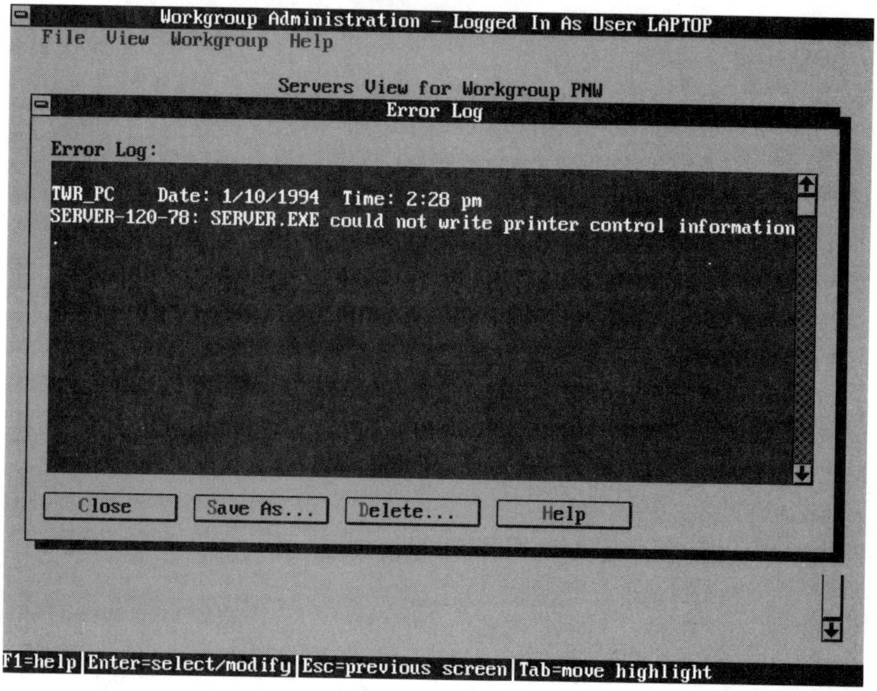

ROUTE MANAGEMENT

If you have a single workgroup and single network, as I have suggested, you won't need to worry about route management. Routes are the highways you define to connect with other workgroup servers. The format is *NETWORK ADDRESS:MACHINE ADDRESS.*

Take a look at Figure 8.36 for a display of routes from within NET ADMIN. Your primary route will be created for you during installation.

TIME SYNCHRONIZATION

The ability to synchronize clocks across a network can be invaluable at times. Some security packages demand accurate times, and some databases are just as picky. Figure 8.37 shows the Synchronize Date/Time dialog box displayed by the NET ADMIN program.

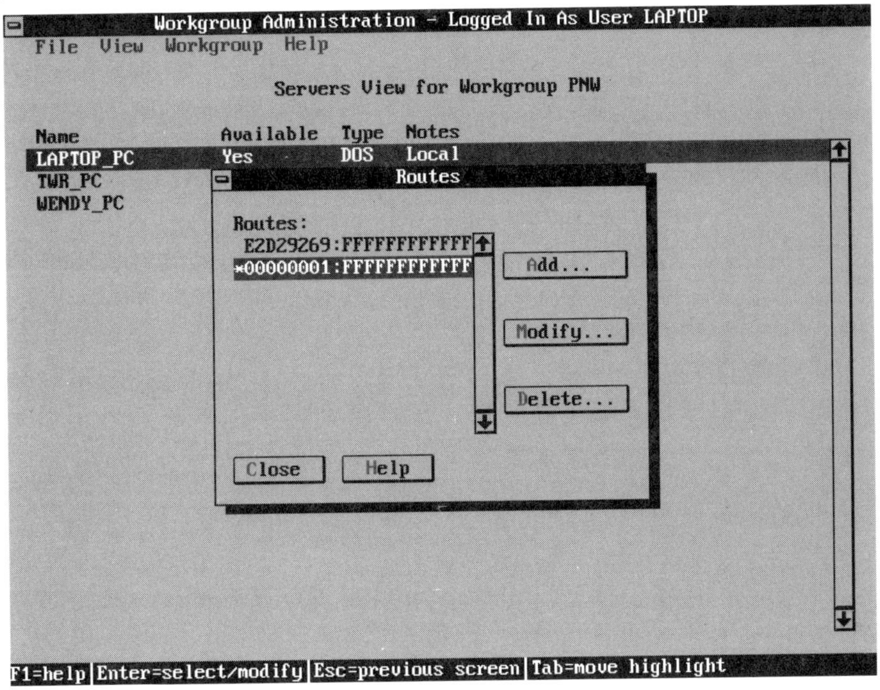

FIGURE 8.36
Route management through NETADMIN

Fine-Tuning Advanced Settings for Servers

Earlier in the chapter, you got a quick overview of the advanced settings for Personal NetWare servers. To save RAM, you can eliminate unnecessary program features by adjusting particular advanced settings. The default values for Advanced Settings are shown back in Figure 8.30. Remember that these take up about 35 KB of RAM on the server PC, which is small considering the amount of resource sharing that is allowed.

FIGURE 8.37

Synchronizing time the easy way through NET ADMIN

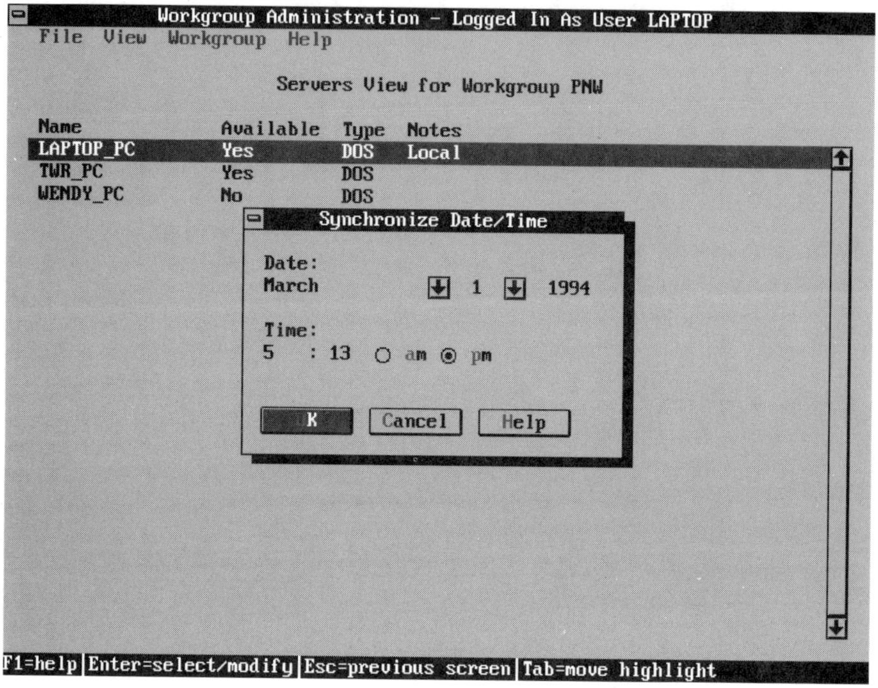

For most users, these settings will be fine. However, some of you might want to change these settings, usually to save as much PC memory as possible. The reason I'm using the DOS version of NET ADMIN rather than the Personal NetWare program in MS Windows is because more details are available under DOS. Notice the range of valid numbers given for each setting? That's not available in the MS Windows version.

Each value you reduce in the Advanced Settings screen reduces the memory required to support the SERVER.EXE program. When memory is important, this is the place to shave those few bytes. Let's go down the list, paying special attention to the changes that can be made if necessary.

Shared directories (0-20)	If your PC is acting as a workgroup server but sharing only a single directory, make that plain in the first line. The number of shared directories listed is not the number of those currently shared, but the number you told the system to prepare to share. If you have only one or two directories shared with no plans to share more, list the actual number. If you plan to only share a printer, set this to zero. Savings per directory: At least 128 bytes.
Shared printers (0-3)	Number of shared printers the system is ready to support. If you don't have a shared printer on this workgroup server, list the number as zero. Savings per printer: Almost 800 bytes.
Connections (2-50)	Concurrent connections supported by this server. Set this to reflect the maximum possible. For example, if there are only two other PCs in your network, make this 3. Savings per connection: 86 bytes.
Client tasks (4-200)	Indicates the number of client tasks that can run concurrently on the server. If the number of connections is low, reduce the number to about two tasks per available connection. If your server is only sharing a printer, make it one task per connection. Savings per task: 100 bytes.
Directory buffers (20-400)	Sets aside RAM to store directory information for file requests by clients. For fewer clients, reduce the default setting. If this server shares only the printer, set the minimum number. Savings per buffer: 24 bytes.

Print buffer size (512-4096)	The amount of RAM each print buffer takes. You can't lower this number below 512 bytes, but if you configure the system without printers, this buffer space is not allocated. That's why you save about 800 bytes if you configure your PC server for no printers at all.
No. of receive buffers (3-20)	Amount of buffers for sending and receiving client requests. Additional RAM required per buffer: 87 bytes.
Receive buffer size (1024-8192)	Number of bytes in each receive buffer. Keep this number tuned to your network transport protocol packet size. For Ethernet, 1024 bytes is fine. Token Ring can support up to 4096 bytes per packet, but pay attention when configuring your Token Ring driver. Too often, many drivers for NetWare default down to 512 bytes, no matter what you set. If you set aside a large buffer size but don't use all of it, that RAM is wasted. In few cases will you need more than 1024 bytes.
Number of IO buffers (0-25)	Amount of IO buffers. An IO buffer is an internal server buffer that reads ahead a bit on every disk read and acts as an internal cache. If you're running NWCACHE, leave this set to zero.
IO buffer size multiplier (2-64)	This number is multiplied by the size of the receive buffer setting. If it is set to 2, and your receive buffer size is set to 1024, the number of bytes used will be 2048.

Service extensions (0-10)	Programming hooks built into the SERVER.EXE program that other software products can use. Currently, the only service extension is SNMP support. If you're not using SNMP, set this value to zero, and some piece of the server code will not be needed. No numbers are reflected in this screen when this value is changed, however.
Use CONFIG.SYS open files	The value set in CONFIG.SYS for FILES= will be used to set the number of open files your server will support. In small workgroups, this works fine. In large groups, or with certain software such as FoxPro, many more open files are necessary than the limit of 255 that CONFIG-.SYS will allow. If this is the case, do not check this box, and set the necessary number of open files for the last Advanced Settings item.
Number of open files (10-1000)	This is not adjustable until the previous item is unchecked. RAM used per open file: 64 bytes.

Fine-Tuning Loadable Modules for Servers

Just as your client software uses loadable modules (Virtual Loadable Modules, or VLMs), so does the SERVER.EXE program. To adjust these modules, press Alt-F from the Properties screen for the server to get to the Server Configuration screen (Figure 8.29), then choose the Loadable Modules button. You'll see the Loadable Modules screen, as shown in Figure 8.38. Each item on this screen can be configured so that it doesn't load during the SERVER.EXE program startup. This will lower the RAM requirements of the SERVER.EXE program.

FIGURE 8.38

Deciding which modules of SERVER.EXE load

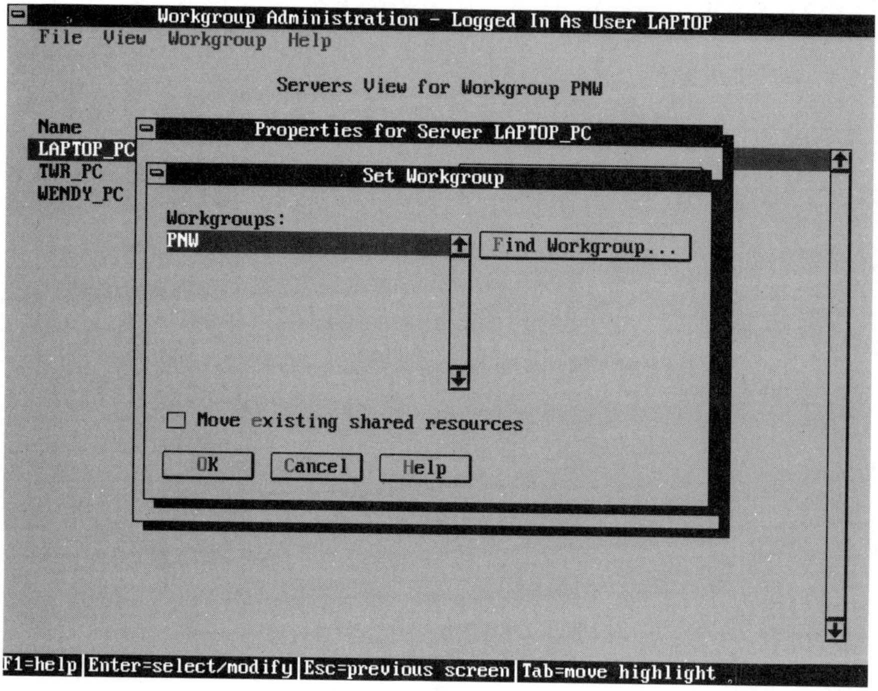

Here's a summary of the loadable modules:

File Sharing	If this PC will be sharing only printers and not any portion of the hard disk, uncheck this box. The numbers in several of the choices in the Advanced Settings screen will become moot if the file sharing sections of the SERVER.EXE program are not loaded.
Print Sharing	If this workgroup server doesn't have any shared printers, uncheck this box. This will save RAM when loading SERVER.EXE, as well as save RAM that would otherwise be used for print buffers.

Security	Many small companies or small workgroups have no security concerns. If this box is not checked, all users in the workgroup will have all rights to all the resources managed by this server. This means every file in every directory will be open for all users to peruse at their leisure, and the user rights discussed earlier will not apply. If that's not a problem for your workgroup, save that RAM.
Full Authentication and Local Authentication	These are related to the security choice previously mentioned. Full authentication enables the requirements for passwords. Local authentication assumes each PC user has passed some other security requirements. In small, trusting groups, passwords are not needed. When Local Authentication is checked, anything entered at the Password prompt is acceptable to the system. In other words, no passwords are required.
Pop-Up Screen	Unchecking this saves quite a bit of memory when loading SERVER.EXE, but eliminates the screen that tells you if the printer is out of paper, or keeps you from accidentally rebooting a PC acting as a workgroup server. If you can remember you may have some connected users before you reboot, and can live without a screen describing the printing error when a printer has a problem, save the RAM.
Reporting	This feature provides the numbers used by the Personal NetWare diagnostics programs. If you have no plans to use any of the diagnostic programs, this feature can be eliminated. If this is not checked, however, no diagnostics information, such as disk space available and traffic levels among the workgroup users, will be available.

Console	Checking this box allows the NET CONSOLE program to run. If running NET CONSOLE is not in your plans, save the RAM.
Salvage	Although this is never mentioned in the Personal NetWare manual, Salvage is a regular NetWare utility that reclaims deleted files. Think of this as an undelete program for a network drive instead of your local drive. This check box allows your favorite undelete program to work on drive letters mapped to other workgroup servers.

Be careful when changing these settings. My earlier warnings about the need for care and good notes before making changes still stand. Change one setting at a time, during noncritical times on the network. During year-end report time is not a good time to experiment. But if you're so inclined, you can configure some significant RAM savings for some workgroup servers using these techniques.

CHAPTER 9

How Do I Use Novell DOS 7?

Without an operating system, your PC is merely bad industrial art pieces connected by cables. The cynical among us may believe it more closely resembles Dr. Frankenstein's monster before the lightning. What is it about DOS that turns this pile of inanimate objects into a powerful information and communications tool?

A Disk Operating System (DOS, pronounced *dahs*) is software that directs the interaction of the various computer pieces with each other and with you, the user. If you bought just Personal NetWare, this chapter will only make you feel bad. If you bought Novell DOS 7, you not only got the best DOS in the business, but you also received all the Personal NetWare networking capabilities covered in this book. Those with only Personal NetWare may want to talk to their dealers about an upgrade to Novell DOS 7.

Details on installing Novell DOS 7 are included in Appendix B. This chapter describes some of the features and functions of the operating system.

A Bit of History

Novell DOS 7 is the culmination of more than a decade of DOS heritage, starting with the first IBM PC back in 1981. The beginnings of Digital Research (DR), the company that developed DR-DOS, go back to the mid-1970's. DR merged with Novell in 1991.

The most popular operating system before DOS was CP/M (Control Program for Microprocessors), written by Gary Kildal, founder of DR. DR started in the same era as Microsoft, with one important difference: DR wrote an operating system decades before the folks in Redmond did. The original MS DOS was bought, not developed by, Microsoft.

Why Do I Need Novell DOS 7?

Turning the industrial art pieces of your computer into performance art, able to crunch spreadsheet numbers and make graphs and write books, is the job of Novell DOS 7. Since people work with other people, the ability to communicate with the PC in the next cubicle or the NetWare file server in the computer room is built into Novell DOS 7. Since some of those people make mistakes, file backup and recovery features are included, along with the ability to "undelete" files and directories that were accidentally deleted. Since some people can't be trusted at all, security features and virus protection are provided.

All the typical functions of DOS are included, of course. Any program written for a PC will run with Novell DOS 7. In fact, programs will probably run better because of DOS 7's memory management and speed enhancers, such as disk caching. Printers are supported, as are modems, CD ROM drives, and the ability to run more than one program at a time (that should keep your boss happy).

Can you do these things with MS or PC DOS? Some of them, but not the networking and multitasking. However, Novell's DOS 7's features are a generation ahead of the options MS DOS does support. If the next generation is available, why stick with the old stuff?

New Features in Novell DOS 7

If you are familiar with DR-DOS 6 (with version 7, the name is changed to Novell DOS), you will find several of its features have been upgraded and improved. If you are only familiar with some version of MS DOS, you will find many features you are not familiar with. Be prepared to be surprised. Most of these features are put into effect by simply choosing options in the Setup program, as explained in Appendix B.

MULTITASKING AND TASK SWITCHING WITH TASK MANAGER

The Task Manager has been upgraded to allow multitasking of software application programs on computers equipped with Intel 80386 and 80486 microprocessors. Multitasking is something most of us are familiar with; it means doing two or more things at the same time.

Novell DOS 7 allows multiple application programs to be loaded in separate virtual PCs within your single PC. *Virtual,* in the computer world, means that something is not real, but usually mimics something that is real. In this case, each session of the multitasking software can run an application and not interfere with other applications running in other sessions. It appears to each application that it has the entire PC to itself. The software is said to be running in a virtual PC, since DOS 7 provides a normal PC environment for the application. The fact that DOS 7 also provides several other normal PC environments has no impact on any single one of the virtual PCs.

While you work, some programs work in the *background*, which means that they do their job at the same time you're doing something else. For example, a word processing program might perform a search-and-replace operation on a long document in the background while you do something else. Because Novell DOS 7 provides more support for the on-screen application, the programs that are running in the background run slower. This keeps the user (you) happy, since the foreground program runs just as fast as it would normally. Since you don't need to wait for the program in the background, you save time.

Another way to handle multiple programs is through *task switching*. With it, DOS 7 again provides a virtual PC for each application running in each session, but only one application is actually running at a time. The other sessions are stopped when they are not on screen. This doesn't bother applications or endanger your files. For example, a search-and-replace operation will stop when you switch to another session with task switching, and it will resume when you again make that program the active session.

Task switching is necessary for those "badly behaved" applications that have trouble with multitasking. These applications bypass the regular rules for software development and use shortcuts. Since the shortcuts usually involve writing directly to the hardware locations on the PC's motherboard, the multitasking software is bypassed. For those programs, task switching allows you to save time by keeping all the programs you need active and ready. Rather than stopping your word processor to look up a phone number in your address database, you can merely use a hotkey to quickly switch to the database. When you're finished, pressing the hotkey again will return you to your word processor, just where you left it. Configuring task switching and choosing hotkeys are described in Appendix B.

MEMORY MANAGEMENT FOR MAKING THE MOST OF RAM

You can never be too rich, too thin, or have too much memory. The original PC supported an astounding 640 KB of RAM, ten times the capacity of CP/M at the time. What would someone need all that memory for?

Today, computers with only 640 KB of memory are looked down upon, and the owners of those machines are pitied. RAM of 4 MB is considered the minimum, especially if that machine will run MS Windows. An amount of 8 MB is better, and non-DOS operating systems, such as UNIX or Windows NT, need to have 12 MB or more before they will even start.

But having gobs of memory doesn't mean all your troubles are over. You must manage that memory, because the initial 640 KB of RAM that came with the original PC is still a limiting factor. Most software requires as much of the first 640 KB of a PC's memory as possible. When you're running several pieces of software—perhaps your main application, networking software, fax software, and a pop-up calculator—each piece will try to use that same 640 KB of RAM. Arranging software in different memory areas than the lower 640 KB is called *memory management.*

The primary memory management for plain DOS is EMM386.EXE. This program turns the memory in your PC into extended and expanded memory for application programs to use.

Some newer programs aren't limited by the lower 640 KB RAM problem. Why? The 640 KB RAM problem arose because of memory control peculiarities in the original Intel 8088 microprocessor chosen by IBM for the first PC. The Intel 286 chip in the next generation AT computers wasn't any better. Only with the Intel 386 and above do the microprocessors handle memory in an intelligent way. Programs that have been written specifically for the 386 and later processor families can bypass the 640 KB limitation to some extent.

This software requires new methods of controlling PC memory, and that's where Novell's DPMI (DOS Protected Mode Interface) and DPMS (DOS Protected Mode Services) come in. These programs take advantage of next generation memory management techniques to provide more memory for newer programs.

ANTI-VIRUS SOFTWARE FOR PEACE OF MIND

Search and Destroy is a modern program that works under DOS and MS Windows to limit your PC's exposure to a harmful computer virus. Search and Destroy comes in two parts: one memory resident (it's available at all times), which you enable through the Setup program, and one that you can run at your discretion.

And if that isn't not enough, each time you start the DOS or MS Windows version of FastBack Express, the file backup utility, a virus scan is performed. This ensures the data you save won't carry a virus that has infected your computer since your last virus scan. Using Search and Destroy and FastBack Express is described later in this chapter.

DISK CACHING FOR HIGHER PERFORMANCE

The disk-caching program, NWCACHE, speeds all your disk operations. Not only does this program increase your computer's performance when reading from the disk, but it also provides options that allow increased performance when writing to the disk.

An added advanced feature of NWCACHE is its ability to lend memory to certain applications. MS Windows, for example, wants as much memory as possible. NWCACHE will run with a large amount of memory when in DOS mode, but give up some of that memory when MS Windows starts. This allows you to balance the needs of the software for RAM versus the need for disk performance.

A disk cache works to improve the speed of your disk reads. When an application reads from the disk, it often needs the same information within a short period of time. By using some RAM as a temporary holding place for information read from the disk, a traditional disk cache provides information to the application considerably quicker than a disk drive will. The more information held in the cache, the faster the performance because it's more likely that the information needed by the application will still be located in the cache area.

Disk reads are tracked to see how old they are, somewhat like shirts are tracked to see if they get donated to Goodwill. Disk blocks that have been used recently stay in the cache, just as shirts that are worn regularly stay in your closet. If the information in a particular block of data in the cache is not needed, it gets replaced by newer information read more recently from the disk. This is how that old shirt gets moved into the Goodwill bag and a new shirt takes its place in the closet.

Novell DOS 7's NWCACHE goes beyond what has been available in disk caches in the past in three important ways:

- It can share some of the RAM from the cache with other programs.
- The lookahead feature will analyze disk-read patterns and get the most likely next block of information into memory before the application program calls for that information.
- The delayed-write and buffered-write options group disk write requests, speeding disk-write operations by reducing the number of separate write operations needed.

This is all well and good, I hear you say, but does this really improve computer performance? Take a look at Figure 9.1. This is the result of the command

```
NWCACHE /S
```

which provides the status of the cache.

The first item says the cache size is 2048 KB (2 MB). The second line tells us that the minimum cache size is 1024 KB, which is 1 MB of RAM available to programs that need it. For TWR_PC, that program is MS Windows.

FIGURE 9.1

Performance savings using NWCACHE

```
NWCache R1.0 Novell Disk Cache
Copyright (C) 1993 Novell, Inc.  All rights reserved.
Copyright (C) 1985, 1990, 1992, Golden Bow Systems.

Cache size: 2048 KB (XMS)
Minimum cache size: 1024 KB
Buffered write drives: A B
Delayed write drives:  C

Current options:
/MUX          Program is loaded into upper and XMS memory using DPMS
/BU=16        Lookahead buffer is located in upper memory, size is in KB
/LEND=ON      Lend memory to other applications - 1024 KB available
/DELAY=5000   Write delay is enabled, time is in milliseconds
/FLUSH=ON     Flush delayed writes before returning the prompt

Disk Usage Statistics:                     Error Statistics:
 Command Requests        #Done   Saved         0 Memory Manager Errors
 Reads:       125509      6209     95%         0 Disk Transfer Errors
 Writes:       24114      3365     86%         0 Errors Ignored by User

C:\SCREENS>
```

Buffered writes are used with removable drives (such as A: and B:, the two floppy drives on TWR_PC), rather than delayed writes. They combine successive write requests into a single disk write for faster access, but flush all information immediately. This makes sure no data gets left in the buffer while a floppy disk is removed from the system.

The delayed-write drive, C:, is the single hard disk in TWR_PC. Down in the Current options box, you see /DELAY=5000. The information for drive C: will either be written to disk within 5000 milliseconds (5 seconds) because the buffer is full or the time has come to flush the buffer to disk.

The other options are displayed with fairly clear explanations. The last option, /FLUSH=ON, avoids a problem that has been reported with other versions of DOS: the delay for writing to the disk is so long, users think it's safe to turn the computer off. When this happens, all information in the buffer is gone for good. So Novell DOS 7 won't return to the command line prompt until the information in the disk buffer is written safely to disk. That doesn't take much toll on performance, because most disk access happens while inside an application program. As you can see in the Reads line in the Disk Usage Statistics box, only one out of twenty disk reads had to be done physically from the disk; 95 percent of the information that the PC needed was in the disk cache.

Disk writes were almost as good. Only one in seven disk-write requests had to be done physically to the disk at the time of request. Six out of seven times, the delayed-write cache held the information until more information was added to the cache. Writing two or more pieces of information at the same time saves the overhead of one full disk-write procedure.

The last box in the bottom right of the screen shows how many errors have occurred. The number speaks for the quality of the software, don't you think?

FILE COMPRESSION WITH STACKER

If you want more disk space (and who doesn't?), Novell DOS 7 offers Stacker, the most advanced file-compression, disk-expanding software available today. By checking a single box in the Setup program, you can have Stacker squeeze more space from your existing, partly used hard drive, leaving you with the same drive letter (usually C:) but many megabytes more disk space.

Another option is to leave drive C: the way it is and use the existing open disk space to create drive D:, the Stacker drive. Either way, you gain disk space with minimal loss of RAM. We'll cover more details on how Stacker works later in the chapter.

FLEXIBLE FILE BACKUP SOFTWARE

A new file backup and restore program, FastBack Express, is included in DOS 7. Both MS Windows and DOS versions are available. The software can back up files with compression, getting more files on the floppy diskettes than ever before. Any DOS device, such as many tape backup systems, can be used as the backup media. If you are connected to a network, the software automatically understands that and allows you to back up to a network drive if you like.

The restore function is improved as well. All files or only certain files can be restored. Virus scans during the start of the FastBack Express program ensure system integrity.

Both the DOS and MS Windows versions are attractive and easily understood. The goal here is to make you want to back up your files and keep your data safe. Using both versions of FastBack Express is described later in this chapter.

EASY INSTALLATION UNDER MS WINDOWS

After installing Novell's DOS 7 (see Appendix B), a Novell DOS group will appear in your MS Windows Program Manager screen. Many of the utilities, such as Search and Destroy, FastBack Express, and the networking commands, have MS Windows versions.

No extra work is required for DOS 7 to be useful under MS Windows. The Novell DOS 7 group includes such extras as an on-demand screen lock with a mandatory password.

Other Handy Features in Novell DOS 7

Novell DOS 7 has many features that aren't in MS DOS. The earlier version, DR-DOS 6, had memory management, disk compression, and task switching several years before MS DOS. Novell DOS 7 continues that lead in the features race. The following sections describe some of the extra features you'll appreciate.

GETTING TWO-COLUMN DIRECTORY LISTINGS WITH DIR /2

Most commands have *switches*, which are extra characters usually following a slash. These switches modify the command in some way. With the

DIR (DIRectory) command, the most common switches are /P, for page-at-a-time display, and /W, to display only the file names in wide format across the screen. With Novell DOS 7, you get a unique switch: /2.

This /2 switch displays all the normal file information that normally comes with the basic DIR command, with one added attraction. If you type DIR on any MS DOS machine, you get the file name, followed by the file size and the date and time the file was either created or last modified. Then there's a half-screen of blank space.

DIR /2 shows the same information as DIR, but in two columns down the screen. This is handy, since you don't need to use the /P (page) switch as often. A full directory listing of up to 50 files can be displayed at one time. Try this command to see the results of the /2 switch:

```
DIR \NWDOS /2
```

AVOIDING FILE LOSS WITH DISKMAP

The DISKMAP command copies your FAT (File Allocation Table) to disk, giving you a headstart in saving accidentally deleted files. DISKMAP doesn't take up any of your computer's RAM, and it will be run every time you start your computer if configured properly in the Setup program (see Appendix B).

If someone accidentally erases a file on your computer while you're at lunch, DISKMAP will help you get that file back. With some other versions of DOS, you must know the name of the file or files to recover. With DISKMAP and Novell DOS 7's UNDELETE command, that's not necessary. You can just type the command

```
DISKMAP C:
```

As a test, I deleted the AUTOEXEC.BAK and CONFIG.BAK files from my root directory on LAPTOP_PC. These files were left by the Edit program, which makes a copy of the original version of all files that are edited. As you can see by the highlighted bar on the CONFIG.BAK file, it can be undeleted without problem. The file just above it, AUTOEXEC.BAK, had just been recovered before this picture was made. See Figure 9.2 for the details.

FIGURE 9.2

Running DISKMAP makes UNDELETE work better

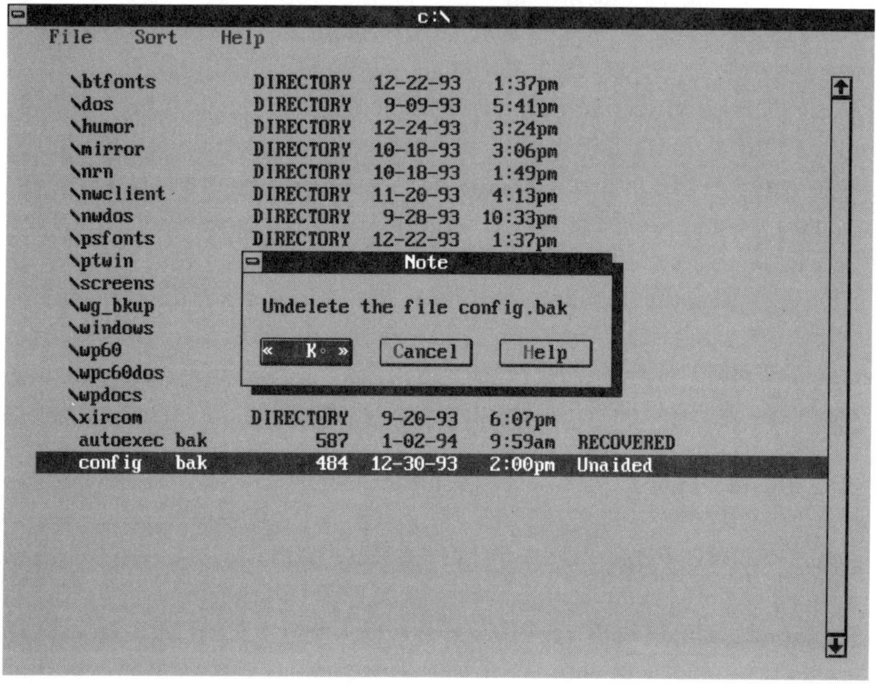

PROTECTING YOUR FILES WITH LOCK

To keep people from deleting files at your computer while you're on a coffee break, Novell DOS 7 includes the Lock program. This can be started automatically in your AUTOEXEC.BAT file or anytime from the command line. The MS Windows version will replace your regular MS Windows screen saver if you configure the Control Panel and Desktop that way.

When Lock is enabled, you must use a password to unlock the PC. This can be the master password you set through the Setup program, or it can be a password you specify when you run the Lock program from the command line, in the format

```
Lock PASSWORD
```

EXTENDING MEMORY WITH NWCDEX

Since more and more computers are requiring CD ROM drives today, Novell DOS 7 includes the NWCDEX.EXE program, an improvement over the MSCDEX.EXE program.

NWCDEX uses less conventional RAM, and it is written to take advantage of Protected Mode. That means DPMS will support all CD ROM drive functions while taking less conventional memory than MSCDEX. This file is placed in the AUTOEXEC.BAT file to load into high memory if possible.

PROVIDING SECURITY WITH PASSWORD

Continuing with security, the Password program can assign passwords to directories and even individual files. Varying levels of security can be set, ranging from protection against files being deleted to files or directories being completely out of reach for any user without the password. The master password for the computer can be configured in the Setup program, under Data Protection and Security. The command line program can begin at your discretion. For example, enter the command

```
PASSWORD C:\BUDGET /R:secret
```

to run Password and assign the password secret to the BUDGET directory.

You can also assign a master password through the Setup program. Configuring your system with a master password protects the hard disk, even when the computer is booted from a fraudulent floppy disk.

RENAMING DIRECTORIES WITH RENDIR

RENDIR (REName DIRectory) is a command that's been in NetWare for many years. It has been frustrating to try to rename directories on standalone PCs with no NetWare connections. Now computers with Novell DOS 7 can rename directories at the drop of a chapeau.

RENDIR is a DOS command in the \NWDOS directory, called an *external command* since it isn't included in the COMMAND.COM program. You don't need to configure anything in the Setup program to use this command. Its format is

```
RENDIR OLD-DIRECTORY-NAME NEW-DIRECTORY-NAME
```

CHANGING TIME AND DATE STAMPS WITH TOUCH

Long a favorite utility in the UNIX world, TOUCH finally comes to DOS. TOUCH changes the time and date stamps of a file or group of files. Any DOS wildcard command is supported. For example, the following command will reset the dates of all *.WK1 spreadsheets in the current directory to Feb 2, 1994:

```
TOUCH *.wk1 /D:02-02-94
```

DELETING MULTIPLE FILES WITH XDEL

XDEL (eXtended DELete) answers a question DOS users have been asking for years: "How can I delete multiple files in subdirectories with one command?" With DOS before Novell DOS 7, if you had four subdirectories' worth of files to delete, you needed to manually delete the files in each directory. Not that I'm particularly lazy, but this can sure be a pain with some of the twisted installation setups I see.

With Novell DOS 7, a single command will do it all. For example, to delete all files with an .WK1 extension in the current directory and all subdirectories, enter

```
XDEL *.WK1 /S
```

LISTING FILE FEATURES WITH XDIR

Since Novell DOS 7 includes features beyond regular DOS, it includes a new command to display these features: XDIR (for eXtended DIRectory). This command shows files in alphabetical order with security attributes and the percentage of file compression. As you can see in Figure 9.3, the \NRN directory on LAPTOP_PC has a few files that have 8:1 compression, but the average ratio is 1.8:1.

```
C:\NRN>xdir
DIRECTORY                        10-18-93   1:49p  c:.
DIRECTORY                        10-18-93   1:49p  c:..
------      121,278  2.7:1    9-22-93   9:36a  c:aiomdms.mdc
------          129  8.0:1   10-17-93   7:12p  c:dialcon.001
------      198,473  1.6:1    9-20-93   2:56p  c:dialcon.exe
------       12,716  2.3:1    9-20-93   1:05p  c:dialcon.hlp
------           79  8.0:1   10-17-93   9:44p  c:dialcon.trc
------       30,051  1.6:1    4-23-93   8:58a  c:ipxodi.com
------      108,619  1.6:1    6-04-91   4:09p  c:login.exe
------       23,675  1.5:1    1-31-91   4:13p  c:logout.exe
------        8,780  1.7:1   11-05-92   2:40p  c:lsl.com
------       48,133  1.5:1    1-21-91  11:20a  c:map.exe
------          207  8.0:1   10-17-93   6:41p  c:net.bak
----h-          207  8.0:1   10-17-93   7:12p  c:net.cfg
------       77,582  1.5:1    2-17-93   1:41p  c:netx.exe
------       38,421  2.2:1    9-22-93  10:08a  c:nrn.com
------          631  8.0:1    9-14-93   3:59p  c:readme.nrn
------        3,118  2.7:1    7-24-90  12:00p  c:sys_err.dta
------        3,722  2.0:1    7-24-90  12:00p  c:sys_help.dta
------       12,468  2.7:1    7-24-90  12:00p  c:sys_msg.dta
total files 18   total bytes 688,289   disk free space 39,718,912
average compression ratio 1.8:1

C:\NRN>
```

FIGURE 9.3
The XDIR command showing a password-protected file

The second thing you might notice is the small *h* in the first column of the listing for the NET.CFG file. Since NET.CFG is a file that is critical to the network, I placed a password on the file. That password shows up as the *h* in the middle of the dashes.

DOSBook: The Best PC Help System Around

Everyone needs help with their computer now and then. To provide that help, Novell DOS 7 includes a complete set of on-line documentation called DOSBook.

Start DOSBook by typing

```
DOSBOOK
```

on the command line. You'll see the opening screen, welcoming you to DOSBook, as shown in Figure 9.4. This screen allows you to jump to any of the five major areas of DOSBook.

Another way to quickly reach help for a particular command is to type

```
DOSBOOK COMMAND-NAME
```

on the command line. This takes you directly to the reference page for that command.

FIGURE 9.4

DOSBook at your service

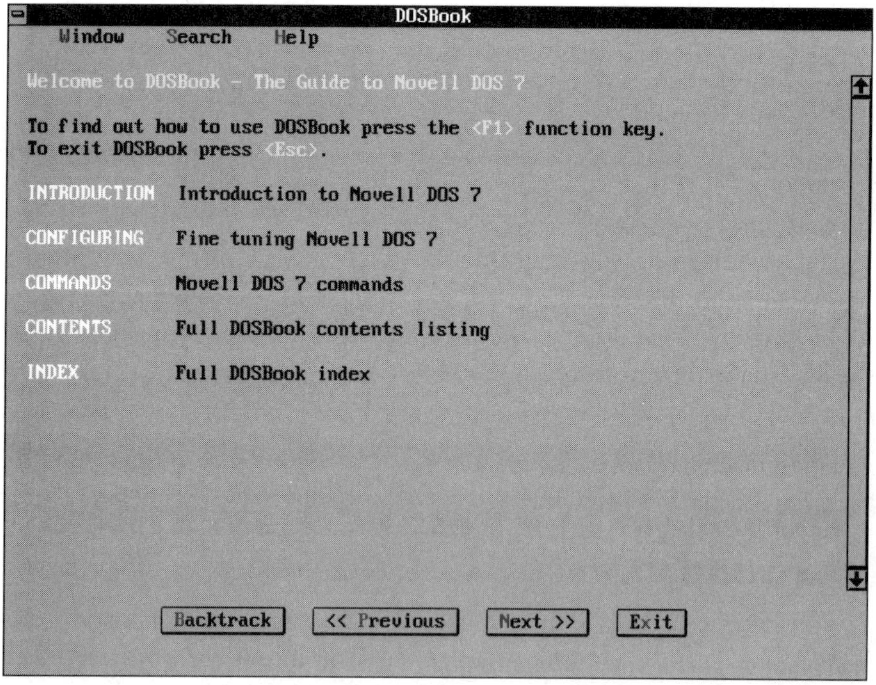

DOSBOOK HOTSPOTS

DOSBook uses hotspots, just as in the MS Window Help function, although the Novell DOS 7 manual calls them glossary keywords. When you highlight those words by advancing the cursor with the Tab key, a special window pops open as long as you hold down the Enter key (or the mouse button if you're using a mouse). See Figure 9.5 for an illustration of these amazing hotspots.

The hotspots are in green and usually in lowercase letters. The words and phrases that jump to new sections in DOSBook are red, and they contain at least some uppercase letters. Color is the best indicator, but if you have a monochrome screen like LAPTOP_PC, take what clues you can.

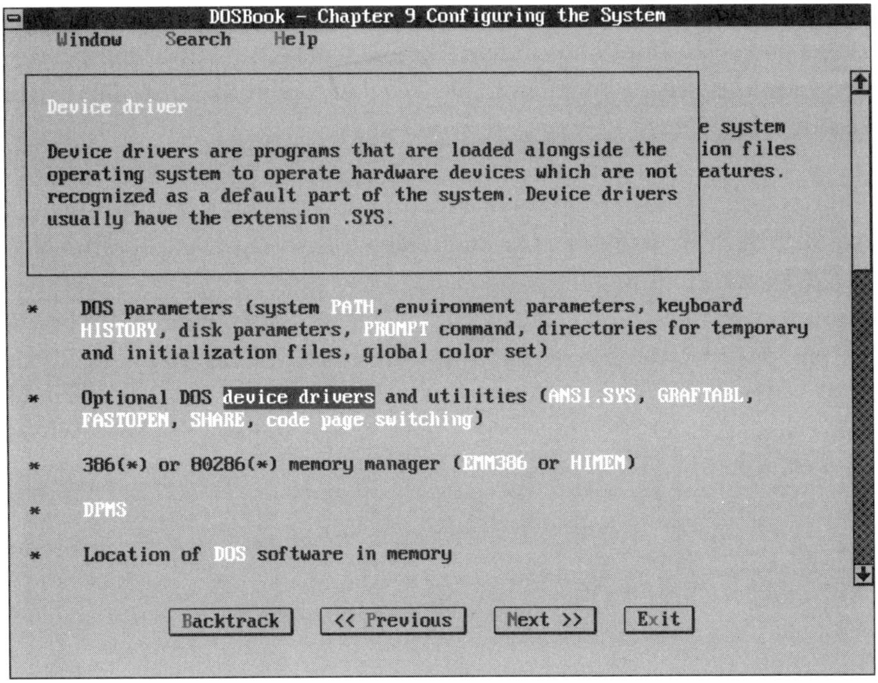

FIGURE 9.5
Highlighting a hotspot word in DOSBook

DOSBOOK COMMAND BUTTONS

Notice the command buttons at the bottom of the screen in Figure 9.5. If you accidentally jump to a new section when you wanted a hotspot explanation (because you don't have a color monitor), use Alt-B for Backtrack. That will return you from whence you came, like breadcrumbs in the fairy tale forest.

The next two command buttons, labeled Previous and Next, move you forward and backward through the pages of DOSBook. This is akin to paging through a physical book.

The last command button, Exit, takes you back to the DOS command line.

OTHER DOSBOOK FEATURES

Need a hardcopy of a section, as you can get by printing MS Windows Help screens? Nothing shortchanged here just because we don't have icons. Press Alt-W to see the Window menu. The first choice is to print the current section.

Can't find what you're looking for by perusing the pages in logical order? Then search intelligently. There's a menu labeled Search, but the quickest way to acquire wisdom is just to start typing the word you want to find. The Index Search window will pop open, and a text field will display your typed characters. Press Enter when you're finished, and the command you typed, or the closest word the system could figure out, is highlighted in the DOSBook Index. From there, you can press Enter to see information about your command. Figure 9.6 shows the Index Search window on the trail of recreation.

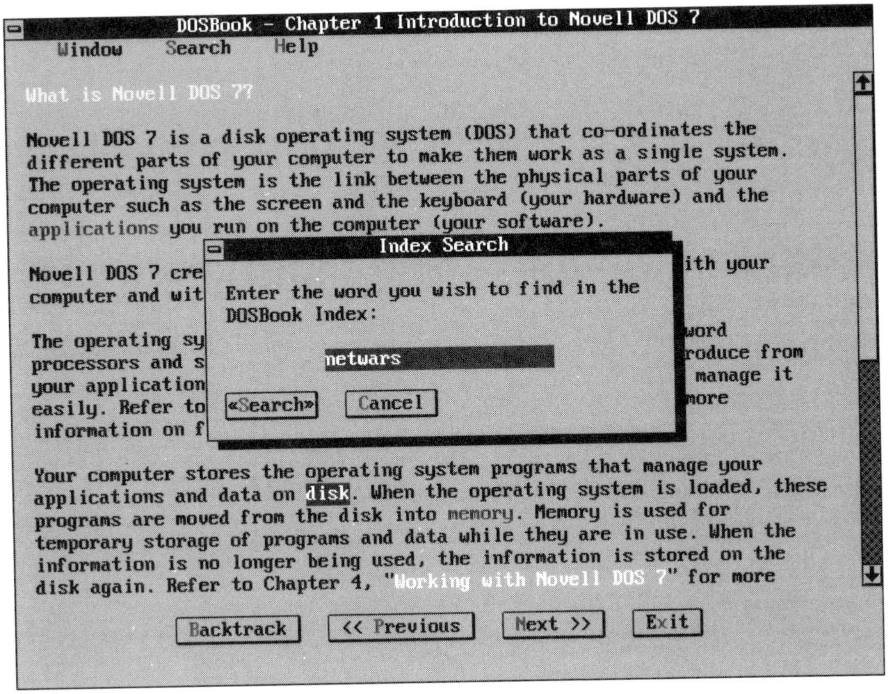

FIGURE 9.6

If you can type it, DOSBook will search for it

Using Edit

Those of you new to computers may never know the curse of using EDLIN. A line editor, rather than a full-screen text editor, EDLIN came along with the first version of MS DOS back in 1981 and still persists today. If you ever need a testament to the persistence of bad ideas and bad products, EDLIN is it.

The Edit program included with Novell DOS 7 is a full-screen text editor. Menus and generous Help screens are included, along with the original WordStar keystrokes for most functions. Another piece of nostalgia today, WordStar was the first decent word processor that became popular on CP/M computers and cornered the early PC market. The early computer pioneers learned the WordStar convoluted Ctrl key commands so well they are unable to forget them to this day. Why does Ctrl-Y delete a line of text in Edit? Because WordStar did it that way.

Enough reminiscing. Edit is the tool to use to create a new text file, edit a text file, or browse through a text file. A *text file* is one where standard ASCII characters define all the letters and numbers, and no special formatting is used within the file itself. The best examples of text files are CONFIG.SYS and AUTOEXEC.BAT. In the MS Windows directories, all the files with the extension .INI are text files as well, and they can be read and edited using the Edit program.

To run the program, type

```
EDIT
```

on the command line. Figure 9.7 shows the opening screen, labeled Select File to Edit.

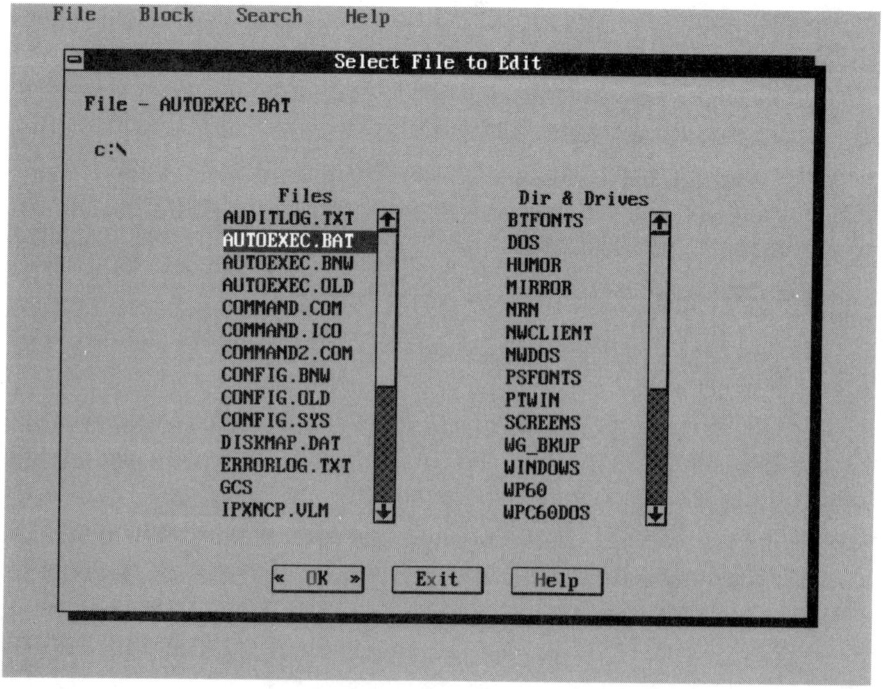

FIGURE 9.7

Preparing to edit AUTOEXEC.BAT using Edit

To create a new text file, type a name for the new file in the File text box. Edit will check to confirm that you want to create a new file.

RETRIEVING A FILE

To move to a list box on the Select File to Edit screen, press the Tab key to go forward or Shift-Tab to go backward. You can either type the file name directly into the File text box or highlight it in the Files box and have Edit fill in the name automatically. In Figure 9.7, you can see AUTOEXEC.BAT is highlighted.

Press Enter to retrieve the highlighted file. Be aware that Edit makes no distinction between files it can and cannot edit. For example, the fifth file in the list in Figure 9.7 is COMMAND.COM, definitely not a text file. Be careful in choosing your files to edit.

EDITING A FILE

Figure 9.8 shows the AUTOEXEC.BAT file after being retrieved into Edit. Pressing Alt and the first letter of each menu drops down that menu. Pressing F1 calls context-sensitive Help screens.

As indicated by the notation Ins on the bottom-right status line, Edit is now in Insert mode. Characters typed will be inserted into the text, not overwrite other characters. Press the Insert key to toggle between modes.

The bottom-left status line tells the name of the file being edited, the total number of characters in the file (340), and which column the cursor is on (column 1).

Extra features in Edit beyond the norm for some text editors include the ability to save portions of the current file to disk and search-and-replace features. Do you have a text file referencing *Abby* but you now need to reference *Michelle*? That's a good chore for search and replace.

FIGURE 9.8

Editing a text file with Edit

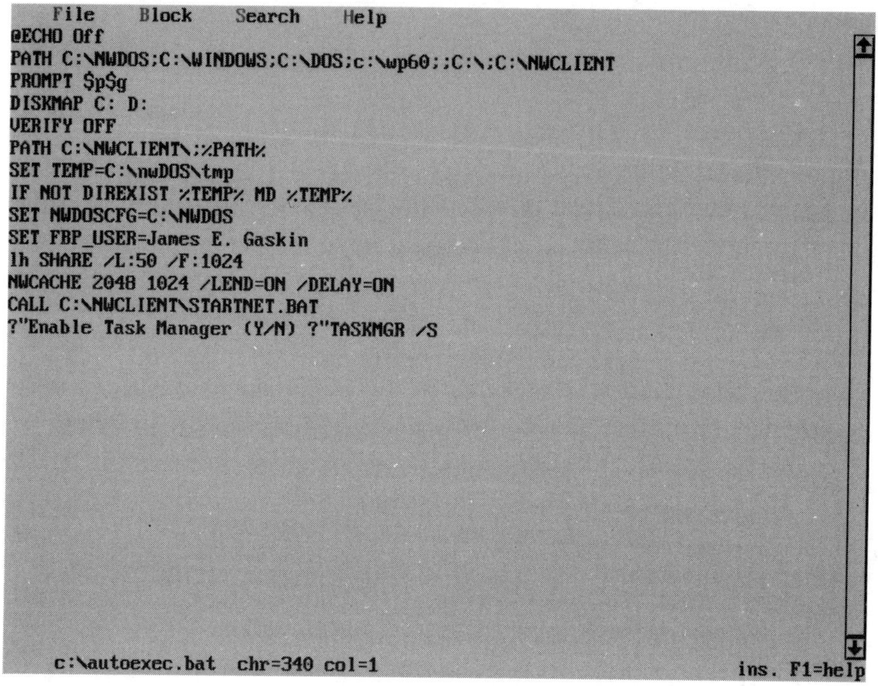
File Block Search Help
@ECHO Off
PATH C:\NWDOS;C:\WINDOWS;C:\DOS;c:\wp60;;C:\;C:\NWCLIENT
PROMPT pg
DISKMAP C: D:
VERIFY OFF
PATH C:\NWCLIENT\;%PATH%
SET TEMP=C:\nwDOS\tmp
IF NOT DIREXIST %TEMP% MD %TEMP%
SET NWDOSCFG=C:\NWDOS
SET FBP_USER=James E. Gaskin
lh SHARE /L:50 /F:1024
NWCACHE 2048 1024 /LEND=ON /DELAY=ON
CALL C:\NWCLIENT\STARTNET.BAT
?"Enable Task Manager (Y/N) ?"TASKMGR /S
c:\autoexec.bat chr=340 col=1
ins. F1=help

The Block menu includes commands for copy, move, and delete functions, as you would expect. There's also a handy Block menu command that saves the highlighted block.

One feature not found in any other text editor is the ability to call up DOSBook from within Edit (by choosing DOSBook from the Help menu). Since Edit is often used to modify one of the configuration files for your computer, having the complete reference available in DOSBook makes sense. Figure 9.9 shows DOSBook called from within Edit.

FIGURE 9.9

The complete DOSBook is available within Edit

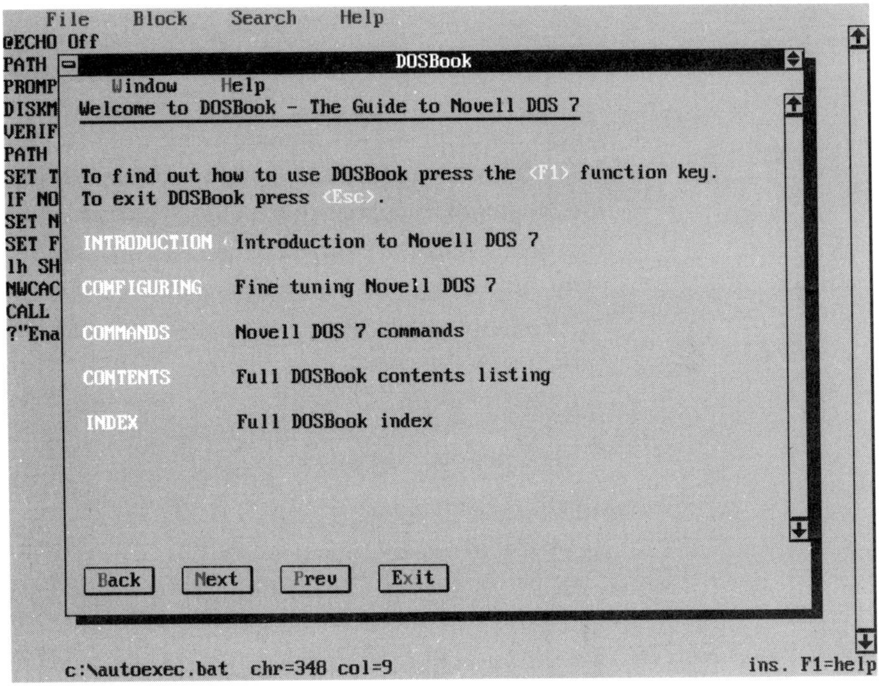

Backing Up Your Disk

We've talked about disk backup. I've threatened you with dire consequences if you don't back up your files regularly, like every day. I know you won't back up enough, but my conscience is clear; I've warned you all I can.

Novell DOS 7 includes programs to help the backup process. You can't say it's too hard to back up, because these programs make things easy.

One of the more popular backup utilities around since the early DOS days is FastBack. Novell DOS 7 includes FastBack Express in both DOS and MS Windows versions. Let's look at the DOS version first.

FASTBACK EXPRESS FOR DOS

Configuration of FastBack Express is done within that program itself, not with the Setup program. You can see on the opening screen, shown in

Figure 9.10, that there are at least four ways to choose which files to back up. Type

FBX

from the command line to start the DOS version of FastBack Express.

FastBack Express allows you to back up any drive seen by your PC, including all the network drives. It also allows you to back up to any drive that your PC can see, including all the Personal NetWare volumes and NetWare file servers you have mapped.

This shows good work on the part of the programmers, but don't think that FastBack Express replaces your need for a solid backup tape system and plan. Using someone else's disk drive is fine for storing backup copies of important files, but not for your regular backup routine.

Try backing up to floppy disks one time, and I'll guarantee you a weekly backup will come lower on your priority list than septic tank repair by hand. Get a tape system.

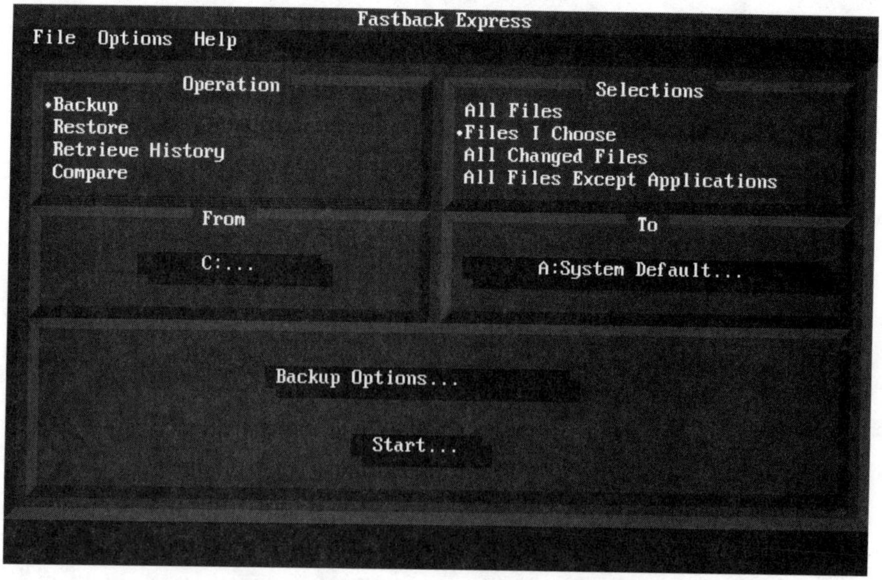

FIGURE 9.10
The opening screen of FastBack Express for Novell DOS 7

FASTBACK PLUS EXPRESS FOR MS WINDOWS

Not to leave out the mouse-friendly, an MS Windows version of FastBack Plus Express is included in Novell DOS 7 as well. All the same features from the DOS version are here. Click on the FastBack Plus Express icon in the Novell DOS group to start the program. Figure 9.11 shows the screen for choosing files to back up.

Optimizing Your Hard Disk

Did you know your computer scatters files around your hard disk like you do around your desk? And for the same reasons you do: there's no room to put these files where they belong.

The technical term for these scattered files is *noncontiguous*. Files are stored in blocks of data, and each file is written into the first available space. But when files grow, they no longer fit into the space they did originally. They then must leave a pointer to the next open space where there's room for the next data blocks. Then of course, that space gets filled, and they

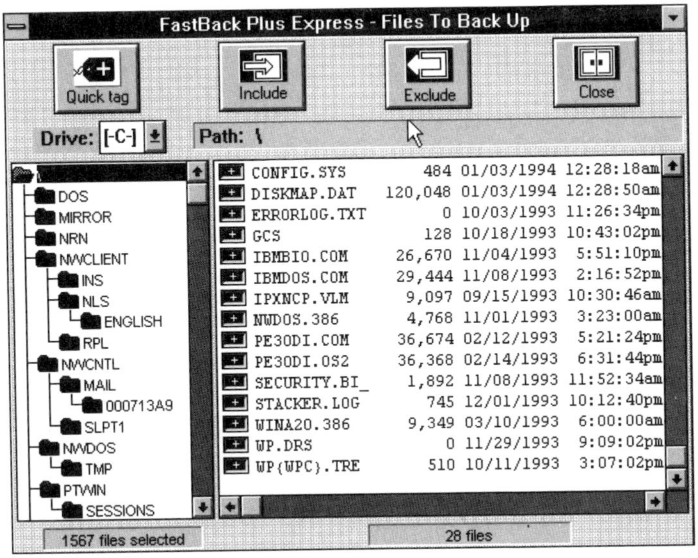

FIGURE 9.11
Choosing files to back up from LAPTOP_PC

overflow again, and blocks for this file are stored in a third place.

If you have an active hard disk, this happens quite a bit. Novell DOS 7's Disk Optimizer utility restacks all your files so the data blocks for each file are next to each other. These consecutive blocks, as you might guess, are technically called *contiguous*.

In Figure 9.12, the little dots are data blocks. See the big open space about two-thirds down the disk? That's the result of an active disk, deleting some directories. Disk Optimizer will fill that space in while consolidating all the file blocks. To start this program from the command line, type

```
DISKOPT
```

Notice that the upper-right corner tells us this is a Stacker drive. You'll find information about this Stacker drive in the next section, but it's not your typical hard disk configuration. Disk Optimizer is specially written by Novell to work with the Stacker drive-compression technology.

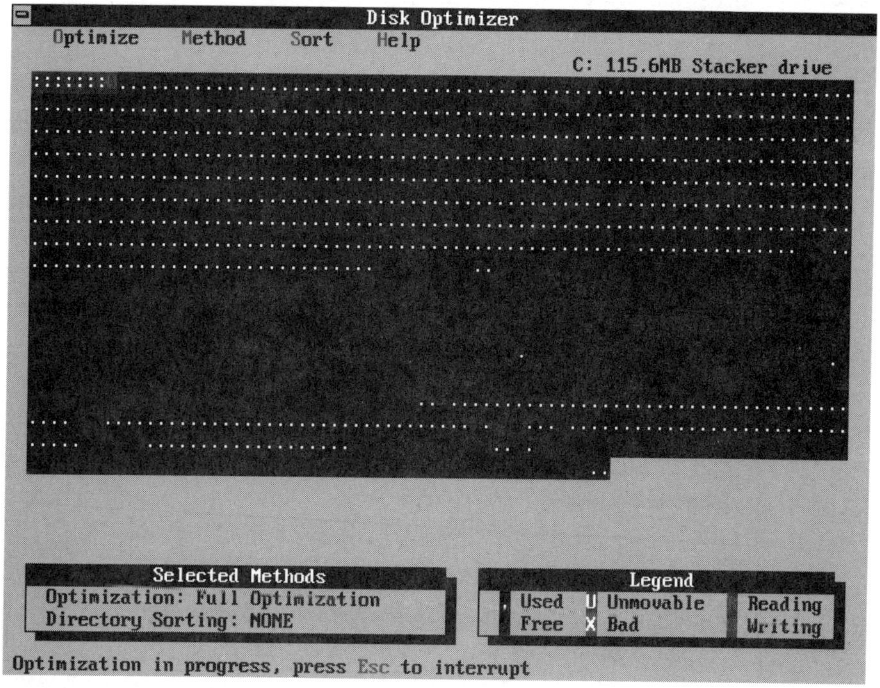

FIGURE 9.12

Don't you wish it were this easy to organize your desk?

Disk Compression: More Disk Space for Almost Free

Here's the beauty of the Stacker program: the physical disk in Figure 9.12 is only 60 MB. But wait, you say, the upper-right corner of the picture says it's a 115.6 MB Stacker drive. That's right. It's only a 60 MB drive physically, but Stacker enables that disk to hold 115 MB of information.

The term *disk compression* is backwards; it should really be disk expander, but more often it's called data compression. That's the apparent result when you compress all the files on the disk. Ever wad up your clothes really tight to get more in the suitcase? That's the same idea. If you make every file smaller, you have room for more files.

The data compression is configured through the Setup program. Figure 9.13 is the Disk Compression screen (see why everyone's confused—even

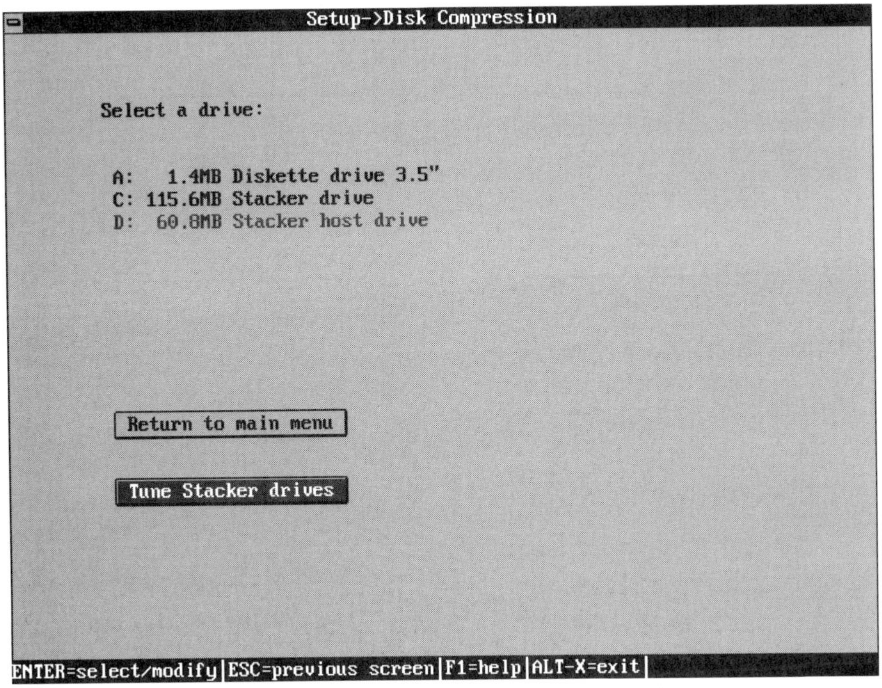

FIGURE 9.13
The 60.8 MB host drive became a 115.6 MB Stacker drive

the program screens say disk compression) in Setup. Since LAPTOP_PC is already stacked, as evidenced by Figure 9.12, Figure 9.13 offers me the chance to run Stacker on a floppy drive. See Appendix B for more details on configuring Stacker drives.

If you do stack a floppy drive, it can be used with non-Stacker equipped computers by loading a driver from the floppy to the second computer. The operation to load those files on the stacked floppy is automatic. It's weird to get well over 2 MB on a regular 3.5-inch floppy disk, but certainly handy at times.

Protecting Yourself Against Viruses

A computer virus is a rogue program that lives to cause mischief. Of course, if your PC has been infected by a virus, you learn two important things: mischief is not a strong enough word, and safe computing is becoming as important as safe sex.

Novell DOS 7 includes several options for your peace of mind. First, the Data Protection and Security option in the Setup program sets a resident Search and Destroy program to load every time you start your computer. The TSR (terminate-and-stay-resident program) will monitor files the entire time your computer is on.

If you rarely work with diskettes from other computers, your chance of getting a virus is lessened. In that case, you may prefer to run Search and Destroy on a regular basis, rather than have it loaded every minute your computer is on. If that's the case, you can use either the DOS or MS Windows versions of the program included with Novell DOS 7.

The Novell DOS group in MS Windows has an icon for Search and Destroy. Figure 9.14 shows the Scan options for the MS Windows version of Search and Destroy. For those that prefer a true feeling of power and control, suspect files can be dragged from the File Manager onto the Search and Destroy icon. When the mouse button is released to drop the file, Search and Destroy will start examining the file.

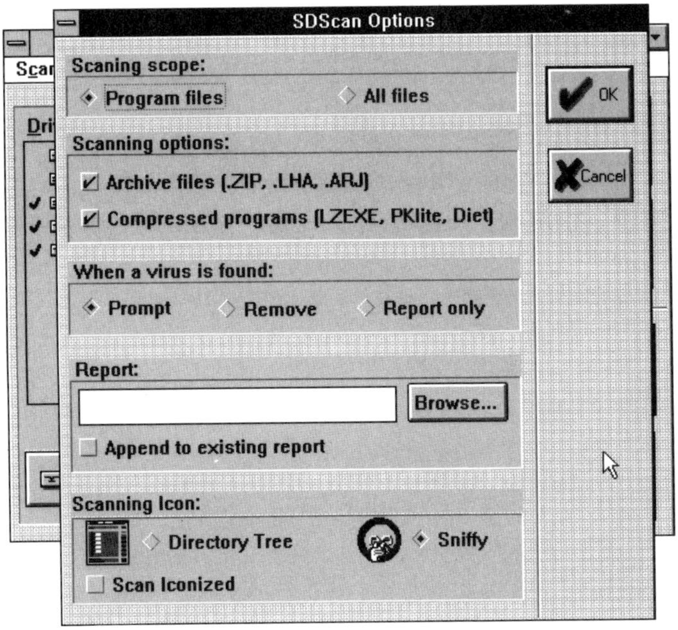

FIGURE 9.14
Search and Destroy Scan options

The DOS version can be run from the command line at any time. Just type

```
SDSCAN
```

and feel your peace of mind improve as every file is individually examined for a virus.

APPENDIX A

How Do I Install Personal NetWare?

The world of personal computers is too varied to provide exact instructions for installing your particular software configuration on your particular computers. So the plan here is to provide a general outline. You'll also get some of the philosophy of installation. If you can understand the goal of the installation process, you can overcome the little aggravations that may appear.

What the Manual Doesn't Tell You about Planning Your Network

The best advice I can give you for setting up your network is this: don't expect to get it perfect the first time. And don't let anyone make you feel bad about that.

This is the classic no-win situation. You must make all the important decisions before you have any real idea of what you're doing. There is no time to grow into networking gradually, since the network either "is" or "isn't." When you boot the software on your first Personal NetWare server, you're committed. Remember the joke about the difference between involvement and commitment? If you're talking eggs and bacon, the chicken is involved; the pig is committed.

The evening you sit down to install the first two or three computers in your new network, you become committed. People will ask the next morning to see the new network. They are interested, even though they don't know exactly what it is or what it's supposed to do. So not only do you have the new technical areas to worry about, you have the attention of everyone in the office.

Your job is harder than setting up a standard NetWare file server network, because you must change the way people think about their own PCs. With a NetWare server, you add something new to the resources of the PCs: the new server. With Personal NetWare, you must add some extra complexity to existing PCs to provide access to the shared resources.

If you don't know already, you will soon discover that people have a strange relationship with their PC. It is more to them than hard disks and glass and wires falling off the back of their desk. The attachment to a PC becomes much stronger than the attachment to the copier or fax machine. It's not just the fact that the PC stays on the person's desk, because people don't feel as strongly about their phone as they do about their PC.

Remember the human side of the network. Remember to tell people the great advantages they'll get with this new network. But always remember that people become attached to their PCs, so treat the machines with more respect than mere hardware deserves.

Networking Components

The Personal NetWare manual is neutral when discussing network interface card types and network topologies, but I'm not. Unless you're part of a large company with established network guidelines, buy 10Base-T Ethernet interface cards and network cabling.

This is not the place for a long-winded discussion of network protocol types and the advantages and disadvantages of each. Just trust me when I direct you toward 10Base-T Ethernet, even for small networks.

YOUR NETWORK CABLING TYPE

10Base-T is the type of Ethernet that transmits signals over UTP (unshielded twisted-pair wire), the same as phone cable. Ethernet also uses thick (expensive) and thin (less expensive, but still more expensive than UTP) coax cable. The thin coax looks like the cable for cable television. The thick coax looks like a yellow water hose. If you're lucky, you'll never see or deal with thick coax. If you're smart, you won't install thin coax.

Coax connects all the computers together like a daisy chain. If the chain breaks, nothing works. UTP connects your computers together like the phone system. If the phone cable gets broken between your desk and the wall, it doesn't bother the phones in the next office.

Taking the phone analogy a bit further, physically wiring the network is easier with 10Base-T. Since it's the same wire type used by phones, you can find more companies that can install this type of wiring.

Like your phone, the wire from each desk goes back to a central point, called a *hub* or *concentrator* by 10Base-T types. This wiring hub or concentrator makes the network portion of things work properly, and it requires no setup or fancy installation. Each computer's cable eventually plugs directly into this hub. As your network grows, hubs can be connected together, and the network can expand with little problem. Take a look at Figure A.1 for a simple, graphic definition of a 10Base-T network.

The area labeled wiring closet in Figure A.1 may not be an actual closet, of course. You may not know where it is, but there's a place where all the phone wires from all the phones come together, and I don't mean a singles'

FIGURE A.1

A diagram of a 10Base-T network for your workgroup

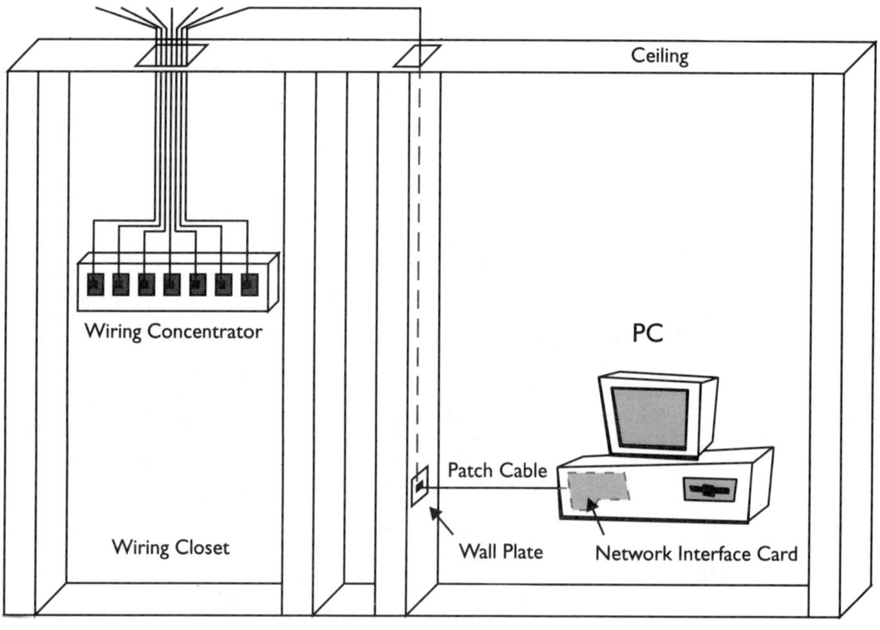

bar. The person or company that installed your phone system knows where it is, and that's where you want to put your wiring concentrator.

10Base-T cabling uses two pairs of wires. Your phone may use two pairs, or it may use only one pair. Your phone at home uses only one pair. Don't call a pair "two wires," because that's not the same thing.

For your network to run properly, the two wires in a pair must be physically twisted around each other. That is, believe it or not, where they got the name twisted pair. All the wire in your network must be twisted pair, unlike your phone system. Often, the piece of phone cable that goes between your phone and the wall is not twisted. It's called *flat satin* cable, because the cable is flat and the plastic sheath is usually a silver-satin color. The cable is flat because the wires inside are running alongside each other, rather than being twisted around each other. But for network cabling, twisted is not only better, it's mandatory.

The two pairs of wires for your network can be inside the same bundle of wires that connects your phones. That's why I say that the people who installed your phone system may be able to install your network cabling. If they're at all hesitant, however, get a network cabling specialist. The price should be comparable.

There is an extra expense with 10Base-T cabling over that for thin Ethernet. The wiring concentrator is not needed with the coax. However, the concentrator will keep your network running longer and with much less hassle than the coax. The price differential is less than $100 per PC between coax and 10Base-T with a wiring concentrator. The cabling cost is usually less for 10Base-T, so you may well pay for the concentrator with the money you save from the cabling. Even if you don't, get the 10Base-T system anyway.

Tell the cable people you want Data Grade UTP Level 4 or above. Show them the wiring pin diagrams from the instruction book that came with your 10Base-T Ethernet network interface cards. Make sure they guarantee every cable works with data networking, not just phone signals. Networks are much more demanding of the cable quality than are phones. Don't let them test the cable runs with a phone-type tester and think that's enough.

Can you do this yourself? No. Unless you're a cable company adding networking to your own offices, don't try this on your own.

YOUR NETWORK INTERFACE CARD

Dozens of 10Base-T Ethernet network interface cards are available. Prices range from under $100 to more than $400, depending on the type of computer you have. If you have a standard ISA bus computer, as most people do, you will be hard pressed to pay more than $200 for a card. Expect to pay lots more for MicroChannel or EISA cards (but note that you can now use ISA cards on any EISA PC). Expect to pay a bit more for local bus cards, but there's little reason to pay the difference and limit your number of potential suppliers this way.

Whose card should you buy? I don't care, as long as the card supports Novell's ODI network drivers. The big names in the business are 3Com, SMC, IBM, HP, Cabletron, Compex, Eagle, IMC, Microdyne, Racal Interlan, and Thomas Conrad. The newer entrants into the market include Intel and National Semiconductor, suppliers of many Ethernet component parts over the years. 3Com made the first card (and invented Ethernet, by the way) and still makes a great "name brand" card. The network used in writing this book includes 3Com, SMC, and Thomas Conrad interface cards, along with a parallel-port Ethernet adapter from Xircom. All of these mix and match without a problem.

Now comes the sticky part: installing the network interface card into a PC. Open your Personal NetWare manual to Section 2. The gist of this section is to show you, with two good tables, how to configure the network interface card to work together with all the things going on in your PC already.

Think of your PC as a bookshelf. Plenty of books are in place already, with just a few spaces open. You must put the correct book in the appropriate space on the shelf. Sometimes the shelf is full, but usually there's room for one more. You just may have to rearrange a few things.

All network interface cards have default settings for their IRQ (interrupt request line) and I/O (basic input/output port) memory addresses. Too often these settings conflict with standard PC equipment. That's why the table in Section 2 of the Personal NetWare manual is important.

If you have two active serial ports on your PC (such as a mouse and a modem), you can't use IRQ 3, one of the most popular default settings for network interface cards. Be careful with this setting, because even if you don't see two physical serial ports on the back of your computer, that IRQ setting may be used by the PC anyway. IRQ 5 is a good choice, but CD ROM drive controllers like that setting as well, so be careful. Network interface cards tend to be more flexible in settings than most other cards, because they've been fighting this configuration battle for ten years.

With a 386 or higher processor, you have a lot more options. IRQ settings of 9 through 12 and IRQ 15 are good choices. The 3Com 3C509 card in TWR_PC comes with a default setting of IRQ 10. I haven't seen anything conflict with that setting.

The next hurdle is the I/O port address. The most popular I/O address on network interface cards is 300, which is generally open. If it isn't open, because of a CD ROM drive or the like, try 340, then 240, then 2A0.

Some network interface cards use a base memory address, such as C800 or D000, but the newer ones usually don't use these addresses. The problem with cards that use these addresses is that they may conflict with your memory management software. You may need to move this address around a bit to find a location that doesn't scramble your memory manager.

Keep a sheet of paper beside you when installing a card for the first time, and write down these settings. Write them down each time you try one, and don't erase the ones that didn't work, just mark through them. Since few PCs are identical, what doesn't work on one PC may be the only viable option on the next PC. Besides that, you'll need these addresses when you configure the Personal NetWare software.

Installing the Smart Way: From the Server

If you are upgrading from NetWare Lite or adding Personal NetWare to an existing network with a Novell file server in place, all the Personal NetWare installation can be done from the network server. Of course, if you don't have a network yet, this method won't work for you. If you do have a network but it consists of less than eight users, this centralized installation method isn't worth the trouble to set up. However, if you have lots of users to install, or just dislike feeding a few floppies to machine after machine, this method can save you some time.

To begin, create a directory on your server just for this project. Name it something simple like \PNW, or \INSTALL. Copy all the Personal NetWare diskettes to that directory by using the following command:

```
XCOPY A:*.* F: /S /E /V
```

This example is guessing that your floppy drive is drive A:, and the network drive you have mapped to the server is drive F:. You want to use the XCOPY command because it reads several files at once, then writes them all at once, which makes the file copy process go more quickly. The normal COPY command reads and then writes each file separately.

The switches (/S /E /V) work with the XCOPY command as follows:

- /S copies all subdirectories.
- /E copies any empty subdirectories found.
- /V verifies each copy operation.

After the files are copied to the server, you run the installation program from that mapped drive. For example, if drive F: is the mapped drive, go to that drive before you type

```
INSTALL
```

The program will still reference your hard disk drive (C:) as the place to locate the files necessary for Personal NetWare.

What you won't need to do with this method is swap floppy disks and wait so long. Although only three floppy disks come with Personal NetWare, it still takes time to swap them. Not as much time as reading from the floppy drive, however. The speed of copying files to your PC will be increased tenfold by eliminating the slow floppy drive from the equipment involved.

Take a book or magazine with you to the installation PC. This helps pass the time as the files are copied. It also distracts you, so you're less likely to browse through the PC owner's desk as you're waiting.

Configuration and Setup

The installation process is the same for both DOS and MS Windows. Call me cautious, but when I have a choice, I prefer to use the DOS installation procedures. I don't want the MS Windows overhead when copying files, and I don't want another MS Windows program to get weird and interrupt the installation.

Before you start, write down the names of the people to be installed on each computer, both their full name and a short network name. Learn where the serial number is for each Personal NetWare package you're about to install, since you need that for the installation. You already have the information for the network interface card for each computer, written down on a piece of paper. You did note those configuration details when I told you to, didn't you?

The Personal NetWare manual, as do all software manuals, tells you to start the installation and answer the questions. They do that because the installation programs change after the manual is printed, and changes in instructions will be handled in the installation program. But I thought you might like knowing what you're getting into.

INSTALLING UNDER DOS

Before you start the installation, unload any TSRs that are running. Even if they don't cause a problem, the more memory you have during installation, the faster the file decompression will go. Most of the large files are in compressed format on the floppy, which is why Figure A.2 shows much more space to be used than three diskettes usually hold.

FIGURE A.2

The Personal NetWare installation program checks your available disk space before starting

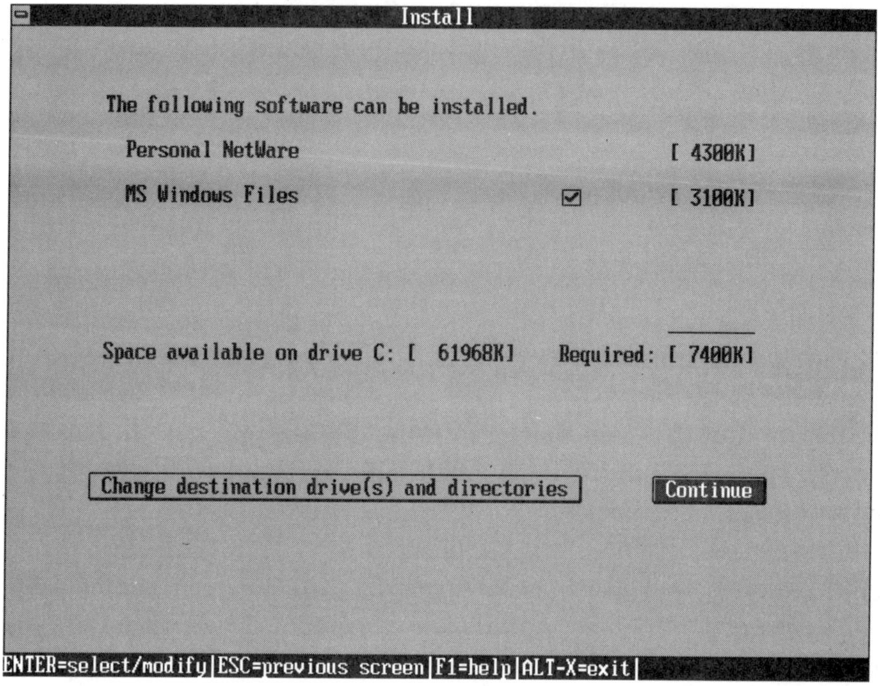

Notice the check box beside the MS Windows Files listing. If you don't want to run any of the Personal NetWare utilities under MS Windows, this is your chance to keep them from taking disk space; just make sure the box isn't checked.

See the text box offering you a chance to change destination directories? Don't do it. Let the installation program put things where it wants to put them, unless you have an extremely good reason not to.

Figure A.3 shows the primary Install screen. Everything branches off from here. I haven't checked the box to Share this computer's resources, because I want to be sure this PC connects to the network before sharing it.

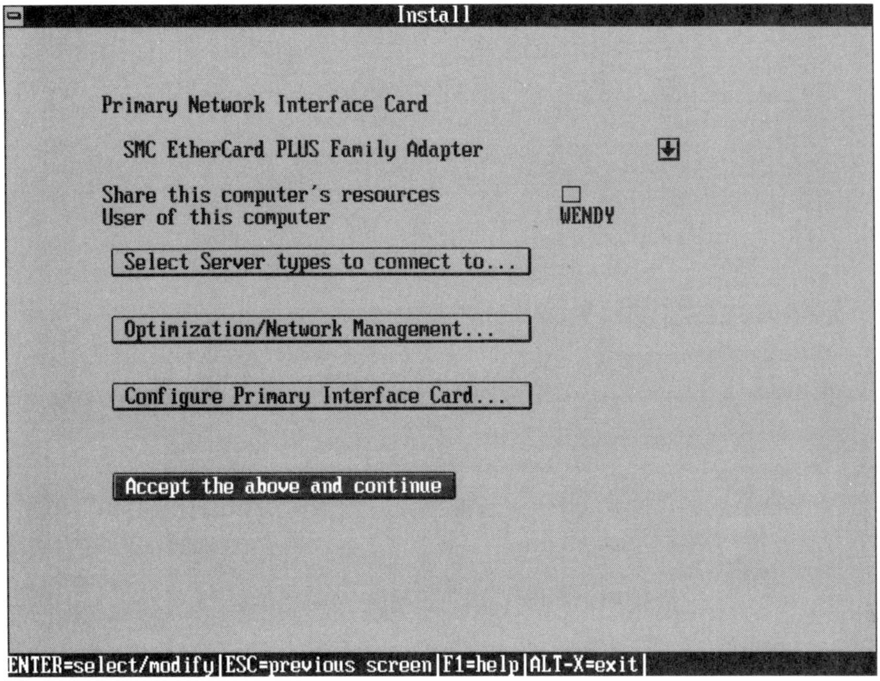

FIGURE A.3

The main installation screen for Personal NetWare in DOS

I've already chosen a network interface card from the pick list, which is indicated by the down arrow to the right of the card name. Pressing Enter on the down arrow shows a list of more than 80 different cards or card families. Figure A.4 shows a portion of the available network interface cards that the installation program knows about. More can be added, as long as your network interface card includes the proper drivers. You can't leave this screen until a name for this PC is provided.

Why don't we configure the card right now? Notice back in Figure A.3 that the last choice is to configure the primary interface card. So we'll get there soon.

FIGURE A.4

Pick a card, any card

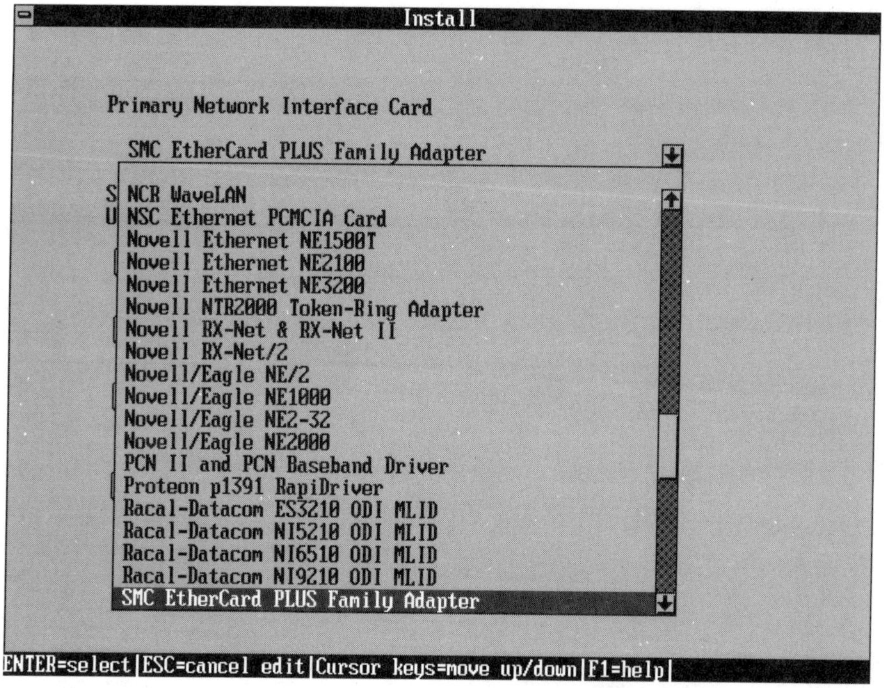

The next choice is choosing which types of NetWare servers to connect to. In the test network, all the different types of servers are available. The screen in Figure A.5 shows I have checked the box for each type of server and typed in the name of my preferred server of each type. These choices are written into the NET.CFG file, as you'll see a bit later. Checking server types you don't have gains nothing and takes extra RAM.

Following the choices down the screen in Figure A.3, our next stop is Optimization/Network Management. This screen is shown in Figure A.6. The details of DPMS software and the rest of the options are explained in Chapter 8. Notice I haven't checked the box for Load SNMP Agent, but I have checked the one for Load NMR Network Management module. SNMP is a rare sight on NetWare networks, but the NMR is necessary if you want to see information about this PC using Personal NetWare diagnostics.

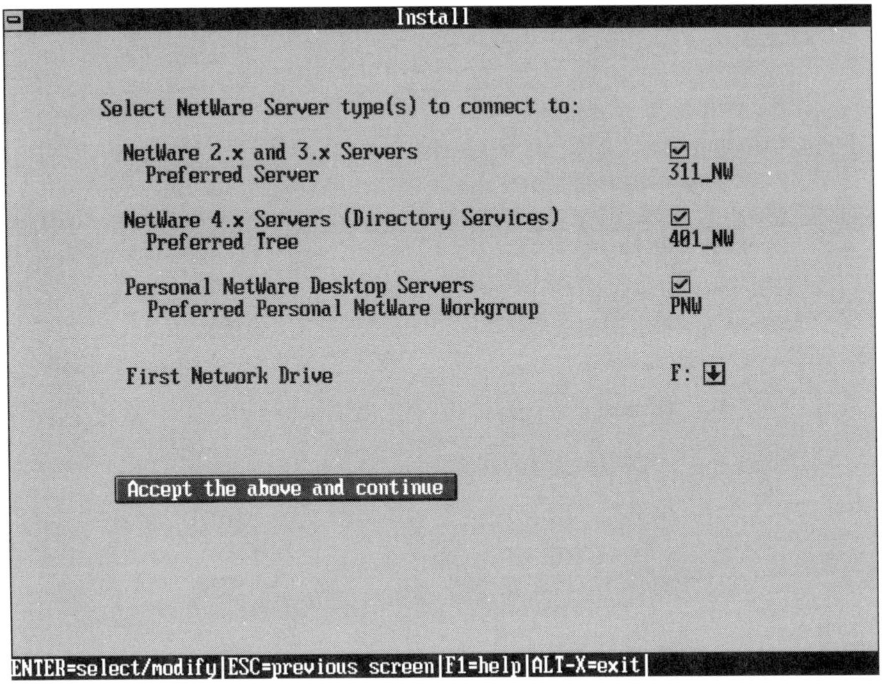

FIGURE A.5

Configuring your connections to various server types

The only Configure button in Figure A.6 is for NWCACHE. Figure A.7 shows the screen behind this button, with the default choices made by Personal NetWare for cache size. This PC, owned by Wendy, has only 6 MB of RAM. The installation program takes that into account when setting the maximum and minimum sizes for the NWCACHE.

The Allow write delays check box isn't checked when this screen appears, but I checked it. This helps performance, and Wendy's PC is already on a battery backup system (MinuteMan from Para Systems, Carrollton, Texas), so there's little danger. The box for allowing memory lending from NWCACHE is checked by default.

FIGURE A.6

Checking off the items for network optimization and management

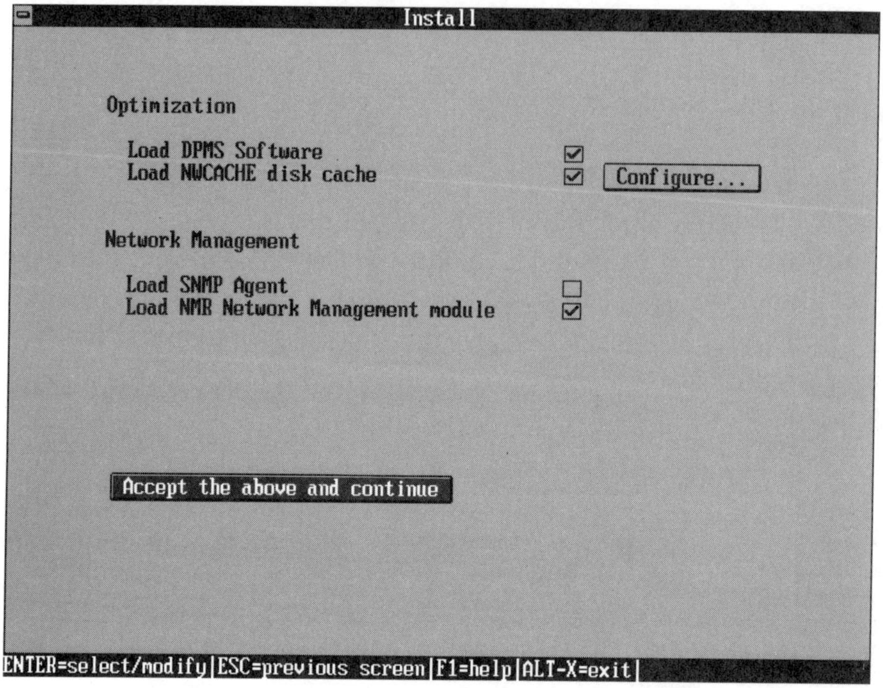

Now we return to our network interface card configuration. Figure A.8 shows the screen that configures all the details for the network interface card. These values are written into the NET.CFG file.

The Frame Types options are important. NetWare has always had a frame type of Ethernet_802.3, an early form of the Ethernet protocol packet. The rest of the world has moved to either Ethernet_802.2 or Ethernet_II frame

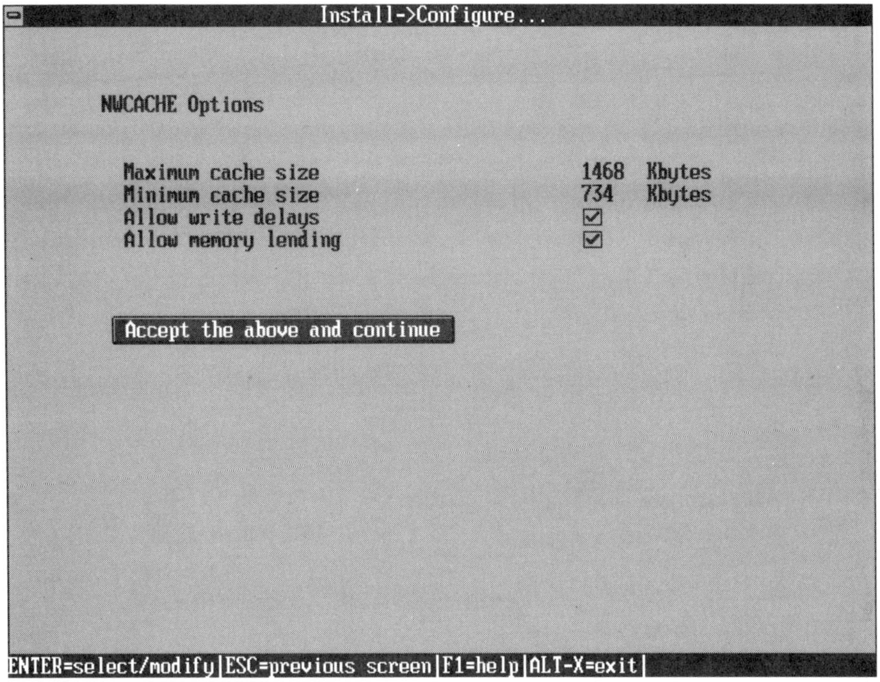

FIGURE A.7
Configuring NWCACHE options

types. Because of this move, Novell recommends changing to the Ethernet_802.2 frame type when possible. In an existing network, especially one with older NetWare servers, Ethernet_802.3 will be in use and can't be changed.

The list of choices available for each option is shown when you press Enter on the down arrow to the right. Figure A.9 shows the options for the SMC card in Wendy's PC as far as IRQs are concerned. The more modern cards support enough IRQs and I/O ports to fit with most PCs. The default values for the SMC card work for Wendy's PC. They wouldn't work for TWR_PC, however, because the CD ROM I installed there needs IRQ 5.

FIGURE A.8

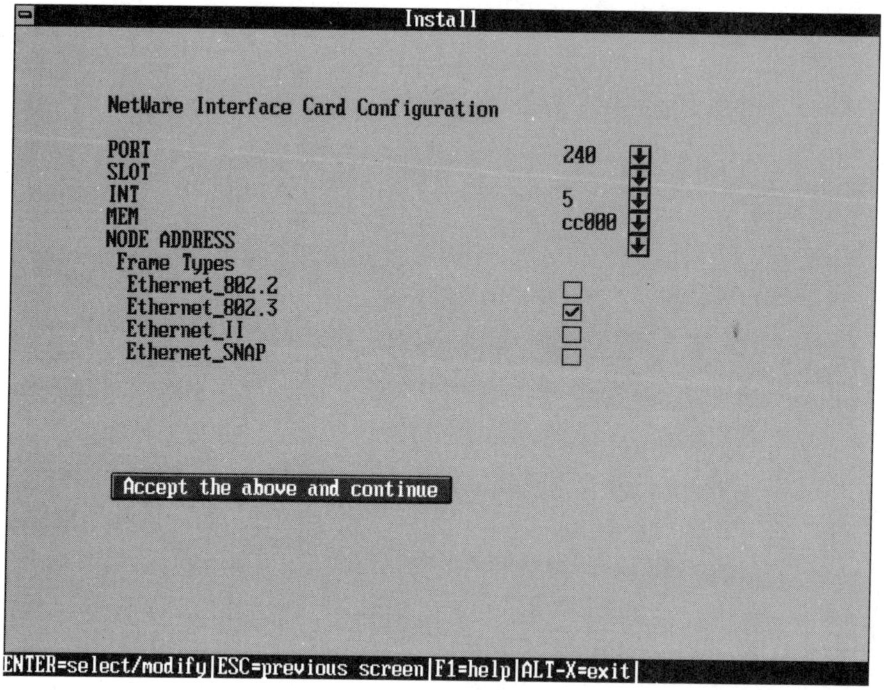

The reason to write down your network interface card parameters

Since all the submenus from the original screen in Figure A.3 have been addressed, there's nothing left to do but install Personal NetWare. Figure A.10 shows the last chance you have to change your mind before installation. The file locations shown are the defaults, as I suggested.

INSTALLING UNDER MS WINDOWS

The MS Windows version of Personal NetWare's installation program is almost the same as the DOS version. Following the manual's instructions,

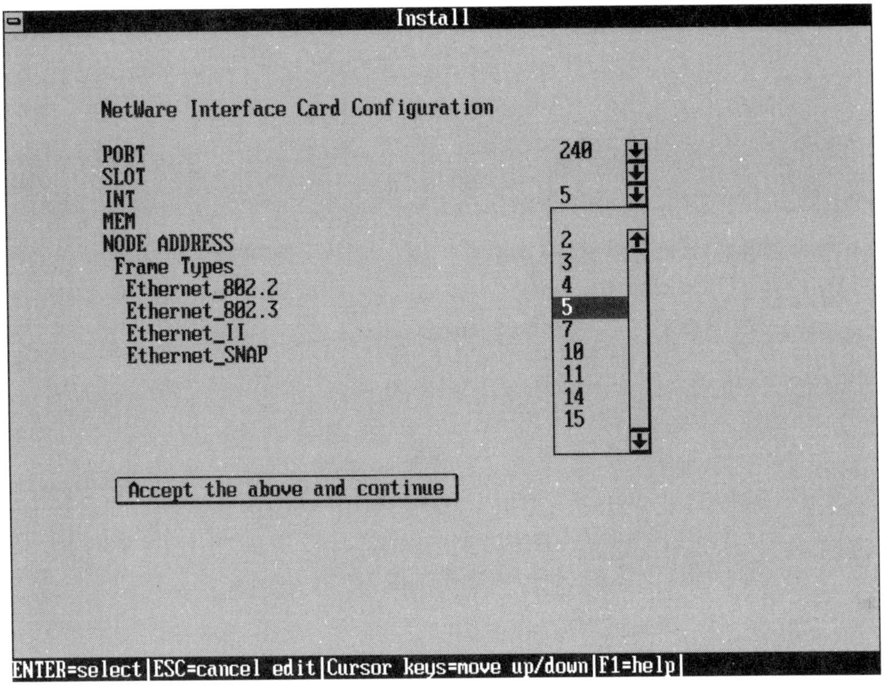

FIGURE A.9

Changing IRQ values on the network interface card

I put the floppy disk into drive B: (in Wendy's PC) and chose Run from the File menu in Program Manager. Typing

```
B:INSTALL
```

started the process and displayed the screen shown in Figure A.11.

FIGURE A.10

Last stop before networking becomes a reality

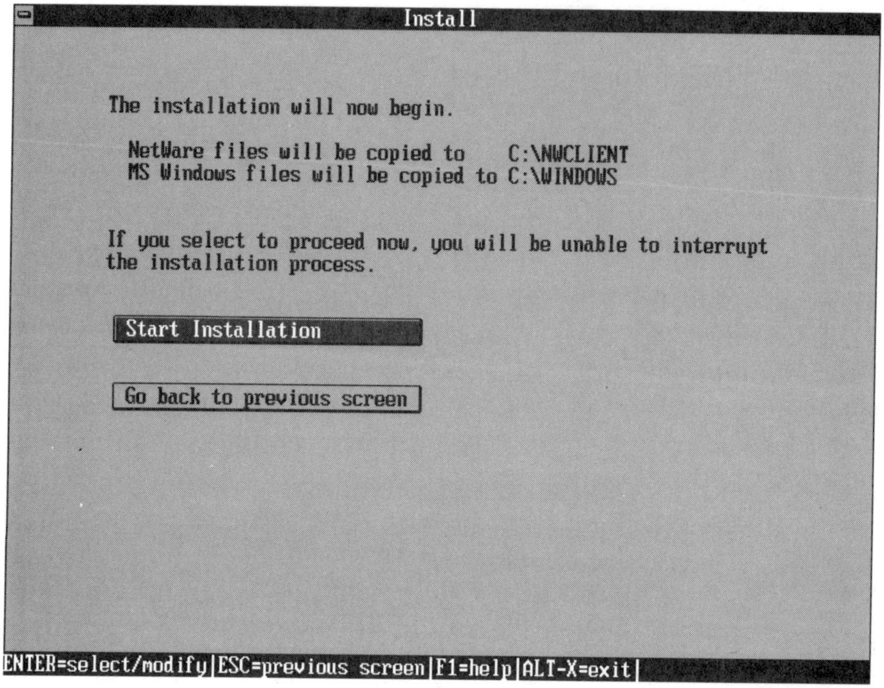
Install
The installation will now begin.
NetWare files will be copied to C:\NWCLIENT
MS Windows files will be copied to C:\WINDOWS
If you select to proceed now, you will be unable to interrupt the installation process.
Start Installation
Go back to previous screen
ENTER=select/modify|ESC=previous screen|F1=help|ALT-X=exit

You must fill in all of these text boxes to continue. The OK button stays gray until all three answers are given. When you finish and choose OK, the installation program confirms the source and destination of all the files. Keep the default values if at all possible. Doing so will save you time and trouble later on, believe me. These default values are shown in Figure A.12.

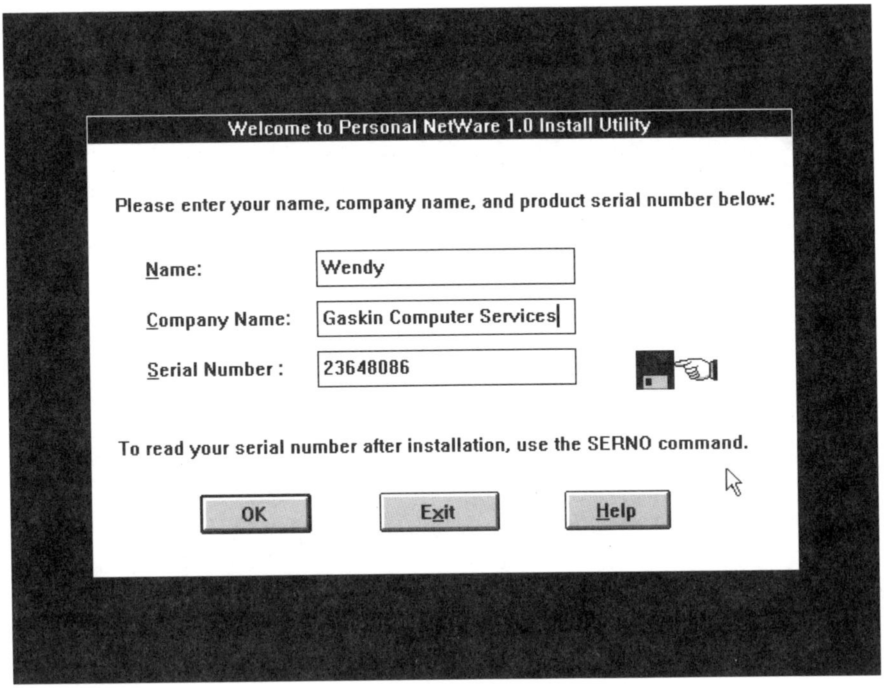

FIGURE A.11
Identifying the user of this PC in the MS Windows installation routine for Personal NetWare

Figure A.13 should remind you strongly (okay, exactly) of Figure A.3. See the discussion of these options earlier in the chapter for details.

Figures A.14, A.15, and A.16 should look just as familiar if you read the section about installing under DOS. Pretend this is a silent documentary and take a look.

FIGURE A.12

The source and destination details for the MS Windows installation of Personal NetWare

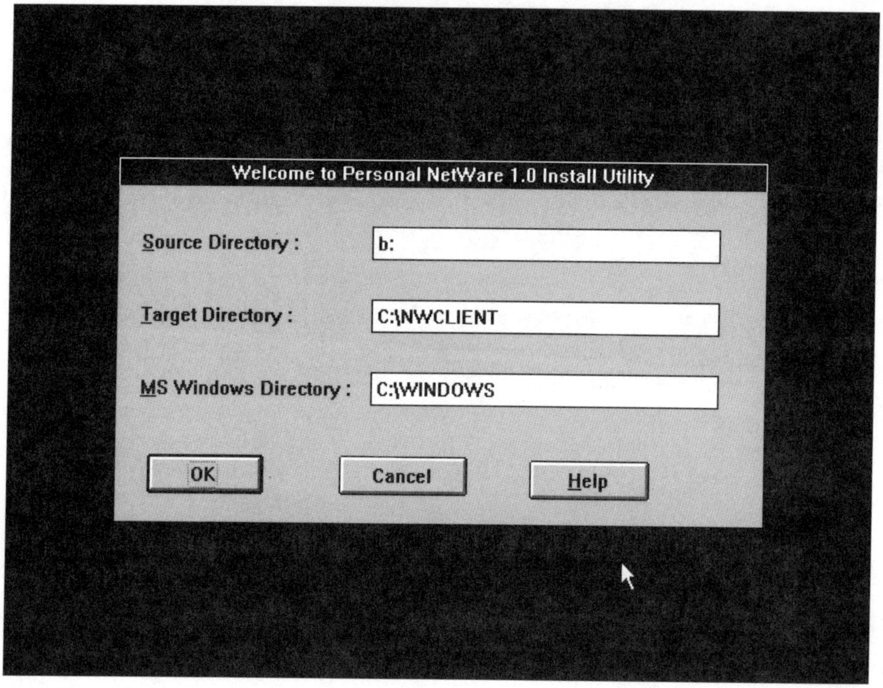

The Resulting Files

All the choices you make in the installation process are written into the NET.CFG and STARTNET.BAT files. If you installed Personal NetWare under MS Windows, changes are made to some of that program's files.

THE RESULTING NET.CFG FILE

Take a look at the NET.CFG file from Wendy's PC:

```
Link driver SMC8000
 PORT 240
 INT 5
 MEM cc000
 FRAME Ethernet_802.3
```

```
Netware DOS Requester
 FIRST NETWORK DRIVE = F
 NETWARE PROTOCOL = PNW,BIND,NDS
 PREFERRED SERVER = 311_NW
 PREFERRED TREE = 401_NW
 PREFERRED WORKGROUP = PNW
 WORKGROUP NET = 00000001:FFFFFFFFFFFF
 VLM = AUTO.VLM
 VLM = NMR.VLM
```

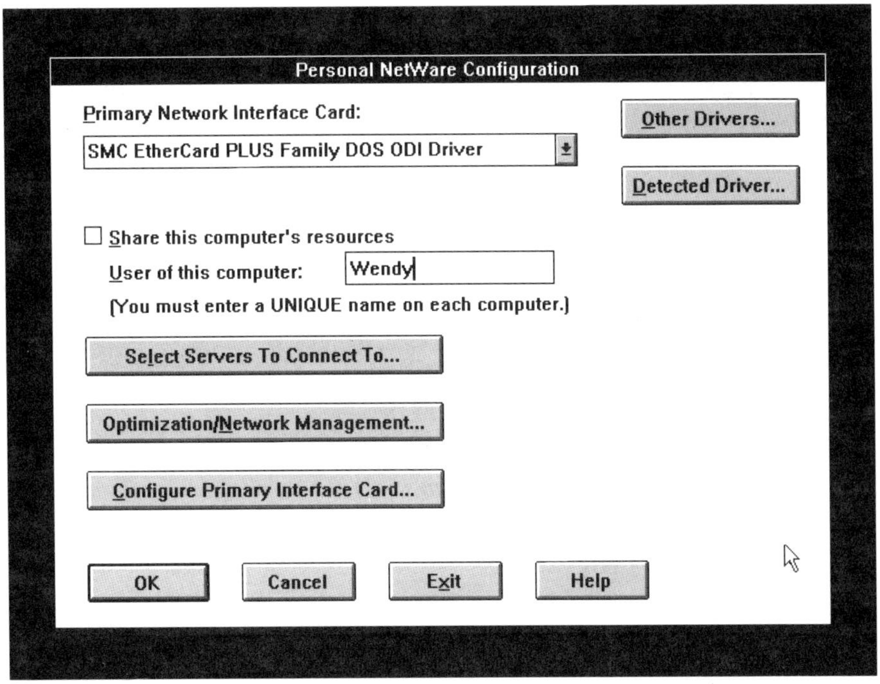

FIGURE A.13 *The main installation screen under MS Windows*

You can tell where every line of this file came from, except perhaps the VLM=AUTO.VLM command. That command automatically reconnects to workgroup servers that disappear, as they tend to do. It's added when you ask to connect to workgroup servers. The installation programmers know that PC users forget about the network and turn off their PCs, even when they're acting as servers.

FIGURE A.14

Connecting your client to preferred servers

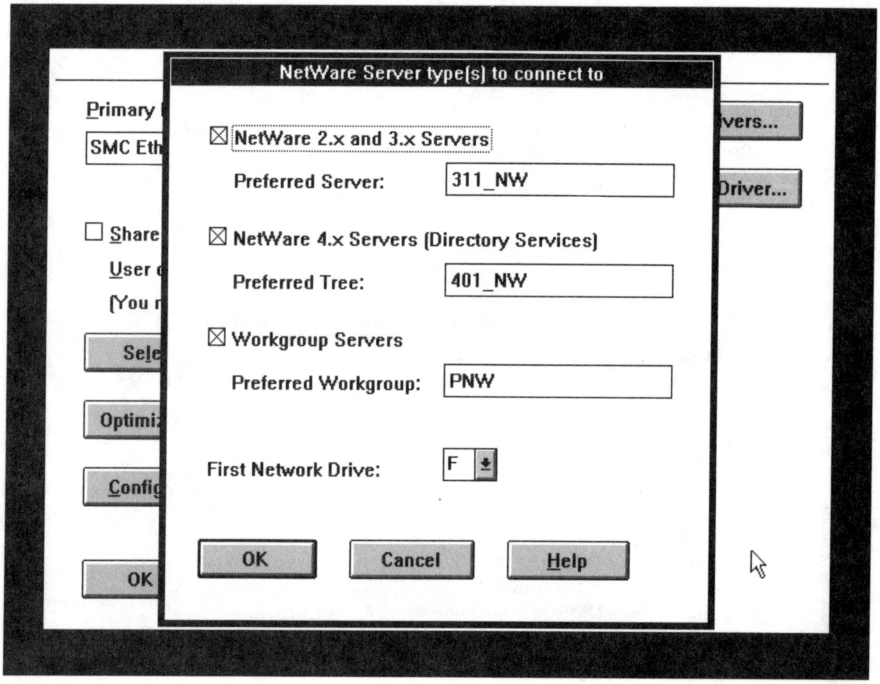

THE RESULTING STARTNET.BAT FILE

The STARTNET.BAT file is also created by the installation process. Such things as NWLANGUAGE=ENGLISH are easy to decipher. The DPMS software is checked in Figures A.6 and A.15, for example. These four lines:

```
LH LSL
LH SMC8000
LH IPXODI
VLM
```

start the NetWare client software drivers to work with the chosen network interface card. In this case, the card is listed as the SMC8000, the driver for

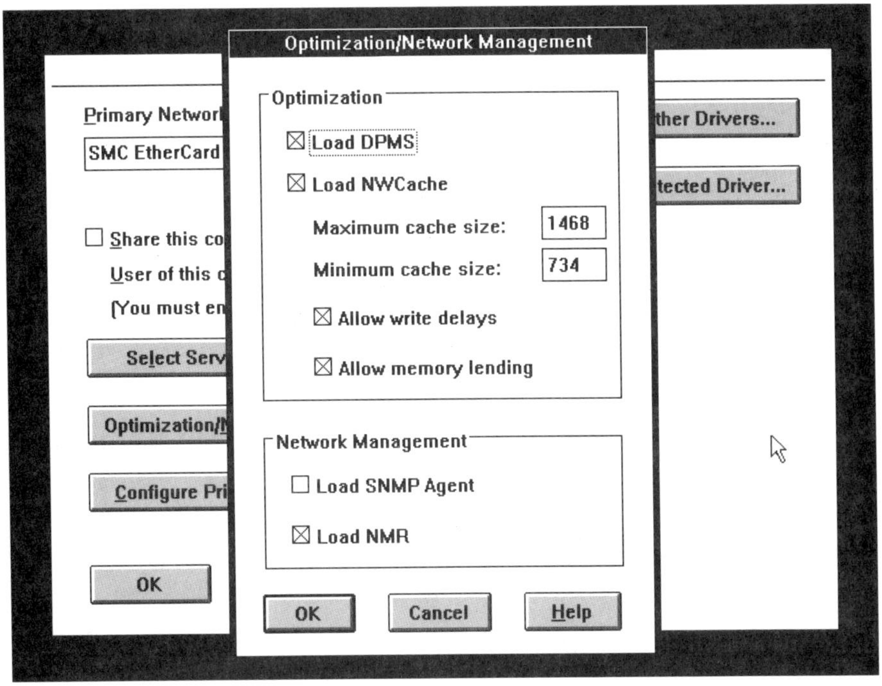

FIGURE A.15
Network optimization and management setup

the SMC family listed in Figures A.3 and A.16. The command VLM loads the VLM files. The VLM files wanted are described in NET.CFG:

```
@ECHO OFF
SET NWLANGUAGE=ENGLISH
C:
CD C:\NWCLIENT
REM DPMS should be loaded before NWCACHE
DPMS
NWCACHE 1468 734 /LEND=ON /DELAY=ON
LH LSL
LH SMC8000
LH IPXODI
VLM
CD \
C:\NWCLIENT\NET LOGIN
```

FIGURE A.16

Configuring the network interface card under MS Windows

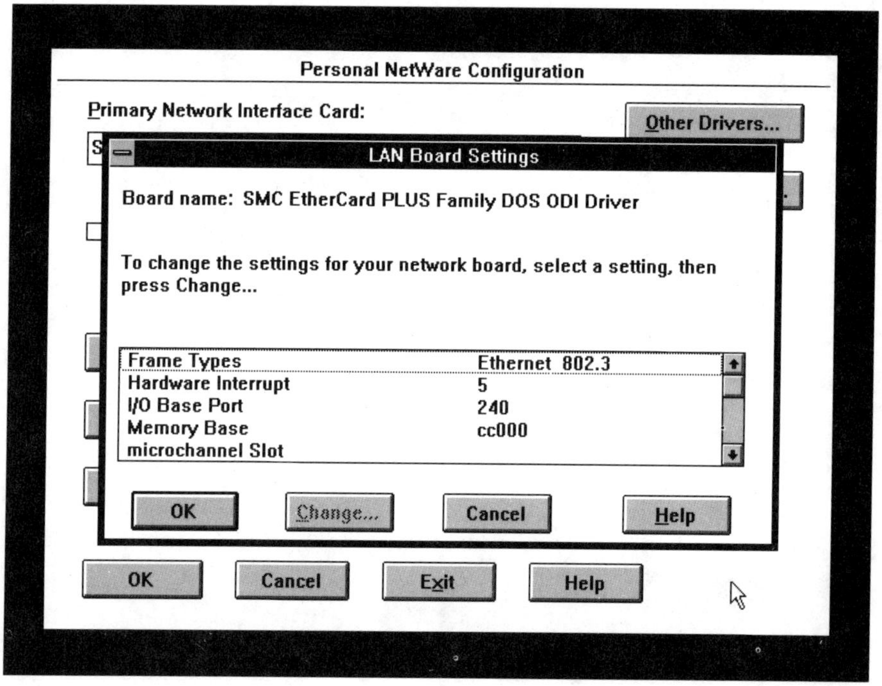

Use the NET.CFG and STARTNET.BAT files listed here as guidelines for the ones that are created during your installation process. Yours won't be exactly the same, but enough similarity will exist for you to have a comfortable feeling if they look right.

CHANGES TO MS WINDOWS FILES

The README.TXT file included in your Personal NetWare diskette set provides more details than you may want for some of the MS Windows information. Every program that installs into MS Windows makes changes to your system files. At least Personal NetWare details which files and what changes are made during installation.

WHERE FILES ARE PLACED

Personal NetWare files live three main places after installation. The \NWCLIENT directory is the main one. That's where all the executable and configuration files are located. Two directories are created under \NWCLIENT, but you have no reason to change anything in either of those.

A directory named \NWCNTL is created also, one level below the root directory, as is \NWCLIENT. There is nothing here that you change, either. The files in this directory are used by other Personal NetWare clients and servers to synchronize network services and the like. If you change or delete any of these files, your network will blow up. Don't mess with these.

Under the \WINDOWS directory lives a NetWare directory labeled \NLS. This directory contains about a hundred small files that control how Personal NetWare interacts with MS Windows. Don't change these, either.

Creating Your Workgroup

When you install your first Personal NetWare software onto a PC, a workgroup must be created. This happens automatically in the installation process. One option is to use the PNW name, as the default setting suggests, if you have only one workgroup. However, your users will feel more comfortable if you give the workgroup a name they can relate to, such as Accounting or Sales.

Once you create the workgroup, you should run the NET program to see if it appears. You may need to log in to the new workgroup, since the NET LOGIN statement at the end of your STARTNET.BAT file won't do anything if there's no workgroup.

Once you create the workgroup, create a user or two by starting the NET ADMIN program. See Chapter 8 for details.

VLM Files

The VLMs listed in Table A.1 are called the core VLMs. These are automatically load by default. You shouldn't change any references to these files in the NET.CFG yourself. Use the SETUP program to make those changes.

TABLE A.1
Core VLM Files Added Automatically during Personal NetWare Installation

VLM MODULE NAME	DESCRIPTION	REQUIRED/ OPTIONAL
CONN.VLM	Connection table manager	Required
IPXNCP.VLM	Transport protocol using IPX	Required
TRAN.VLM	Transport protocol manager	Required
SECURITY.VLM	NetWare enhanced security	Optional
NDS.VLM	Protocol support for NetWare Directory Services	Required for NetWare 4.*x*
BIND.VLM	Protocol support for NetWare Bindery	Required for NetWare 3.*x* and 2.*x*
PNW.VLM	Protocol support for Personal NetWare	Required for Personal NetWare
NWP.VLM	NetWare protocol multiplexer	Required
FIO.VLM	File input/output control	Required
PRINT.VLM	Printer redirection	Required to print to a network printer
GENERAL.VLM	Miscellaneous control functions for NETX.VLM and REDIR.VLM	Required
REDIR.VLM	DOS redirection	Required
NETX.VLM	NetWare shell (earlier versions) compatibility	Optional, but necessary for many applications

The VLMs listed in Table A.2 must be loaded on purpose. To do so, changes must be made in your NET.CFG file. Of the VLMs shown in Table A.2, the AUTO.VLM file is the most interesting and useful to the majority of NetWare users. With this program loaded, your PC will reconnect to any workgroup servers that disappear and reappear. Although this is not listed as a core VLM, it will be loaded automatically if you specify a preferred workgroup during installation.

TABLE A.2
VLM Files You Can Add

VLM MODULE NAME	DESCRIPTION	NETWARE VERSION SUPPORTED
AUTO.VLM	Auto reconnect to servers	Personal NetWare 4.*x* servers
MIB2IF.VLM	Files to allow the management of your station	All
MIB2PROT.VLM	Files to allow the management of your station	All
NMR.VLM	NetWare management responder	All
PNWMIB.VLM	Files to allow the management of your station	Personal NetWare
RSA.VLM	RSA encryption for security	Personal NetWare 4.*x* servers
WSASN1.VLM	Files to allow the management of your station	All
WSREG.VLM	PC registration to network management station	All
WSSNMP.VLM	PC network management client software	All
WSTRAP.VLM	PC software to send error messages to management station	All

Migrating from NetWare Lite

If you have NetWare Lite, many of the details concerning network interface cards and cabling are no mystery to you. If you're upgrading from NetWare Lite, the Personal NetWare manual describes this process in Section 2.

Here's the short version:

1. Make the NetWare Lite server a Personal NetWare server.
2. Log in as SUPERVISOR.
3. Type the program name **NLMIGRAT** (Netware Lite MIGRATe) from the command line.

Passwords are encrypted and cannot be transferred. Although this changeover process works, plan for it to take some extra time if you have modified NetWare Lite configuration files. Automated programs such as this are never as smart about figuring out what you did as they should be. I just hope you can remember what you did. I always forget and need to start all over.

APPENDIX B

How Do I Install Novell DOS 7?

Novell DOS 7 has the same look and feel as the Personal NetWare DOS utilities. Or, I could say Personal NetWare has the same look and feel as Novell DOS 7. Take your pick. The bottom line is that they look similar.

There is no planning to concern ourselves with when installing Novell DOS 7 as there is with Personal NetWare. You needn't plan what kind of disk drive or video board will be used with Novell DOS 7, because all types are supported. And since Novell DOS 7 exists on only one computer at a time, details about cabling and network interface cards don't matter until you get to the Personal NetWare section.

Installing the Smart Way: From the Server

If you are upgrading a PC that has a current network connection, all the Novell DOS 7 installation can be done from the network server. This won't work when installing Novell DOS 7 on new PCs or on PCs that don't have a network connection.

For less than eight users, the centralized installation method isn't worth the trouble to set up. However, if you have lots of users to install, or just dislike feeding a few floppy disks to machine after machine, this method can save you some time.

See Appendix A for details on installing from a server. Use the same procedure to copy the Novell DOS 7 diskettes to a server for installation as that described for Personal NetWare.

Starting the Installation

If the target computer already has some version of DOS installed, place the first Novell DOS 7 disk in the floppy drive and type

```
A:INSTALL
```

This assumes drive A: is the drive containing the floppy. Use B: instead if you're installing from that drive. This will start the installation process and present the screen shown in Figure B.1.

If a version of DOS is not running on the target computer, use the bootable first installation disk to start the computer. Place that first disk into the floppy drive and either reboot or turn on the computer. The necessary system files on the Install disk will provide enough system information to start the installation program.

In Chapter 9, I mentioned that Novell DOS 7 includes virus protection utilities. As a sign of how serious Novell is about this, Figure B.2 shows the next screen in the installation process. You are offered the chance to run the virus scan program before continuing the installation.

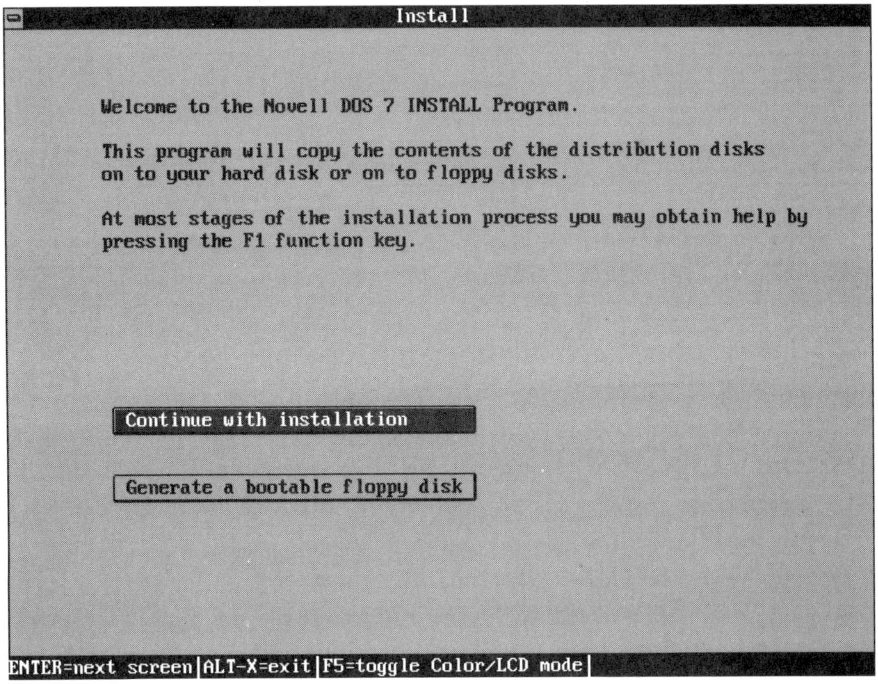
Install
Welcome to the Novell DOS 7 INSTALL Program.
This program will copy the contents of the distribution disks
on to your hard disk or on to floppy disks.
At most stages of the installation process you may obtain help by
pressing the F1 function key.
Continue with installation
Generate a bootable floppy disk
ENTER=next screen|ALT-X=exit|F5=toggle Color/LCD mode|

FIGURE B.1
The initial installation screen for Novell DOS 7

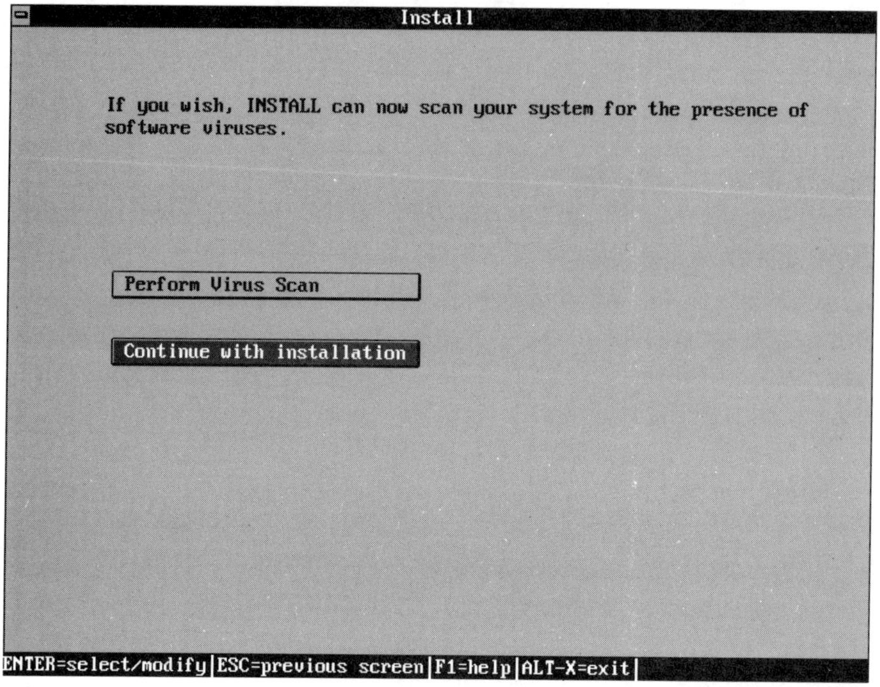

FIGURE B.2
Making sure the target computer is free of viruses

If this target PC is being upgraded from an earlier version of DOS, it makes sense to check the system. The virus scan works quickly, so you won't be delayed for long.

The installation program will ask if you wish to install all the MS Windows and networking portions of Novell DOS 7. Figure B.3 shows the default locations for all the components. You'll see a drive D:, because this was copied from LAPTOP, which has the Disk Compression utility active. The DOS system files shown in the figure refer to the low-level boot files necessary to start the computer.

After it copies the files and reminds you to send in your registration card, the installation program will be finished. Take the offered chance to peruse the README.TXT file for any last-minute changes in the program that are not reflected in the manual. Then allow your PC to be restarted, running with Novell DOS 7.

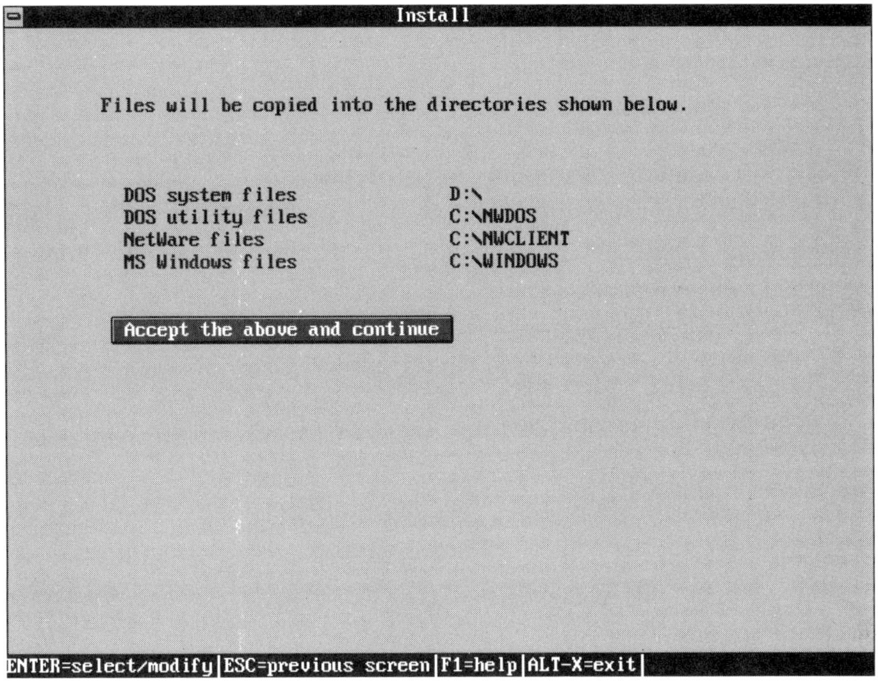

FIGURE B.3
The default placement for Novell DOS 7 files

If you installed Novell DOS 7 under MS Windows, a Novell DOS group will appear in your Program Manager screen. This group includes icons for the utilities, such as Search and Destroy, FastBack Express, and the networking commands.

Setup and Configuration

Normally, configuring the startup options for your PC is a manual process. Editing the CONFIG.SYS and AUTOEXEC.BAT files a dozen times to make things work together properly is not out of the question. With Novell DOS 7, those days are past.

To configure disk compression, memory management, multitasking, and networking, you run the Setup program. Change directories to \NWDOS and type

```
SETUP
```

to start the program. Figure B.4 shows the opening screen of the Novell DOS 7 Setup program. Everything that used to be done manually, tweaking command lines and praying that a typo doesn't crash the system, can now be done from the Setup program.

USING THE SETUP PROGRAM

You are right in guessing that the first menu choice, the one highlighted in Figure B.4, deals with most of the settings in the CONFIG.SYS and

FIGURE B.4

Starting the configuration process with the Setup program

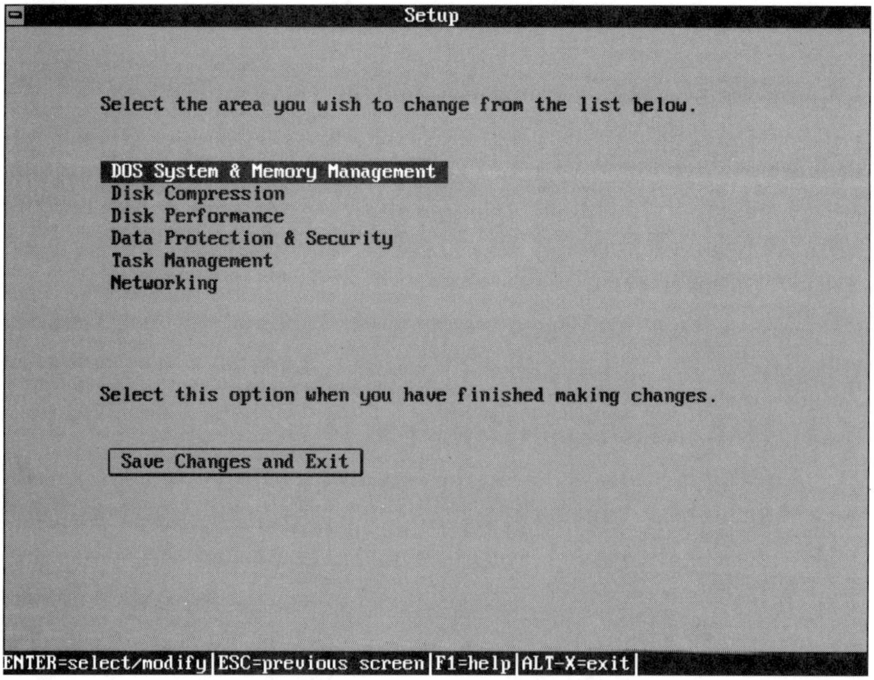

AUTOEXEC.BAT files. After all, memory management and DOS system setup are the primary functions of these two crucial files.

See the last option on the list, Networking? If you have the full Novell DOS 7 package, this is how you gain entry to all the network-specific setup screens. Figure B.5 shows the main Networking screen in the Setup program.

Getting help in the Novell DOS 7 Setup program is easy. In fact, if you sit and stare at a screen too long, Setup will remind you that help is only an F1 keypress away. Figure B.6 shows what happens if you start daydreaming when you're supposed to be configuring your computer.

As in all the screens in Setup, options are listed across the bottom status line. In this case, we see the only option is to press Enter to continue.

Let me provide a couple of quick hints for using this Setup program. If you make what might be a mistake, don't worry. Press Alt-X to jump the program back to an exit screen. This screen, shown in Figure B.7, allows you to drop back to DOS without saving any changes. The bad news is

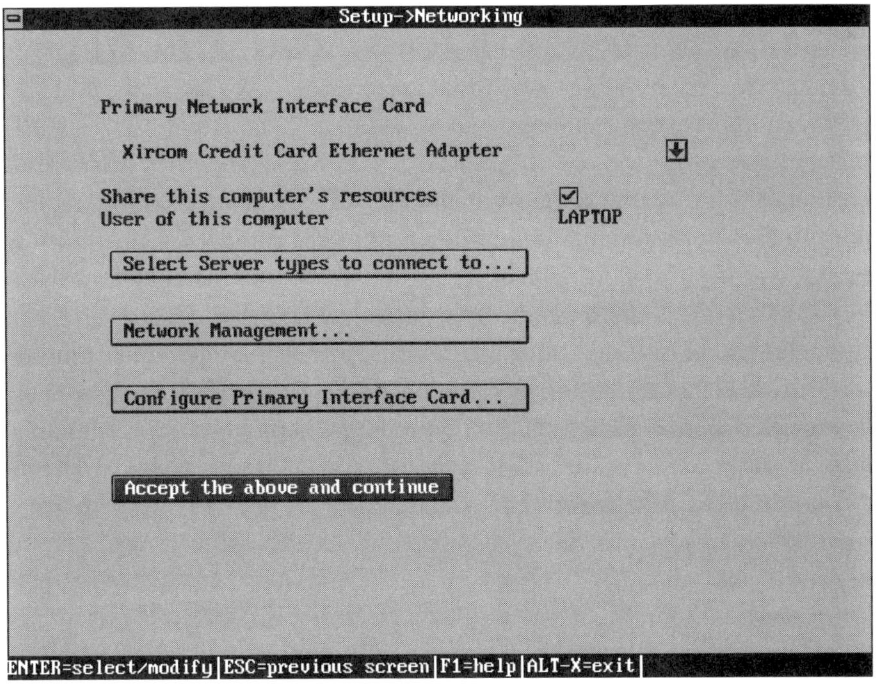

FIGURE B.5
The networking screen in the Novell DOS 7 Setup program

FIGURE B.6

An example of a persistent Help system

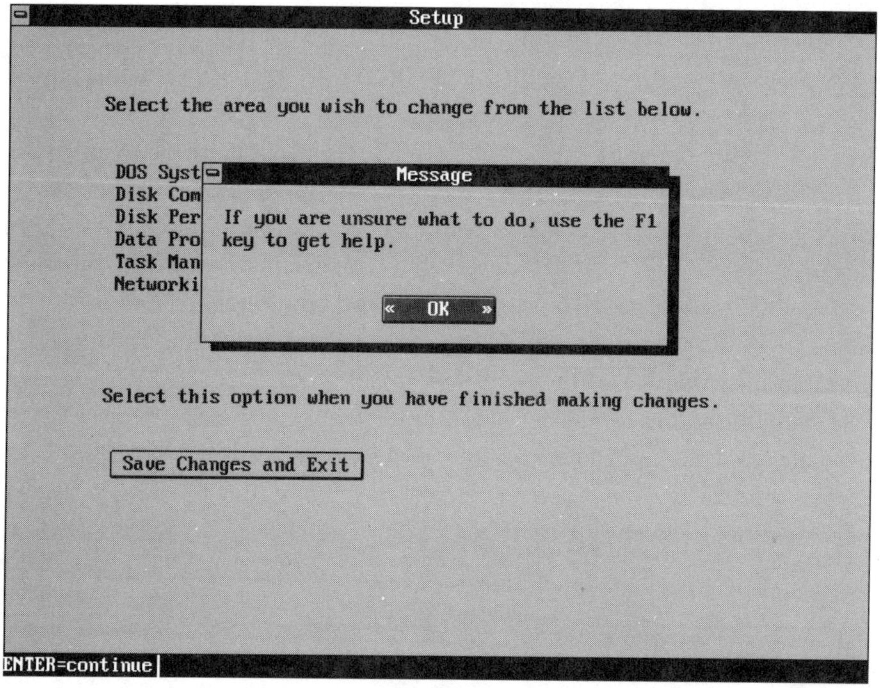
Setup
Select the area you wish to change from the list below.
DOS Syst
Disk Com
Disk Per
Data Pro
Task Man
Networki
Message
If you are unsure what to do, use the F1 key to get help.
« OK »
Select this option when you have finished making changes.
Save Changes and Exit
ENTER=continue

that you will lose all the changes, good and bad, you made in that last session. But the good news outweighs the bad. If you got confused and aren't sure what to do in a screen, you can bail out. The status line at the top shows I was in the screen to configure Disk Performance when I pressed Alt-X. Now Exit to DOS is highlighted. If I choose that option, all the changes I made will disappear.

Another trick is to save your NET.CFG and STARTNET.BAT files under another name before starting to configure any of your networking options. If you visit the Networking screen (Figure B.5) and aren't careful, the wrong card identifier can be placed into the Primary Network Interface Card field. If you carefully erase the contents of that field before exiting, the Setup program will think you have *no* network interface card, and it will modify your NET.CFG and STARTNET.BAT files to reflect that. Either way, things won't work.

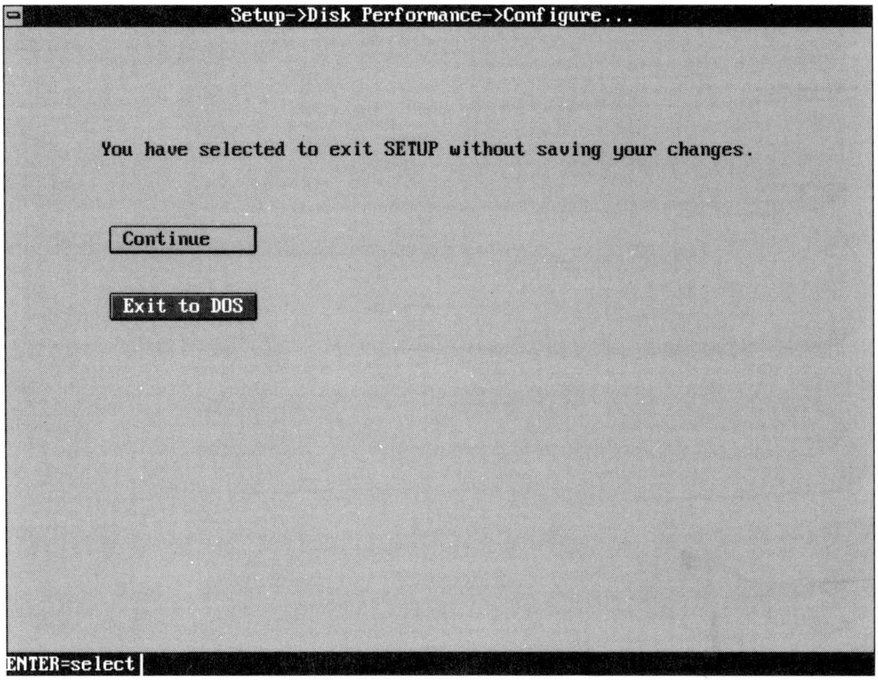

FIGURE B.7
The "bail-out" screen from the Setup program

When this happens, your boot procedure sounds like a beeper convention, because each network parameter that tries to load beeps on the error it finds. The error is usually the fact the somehow the Primary Network Interface Card field got set to the wrong thing. Life will continue normally after you copy your old NET.CFG and STARTNET.BAT files back into the \NWCLIENT directory and reboot. Then you will hear only one beep from your PC, and your network will live again.

Don't think this won't happen to you. Before we explore Setup, make copies of NET.CFG and STARTNET.BAT. While you're at it, copy CONFIG.SYS and AUTOEXEC.BAT to a safe place for good measure. It's not sissy; it's smart.

SETTING THE CONFIG.SYS FILE

The CONFIG.SYS file from a Novell DOS 7 PC looks similar to one from MS DOS. Tell me which operating system the following comes from:

```
DEVICE=C:\NWDOS\EMM386.EXE MULTI DPMI=ON /F=NONE
DEVICE=C:\NWDOS\DPMS.EXE
BUFFERS=30
FILES=50
DOS=UMB
DEVICEHIGH=C:\NWDOS\ANSI.SYS
LASTDRIVE=Z
HISTORY=ON,512,ON
COUNTRY=1,,C:\NWDOS\COUNTRY.SYS
FCBS=4,4
DEVICE=C:\NWDOS\SETVER.EXE
DOS=HIGH
SHELL=C:\COMMAND.COM C:\ /E:512 /P
BREAK=OFF
FASTOPEN=512
DEVICEHIGH=C:\NWDOS\STACHIGH.SYS
STACKS=9,256
```

Okay, it's a pretty safe bet this CONFIG.SYS file was created by Novell DOS 7. It's from LAPTOP_PC, the server and client that star in many examples in this book. But the only way to tell this is a Novell DOS 7 CONFIG.SYS file rather than from MS DOS is by noticing the ***C:\NWDOS*** at the beginning of many lines.

You can scour the manual for every switch option for lines like

```
SHELL=C:\COMMAND.COM C:\ /E:512 /P
```

to figure it out for yourself, or you can use the Setup program. I prefer the latter.

As an example, take a look at Figure B.8. Here, I was setting the BUFFERS, FILES, and FCBS (File Control Blocks) parameters. These are the third, fourth, and tenth lines of my CONFIG.SYS file listed earlier. Being unsure, I asked for help on the BUFFERS setting, which is just what the Help screen provides.

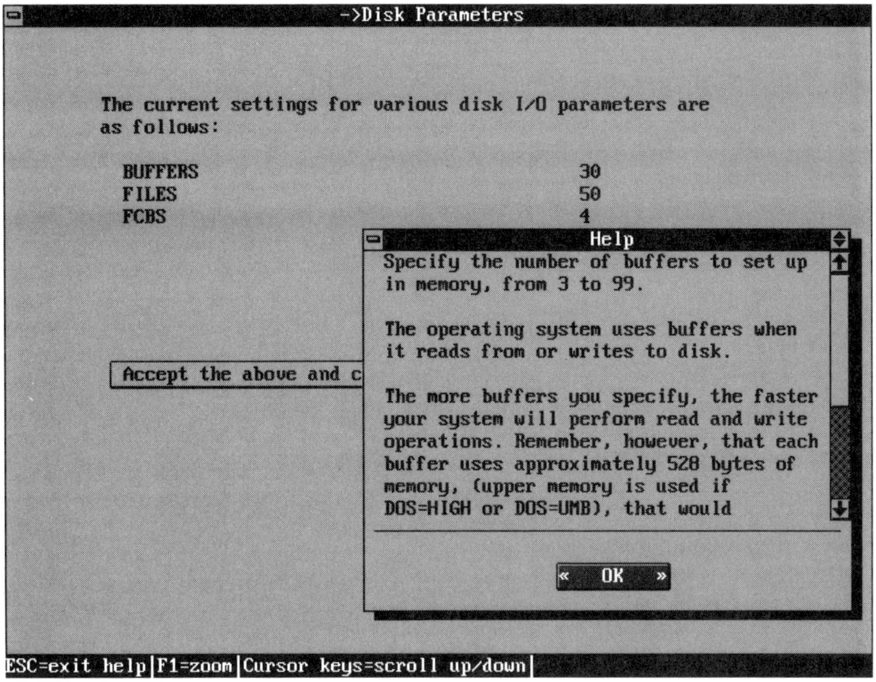

FIGURE B.8

Configuring my CONFIG.SYS file from the Setup program

The amounts for FILES and BUFFERS have been set higher than the Help screen recommends because LAPTOP_PC is a server for the workgroup. These two settings were modified by changing the values of the file server program, detailed in Chapter 8.

Curious about the SHELL= statement? Where do you specify that E: 512 setting? Take a look at Figure B.9, showing another screen in the Setup program. It also shows where the BREAK= statement came from. VERIFY is off. This setting forces DOS to verify everything written to the disk. The default is OFF, because computers are generally reliable, and verification slows down performance. But the setting shows up in the AUTOEXEC.BAT file, not in the CONFIG.SYS file.

The LASTDRIVE setting in the CONFIG.SYS file tells the NetWare DOS Requester what drives are available for network mapping. Since I said LASTDRIVE=Z, the NetWare networking client files know that every drive

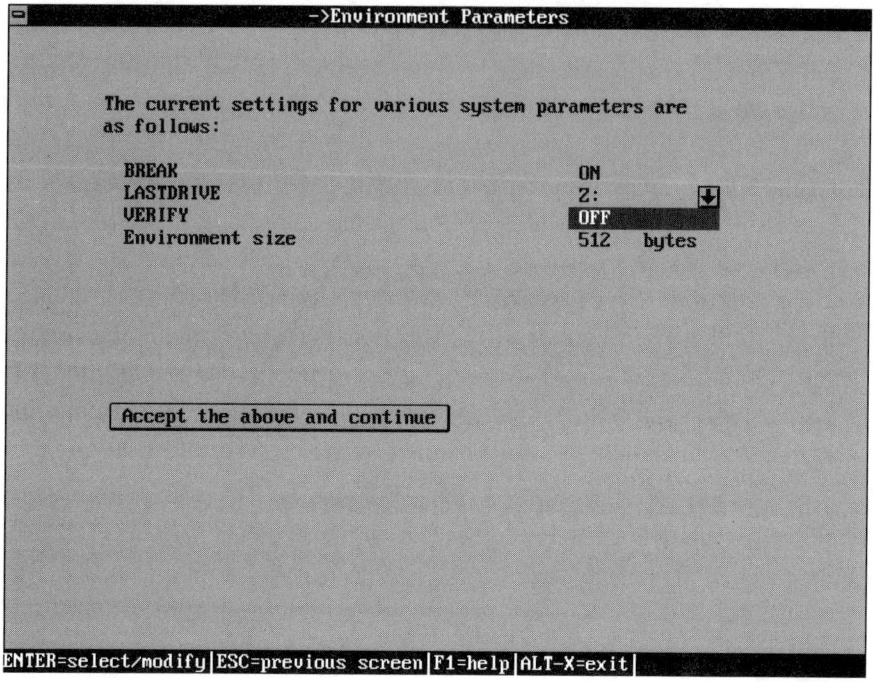

FIGURE B.9

The Setup screen to configure environment parameters

is available, so drives can be mapped from A to Z. But remember that drives A: through E: are commonly reserved for local DOS drives. You can see how that can get filled up, since adding the CD ROM to TWR_PC used drive D:.

If you do much PC setup with some other version of DOS, you know one of the hassles is deciding which device drivers and TSRs go in CONFIG.SYS and which go in AUTOEXEC.BAT. Figure B.10 is an example of the Novell DOS 7 Setup program's one screen for configuring both files. Notice the FASTOPEN=512 line in CONFIG.SYS? The line

```
lh SHARE /L:50 /F:1024
```

is fourth from the bottom of the AUTOEXEC.BAT file, shown just ahead. Take a look at Figure B.10 to see both of them being configured.

One of the special features of Novell DOS 7 is the ability to selectively load drivers in the CONFIG.SYS file. By putting a question mark (?) at the beginning of a command in CONFIG.SYS, you can have the system stop

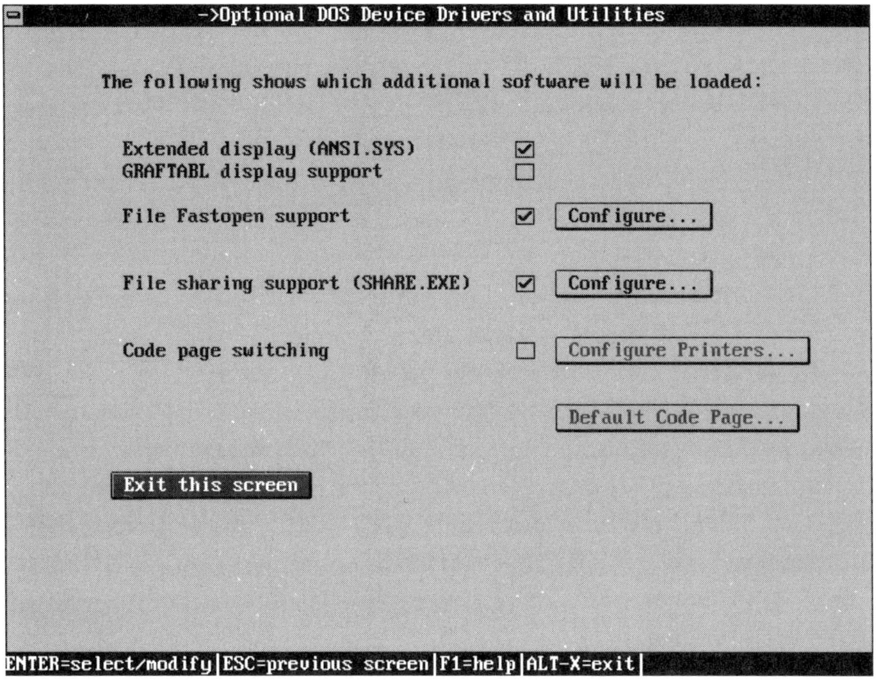

FIGURE B.10
Configuring CONFIG.SYS and AUTOEXEC.BAT with one screen

executing the file until you answer either yes or no. For example, if the line is written

```
?DEVICE=C:\NWDOS\NWCDEX.EXE
```

the execution of CONFIG.SYS stops and the system displays

```
DEVICE=C:\NWDOS\NWCDEX (Y/N) ?
```

If you type Y, NWCDEX (NetWare CD rom EXtensions) loads, and you will have access to the CD ROM drive on your system. If you type N, this driver won't load, and you won't have access to the CD ROM drive. Why would you not want to load this driver? Perhaps you're having trouble with your computer, and you want to check the boot sequence carefully. Perhaps you have just added the CD ROM and you want to be sure it loads properly before loading this driver automatically. Who knows why you do the things you do? Go for some therapy so you can blame your parents for everything.

Taking this capriciousness to the next level, the SWITCH command allows you to choose completely different configurations on startup. If booting without the CD ROM drive will be done a lot, two different configurations could be described, labeled CONFIGURATION 1 and CONFIGURATION 2 within the CONFIG.SYS file. The SWITCH command stops the execution of CONFIG.SYS and asks which configuration should be executed. When the answer is supplied, the program jumps to the label for the chosen configuration and continues.

People often use this option if they go back and forth between loading MS Windows or some particularly large drivers for network access. If you want to configure memory differently within CONFIG.SYS for running MS Windows and staying with DOS, the SWITCH command offers the only efficient method of choosing your configuration at boot up time.

For those computer owners that like to get a fresh cup of coffee when their computer boots in the morning, a TIMEOUT command in CONFIG.SYS specifies how long the system will wait for an answer to either the ? or SWITCH command. If no response is forthcoming within the number of seconds specified, the ? is answered No, and the first configuration is run for SWITCH.

For the occasional troubleshooter, there are two other tricks to control your PC's boot procedure. After the computer beeps, immediately press either F5 or F8 once. F5 bypasses both CONFIG.SYS and AUTOEXEC.BAT. F8 effectively puts a question mark before each statement in both files. Execution stops and waits at each command for either a Y or N response to execute or bypass each line of these two files.

SETTING THE AUTOEXEC.BAT FILE

If the CONFIG.SYS file from a Novell DOS 7 PC looks normal, then the AUTOEXEC.BAT file should as well. See for yourself if this looks like a traditional AUTOEXEC.BAT file:

```
@ECHO Off
PATH C:\NWDOS;C:\WINDOWS;C:\DOS;c:\wp60;C:\;
PROMPT $p$g
DISKMAP C: D:
```

```
VERIFY OFF
PATH C:\NWCLIENT\;%PATH%
SET TEMP=C:\nwDOS\tmp
IF NOT DIREXIST %TEMP% MD %TEMP%
SET NWDOSCFG=C:\NWDOS
lh SHARE /L:50 /F:1024
NWCACHE 2048 1024 /LEND=ON /DELAY=ON
CALL C:\NWCLIENT\STARTNET.BAT
?"Enable Task Manager (Y/N) ?"TASKMGR /S
```

There may be a few more items in this file that indicate we're not in MS DOS anymore. Of course, the second line references the C:\NWDOS directory, a clear giveaway now that you know the tricks. The fourth line references the DISKMAP command, which doesn't exist in MS DOS, and the eleventh line calls the NWCACHE program.

All these items are again configured without resorting to a text editor. Everything you see here has been set up by using the Setup program.

Take the NWCACHE line as an example. The translation of

```
NWCACHE 2048 1024 /LEND=ON /DELAY=ON
```

is that I want to run the disk caching software, allow 2048 KB in the cache to start, and keep at least 1024 KB in the disk cache. Keep it when? When I LEND extended memory to MS Windows. I will DELAY writing to the disk, hoping to collect more data to write to the disk, so I can write all the data in one operation, rather than in multiple, small write operations. Figure B.11 shows the screen in Setup where all this is configured.

This same screen appears in the Setup program for Personal NetWare also, since NWCACHE is included in Personal NetWare.

Notice the last line in the AUTOEXEC.BAT file:

```
?"Enable Task Manager (Y/N) ?"TASKMGR /S
```

This is a living example of the ? command switch that was described in the previous section for CONFIG.SYS. It gives me a choice each time I boot up the computer of whether or not to enable task switching. The Task Manager and task switching are covered a little later in this appendix.

FIGURE B.11

Configuring the disk cache parameters in Novell DOS 7

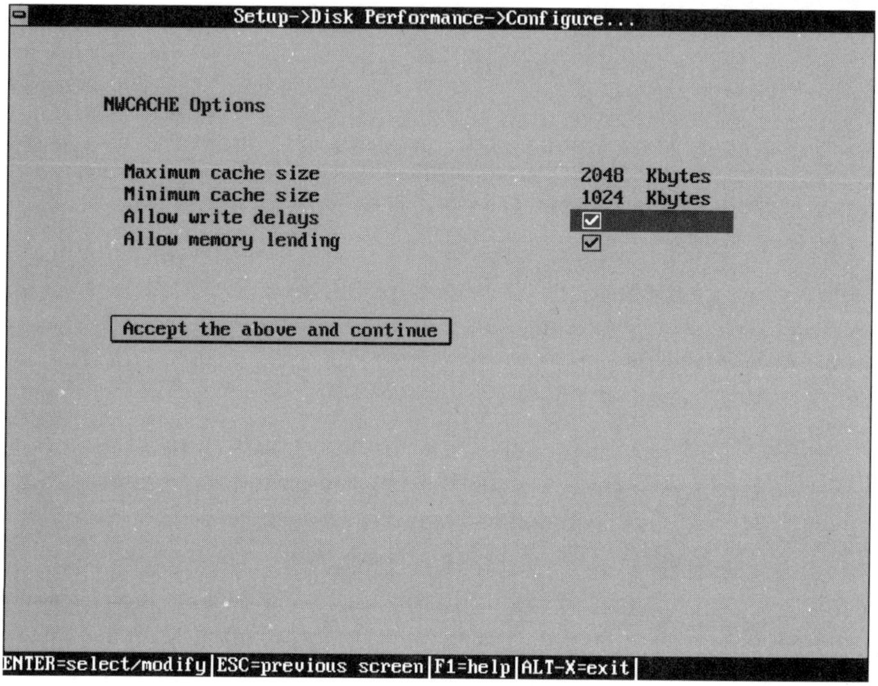

MEMORY MANAGEMENT WITH DPMI AND DPMS

Managing memory is one of the most important jobs of an operating system. All computer systems, from the smallest Personal Digital Assistant to the largest mainframe, need all they memory they can get and then some. Novell DOS 7 provides several ways to help you squeeze as much memory as possible from your recalcitrant computer.

The most important memory management happens in the CONFIG.SYS file. The first two lines set the memory management for LAPTOP_PC. The first line:

```
DEVICE=C:\NWDOS\EMM386.EXE MULTI DPMI=ON /F=NONE
```

tells the system to load the EMM386.EXE program from the \NWDOS directory. This is the primary memory management program for Novell DOS 7. The MULTI statement supports the Task Manager, which controls task switching and multitasking. The statement DPMI=ON controls the loading of DOS Protected Mode Interface, a program to allow the memory management software to support multiple DOS sessions running on one PC when using multitasking or task switching. The statement /F=NONE disables the support for EMS memory, because none of the programs running on LAPTOP_PC require expanded memory.

The second line

```
DEVICE=C:\NWDOS\DPMS.EXE
```

loads the DPMS (DOS Protected Mode Services) program. DPMS is set by running Setup and choosing DOS System and Memory Management, then Memory Manager, and checking the box labeled Load DPMS software.

Figure B.12 shows this screen in the Setup program. One of the options is deciding where DOS should reside. The list box for the Location of DOS software option is open, and Upper Memory is highlighted. This allows programs such as NWCACHE and SERVER to run outside conventional

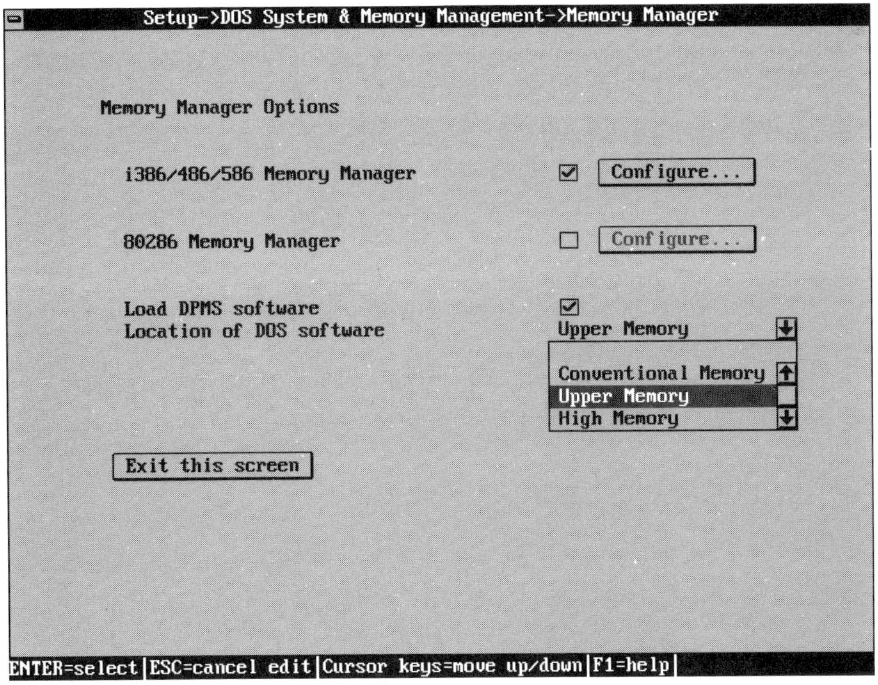

FIGURE B.12

Configuring the memory profile of LAPTOP_PC

640 KB memory. With these programs and others running in Protected Mode, the impact on conventional memory is much lower. Upper Memory will be chosen by default, so don't worry about it.

The goal of Novell DOS 7 goes beyond that of a single PC. Novell DOS 7, for the first time, makes networking an integral part of the PC operating system. Using DPMS and DPMI are ways to provide that support while leaving plenty of conventional RAM for applications.

DISK PROTECTION AND SECURITY

Novell DOS 7 includes several options for your peace of mind. The Data Protection and Security screen in the Setup program, shown in Figure B.13, includes the following choices:

- The DELWATCH File recovery utility tracks all deleted files and stops DOS from using the same disk space as those deleted files. This guarantees success with recovering deleted files (as long as your disk has enough open space for new files).
- The DISKMAP File recovery utility copies your FAT (File Allocation Table) to disk each time you turn on your computer, which makes it easier to recover deleted files (although it doesn't guarantee that you'll be able to get those files back).
- The Search and Destroy Anti-Virus utility monitors files for viruses the entire time your computer is on.
- The DOS screen saver/system lock option locks your computer and puts up a screen saver while you're away. You can configure it with a password, which must be used to unlock your computer, or provide the master password used in the Setup program.

See Chapter 9 for more details on these utilities.

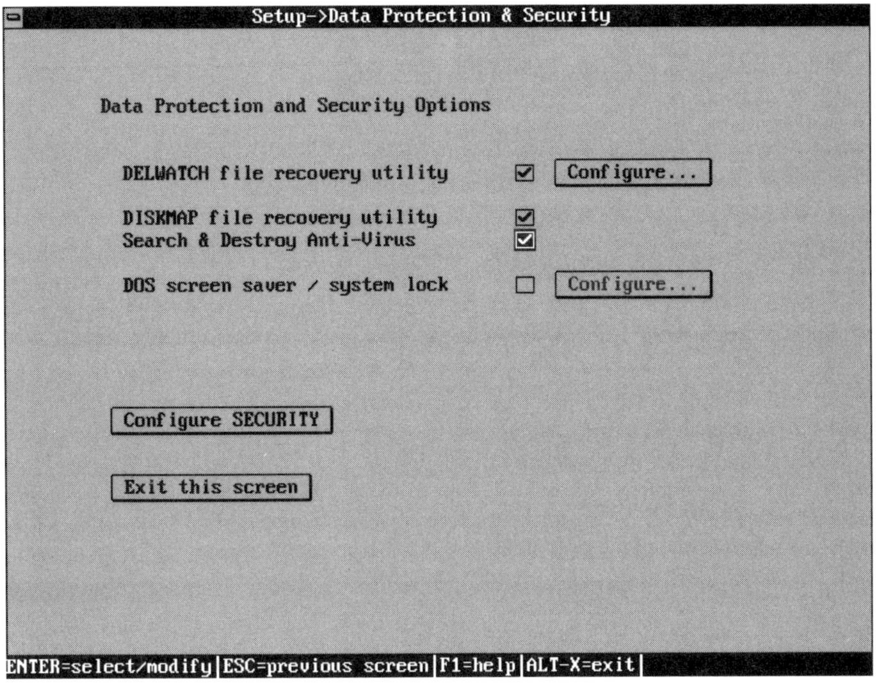

FIGURE B.13
The Data Protection and Security screen in the Setup program

MULTITASKING AND TASK SWITCHING

The ability to do several things at once has been mastered by parents for decades, but only in the last few years have computers been able to duplicate that feat. That this can now be done on your basic PC is a wonderful testament to advancing technology.

Of course, it only looks like the computer is doing several things at one time. Your mother couldn't really be doing laundry ***and*** know you were trying to saddle the dog in the backyard, but the effect is the same. In the case of the computer, the CPU (central processing unit) is so fast it can juggle several things at once, and all the applications get the service they need. Technology can't yet explain the power of mothers.

Task switching is technically easier than multitasking, and Novell DOS has supported task switching for several years. With task switching, the foreground application (the one on the screen at the moment) is active. The background applications (the ones you can't see) are stopped. They will become active only when they are in the foreground.

Multitasking provides processing power to both foreground and background applications. Normally, the scale is weighted heavily to the foreground application, but the ratio is adjustable. Since you aren't actively waiting for things to happen with the background tasks, the fact that they're a little slower is acceptable.

Figure B.14 shows the primary Setup screen for task management. The top status line shows how I reached this screen.

Tons of keys are available for use as hot keys. The problem becomes finding an easy-to-remember combination that isn't taken by your application programs. The default is Ctrl-Esc, which conflicts with MS Windows. I use WordPerfect as my word processor, and since I was raised on early DOS versions of WordPerfect, I still use the Alt and Ctrl key combinations to perform

FIGURE B.14
Configuring multitasking

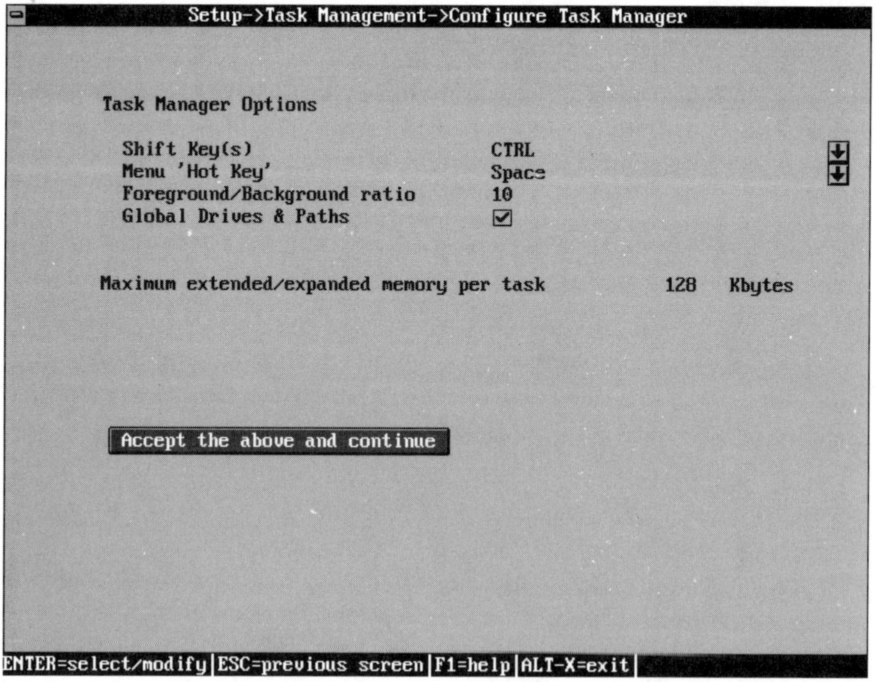

many functions. Ctrl-F8 may not mean anything to you, but it means Fonts to me, even while using the MS Windows version of WordPerfect.

I settled on the Ctrl-spacebar combination, since it's easy to remember and I don't have any applications that already use that combination. You may need to spend some time searching for the combination that works best for you, but you're welcome to try Ctrl-spacebar. Figure B.15 shows some of the options available for key combinations.

There are considerations when configuring Task Manager for either task switching or multitasking. If you refer back to Figure B.14, you'll see Global Drives & Paths as the last option in the group of four. This keeps all your drive mappings the same in all your different application windows.

This should tell you that network drivers and your login scripts must be run before the Task Manager is started. Other drivers and programs that need to be loaded included print spoolers, mouse drivers, and other TSRs

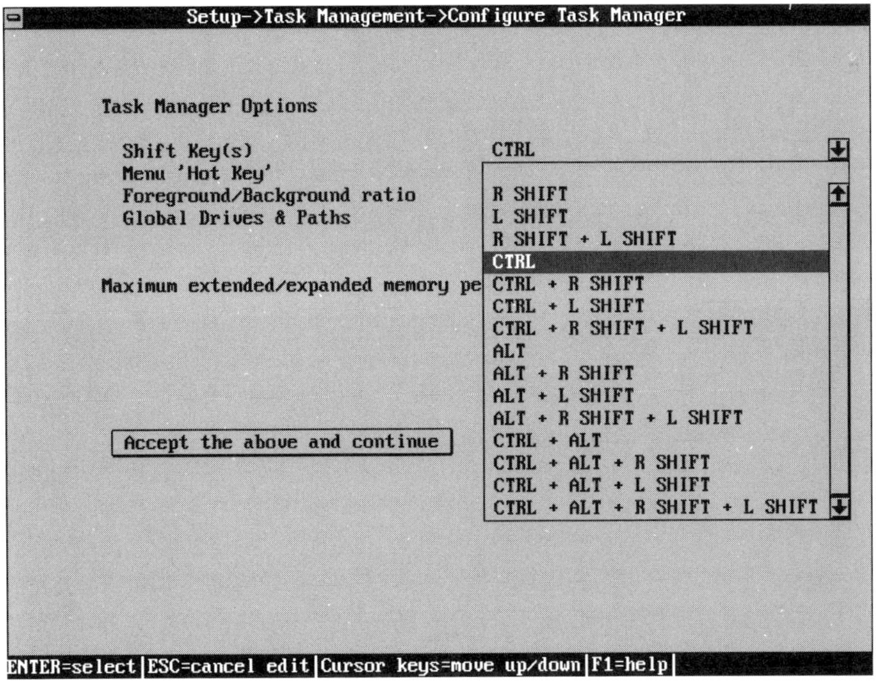

FIGURE B.15
The pick list for Task Manager hotkeys

that start from your AUTOEXEC.BAT file. When starting, put everything before Task Manager; and if that works, leave it alone.

The key combinations picked in the screen shown in Figure B.15 call up the Task Manager menu. This menu suspends all else in the foreground while displaying a list of open tasks. It's the switching center between tasks. See Chapter 9 for further discussion of Novell DOS 7's task-switching and multitasking capabilities.

DISK SPACE MANAGEMENT

Stacker, the Novell DOS 7 data-compression software, is activated through the Setup program. You can use it with the same drive letter (usually C:) or create a separate Stacker drive (drive D:). Either way, you gain disk space with minimal loss of RAM.

Figure B.16 shows the Setup screen for enabling Stacker. Before stacking the drive, Novell DOS 7 will force you to close any TSRs, such as the SERVER.EXE program. If a file is modified during compression, an error will result and the wrong consequences will ensue.

A driver must be loaded every time your computer starts to support this stacked drive. The configuration of loading this driver into upper memory is handled by the Setup program. A single line is added to CONFIG.SYS:

```
DEVICEHIGH=C:\NWDOS\STACHIGH.SYS
```

The amount of RAM taken by this driver is 20.5 KB. You make up your own mind, but I felt that 20 KB of RAM in exchange for another 55 MB of disk space (especially on LAPTOP_PC) is worth the trade.

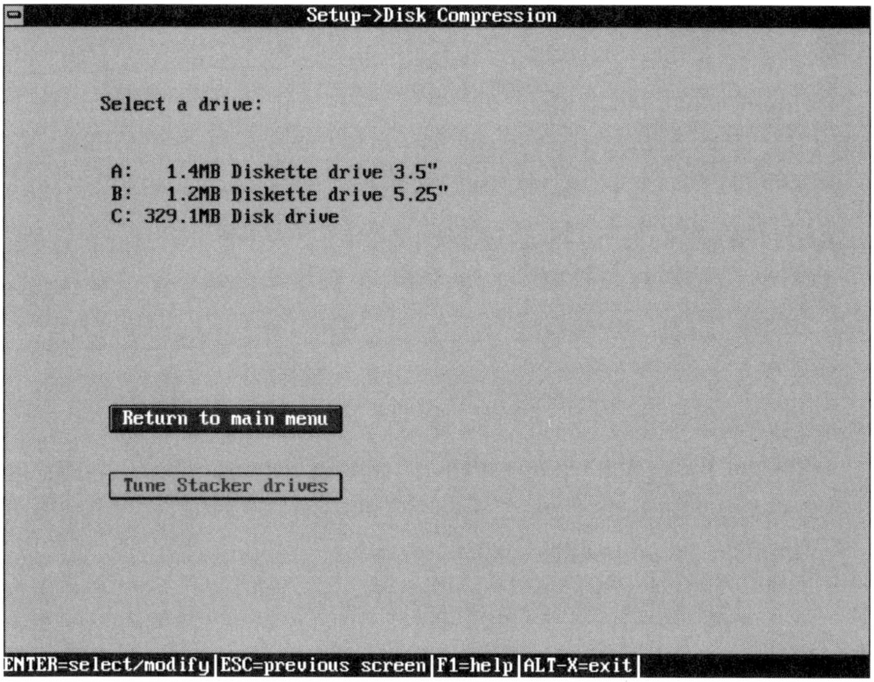

FIGURE B.16
Enabling Stacker for data compression

APPENDIX C

How Do I Make Things Right When They Go Wrong?

You don't manage a network, you manage the *changes* to that network. And changes to a network bring problems to the network more often than not. So if you don't have changes, you don't need to be concerned about much management.

Ah, but everything changes, right? Change is the only constant, especially when discussing computers. So prepare yourself for spending time managing those changes and the problems they can cause.

What Part Is Broken?

One day, one of your co-workers will appear beside your desk and say, "My computer won't work right." This is akin to telling the mechanic, "There's something wrong with my car." Usually, it costs much more to fix a car than your network, so you can relax. Your radio stations won't get changed, either.

Hardware components break down rarely. You will spend less than one percent of your network management time with broken hardware. But people are comfortable with the idea that mechanical things break, so they will always assume some piece of equipment is broken when there's a problem.

Software doesn't break either. "Bit rot," a condition where software gradually deforms on the hard disk over time, does not exist except in computer jokes. If a program worked yesterday but not today, *something changed.* Changes cause problems. If you don't believe me, wait for your children to get older.

Your Computer Won't Boot and You Want to Blame the Network

Blaming the network when your computer won't boot is justified only one time: when you first install the network interface card. Remember all that talk about different IRQs and I/O address ports and base memory addresses? If the network interface card conflicts with something already in your PC, there's a chance the computer won't start.

CHECKING THE NETWORK INTERFACE CARD

If you have just installed a network interface card, and turned to this appendix because the computer didn't start properly, go back to Appendix A. The problem is most likely in the IRQ (interrupt request line) setting. But check to make sure by pulling the network interface card out of the PC and turning it back on. If your computer boots normally then, you know the network interface card is the culprit. If your computer still doesn't boot, something else is wrong.

CHECKING THE CONFIG.SYS AND AUTOEXEC.BAT FILES

With Novell DOS 7 and some versions of MS DOS, the CONFIG.SYS and AUTOEXEC.BAT files can be bypassed or processed command by command. After the POST (Power On Self Test) for the computer is finished, it will beep one time. Immediately after that beep, press and release the F5 key one time only. The CONFIG.SYS and AUTOEXEC.BAT files will be bypassed. None of the drivers or programs in those two files will run. DOS will boot the computer, then ask you to verify the time and date. By default, if there's no CONFIG.SYS or AUTOEXEC.BAT file, the correct time and date must be verified upon booting.

Instead of pressing F5 after the POST, you can try pressing F8. POST will display each statement in CONFIG.SYS and AUTOEXEC.BAT with a yes or no question. Each statement can be executed or bypassed, depending on your choice. This can help you isolate your problem.

Pass through the commands and answer affirmatively to process each one. Eventually, you will lock up your computer. The command you just agreed to process is the culprit. Write down that command, or at least make a note.

Restart the computer and press F5 this time after the POST. Go to the file containing the bad command and start the editor. You will need to type the full path statement to that file, since your PATH statement was bypassed. For example, to edit the CONFIG.SYS file, from the root directory, type

```
\NWDOS\EDIT CONFIG.SYS
```

Go to the line that broke your computer. At the beginning of the line, insert

```
REM
```

followed by a space. That tells your computer this statement is only a REMark, not a command statement to be processed. Then save the file, and restart the computer.

Older versions of DOS will burp when they hit this REM statement, and display something along the lines of

```
UNRECOGNIZED COMMAND IN CONFIG.SYS
```

Ignore that. You want to see if everything else works properly.

Things won't work quite right, because that command was in that file for a reason. You just want to see if the computer starts more or less properly. If it boots up, but the later commands that relied on the command that's now a remark don't work right, you know what's wrong. Just go back to that command line and fix your typo or other mistake.

GOING BACK TO BASICS

I may be ahead of myself in the previous section. Before all else, make sure the computer is plugged in to the wall and into a socket that provides electricity. Make sure the monitor is plugged into the computer. Check the power cord for the monitor as well. Make sure the keyboard is plugged in.

If I said these things at the beginning, you would have felt insulted and ignored them. If you've read this far, something must really be wrong, and you can't figure out what it is. So now, since you're getting desperate, check the cables and plugs.

Also check the brightness knob on the monitor. I once drove across town in a snowstorm to service a system that had been installed only two days before. What was the problem? Someone had turned the monitor's brightness level down to zero. The customer said the computer didn't work, because she couldn't see anything on the monitor.

Your Computer Won't Start the Network Client Software

Now that your computer boots all the way up, it must run the network client software properly. If it hangs here, there are a couple of places to check:

- Remember what you just changed, and reverse that change. This will fix 90 percent of software startup problems. You (or the owner of the computer, if you're helping someone) made a change, probably the day before. When the computer started up this morning, the change caused it's mischief and you're stuck. Reverse the change and get unstuck.
- Check the STARTNET.BAT file. Move to the \NWCLIENT directory and type

  ```
  TYPE STARTNET.BAT
  ```

  Make sure the file is longer than zero bytes, in case the Setup program made a mistake. The file is short enough to fit onto one screen without scrolling. Look for obvious errors.
- Check your AUTOEXEC.BAT file. The STARTNET.BAT file is called from there, STARTNET.BAT is run, and then execution of AUTOEXEC.BAT continues. Make sure the lines before and after the reference to STARTNET.BAT haven't been changed.
- Make sure all the files referenced by the STARTNET.BAT file are where they belong. The \NWCLIENT directory should include VLM.EXE, LSL.COM, IPXODI.COM, and the COM file for your network interface card. There should also be about two dozen files with the .VLM extension. If any of these files are missing, the network client software will be unable to perform properly.

You Can Start the Software, but You Can't See the Network

You've turned to this section because you've gotten the PC to boot up and the client software loads properly, but you can't find the network.

If there is a problem with the network interface card driver file, none of the other network files will load. This should tell you to step back one section, and get the network client software under control again.

Another possibility is that a cable connecting your PC to the wiring concentrator is missing. Then you obviously aren't going to have any luck finding a network. Check the cable going from your PC to the wall and from the the wiring mess in the closet to the concentrator. If you're using 10Base-T, there are usually lights on the network interface card, the wiring concentrator, or both. When the cable connects your PC to the wiring concentrator, a link light should indicate that fact on your PC card.

If there is no link light, that indicates a physical wiring problem between your PC and the wiring concentrator. Have people been wiring new phones in your office? If so, they probably dislodged your connection by accident as they were adding the new wiring.

Don't overlook anything here. Even if the new cable installers didn't disconnect you, did they unplug the wiring concentrator? I've seen them do that so they'll have a plug for their radio. Check it out.

If nobody has been around, make sure your patch cable (between your PC and the wall plate) is in good shape. They often get stepped on or have chairs rolled over them. The cable will last for a while under that stress, but will give up eventually. Replace the patch cable with a good one and see if that helps.

You Can See the Network but Can't Use Resources

Once the physical cable is working, and the software on your PC is in good order, you should be in good shape. But you say you can't find any of your resources?

Make sure the computers with the resources you're looking for are up and on the network. If you come in on Saturday and the three servers were turned off Friday night, you'll need to start them up again. This may look curious if your PC is a client only, with odd error messages referencing a missing workgroup. A server will at least provide your own workgroup resources.

The second place to check is your workgroup. If you have several workgroups, you may be logged in to the wrong one. Use the NET program (choose Include from the View menu to see other workgroups) or the NET WGFIND command from the DOS command line.

You Can Do Everything but It Seems Wrong Somehow

Everything is there, but it's not right. It's so slow, it's like you're slogging through molasses. Or everything has a different name and look to it, like you woke up in another dimension on Twilight Zone.

Several things make the network slow. It may be getting busy. Have you added a department or two? Are there more people running MS Windows than before? Have you installed some new applications on the various file servers scattered around?

It's a simple fact of life: the more traffic, the slower the travel. Same on the ride to work during rush hour, isn't it? But more traffic alone doesn't cause consistently slower performance. The usual symptom of more traffic is the occasional slight delay, such as while you're copying a file across the network or loading an application.

The performance of the servers will cause these effects more often than the pure traffic levels. 10Base-T Ethernet can transfer several megabytes a second of information without a problem. Your PC, however, can't.

Use the network diagnostics programs to check the load on your workgroup servers (see Chapter 7). It's common for servers to get loaded little by little, with no problems until some threshold is crossed in the peformance curve. Then things bog down.

Check that the owners of the program aren't using their PC for something new. If a PC starts making presentation graphics or sorting databases more often, that will have an impact on its ability to share its resources with the workgroup.

One way I like to check PCs with MS Windows is to start the screen saver program within MS Windows and watch. If the PC is being asked to do lots of workgroup printing or copy lots of files, the screen saver motion will jerk or stop for seconds at a time. That's a clear indication that the server is overworked.

Are things just wrong? Do the people you work with believe you can perform feats of magic and that monkeys fly? Click your heels three times while saying, "There's no place like home," and everything will be fine again (although it may be in black and white).

Who Do You Call when You Give Up?

At least two sources provide reliable NetWare support. The most popular is NetWire, on CompuServe.

NetWire is Novell's umbrella name for all the forums available on various Novell products. Novell DOS 7 has an area to itself already, with a wealth of information concerning previous and current versions of the software. Personal NetWare itself will have a forum section to start with, but demand may push the creation of a special forum just for Personal NetWare users.

The other reliable option is 1-800-NETWARE, especially the FaxBack service. After dialing 800-NETWARE, press the * key on the telephone keypad, then follow directions.

Both these sources, along with the original dealer who sold you Personal NetWare and/or Novell DOS 7, should go a long way toward answering your technical questions. CompuServe can provide enormous help, especially for those new to networking.

APPENDIX D

The Complete NET Command Reference

A total of 35 commands work from the DOS prompt, without any fancy menus and programs. All these commands start with NET.

Why should you type a DOS prompt line, such as

```
NET SEND "Let's eat!" Marilyn
```

rather than starting the NET program and using the Send menu option? Why should you make an effort to learn some of these commands, along with their different variables? Here are some good reasons to use NET commands:

- They are often quicker than running the NET.EXE program.
- Some commands work only on the command line.
- Command results can be redirected to files or printers to provide historical records.
- NET command lines can be put into batch files.

The NET Commands

Let's face it, the manual covers the NET commands in complete detail. The Help screens are so good you get a complete explanation whenever you type

NET HELP *COMMAND*

So why should this appendix repeat everything that's in the manual or Help screens?

But this book can do what the manual can't. The manual must cover every option for every command, no matter how rarely used a particular command is. When you look at the manual, you have no idea which commands are really worthwhile and which ones will never be used. To help you out, this appendix provides the inside lowdown on which commands are useful, which aren't, and which should be avoided. If you're better off ignoring a command and doing that particular function through the NET.EXE program, I'll tell you.

Ratings are done with stars; the more, the better. A rating of one star, the lowest, means you probably won't have any use for this command. A rating of four stars, the highest, means you will most likely use this command quite a bit.

NET ADMIN

Quick Explanation: This is cheating. NET ADMIN starts the main DOS administration program for Personal NetWare. You already know this unless you skipped Chapter 8. Go back to the second half of Chapter 8 to learn about NET ADMIN and see many screens from that program.
Rating: (1–4 Stars): ****
Useful Variations: Not applicable
Better than NET.EXE?: It's an interactive program like NET.EXE.

NET AUDIT

Quick Explanation: Tells if network auditing is on or off.
Rating (1–4 Stars): *
Useful Variations: NET AUDIT "message" places a message in the audit log.
Better than NET.EXE?: No. There are better places to put important messages than buried inside the audit log, which is full of log ins and log outs.

NET CAPTURE

Quick Explanation: Lists currently captured printer port assignments and connects a printer port to a workgroup printer.
Rating (1–4 Stars): **
Useful Variations: NET CAPTURE DEL LPTn deletes the printer assignment to that LPT port. Every print control option can be set from the command line.
Better than NET.EXE?: No. With NET.EXE, you can see all the print control options for available printers. With NET CAPTURE, you must remember them all. Your regular printer connections should be made in STARTNET.BAT.

NET CONNECT

Quick Explanation: Lists all servers (both workstation and NetWare) you have connected.
Rating (1–4 Stars): **
Useful Variations: NET CONNECT server-name\user-name
Better than NET.EXE?: No. NET.EXE displays all available servers for you.

NET CONSOLE

Quick Explanation: Displays all clients connected to your server and their open files. Works as a screen saver as well.
Rating (1–4 Stars): ****
Useful Variations: Cursor keys control the "snake" on the screen; + and – keys increase and decrease snake length; Ins and Del increase and decrease snake speed.
Better than NET.EXE?: Yes.

NET CONTEXT

Quick Explanation: Displays or changes your current NetWare 4.*x* context.
Rating (1–4 Stars): *
Useful Variations: NET CONTEXT new-context
Better than NET.EXE?: No. NET.EXE displays all available contexts for you.

NET DIAGS

Quick Explanation: Starts the DOS diagnostics program.
Rating (1–4 Stars): ****
Useful Variations: Not applicable
Better than NET.EXE?: It's an interactive program like NET.EXE.

NET DOWN

Quick Explanation: Downs the PC server program on your PC, closing all files and disconnecting all clients.
Rating (1–4 Stars): ****
Useful Variations: NET DOWN server-name closes the server program on the named server.
Better than NET.EXE?: Yes. The DOS version doesn't have this option.

NET HELP

Quick Explanation: Displays a list of all NET commands.
Rating (1–4 Stars): ****
Useful Variations: NET HELP command
Better than NET.EXE?: Yes. It provides details about particular commands.

NET INFO

Quick Explanation: Displays the names and versions of all Personal NetWare software running on your PC, including the name of your server, your workgroup, and the machine address.
Rating (1–4 Stars): ***
Useful Variations: Not applicable
Better than NET.EXE?: Yes. This information isn't available through NET ADMIN in any one place. Administrators may find it valuable for troubleshooting.

NET JOIN

Quick Explanation: Connects your PC to a different workgroup, modifying your software to make this new workgroup your default workgroup the next time you log in.
Rating (1–4 Stars): *
Useful Variations: Not applicable
Better than NET.EXE?: No.

NET LINK

Quick Explanation: Sets several background communications parameters for maintaining contact with servers in large or busy networks.
Rating (1–4 Stars): **
Useful Variations: NET LINK SAVE saves new parameters in your NET.CFG file.
Better than NET.EXE?: Yes. It isn't available in NET.EXE. Administrators may find it useful in certain network situations.

NET LOGIN

Quick Explanation: Initiates the login process to connect the user to the workgroup.
Rating (1–4 Stars): ****
Useful Variations: NET LOGIN @batch-file-name. Also uses the PNW-LOGIN.SCR script saved by the NET program to automate all network connections.
Better than NET.EXE?: Yes. It's particularly useful with PNWLOGIN.SCR or specific batch files created for special purposes.

NET LOGOUT

Quick Explanation: Disconnects the user from all workgroup and other network resources.
Rating (1–4 Stars): ****
Useful Variations: NET LOGOUT /W disconnects just the workgroup; NET LOGOUT /B disconnects just the NetWare 2.*x* and 3.*x* servers; NET LOGOUT /T disconnects just NetWare 4.*x* directory trees; NET LOGOUT server-name disconnects a specific workgroup server.
Better than NET.EXE?: Yes.

NET MAP

Quick Explanation: Lists all drive connections.
Rating (1–4 Stars): ***

Useful Variations: Can add or delete drive mappings from the command line.
Better than NET.EXE?: Yes, for a quick look at current connections. No, for connecting new drive mappings. NET.EXE lets you choose from a list of all the available servers.

NET NTIME

Quick Explanation: Synchronizes the time and date of all servers in your workgroup to your computer's time and date.
Rating (1–4 Stars): **
Useful Variations: NET NTIME NOW synchronizes immediately, without the Y/N prompt.
Better than NET.EXE?: Yes. It's quicker than NET.EXE, because the Sync Server Time choice is several menu levels deep. However, this command won't be used often unless time stamps are vitally important on your network.

NET PLIST

Quick Explanation: Lists all available printers in your network.
Rating (1–4 Stars): **
Useful Variations: NET PLIST wildcard* works with the wildcard to show all printers starting with the letter. Can also show specific printer information.
Better than NET.EXE?: No. It requires at least one more command to connect to a printer after viewing the list. Both operations are on one screen in NET.EXE.

NET PRINT

Quick Explanation: Prints files to previously captured NetWare printers.
Rating (1–4 Stars): ****
Useful Variations: Allows wildcards, and you can specify the printer port or printer name when you're connected to more than one printer.

Better than NET.EXE?: Yes. However, you need to remember to send only appropriate text files or special print-to-disk files to the printer. Use your application's print functions for normal printing to captured printers.

NET RECEIVE

Quick Explanation: Controls message reception at your PC.
Rating (1–4 Stars): **
Useful Variations: NET RECEIVE ON turns on message reception; NET RECEIVE OFF turns off message reception; NET RECEIVE number-of-seconds specifies the amount of time the message remains on your screen.
Better than NET.EXE?: No. This parameter isn't changed often. The command is rarely used unless you have a job that takes a long time to run on your PC and you want to be sure no messages interrupt that job.

NET RIGHTS

Quick Explanation: Displays your rights to use files in the current directory. This command can set rights for your own shared directories from the command line.
Rating (1–4 Stars): **** for checking rights; * for setting rights
Useful Variations: None
Better than NET.EXE?: No. The NET Help screen takes a screen and a half just to explain all the variations. Use NET ADMIN to set rights for directories on your PC server and others you manage.

NET SAVE

Quick Explanation: Saves your current connection settings into a batch file named PNWLOGIN.BAT in your current directory.
Rating (1–4 Stars): *
Useful Variations: NET SAVE batch-file-name saves the connection settings with the name you provide.

Better than NET.EXE?: No. NET.EXE provides an easy way to see your connection arrangements before you save them. It also saves the file PNW-LOGIN.SCR to a specific directory each time, rather than the current directory. If you use both NET.EXE and the NET SAVE command, the PNWLOGIN.SCR script saved by NET.EXE will take control when the login process starts.

NET SEND

Quick Explanation: Sends a short message to other workgroup users.
Rating (1–4 Stars): ****
Useful Variations: NET SEND "message" Marilyn sends a message specifically to Marilyn; NET SEND ALL sends it to everyone who has message reception turned on.
Better than NET.EXE?: Yes. It's quick, and it's easy to remember the command syntax.

NET SETDOG

Quick Explanation: Sets the frequency of server checks to make sure all connected clients are still running.
Rating (1–4 Stars): *
Useful Variations: NET SETDOG number-of-minutes
Better than NET.EXE?: Yes. The command line is the only place to set this parameter.

NET SETPASS

Quick Explanation: Changes your workgroup password.
Rating (1–4 Stars): **
Useful Variations: Can be used to change passwords on NetWare servers and directory trees as well as your workgroup.
Better than NET.EXE?: No. It doesn't have any advantages over NET.EXE. If your password is set to expire, you will be asked for a new one when you log in. If you have a single login name for the entire network, you must use

the same password on all systems, which means that you would need to use NET SETPASS for every server you access.

NET SHARE

Quick Explanation: Shares a local resource from your PC (it must be running as a server to share).
Rating (1–4 Stars): **
Useful Variations: NET SHARE path-name shares a directory; NET SHARE port-name shares a printer.
Better than NET.EXE?: No. It's easier to track all shared resources through NET.EXE, which offers better help and support. However, the command may be useful for quick, temporary share operations.

NET SLIST

Quick Explanation: Lists all available servers (both workgroup and NetWare).
Rating (1–4 Stars): ***
Useful Variations: NET SLIST /B shows Bindery servers (NetWare 2.*x* and 3.*x*); NET SLIST /T shows NetWare 4.*x* directory tree servers; NET SLIST /P pauses at each full page of display.
Better than NET.EXE?: Yes, for a quick check to see if a particular server is still up and running.

NET SYNC

Quick Explanation: Synchronizes client and server connections between computers within a workgroup.
Rating (1–4 Stars): *
Useful Variations: Special strings to identify workstations trying to synchronize.
Better than NET.EXE?: Not applicable. Although using this avoids the problems of a client looking for a server that's not yet active, it depends on all servers and clients being started at the same time. The best option is to leave the servers up all the time so they're always available for clients. That's

why you're going to buy a battery backup system for each workgroup server, remember?

NET TIME

Quick Explanation: Sets your PC's clock to the clock of the server connected to your active drive letter.
Rating (1–4 Stars): **
Useful Variations: NET TIME server-name sets your clock to the named server's clock.
Better than NET.EXE?: Yes. It's quicker if you need to synchronize your clock before certain time-critical operations. This feature is not important to most users.

NET ULIST

Quick Explanation: Lists the users currently logged in to the workgroup or a NetWare server, with their physical addresses.
Rating (1–4 Stars): **
Useful Variations: NET ULIST server-name shows only those users connected to the named server.
Better than NET.EXE?: No. If you want to see a list of users, it's usually because you want to take another action, such as a send message. These multiple-command functions work best in NET.EXE.

NET USER

Quick Explanation: Starts the NET program in user mode (the default you're used to).
Rating (1–4 Stars): *
Useful Variations: None.
Better than NET.EXE?: It's the same as NET.

NET VLIST

Quick Explanation: Lists all shared workgroup directories and NetWare server volumes you have available.
Rating (1–4 Stars): **
Useful Variations: NET VLIST volume-name shows just the named volume and server.
Better than NET.EXE?: Yes, but only for a quick check of available volumes for troubleshooting if something doesn't work properly.

NET WAIT

Quick Explanation: Pauses batch file execution for a specified number of seconds.
Rating (1–4 Stars): *
Useful Variations: NET WAIT seconds
Better than NET.EXE?: Yes. There's no comparable command in NET.EXE. However, it's unusual for an automatic delay in a batch file to be the best way to perform a function.

NET WGFIND

Quick Explanation: Lists all workgroups on the network.
Rating (1–4 Stars): *
Useful Variations: You can use common DOS wildcards in workgroup names, as in NET WGFIND DALL*.
Better than NET.EXE?: No. If there are multiple workgroups, finding them with the NET.EXE program makes it easier to connect to the new workgroup. However, it's good to use before running diagnostics programs.

NET WGLIST

Quick Explanation: Displays all workgroups included in your network's routing information tables.
Rating (1–4 Stars): *
Useful Variations: None

Better than NET.EXE?: No. But note that this command causes less network traffic than NET WGFIND. NET WGFIND sends queries onto the network, asking for all other senders and workgroups to respond with information.

NET XLIST

Quick Explanation: Displays all current service extensions running on your Personal NetWare server.
Rating (1–4 Stars): *
Useful Variations: None
Better than NET.EXE?: No.

APPENDIX E

Glossary

ASCII: American Standard Code for Information Interchange; a standard way of encoding letters, numbers, and punctuation as bits in a file. Typically, ASCII is a standard used for moving text files from one computer to another, as well as for printing files without an application.

Attributes: Attributes are assigned to NetWare files and directories. They control such things as whether the file or directory can be shared by several users, whether it can be deleted, and so on. Attributes override any trustee rights a user may have. Attributes are sometimes called flags. Personal NetWare does not use NetWare attributes, since the files being shared are DOS files.

Audit log: A file created by Personal NetWare to keep track of server activity. It includes entries for each time a server becomes available or is taken down, and each time a user logs in or out. Personal NetWare users can also make special entries in the log.

AUTOEXEC.BAT file: A batch file, which is a file that executes several commands automatically for the user. The AUTOEXEC.BAT file located on a workstation's boot disk calls the STARTNET.BAT file to start the network resources configured for that PC.

Backup: A copy you make of an application or of files. If you lose files because of a system failure or an accident, you can restore the backup copy.

Batch file: An ASCII file that contains a series of commands that execute when you run the file. A batch file's name has the extension .BAT. Common batch files on boot disks are AUTOEXEC.BAT and STARTNET.BAT.

Boot disk: A floppy diskette or workstation hard disk that contains the files necessary for booting the workstation with DOS. Most boot disks for NetWare workstations also configure the workstation's environment, load the NetWare client files, and log the user in to the network.

Booting up: Turning on a computer so that its operating system and other necessary files load.

CD ROM: Compact disk, read-only memory; a technology that allows for the storage and retrieval of large amounts of data on a small compact disk.

Client: A device, such as a workstation, that requests services from a workgroup or network server.

Client/server network: Typically refers to a system in which two computers are used to process an application program. The client handles the user interface portion, while the server handles the data processing. A broader definition is the distribution of an application program into parts, serviced either by different computers or different programs within the same computer.

Command line utilities: Personal NetWare utilities that let you perform a network task. You execute command line utilities by typing a command at the system prompt.

CONFIG.SYS: A DOS file that allows you to customize the DOS environment for a workstation so that certain applications run more efficiently under DOS. You also load device drivers from CONFIG.SYS. If you are using Novell DOS 7 or MS DOS, this file was created when you installed that operating system.

Database: A collection of information that is accessible to computer programs. The database can be an integral part of a program, or it can be a separate file accessed by a database program. One example of a simple database is a collection of telephone numbers with names and addresses.

Dedicated: A computer on the network that is reserved for one specific task. For example, you can use a dedicated workstation as a print server.

Default: The choice a program makes if a user does not select another choice. Your default directory is the directory in which you are currently working.

Disk cache: An area of computer RAM used to store frequently accessed disk information. Servicing application requests for information from RAM rather than from the disk itself improves the computer's performance. The NWCACHE program handles disk caching in Personal NetWare.

DOS Requester: See **NetWare DOS Requester**.

DPMI: DOS Protected Mode Interface; a program to allow the memory management software to support multiple DOS sessions running on one PC when using multitasking or task switching.

DPMS: DOS Protected Mode Services; a memory control utility that allows programs written with DPMS awareness to execute in the protected mode of 80386 and higher microprocessors. These programs take little or no conventional memory when running. In Personal NetWare, SERVER.EXE and NWCACHE.EXE use DPMS if available.

Drive mapping: Assigning letters to directories on local disks or to network directories. Mapping drives to directories makes it easier for both users and applications to find files located in those directories.

Driver: Software that allows hardware and software to communicate with each other. For example, LAN drivers allow network communications to travel across network interface cards and cables, printer drivers allow your printers and applications to communicate, and tape drivers allow tape backup systems to receive network data from the backup program.

Effective rights: The sum of trustee rights that a user can ultimately exercise in a directory or file, taking into consideration specific user and group trustee assignments, security equivalences, rights inherited from parent directories, and the Inherited Rights Filters assigned to the directory or file.

Error log: Whenever an error occurs with the workgroup server, Personal NetWare records the error in an error log file, which you can view and print.

Ethernet frame type: The format that Ethernet uses to send packets of data across the network. NetWare versions 2.2 and 3.11 use an Ethernet frame type called 802.3. In NetWare 3.12, Novell changed the default frame type to 802.2, which is an industry standard. Personal NetWare supports the four frame types available under ODI.

Executable file: A program file that performs a task. For example, the executable file that runs WordPerfect is WP.EXE. Common executable file name extensions are .EXE, .COM, .BAT, and .NLM.

Fake root: Some applications require that they be installed at the root of the volume. If you would rather install the application in a subdirectory, you can map a fake root on a NetWare server to the subdirectory that contains the application. Then the application will think it is located at the root of the volume instead of in a subdirectory.

File server: The computer on the network that has the NetWare operating system running on it. The file server controls file and print sharing on the network and regulates network communications.

Frame type: See **Ethernet frame type**.

Inherited Rights Filter: A list of the trustee rights that users are allowed to inherit from a trustee assignment to a parent directory. An Inherited Rights Filter is assigned to every directory and file and affects only inherited rights, not explicit trustee assignments. In NetWare version 3.*x*, this list is called the Inherited Rights Mask.

Internal router: See **Router**.

I/O address: Input/output address; used by the computer's microprocessor to communicate with peripheral boards. No two boards in the same computer can share the same address, so part of the board installation process is locating an open I/O address.

IPX: Internetwork Packet eXchange; a network-level protocol developed by Novell to move communications packets from one computer to another across a network.

IRQ: Hardware interrupt, used by peripheral devices to let the computer know that they are waiting to be serviced. No two boards in the same computer can share the same IRQ, so part of the board installation process is locating an open IRQ.

Loadable module: See **Virtual loadable module**.

Local area network (LAN): See **Network**.

Local drive: A disk drive on the user's workstation; as opposed to a network drive, which is mapped to a directory located on the file server. In Personal NetWare, a drive in a PC can be both a local drive for that PC and a network drive to another PC.

Local printer: A printer that is attached to a file server or workstation that is running the print server.

Logical drive: An internal representation of a drive by an operating system (such as NetWare, Personal NetWare, or DOS). Usually refers to a DOS drive letter used to connect to another volume somewhere on the network.

Log in: The procedure by which a user accesses the network. To log in to a NetWare network, type LOGIN. The LOGIN utility executes a login script, which sets up a user's working environment. The Personal NetWare equivalent is NET LOGIN.

Log out: The procedure by which a user exits the network. To log out of the network, type LOGOUT. The Personal NetWare equivalent is NET LOGOUT.

Login script: A file on a NetWare server that contains commands that set up a user's workstation environment. For example, a login script may set up drive mappings, display messages on the user's screen, and so on. The login script is executed by the LOGIN utility. Personal NetWare uses the PNWLOGIN.SCR file as a login script.

Memory management: Arranging software in different memory areas than the lower 640 KB of conventional memory.

Menu program: A program that allows users to select tasks from a list of options displayed on the computer screen.

Multitasking: Multiple application programs loaded and running in separate virtual PCs within your single PC. Each session of the multitasking software can run an application and not interfere with other applications running in other sessions.

NDS: NetWare Directory Services; a global, distributed, replicated database that maintains information about every resource on the network. Based on the developing international directory specifications known as X.500.

NET.EXE: The primary DOS network program in Personal NetWare. Through the NET program, users can accomplish most Personal NetWare networking operations.

NETBIOS: Network basic input/output system; an IBM-developed application interface for network communications.

NET.CFG: A file that allows you to customize the NetWare environment on a workstation. You can use the NET.CFG file on workstations with either ODI drivers or dedicated IPX drivers. The SHELL.CFG file is a similar file that can be used only on workstations with dedicated IPX drivers.

NET LOGIN: The NET command that starts the login and connection process in Personal NetWare.

NET LOGOUT: The NET command that disconnects the user from all workgroup and NetWare file servers.

NetWare: A network operating system from Novell, Inc., which lets you connect a variety of computers together so that users on all these computers can share the same files, applications, printers, and so on.

NetWare 4.*x* domain: Refers to the NetWare Directory Services (NDS) used by NetWare 4.*x*. In large, enterprise networks, a domain is a description of a machine, department, or site for naming purposes.

NetWare DOS Requester: The workstation client software shipped in Personal NetWare and NetWare 3.12. The DOS Requester replaces NETX, EMSNETX, and XMSNETX.

NetWare loadable module (NLM): A NetWare version 3.*x* software program that runs on the file server and adds a particular feature to the network. For example, the SBACKUP.NLM loadable module allows you to back up network files from your file server.

Network: A group of computers that are connected so that they can share files, applications, and other resources (such as disk space and printers). The NetWare operating system runs on the file server computer and controls communications across the network.

Network diagnostics: The programs provided by Personal NetWare in both DOS and MS Windows versions to monitor network performance and node configuration details. The information provided by the various diagnostics programs includes number of packets on the network, disk space used and available on all servers, and server configuration files.

Network drive: A letter (such as F: or Y:) that is mapped to a directory located on the file server.

Network interface card: A circuit board that allows a computer to communicate on the network. Each workstation and file server on the network must have a network interface card installed in it. Network cables connect the boards to the rest of the network. Network interface cards (NICs) are sometimes called network boards or network adapters.

Network operating system: The software that runs on the file server and controls network communications, including file sharing and print services. NetWare is a network operating system.

NetWare server: A dedicated PC running NetWare 2.*x*, 3.*x*, or 4.*x* software. A NetWare server cannot act as a PC workstation and run application programs. In this book, ***NetWare server*** is used to differentiate the dedicated NetWare operating system software and supporting hardware from a workgroup server running both SERVER.EXE and typical PC application programs.

Network supervisor: The user who has rights to modify any file on the file server and to install or modify network resources.

Node address: Physical workstation address; each workstation must have a unique node address. Some network interface cards (Ethernet) have unchangeable node addresses assigned at the factory. Token Ring cards have a unique node address assigned, but this address can be changed in software.

Nondedicated: A computer on the network that is not limited to one task. For example, a nondedicated file server can also be used as a workstation.

NWCACHE: The disk caching program included with Personal NetWare. This program supports all types of normal and compressed drives, shares its RAM with other programs, and loads into high memory by using DPMS.

ODI driver: Open Data-Link Interface driver; a type of driver installed on a workstation. ODI drivers can handle more than one type of protocol. In addition, ODI drivers can handle different types of Ethernet.

Operating system: A program that controls the way a computer handles communication between data and hardware. PCs can use operating systems such as Novell DOS 7, MS DOS, or OS/2. NetWare is a network operating system that controls the entire network's communications.

Parent directory: Any directory that contains other directories (called *subdirectories*).

Password: A word, phrase, or other combination of characters you type to prove that you are authorized to log in to the network. Each user should have a unique user name and password to make sure that the network cannot be accessed by unauthorized people.

Patch: A small program designed to fix a bug in a product that has already been released.

Path (directory): The series of directories you follow to reach a particular file. For example, if you've stored a file called ARTICLE in a subdirectory called LENSES in another directory called PHOTO on the volume VOL1:, the directory path to that file is VOL1:PHOTO\LENSES\ARTICLE.

Path (DOS): DOS allows you to set paths to directories. These paths tell DOS which directories to search through when looking for executable files that are not found in your current directory.

Peer-to-peer network: A type of network in which every workstation is equal, and all workstations can share their resources with the other workstations.

Peripheral: A device, such as a printer, modem, or tape drive, that is attached to the network or workstation.

Port: An outlet on a computer that allows the computer to communicate with printers, modems, or other peripheral devices.

Print job: A file that has been sent to be printed.

Print queue: A directory on the file server that holds a print job temporarily until the print server is ready to take the print job and send it to the printer. Print jobs are held in the print queue in a first-come-first-served order.

Print server: NetWare software that controls how print jobs are taken from print queues and directed to printers. The print server software can be installed on either a file server or a dedicated workstation on a NetWare network. Personal NetWare servers can only share printers.

Prompt: The mark the operating system or application puts on the screen to indicate that it's ready to accept another command. In DOS, the DOS prompt usually shows the drive you are currently working in, followed by an angle bracket (>). On a NetWare file server, the console prompt is a colon (:).

Protocol: A formal description of message formats and the rules two or more machines must follow to exchange those messages.

RAM: Random-access memory; the memory used by the computer to manipulate and temporarily store information. This memory is dynamic, which means that any information stored in it will be erased when the computer's power is turned off. Some applications require a large amount of RAM to run successfully.

Restore: To retrieve files from a backup disk or tape and place them back on the network.

Rights: See **Trustee rights**.

Router: A software connection between two different networks that allows the two networks to communicate with each other. When a file server contains two or more network boards, each connecting to a different network, the router that connects those networks is called an internal router. When networks are connected through a workstation that contains two or more network boards, it is called an external router.

Search drive: A special type of drive mapping to a NetWare server directory. If a search drive is mapped to a directory, the system will look in that directory for executable files if it can't find them in a user's current directory. For example, the NetWare utilities are located in the SYS:PUBLIC directory. A search drive to that directory is placed in the system login script so that the utilities can be executed by users no matter which directory those users are currently using. Personal NetWare relies on the DOS PATH statement; there are no Personal NetWare search drives.

Security: The NetWare features that protect your network data. NetWare security includes user passwords, user account restrictions (which limit when users can log in), trustee rights (which are assigned to users to control the tasks they can perform with directories and files), and file and directory attributes (which are assigned to directories and files and limit all users' access to them).

Spooler assignments: Spooler assignments give a corresponding printer number (0 through 4) to a print queue name so that applications that require printer numbers can communicate with NetWare.

STACKER.EXE: A program used by Novell DOS 7 to increase disk capacity by reducing the amount of physical disk space each disk file uses. This is accomplished by eliminating repetitive pieces of information. A drive can be stacked any time, and both hard disk and floppy disk drives can be stacked to become Stacker drives.

Stand-alone: Any device, such as a computer or a printer, that is not connected to a network.

STARTNET.BAT: A batch file that is automatically created during the DOS Requester installation. This batch file loads the LSL, LAN driver, and IPXODI files, then executes the VLM.EXE command, which loads all the necessary VLM files. Most of these commands are put into the AUTOEXEC.BAT file in previous versions of NetWare. If this workstation was previously using NETX, you will need to edit the AUTOEXEC.BAT file and remove any lines that loaded the LSL, LAN driver, IPXODI, IPX, or NETX files.

Subdirectory: Any directory that is contained within another directory.

Surge suppressor: A device that provides some protection for hardware against power peaks that occasionally come through the power-supply line.

Task switching: One of Novell DOS 7's methods of providing a virtual PC for each application program. With task switching, only one application is actually running at a time. The other sessions are stopped when they are not on screen.

Trustee: A user or group who has been granted rights to work in a network directory or file.

Trustee rights: The means by which you control what a user can do to a particular directory or file. For example, trustee rights regulate whether a user can read a file, change it, change its name, delete it, or control other users' trustee rights to it. Trustee rights are assigned to individual users, and one user's rights can be different from another user's rights to the same directory.

TSR: Terminate-and-stay-resident; a program that leaves some or all of its operations in the computer's memory. This keeps the program available at all times. SERVER.EXE and NWCACHE.EXE are TSR programs.

Universal NetWare Client: An umbrella name given to all the Personal NetWare client programs that allow the user to access the resources of all types of NetWare servers.

UPS: Uninterruptible power supply; a device that provides alternative power to your file server if the main power supply is interrupted.

User account: The definition of a network user. Every person who wants to log in to the network must have a network user account.

User account restrictions: A means by which you can restrict users' work with the network in various ways. For example, you can limit the hours that a user can log in to the network, the workstations he or she can use, the amount of disk space that user can fill up, or the length of time he or she can use the same password. You can assign account restrictions on a systemwide basis or to individual users.

Utilities: NetWare programs that allow you to perform tasks on the network. There are workstation utilities and server utilities. Generally, you use workstation utilities to work with users, files, directories, and so on. You use server utilities to change the way the file server operates. Some utilities are command line utilities, which you execute by typing a command. Other utilities are menu utilities, which you execute by selecting an option from a menu displayed on the screen.

Virtual disk: A portion of the computer's RAM that is configured to look like a fast disk drive. File operations to and from a virtual disk are much faster than those on a normal disk. When the computer is turned off or rebooted, the information in the virtual disk is lost.

Virtual loadable module (VLM): A file loaded on a DOS or MS Windows workstation as part of the DOS Requester workstation software. VLMs replace NETX, EMSNETX, and XMSNETX. VLMs are required for Personal NetWare and are recommended for use with NetWare servers.

Volume: The top level of NetWare's directory structure. A volume is a portion of the file server's hard disk. The volume contains directories and files. A NetWare file server must have at least one volume, called SYS: (for system), which contains all the files required to run NetWare. In Personal NetWare, shared directories on workgroup servers appear as NetWare volumes.

Wildcard character: A character that can match any other character; used in specifying file names. The asterisk (*) stands for any series of characters. The question mark (?) represents any single character.

Workgroup: A group of users on a network that wish to share resources. At least one computer must be acting as a Personal NetWare server to support the workgroup.

Workgroup server: A PC in a workgroup that is running the SERVER.EXE program. Also called a *desktop server*.

Workstation: A PC that can be used to accomplish daily work. Workstations on a NetWare network can be PCs (running DOS or OS/2) or Macintoshes. A NetWare workstation contains a network interface card, which connects it to the network cabling, and workstation software, which communicates with the file server.

Index

Note to the Reader:

Boldfaced numbers indicate pages where you will find the principal discussion of a topic or the definition of a term. *Italic* numbers indicate pages where a topic is illustrated in a figure.

NUMBERS AND SYMBOLS

A

B

C

D

E

F

G

H

I

J

L

M

N

O

P

Q

R

S

X

A Quick Guide to Personal NetWare for DOS

(See Inside Front Covers for Instructions on Personal NetWare for MS Windows)

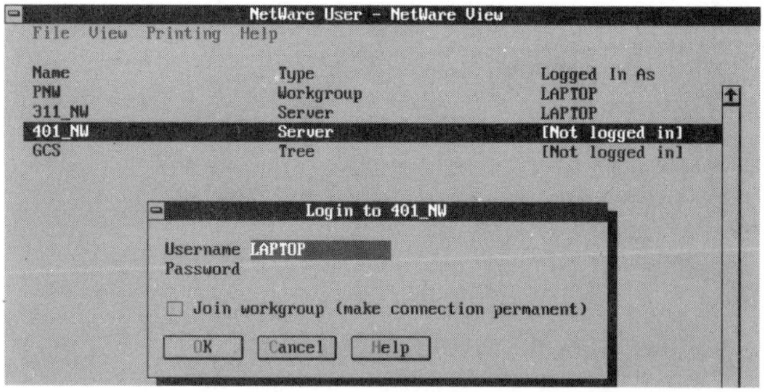

To Connect to a Network Server

(1) Type **NET** from the DOS command line to start the NET.EXE program. (2) In the NetWare View screen highlight the desired server, then press Enter. (3) In the Login window, enter your name and password, then press Enter.

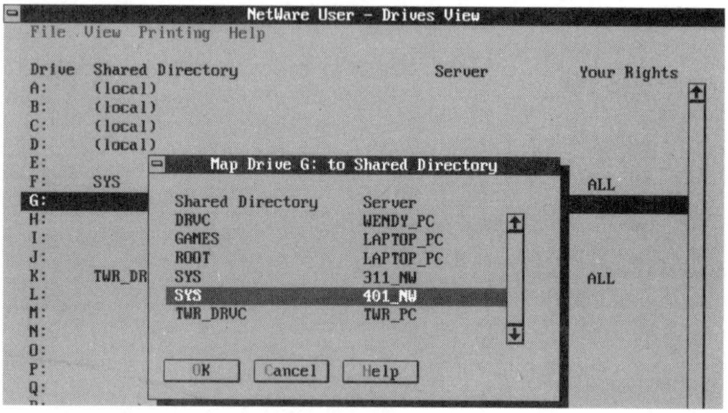

To Map Drive Letters to a Server

(1) Type **NET** from the DOS command line to start the NET.EXE program. (2) Press Alt-D to see your available drives. (3) Highlight the drive you want to connect to a NetWare server, then press Enter. (4) In the Map Drive to Shared Directory window, highlight the server to which you want to map the drive, then press Enter. (5) Press Alt-O to confirm the drive mapping.

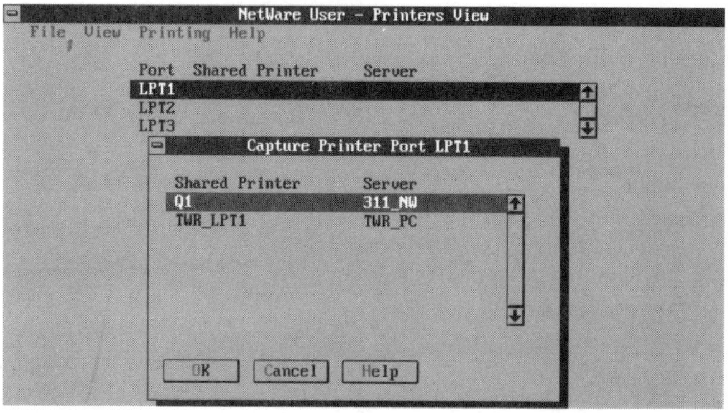

To Print to a NetWare Server Printer

(1) Type **NET** from the DOS command line to start the NET.EXE program. (2) Press Alt-O to see your LPT settings. (3) Highlight the desired parallel port (usually LPT1), then press Enter. (4) In the Capture Printer Port LPT window, highlight the desired printer, then press Enter. (5) Exit NET and start your application.